DATE DUE			

MUSLIMS OF THE SOVIET EMPIRE

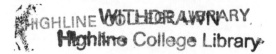
ALEXANDRE BENNIGSEN

S. ENDERS WIMBUSH

Muslims of the Soviet Empire

A Guide

INDIANA UNIVERSITY PRESS
BLOOMINGTON AND INDIANAPOLIS

Manufactured in Great Britain

Library of Congress Cataloging-in-Publication Data

Bennigsen, Alexandre.
  Muslims of the Soviet empire.

  Bibliography: p.
  Includes index.
  1. Muslims—Soviet Union. 2. Islam—Soviet Union.
I. Wimbush, S. Enders.   II. Title.
DK34.M8B46   1985   947'.0082971   86–15343
ISBN 0-253-33958-8

1 2 3 4 5 91 90 89 88 87

ACKNOWLEDGMENTS

Our thanks must go especially to the Stiftung Volkswagenwerk for its generous and timely support for this project.

Many individuals stimulated our thinking on a wide range of issues discussed herein and provided specific information on the Muslim groups under study. It is impossible to list the nature of their contributions, but we would be remiss to fail to acknowledge their help and encouragement. We particularly wish to thank our colleagues and friends Alexander R. Alexiev (the Rand Corporation), Jeremy R. Azrael (the Rand Corporation), Hans Bräker (Bundesinstitut für ostwissenschaftliche und internationale Studien, Cologne) who also contributed the Foreword, Nadir Devlet (Marmara University, Istanbul), A.G. Rawan Farhadi (University of California, Berkeley), the late Joseph F. Fletcher, Jr. (Harvard University), Paul Goble (US State Department), Mehmet Gonlubol (Middle East Technical University, Ankara), Paul B. Henze (the Rand Corporation), Michel Heller (CNRS, Paris), Guy Imart (Université d'Aix-en-Provence), Halil Inalcik (University of Chicago), Kemal H. Karpat (University of Wisconsin-Madison), Sir John Lawrence (Keston College), Chantal Lemercier-Quelquejay (CNRS, Paris), Daniel C. Matuszewski (International Research and Exchanges Board, New York), Lt.-Col. N.L.D. McLean (London), David Morison (Central Asian Research Centre, London), Hasan Oraltay (Radio Liberty, Munich), Alexandre Popovic (CNRS, Paris), Azade-Ayse Rorlich (University of Southern California), Michael Rywkin (City University of New York), Garip Sultan (Radio Liberty, Munich), Mahmud Tahir (Ankara), George B. Tanham (the Rand Corporation), Albert and Roberta Wohlstetter (Pan Heuristics, Los Angeles), and Masayuki Yamauchi (University of Tokyo).

Dawn Jamison read the proofs and compiled the index — two heavy tasks, especially in a work of this kind, which she performed with her usual good sense, humour and unflappability; for this we are greatly in her debt. We wish to thank as well Catherine Berendei, who did all the cartography to our demanding and frequently changing standards, and Caroline Gray, who prepared most of the manuscript.

Les Codouls and Ruères   A.A.B.
June 1986   S.E.W.

FOREWORD

by Hans Bräker

Alexandre Bennigsen and S. Enders Wimbush have teamed for many years to conduct research on Soviet Muslims. Together and singly, they have produced an impressive collection of books and articles dealing with most aspects of Islam in the Soviet Union and of nationality problems in the Soviet empire more generally. Their most recent effort together, *Mystics and Commissars: Sufism in the Soviet Union* (London: C. Hurst and Co.; Berkeley/Los Angeles: University of California Press, 1985) is typical of their commitment to detailed research and provocative analysis, which harmoniously reflects their different academic training and generations.

Their new book, *Muslims of the Soviet Empire*, continues this intellectual blending at different levels, but it is much more of a straightforward reference work than their previous offerings. The authors' aim is to set out the basic information about the many and diverse Muslim peoples of the Soviet state (Part II) and to examine in their basic outlines the domestic and foreign influences which contribute to the Soviet Muslims' social and political evolution (Part I). I am sure that Bennigsen and Wimbush will forgive me for saying that I wish this important encyclopaedia had been available ealier. At the very least it would have provided specialists with the kind of minutiae they are unlikely to find easily elsewhere, and certainly not in such a systematic and compact form; such as the clanic composition and geographic distribution of the two great federations of Kirghiz tribes, or the *lingua franca* of the tiny Rutuls of Daghestan.

They might have intercepted as well the lemming-like rush of too many of today's "political scientists" to explain Soviet Muslim reality in terms of the Soviet concepts of social engineering and social science theory more broadly rather than as the inescapable sum of its anthropological parts. Political science has told us little about what makes Soviet Muslims what they are and why they behave as they do. Indeed, it has probably obscured some of the most important aspects of their psychological make-up, such as the critical importance of Islam.

Muslims of the Soviet Empire is not about grand social theories, however; it is about bits and pieces. And it is a timely contribution. Since the mid-1970s this branch of the world Muslim tree has cast its shadow more and more over our awareness of the extended Russian empire and its evolution. A thorough understanding of the dynamics of Soviet Muslim society is now *de rigueur* for an accurate understanding of the course of Soviet development specifically and of the entirety of Central Asia, stretching from western China to eastern Anatolia, more generally. This book provides the basic building-blocks for understanding of this kind.

In particular, Benningsen and Wimbush emphasise, as they have in their earlier works, why it is that an appreciation of the Islamic factor should constitute the central pillar of our research. Other aspects of Soviet Muslim development, such as rapid demographic increases, have probably been more important in bringing Soviet Muslim issues to the fore than the spectre of the attachment of more than 50 million individuals, deep inside the Communist camp, to the community of Islam, the *umma*. Yet today demographic dynamism among Soviet Muslims loses its real significance when it is considered apart from questions of the Soviet Muslims' self-identity and, in particular, their adherence at least to a body of Islamic traditions and psychological pre-dispositions, if not to Islam's religious rites and routines.

Few observers are more eloquent — or more violent — about the political importance of Islam's staying power, indeed its growth, among Soviet Muslims than Soviet officials themselves. Witness, for example, the extraordinary spectacle of several of the First Secretaries of the Soviet Central Asian republics speaking at considerable length in their keynote speeches to their respective republic Party congresses for 1986 about "illegal religious organisations", the rise of pan-Islamism, the "flirtation" even of Party officials with Islamic rites and customs, and the failure of Soviet anti-religious propagandists to understand the "political acuteness" of the Islamic problem in the USSR.[1] There are many other indications at lower official levels of this concern about Islam's political threat — as there have been for some years. Such high-level, candid articulation of the problem in a forum as important as a republic Party congress should alert us all that the Soviets themselves now admit that Islam's power and influence within the empire itself has reached dangerous proportions and that action will probably be taken against it.

We do not need to look far for the immediate reasons for Islam's heightened profile within Soviet borders. Clearly knowledge of events

[1] See, for example, *Pravda Vostoka*, 31 Jan. 1986, and *Kommunist Tajikistana*, 25 Jan. 1986.

and ideas from the Islamic revolution in Iran and, particularly, Soviet engagement in Afghanistan have found channels into the Soviet Union and have found resonance among Soviet Muslims. In an earlier examination of the impact of these events on Soviet Muslims Alexandre Bennigsen dismissed the idea that their influence had ''spilled'' into the Soviet Muslim regions; instead, they had ''dripped'' in, which was sufficient to cause serious Soviet concern.[2] In the light of what we are now hearing from the Soviets themselves, Bennigsen might wish to reconsider whether he was over-cautious in his characterisation of the Soviet Union's faulty political plumbing. It is evident to nearly everyone at this stage that the Soviets are experiencing rather more than a trickle of unwanted Islamic influence from these sources, and they may in fact be in the midst of a stream.

Iran and Afghanistan are not the only answers, however. We would be seriously mistaken to believe that Muslim society in the Soviet Union lacks the internal dynamism to produce its own regeneration. Most observers have simply failed to see that the Soviet Muslim lands never lost whatever it is that Soviet social engineering is supposed to have destroyed. Certainly, Islamic belief and Muslim politics have taken new and frequently imaginative forms, but Islamic culture never disappeared. The bedrock for intense belief and provocative political activity remains as solid as ever.

The Muslim peoples of the Soviet Union have suffered, at the hands of Western so-called ''Soviet specialists'', an unwarranted isolation from the issues of the larger Muslim world. Of course, no one would be so rash as to claim that the Central Asian Uzbek is preoccupied with the Arab-Israeli conflict; but one need not have such a preoccupation to feel part of the larger Islamic community. Western preoccupations with the Islamic issues we know and are frequently involved in has led too many otherwise intelligent people to remain ignorant of the fact that the centre of the Muslim world is considerably further east than Cairo or Tripoli and that the historical evolution of Central Asia, of which Soviet Muslims are a part, shares very little with the historical evolution of the Arab lands.

I would like to think that we have reached a point where serious students of history will be able to impress their colleagues — and even politicians — with the importance of grasping what we might think of

---

[2] See his ''Mullahs, Mujahidin and Soviet Muslims'', *Problems of Communism*, November–December 1984.

as the Central Asian concept — that is, an understanding and appreciation of the common historical, religious, linguistic and cultural forces
which are largely responsible for shaping the Central Asian region and
which distinguish it so starkly from the evolution of other parts of the
Muslim world. I say I would like to think that this could be the case, but
I realise that old analytical concepts — "the Middle East", "South
Asia", "the Sub-continent" and so forth — die hard. They continue to
exist, challenged at the expense of a more accurate and more rewarding
understanding of Central Asia and, in particular, of Soviet Muslims.

Muslims of the Soviet Empire will help to break down these self-imposed
barriers and to illuminate a part of the Muslim world which has remained
too long a backwater in our thinking. In the development of more far-
ranging and far-reaching intellectual horizons it will become a rich
resource.

CONTENTS

PART TWO

7. The Muslims of Central Asia   45

       (i) *The Uzbeks*   50
      (ii) *The Kazakhs*   63
     (iii) *The Kirghiz*   73
      (iv) *The Tajiks*   85
       (v) *The Turkmen*   93
      (vi) *The Dungans*   106
     (vii) *The Karakalpaks*   108
    (viii) *The Uighurs*   115
      (ix) *The Baluchi*   120
       (x) *The Pamirian peoples*   121
      (xi) *The Ironis*   123
     (xii) *The Central Asian Tsiganes*   124
    (xiii) *The Central Asian Arabs*   125

8. The Muslims of Transcaucasia and the North Caucasus   127

       (i) *The Azeri Turks*   133
      (ii) *The Muslims of the North Caucasus*   146
     (iii) *The Daghestanis*   160
      (iv) *The Chechen-Ingush*   181
       (v) *The Cherkess tribes*   190
      (vi) *The Abazas*   200
     (vii) *The Karachai-Balkars*   201
    (viii) *The Muslim Ossetians*   204
      (ix) *The Shah Dagh peoples*   206
       (x) *The Georgian Muslims: Adjars, Ingilois, Laz*   207
      (xi) *The Kurds*   209
     (xii) *The Abkhaz*   213
    (xiii) *The Meskhetians*   216
     (xiv) *The Talyshes*   219
      (xv) *The Muslim Tats*   220

MAPS

TABLES

Part One

1

INTRODUCTION

The Soviet Union is one of the world's larger Muslim states. This frequently comes as a surprise to Westerners, who are inclined to conceptualise the world of Islam on the basis of the prolific reporting of Middle Eastern events in the last two decades or so. In reality, the heart of the Islamic world lies considerably to the east of the Middle East: Indonesia is the largest Muslim state, with a Muslim population in the vicinity of 130,000,000, followed by Pakistan (79,000,000), India (73,000,000), Bangladesh (72,000,000), and the Soviet Union (50,000,000). All the Middle Eastern states which receive so much media attention in the West currently have Muslim populations smaller than that of the Soviet Union. This being the case, it is anomalous that Soviet Muslims, till recently, have been the object of very little scholarly research or diplomatic attention.

The 1979 Soviet census* lists thirty-six Muslim or partly Muslim groups. They may be grouped as follows:

Turkic	14
Iranian	5
Ibero-Caucasian	15
Chinese	1
Indian	1

Some smaller groups, such as Muslim Georgians or Arabs, are not counted separately in the Soviet census. In 1979, the individual groups were credited in the census with the numbers listed in Table 1; natural population increase in line with known growth trends (see below) allows us to project a conservative 1985 figure of approximately 50 million.

*The next Soviet census is due in 1989, with results to be released perhaps two years later. If the 1979 census is an accurate precedent, we will not get all the important information we seek at any time. All the tables in this study have been updated as of the 1979 information where it was available. Further updating is not necessary, and probably will be not be possible, for at least ten years. The major omission in the 1979 data is the ethnic composition of major cities, hence the incompleteness of some of the tables and explanations.

Table 1.1. MUSLIM NATIONALITIES IN THE 1979 SOVIET CENSUS

	Turks	Iranians	Ibero-Caucasians	Others
Uzbeks	12,456,000			
Kazakhs	6,556,000			
Tatars	6,317,000			
Azeris	5,477,000			
Tajiks		2,898,000		
Turkmen	2,028,000			
Daghestanis				
Avars			483,000	
Lezghins			383,000	
Darghins			287,000	
Kumyks	228,000			
Laks			100,000	
Tabasarans			75,000	
Nogais	60,000			
Rutuls			15,000	
Tsakhurs			14,000	
Aguls			12,000	
Bashkirs	1,371,000			
Chechens			756,000	
Ossetians		542,000[1]		
Kabardians			322,000	
Karakalpaks	303,000			
Tsiganes				100,000[2]
Uighurs	211,000			
Ingush			186,000	
Muslim Georgians				
(Adjars, Ingilois)			150,000 (?)	
Karachais	131,000			
Kurds		116,000		
Adyghes			109,000	
Turks	93,000			
Abkhaz			91,000[3]	
Balkars	66,000			
Dungans (Muslim Chinese)				52,000
Iranians (Persians)		31,000		
Abazas			29,000	
Tats		22,000[5]		
Baluchis (1970)		13,000		
Arabs				10,000[7]
Albanians (1970)				4,000[6]
Afghans (1970)		4,000		
Muslim Armenians				1,000[7]
(Khemshins)				
Total	37,203,000	3,626,000	2,967,000	167,000

1. Less an unknown number of Christian Ossetians.
2. Total of Tsiganes: 209,000; Central Asian and Caucasian Tsiganes are Muslim.
3. Less some 50 percent Christian Abkhaz.
4. Less some 20,000 Yezidis.
5. Less an unknown number of Jewish and Christian Tats.
6. Less an unknown number of Christian Albanians.
7. Not listed separately in 1970.

Our objective is to answer the question, "Who are the Soviet Muslims?" Part I is devoted to a discussion of the historical roots of Islam in the Soviet Union; to a brief examination of the political dynamics that have shaped Muslim life within the Soviet multinational empire; and to a survey of the domestic and regional issues which will increasingly affect the future of the Soviet Muslim community and, in turn, be affected by it. Part II is devoted to a detailed group-by-group examination of the history, culture, demography, and politics of Soviet Muslims. Part III is a bibliography of sources in many languages, which, we hope, will be of use to scholars. Taken together, the three parts are intended to constitute a kind of encyclopedia of Soviet Muslims. We make no claim to treat in depth all of the issues raised herein; rather, this is intended to be a reference work of basic information, including suggestions and guides about where one might look for more complete explanations and data.

From the outset, we wish to establish that the term "Muslim" in this presentational and analytical context is used to designate individuals and groups who before the 1917 Russian Revolution belonged to the world of Islam. In this sense, "Muslim" does not necessarily refer to one who engages in the active religious practice of Islam, for in the Soviet Union, as elsewhere in the Muslim world, Islam represents not only a code of worship but also a cultural outlook and a set of social conventions: a way of life, if you will. Islam transcends the narrow spiritual domain in many places, making it impossible to assert that someone from a Muslim people who eschews the formal religious practice of Islam *ipso facto* ceases to be a Muslim. A Soviet Muslim, in the sense that we use the term, may be a non-believer, but moulded by centuries of Islam he nevertheless preserves certain spiritual, social and psychological attitudes and allegiances which help to determine his political, cultural and social behaviour and values.[1]

Muslim peoples of the Russian empire and its modern-day incarnation, the Union of Soviet Socialist Republics, have played a major historical role in the unfolding of events affecting this one-sixth of the earth's surface. For reasons which will be outlined below, they will probably continue to influence change in the operation and structure of the Soviet empire, perhaps at an even more rapid tempo than in times past. It should be borne in mind that the Soviet Union is a multinational empire which is subjected to the same tensions and strains inherent in all multinational configurations.[2] Whether the Soviet leadership can implement policies which will allow the Soviet empire to escape the disintegrating influences of multi-nationalism as it has appeared in other empires is an open question. Albert Wohlstetter has noted that "the USSR and its satellites have the brittle stability of an explosive mixture in a strong container capped under high pressure."[3] If this is the case, it is becoming clear that Soviet Muslims will be an important chemical agent in the future brew. For this reason alone, the study of who the Soviet Muslims are is important.

2

THE SPREAD OF ISLAM AND RUSSIAN EXPANSION

Islam first came to the territory of the present-day Soviet Union in the seventh century. It was brought to these lands by many different agents, including Arabs, Persians and Caucasians from the south and Turks and Tatars from the north and west. Arabs and Ottoman Turks forced Islam on the inhabitants of the sparsely populated territories by military conquest; later, they reinforced Islam's grip by diplomatic means. Arab, Persian and Volga Tatar merchants helped to spread the doctrine, as did the organised missionary activities of the various Sufi brotherhoods from Central Asia, Eastern Turkestan and the Caucasus.

The character of Islam in each of the areas of the Russian empire was determined largely by the means of penetration. An understanding of these means helps even today to explain some of the seemingly contradictory aspects of Islamic development in the Soviet Union. In areas where Islam was imposed by Arab conquest — e.g. in Central Asia and the Caucasus — Islam tends to be conservative and traditionalist. Where it was brought by merchant colonies or by diplomatic initiatives of the Ottoman Empire, it assumes a more liberal, modernist cast as in the Middle Volga regions. Where the Sufi brotherhoods bear primary responsibility for its propagation, as in the North Caucasus, Islam is radically conservative.

The expansion of Islam on present-day Soviet territory can be divided roughly into five periods:[4]

600– 800 The period of Arab conquest

800–1200 Peaceful penetration along trade routes

1200–1300 The Mongol Empire

1500–1800 The period of Russian expansion

1905–1928 The revolutionary period and the Soviet takeover.

The first period: Arab conquest, 600–800

During this first period, Islam was imposed on eastern Transcaucasia (Azerbaijan) and Central Asia by conquerors. The Arabs penetrated first into the eastern Caucasus, which was largely a Christian region, in the middle of the seventh century. In 639 they entered the territory of Azerbaijan, and in 642 Daghestan. Arabs occupied Derbent for the first time in 652, and once again in 685.

North of Derbent, Arab progress was checked by the Jewish Khazars, and on the western border of Azerbaijan they were stopped by Gregorian Christians. On the other hand, the Islamisation of the territory of Azerbaijan and southern Daghestan was rapid and met with virtually no opposition. In the eighth century the majority of the population was already Muslim; however, small islands of Christians (Udins) and Jews (Dagh-Chufuts-Tats) have survived up till today. In the Daghestan mountains, Arab progress was much slower. The Islamisation process there lasted till the twelfth century, when the last Christian and Jewish communities finally disappeared.

In Central Asia, an area divided among Buddhists, Manicheans and Nestorian Christians, Arab pressure was felt for the first time in the middle of the seventh century. In 673 Arabs crossed the Amu Darya and laid seige to Bukhara. The final Arab conquest of Central Asia south of the Syr Darya took place between 706 and 716; Islam had become the only religion of this territory by the middle of the tenth century. From this time until the end of the sixteenth century, Central Asia was one of the most prestigious cultural areas of the entire Muslim world.

The second period: Expansion along trade routes, 800–1200

Between the ninth and the thirteenth centuries Islam expanded peacefully along important trade routes. Two medieval routes were of particular importance: the north-south route along the Volga, known as the "Fur Road", and the west-east route from the Black Sea to China, the famous "Silk Road". As early as the ninth century, Islam penetrated via Arab merchants and ambassadors into the Bulgar kingdom of the Middle Volga (present-day Tatar territory). In the tenth century, this world centre of the fur trade was already predominantly Muslim, and from this region Islam was spread in the eleventh and twelfth centuries into the Urals (present day Bashkiria).

From Central Asia, Muslim merchants — Arabs, Central Asian Iranians and Turks — brought Islam to the Kazakh steppes north of the Syr Darya, to the Kirghiz mountains, and finally to regions of Eastern Turkestan (present-day Xinjiang). This expanison was somewhat slower, and until the eighteenth century the nomads remained only superficially Islamicised.

The third period: The Mongol empire, 1200–1300

The early thirteenth century represented a major setback for the Muslim world. At the beginning of the period — especially in Central Asia — Mongol rule had a strong anti-Islamic character because there were many Buddhists and Nestorian Christians among the Mongol leaders. But as a result of Sufi brotherhood activity Islam survived, although in a modified form. For a time, Islam ceased to be the religion of the rulers and became rooted in the popular masses.

Sufi missionaries and merchants were the instruments for another significant expansion of Islam from the end of the thirteenth century and the beginning of the fourteenth. By the end of this period, Mongol sovereigns of the Golden Horde and of the Chagatai Khanate became Muslims, a new phase which lasted until the middle of the sixteenth century. During this period the Crimea, the steppe region of southern Russia north of the Black and Caspian Seas, the Nogai Horde, the Kazakh steppes and western Siberia became part of the Islamic world. In the Caucasus Islam, conveyed by the Nogais, penetrated from the north into Kabardian territory. At the end of the fifteenth century, some of the Kabardians, the Balkars, the Karachais and the eastern Cherkess had become Muslim.

As a result of the activities of the Crimean Khanate,[5] Islam had taken root by the sixteenth century in the northwestern Caucasus (Cherkess territory) and in Abkhazia. In the central Caucasus the Ottoman Turks, backed by their superior military power and the prestige of Constantinople, checked Christianity's progress in Kabarda. By the turn of the century, Islam was firmly established in Kabarda and from there penetrated into western Ossetia. By this time, Islam had also spread to southwestern Georgia (Adjaristan), which was occupied by the Ottoman Turks.

The period from 1200–1500 is frequently characterised as the time during which the Russians endured the "Tatar yoke" imposed by the

Golden Horde. The Russians were thus the only Christian nation of Europe, apart from the Spanish and the Balkan peoples, to have experienced a long Muslim domination, and this has left a deep, long-lasting imprint on Russian-Muslim relations.

The fourth period: Russian expansion, 1500–1900

In the mid-1400s the young, centralised Muscovite state began to drive back the enfeebled heirs of the Golden Horde, bringing the Muslim population under Russian rule. In the mid-1500s, Muscovy embarked on its southward and eastward drive. Important Muslim territories were conquered and incorporated into the Russian empire, including Kazan (1552), Astrakhan (1556), and western Siberia (1598); by the end of the seventeenth century, the Russian advance had reached the North Caucasus.

The liquidation of the governing bodies of these territories was followed by a systematic occupation of the former Muslim lands, and Muslims were expelled from all important cities and from the best lands along the rivers. A network of fortresses, inhabited exclusively by Russians, was established at strategic points, reducing the native population to minorities within the framework of Russian settlements.

Muslim lands conquered in the sixteenth and seventeenth centuries were annexed by the Muscovite state of Ivan the Terrible and the first Romanovs. This state was purely Russian and even Great-Russian, indifferent to the problems of relations between the Russians and other nationalities. Muslim principalities were integrated into the Muscovite Tsardom, and Muslim inhabitants were treated as Russian subjects to whom the rights reserved to Christians were denied.

The main principles of policy applied to Muslims during the first part of this period established guidelines for the three different social strata: nobility, religious leaders and masses. Muslim nobility were faced with cooptation — with or without immediate conversion to Christianity — and economic servitude. Those who resisted were liquidated. Muslim religious leaders were expelled from the cities and their mosques destroyed. A programme of forcible conversion to Christianity was implemented in 1565 for large parts of the masses. New converts to Orthodoxy became subjects of the tsar without being russified.[6]

Paradoxically, however, Muslim expansion under the Russian empire throughout the eighteenth century was not impeded by the Russian expansion. In fact, in the late eighteenth century, during the reign of Catherine II, Islam advanced. In contrast to her predecessors, Catherine II had the highest regard for Islam, considering it a "reasonable religion", better suited to the task of civilising Asia than Russian Orthodoxy. In the newly annexed Crimea, Catherine II guaranteed to the Muslim population the right to their possessions, a status equal to that of the Russians, and the right to practice their religion. The name of the Ottoman Sultan Khalif continued to be mentioned at Friday prayers in all Crimean mosques. Crimean landed gentry kept their rights and prerogatives within the established social hierarchy of Russian society without being obliged to adopt Christianity. This ensured their loyalty to the Romanov dynasty, if not to the Russians. Muslim religious leaders retained power and wealth and the clergy's right to *waqf* revenues.

However, these concessions were not without cost to the Crimeans. Under Catherine II, the Crimea was flooded with Russian, German, Greek and Baltic immigrants, and the best properties were requisitioned for their nobilities. From 1783 to 1893, over one million Crimean Tatars and the entire population of Crimean Nogais migrated to the Ottoman Empire.

In 1782, Catherine II created the Muslim Spiritual Assembly of Orenburg, which later moved to Ufa. Its chairman, the mufti, was nominated by the Imperial Minister of the Interior, and his authority extended over the European and Siberian parts of the empire, excluding the Crimea and the Kazakh steppes.

Catherine II was particularly successful when dealing with Volga Tatar merchants. She cancelled all restrictions established by her predecessors on Tatar trade in Bashkiria, Siberia and the Kazakh steppes, and granted important contracts to Tatar trading colonies. The Volga merchants, who served as middlemen between Russia and the still unconquered Central Asians, acted as missionaries, building mosques and schools and thereby bringing Islam to the as yet half-pagan population of Bashkiria, western Siberia, and the Kazakh steppes. It was during the late eighteenth century that the Volga Tatars, especially their merchants and their mullahs, became the undisputed leaders of Russian Islam. It was also during Catherine's reign that Islam finally took root among the nomads and semi-nomads, Kazakhs, Bashkirs, and Nogais, who had formerly been only superficially Islamicised.

The appearance of the Naqshbandiya Sufi missionaries in the North Caucasus marked the second phase of Islamic expansion under Russian rule at the end of the eighteenth century.[7] It was the Sufis who for a century (1784–1878) organised and led the resistance movements of North Caucasian mountaineers to Russian conquest, known as the Murid movements.[8] Because of their efforts, the Chechens, the western Cherkess, and the Abazas became militant Muslims, a characteristic which is still evident today. Following the defeat of the Naqshbandiya in 1865, another Sufi brotherhood, the Qadiriya, took root in the North Caucasus and converted the Ingush to Islam.

The Russians embarked on the conquest of Central Asia in 1855, immediately after the end of the Caucasian wars. They took in succession Chimkent (1855) and Tashkent (1865) and forced their protectorates on Bukhara and Khiva (1873). In 1875 they invaded the Khanate of Kokand, which they abolished the following year, and they rounded off their conquest of Central Asia in 1873–84 with the capture of the Turkmen territory and, around 1900, the occupation of the Pamirs.[9]

With the exception of the two protectorates of Khiva and Bukhara, Central Asia was placed under the military administration of a Governorate General of Turkestan. Native Muslims were not considered to be citizens of the empire. They preserved their own juridical status based on Shariat law and were exempt from military service. The policy of the Russians toward the Muslims of this region was a classic colonial one: they made no attempt to russify the natives or to introduce European civilisation to the territory. Russian authorities tried unsuccessfully to isolate the country, to protect it from all outside influence (especially that of the Volga Tatars), and to maintain it in a state of medieval stagnation, hoping thus to remove any possibility of organised national resistance. To this end Central Asian natives were encouraged to preserve the most archaic forms of Islam.

The conquest of Central Asia and the opening of this huge territory to Russian enterprise produced a radical change in Russian-Muslim relations. In particular, Russian policy included the resumption of attempts at religious and cultural assimilation of Muslims, albeit using more subtle techniques than before. The policy was set in motion by Nikolai Il'minski, a Kazan missionary, and it has come to be referred to as the "Il'minski system".[10] The Muslim reformist movement of the late nineteenth century was a direct result of this new Russian policy.[11]

The final stage: The revolutionary period and the Soviet takeover,
1905–1928

Following the publication of a decree in 1905 announcing religious liberty in Russia, Islam entered its final phase of expansion. During this period, the majority of Muslim Tatars who had converted to Orthodox Christianity in the eighteenth and nineteenth centuries returned to their old faith. Islam spread slowly but steadily among the animist and Christian eastern Finns (Udmurts, Mari, Mordvinians) and Christian Turks (Chuvash). It is possible to generalise by stating that before 1917 all Muslim nationalities of the Russian empire with very few exceptions (Volga Tatars, Bashkirs, some Kurds, the Abkhaz, and some Ossetians) were thoroughly converted to Islam.

The onslaught of Soviet-directed anti-Islamic policies, which date approximately from 1928, brought a halt to Islam's expansion within the territories of the Russian-Soviet empire.[12] Soviet policy towards the Muslims of the reconstituted empire has changed several times. For the purposes of this general introduction, these changes have created seven distinct periods.

The first period is that of the Civil War and the first consolidation of Bolshevik rule, approximately 1917–19. The characteristic feature of this period was the "cavalry raids" by local Bolsheviks against (with some regional exceptions) all religious institutions, including Islam.[13]

The second period, that of Muslim National Communism, lasted from 1919 to 1928.[14] Muslim leaders who joined the Communist Party remained partial to Islamic culture, and exercised authority in all the Muslim republics. Islam was left relatively unhindered, but various administrative measures were adopted by the Bolsheviks to weaken the economic and cultural power of the clerics. These measures included: the liquidation of the *waqfs*, which were the basis of clerical economic power; the suppression of the religious (*shariat*) and customary (*adat*) courts; and the elimination of the confessional school system (*mekteps* and *medressehs*).

The third period, 1928–41, was characterised by a frontal assault on Islam within Soviet borders. This assault resulted in the closing of thousands of mosques and the liquidation or imprisonment of most Muslim clerics. This attack also involved intense anti-Islamic propaganda. In the 1930s, especially, clerics and believers were accused of being spies, saboteurs, counter-revolutionaries and parasites.

A period of more relaxed relations followed, and lasted from 1941 to

1959. The main stimulus for this change was, of course, the Second World War, during which the Soviet official position towards religious institutions underwent a dramatic change in order to secure greater support for the Soviet war effort. An official Muslim organisation was created in late 1942, first in Ufa and then in Central Asia, on the initiative of the Mufti Abdurrahman Rasulaev of Ufa. All anti-Islamic propaganda ceased during the war.

A new offensive against Islam was launched by Khrushchev in 1959, and lasted till he was ousted from power in 1964. The majority of working mosques were closed during this period, their number falling from approximately 1500 in 1958 to less than 500 in 1968 (compare this with the 26,279 mosques that existed in the Russian empire in 1912).

Under Brezhnev (1964–82) the massive campaign against Islam was abandoned as being counter-productive, and direct attacks on the official religious leadership disappeared completely from the Soviet press. Relations between church and state became more normal. Beginning in the late 1970s, several new mosques were opened,[15] and religious authorities, especially those attached to the Muslim Spiritual Directorate in Tashkent, have both travelled widely abroad and entertained foreign Muslim delegations at home. During this period, the Soviet use of Islam as a strategic and diplomatic instrument became marked.[16]

The current period, dating approximately from the Islamic revolution in Iran and the Soviet invasion of Afghanistan, can be characterised by an abrupt backtracking on the relative liberalism of the Brezhnev years. In the early 1980s, a new anti-Islamic campaign was initiated, a reversal predicated on the Soviet leadership's justifiable fears that the Iranian and Afghanistan situations were infecting Soviet Muslim territories.[17] At the time of going to press, Gorbachev's policies toward Islam are not entirely clear, although first indications suggest that at least the beginning of his tenure will be remembered for the vehemence of the anti-Islamic line taken by regional Soviet officials. Recent keynote speeches at the Central Asian party conferences of January 1986 are remarkable for their violent hostility to Islam and the party leaders' perception of the political damage which Islam is causing to their social policies. If we are to assume that these leaders are Gorbachev's men and that they articulate his policies, it is probable that Islam under the new Soviet regime will be more persecuted rather than less so.

3

THE OFFICIAL PRACTICE OF ISLAM IN THE SOVIET UNION

Official Islam in the Soviet Union is composed of several different rites.[18] Most Muslims belong to the Sunni creed and to the Hanafi school (*mazhab*). The Shafe'i school prevails in Daghestan, numbering some 1,400,000 adepts in 1970. The exception in Daghestan are the Nogais, who are of the Hanafi school. Other rites in the Soviet Union are as follows:

The Ja'farite rite of Shi'ism ("the Twelvers" or those who recognise the twelve revealed Imams; the same rite as in Iran). Those belonging to this rite may be grouped as follows: 70 per cent of the Azeris; the Ironis of Central Asia, a heterogeneous nationality composed of descendants of former Iranian prisoners taken by the Turkmen and the Uzbeks during the past centuries and of Iranian merchant colonies in Central Asia (27,000 in 1970); the Muslim Tats of Daghestan and Azerbaijan (10,000 in 1970); and an unknown number of people living in the cities of Central Asia, such as Samarkand, Mary, Bukhara, Krasnovodsk, Ashkhabad (approximately 100,000 individuals). Today the total number of Shi'a Twelvers is around 4,000,000.

The Ismailis of the Nizarit rite (the "Followers of the Aga Khan"). To this rite belong the so-called "Pamirian Peoples" (or Mountain Tajiks, Vakhis, Yazgulams, Ishakashimis, Shugnans, and Bartangs), numbering today not more than 100,000 in the Autonomous Oblast' of Gorno-Badakhshan in the Tajik SSSR.

The Bahais, descendants of émigrés from Iran, living in some cities of Azerbaijan (Baku, Shemakha, Lenkoran, Kuba), in Ashkhabad and Mary (Turkmen SSSR), and in Astrakhan. Their total number is unknown (probably less than 50,000).

The Shi'a extremists ("Ali Illahis" or "Those who deify Ali") are represented by some 10,000 Karapapakhs — a Turkic tribe of eastern Armenia.

The Yezidis ("Devil Worshippers"), Kurds of Armenia (15,000 individuals in 1926; probably around 25,000 today). They are listed sometimes among Muslims, although this is an error: their religion is a syncretist creed of Manichean (dualist) origin. They do indeed worship the devil, who, they believe, repented ("he quenched hell's fires with his tears").

13

The traditional hostility between Sunnis and the Shi'as has been decreasing steadily since the Russian conquest of the Muslim territories in the Caucasus and in Central Asia. In 1905, at the Third Congress of the Muslims of Russia in Nizhni Novgorod, the Sunni and Shi'a delegates decided that the Ja'farite creed of Shi'ism was to be considered as the fifth legal *mazhab*, on a level with the four Sunni *mazhabs*: Hanafi, Shafe'i, Maliki and Hanbali.

Since the Russian Revolution, the rapprochement between the Sunnis and the Shi'a Twelvers has been continuing. No major religious conflict has occurred between them either in Azerbaijan or in Central Asia. The same evolution is observed in the relations between the Sunnis of Tajikistan and the Ismailis of the Gorno-Badakhshan AO. This rapprochement does not apply to the Bahais, who are rejected by the Muslim community, nor to the Yezidis, who are not considered by Muslims as followers of Islam.

The official administration

The Soviet government recognises only the Sunni and the Shi'a of the Ja'farite creed as official "ecclesiastical establishments". During the Second World War, Sunni and Shi'a Islam were endowed with an official administration, which has no parallel in the rest of the Muslim world since Sunni Islam is a highly decentralised religion, has no clergy, and hence has no need for an ecclesiastical establishment.

In the Soviet Union the Islamic establishment has no central organisation, although there exists in Moscow a coordinating centre with a limited responsibility: the Department of International Relations with Foreign Countries, created in 1962, in charge of the relations of the four spiritual directorates with the Muslim world abroad.

Islam is divided geographically among the four spiritual directorates (*Dukhovnye Upravlenia*). Three of them are Sunni; the fourth is mixed, Sunni-Shi'a. Each spiritual directorate is administered by an executive committee elected by a regional congress of believers and composed of both clergy and laymen. It is led by a *Mufti* (or a Shi'a *Sheikh ul-Islam* in Transcaucasia). Official relations between the spiritual directorates and the Soviet government are regulated by the Council of Religious Affairs, which is attached to the Council of Ministers of the Soviet Union and has branches at the republican level.

The most important spiritual directorate is that of Central Asia and

Kazakhstan. It is Sunni of the Hanafi rite. Founded at the First Congress of the Muslims of Central Asia and Kazakhstan, it was convened in Tashkent on 20 October 1943. Its seat is located at Tashkent, Uzbekistan SSR. Its current chairman is Mufti Shams ud-Din Babakhanov, who succeeded his father Zia ud-Din Babakhanov. The vice-chairman (since 1979) is Sheikh Yusufkhan Shakirov. The language used is Uzbek. The directorate is represented in each of the five Turkestani republics by a *kaziyat* (delegation).

The Spiritual Directorate of the Muslims of European Russia and Siberia is the second, and it is also Sunni of the Hanafi rite. Its seat is in Ufa, Bashkir ASSR. The chairman is the Mufti Talgat Taziev (a Tatar born in 1948 in Kazan) elected in 1980, who replaced Abdal-Bary Issaev (elected in 1974). Its language is Volga Tatar.

The third is the Spiritual Directorate of the Northern Caucasus and Daghestan, which is Sunni of the Shafe'i rite. Its seat is in Makhach-Qala (before 1974, Buinaksk), Daghestan ASSR. The chairman is Mufti Mahmud Gekkiev (a Balkar) since 1978, replacing Abdul al-Hafiz Omarov. Since 1978 this directorate has had its own Department of International Relations. The authority of the directorate covers all the autonomous republics and regions of the Northern Caucasus (except Abkhazia, which belongs to the Directorate of Baku) and the territories (*krais*) of Stavropol' and Krasnodar.

The fourth is the Spiritual Directorate of the Transcaucasian Muslims. It is both Shi'a of Ja'fari rite and Sunni of Hanafi rite. Its seat is Baku, Azerbaijan SSR. The chairman since 1980 is the Shi'a Sheikh ul-Islam Alla Shukur-Pasha Zade (Pashaiev), replacing the Sheikh ul-Islam Mir Kazanfer Akbar oglu.

The authority of this directorate covers all the Shi'a (Ja'fari) communities of the Soviet Union and the Transcaucasian Sunni communities: Azeris (30 per cent of the total population), Abkhaz, Kurds, Adjars and Ingilois (Georgian Muslims, 150,000 in 1979), Khemshins (Armenian Muslims, 1,000–2,000 in 1979); and Meshketian Turks (less than 100,000 in 1979). Since 1978 this directorate has had its own Department of International Relations. Its language is Azeri Turkic.

Because of the importance of Central Asia, where 75 per cent of the Soviet Muslims live, the Directorate of Tashkent is especially important. It is the only one to have a publication facility, and the only two official *medressehs* in the Soviet Union are established on its territory. Nevertheless, the other directorates are totally autonomous, not only as administrations but also in canonical matters. There have existed great differences, in particular, between the more progressive and modernist directorates of Tashkent and Ufa and the more conservative Caucasians. Until 1970 the traditionalist mufti of Daghestan, Haji Kurbanov, openly opposed the modernistic activity of the Mufti Zia ud-Din of Tashkent, condemning it as "contrary to the spirit of Islam".

The four spiritual directorates are empowered by the Soviet government to control the religious life of Muslim believers. All the "working" mosques, *medressehs*, and religious publications are placed under their strict supervision. Under Soviet legislation, any kind of religious activity outside the working mosques is illegal and strictly forbidden. All Muslim clerics must be registered with the directorates as well as with the Council for Religious Affairs of the Republic and are paid and nominated by them. Unregistered clerics performing various religious rites are branded as "parasites" and hunted down. The directorates and their registered clerics alone are entitled to represent Islam *vis-a-vis* the Soviet authorities, and it is solely members of the directorates who may represent Soviet Islam abroad.

The small group of registered clerics (probably 2,000–3,000) make up the executives of the four directorates and their delegates in the Republics and regions. They also form the staff of the working mosques: *imam-khatibs* and their assistants, *mutevvalis, muezzins, qadis,* and *mudarris*, designated by the general name of *mullah* (or *akhund* among the Shi'as). We may assume an average of four to five registered clerics for every working mosque.

The composition of this registered group is heterogeneous. We find a few old survivors of Stalin's purges, trained in the pre-1928 Turkestani or Tatar *medressehs*, and also young *ulemas*, graduates of the two Central Asian *medressehs*, who in some cases have finished their education abroad, in Egypt, Morocco, Syria or Libya. Members of this last group may be subdivided into two categories: former Soviet intellectuals who, before joining the Muslim establishment, completed their studies in regular Soviet schools and even in universities; and sons of *ulemas* for whom clerical careers were hereditary (this is especially true of the Caucasus and Central Asia).

4

MOSQUES, MEDRESSEHS AND ISLAMIC PUBLICATIONS

The number of mosques

As noted earlier, only a few of the more than 25,000 mosques that existed in Russia before the revolution are still in operation. An initial, massive destruction of Muslim prayer houses began in 1928 and lasted until the Second World War. During the war some were reopened. *Soviet War News* noted that there were some 1,200 mosques in the Soviet Union.[19] This figure is acceptable, and it would seem that it slowly increased until Stalin's death. In 1959, when Khrushchev launched a second campaign against Islam, the number of mosques was estimated at 1,500. Khrushchev's short but violent campaign lasted until 1964, and during this period, most of the mosques — in particular, almost all village mosques — disappeared. Their number remained static until 1978, when a certain revival of official Islam was marked by the opening of a few new mosques. It is impossible to ascertain the number of working mosques today. The executives of the directorates are very cautious in answering indiscreet questions, and data published by the Soviet sources are vague, incomplete and generally unreliable.

In April 1979 the mufti of Central Asia gave the following information about the working mosques.[20] In Central Asia there are 200 "cathedral" mosques, plus an unknown number of small mosques. (A "cathedral" mosque or *masjid-e juma* is a mosque where Friday prayers can be performed.) In the Soviet Union it is generally a small building. A small mosque or *masjid* is a simple room where prayers can be performed. The total number of working mosques in Central Asia has been estimated at 1,200 by the deputy mufti of Tashkent, Abdulgani Abdullaev, on a Radio Budapest broadcast in Hungarian. However, this figure seems exaggerated; *Muslims of the Soviet East*, April 1978, boasts of only 200 mosques in Central Asia. According to the same source, in the European part of the Soviet Union and Siberia there are over 1,000 cathedrals and small mosques. In Azerbaijan there are 200 cathedrals and small mosques, and in Daghestan and the Northern Caucasus, approximately 300 cathedral and small mosques. More recently, Abdulla Nurullayev, member of the Council of Religious Affairs of the Soviet Union, Council of Ministers, in a talk with Leo Wieland, a German journalist of

17

the *Frankfurter Allgemeine Zeitung* (4 May 1979), advanced the figure of "more than 1,000 registered communities with a mosque".[21]

These figures of working mosques given by the leaders of Soviet Islam and the official representatives of the Soviet government are contradicted by recent figures advanced by other Soviet sources. In 1976 an executive of the Spiritual Directorate of Tashkent speaking to a Western visitor acknowledged the existence of 143 working mosques in Central Asia and Kazakhstan — which seems plausible if this number concerns only the cathedral (*juma*) mosques and not the small ones: *mahalle* mosques or *masjid* are many times this number.[22]

We have more detailed data concerning the Northern Caucasus. Except in Daghestan, almost all the mosques are in cities. According to recent Soviet figures, in 1974 there were 27 working mosques in Daghestan and only two in the Chechen-Ingush ASSR (both opened in 1978). There are no working mosques in the Karachai-Cherkess autonomous oblast' since the deportation of the Karachais in 1943. In the cities of the central and western North Caucasus, the number of mosques may be estimated at ten. Thus the total of working mosques controlled by the Makhach-Qala Directorate is probably not more than 45.

In Transcaucasia the situation is even worse. In 1976 there remained in Azerbaijan 16 working mosques, including two in Baku and one in each important city. Mosques are generally both Shi'a and Sunni, and the ceremony is often attended by believers of both rites.

The number of mosques is slowly growing, and a certain number have been built since the mid-1970s. Four new cathedral mosques were built during the first six months of 1978 in the Uzbek SSR alone.[23]

The general distribution of mosques is significant for the post-war evolution of official Islam in the Soviet Union. In Central Asia, the overwhelming majority of working mosques are to be found in cities. The former situation is thus reversed: while the strength of pre-revolutionary Russian Islam resided in the countryside, Soviet "official" Islam is moving back to the cities because there are not enough registered clerics to run the rural mosques. As to the countryside, except in the Tatar-Bashkir territories where many rural mosques have survived, it remains the realm of "parallel" Islam represented by the Sufi brotherhoods or, simply, by the numerous unregistered *mullahs*.

It must be noted, however, that the "level" of the religious fervour of the population in no way depends on the number of working mosques. The Chechen-Ingush ASSR — a real bastion of the Muslim faith — did not possess a single mosque between 1943 and 1978.[24]

The religious educational institutions

The Tashkent Directorate controls the only two Muslim religious educational institutions, the *medresseh* of Mir-i Arab in Bukhara and the *medresseh* Imam Ismail al-Bukhari in Tashkent. All *mektebs* (lower level schools) and other *medressehs* (medium level) were closed before 1928.

The *medresseh* Mir-i Arab of Bukhara was opened in 1945. It is a medium-level establishment with seven years of courses; students come from all over the Soviet Union, usually after graduating from a Soviet school or even from a university. In 1978 it had some 70 students. Graduates from Mir-i Arab (some 10–15 every year) either become *imam-khatibs* of the working mosques or complete their education at a higher-level *medresseh*, Imam Ismail al-Bukhari of Tashkent.

Founded in 1971, this higher level *medresseh* received the name of Ismail al-Bukhari in 1974. Its first class graduated in 1975, after a four-year course. In 1978 there were 30 students attending. Some students complete their education in various Muslim universities abroad: Al-Azhar of Cairo, al-Baidha of Libya, or the University of Damascus. Graduates from the Tashkent *medresseh* as a rule become executives of the four spiritual directorates. According to our information, the intellectual formation of students in both *medressehs* is relatively good, but is certainly lower than the level of the students of Al-Azhar or of any other Muslim higher educational institution of the Middle East. Soviet Islam possesses today a small but competent and efficient body of Muslim clerics.

Religious publications

The Tashkent Directorate is also the only one of the four spiritual administrations to have any real publishing activity. In 1946, it brought out a quarterly review in Uzbek (in Arabic script): *Urta Asia ve Kazakhstan Müsülmanlarinin Dini Nazariia Zhurnali (Journal of the Spiritual Directorate of the Muslims of Central Asia and Kazakhstan)*. This review was replaced in 1968 by *Muslims of the Soviet East*, a quarterly journal in two editions: the Arabic *Al-Musulmanan fi al-Sharq al-Sufiyati*, first issue in May 1969; and the Uzbek (in Arabic script) *Sovet Sharki Musulmanlari*, first issue in winter of 1968. English and French (1974), Persian (1980) and Dari (1984) editions have been added. The six editions are identical.

The Tashkent journal is the Muslim equivalent of the Orthodox

Zhurnal Moskovskoi Patriarkhii, but it surpasses its Christian counterpart both in presentation and in content. It is an amply illustrated publication, giving an excellent picture of the political and spiritual life of the directorates. It contains the texts of the most important *fetwas*, editorials on religious themes, and detailed historical articles, often signed by scholars from Academies of Sciences and universities of Central Asia.

The directorate also publishes a limited number of books and pamphlets. These have included a collection of *fetwas* by the former Mufti Ishan Babakhan (1945); a remarkably beautiful art album of Soviet Islamic monuments (1956); five or six editions of the Quran (number of copies unknown, except for the last edition in 1977, which had 10,000 copies); and a religious calendar (10,000 copies) giving the equivalent of the Hijri and Christian calendars, and the dates of religious and Soviet holidays, in Uzbek and Arabic scripts. In 1970 the directorate brought out a collection of *hadith* of Imam al-Bukhari, *Al-Adab al-Mufrad* (number of copies unknown) and in 1973 his second big collection of *hadith*, *Jami' al-Sahih* (number of copies unknown).

The Spiritual Directorate of Ufa has published since the Second World War an edition of the Quran and one catechism, *Islam ve Islam dini (Islam and Muslim Faith*, Ufa, 1957, 69 pages in Kazan Tatar and in Arabic script). The directorate also publishes a religious calendar in Tatar and Arabic script.

The other legal activities of the directorates are modest. No *shari'at* courts are left (the last one was closed in 1928). There are no *waqfs* to administer justice, and all social and economic activity is strictly forbidden to the religious associations. The collection of *zakat* came to an end in 1928. Muslim parishes depending entirely on the *sadaka* (the voluntary contribution of the believers) are wealthy and prosperous, but their intellectual and spiritual life is limited to prayers, to *fetwas*, and to the predication of the *imam-khatibs*.

It is obvious that official Islam alone could not maintain religious feeling among masses of believers. There are too few mosques left, and too few registered clerics to satisfy the spiritual needs of the believers and to perform the necessary rites. Without the activity of "parallel" Islam (see below), religion in Muslim territories of the Soviet Union would have lapsed long ago into ignorance and indifference.

5

PARALLEL ISLAM

The dynamic "parallel" or non-official Islam[25] — more powerful than official Islam — is based on the Sufi brotherhoods (tariqa: the path leading to God).[26] The tariqa are semi-secret societies. The adept (murid) is accepted into the brotherhood after a ritual of initiation and remains under the control of his master (murshid). Throughout his life, even if he is only a lay brother, he must follow a complicated and compulsory spiritual programme. In this programme permanent prayers, invocations and litanies — loud or silent zikr — accompanied by peculiar breathing and physical movements, play an important part and prepare the adept for a state of intense mental concentration. The tariqa represent perfectly structured hierarchical organisations, endowed with an iron discipline which is certainly stronger than that of the Communist Party.

Two tariqa dominate Soviet Islam: the Naqshbandi, founded in the fourteenth century in Bukhara and introduced into the North Caucasus in the late eighteenth century; and the Qadiri, a Baghdad order founded in the twelfth century and introduced into the North Caucasus at the end of the nineteenth century. Both orders have a long tradition of holy wars and of resistance to the Russian conquests in the Caucasus, in the Middle Volga region and in Central Asia. Imam Mansur in the eighteenth century, Sheikh Shamil in the nineteenth century, Imam Najmuddin of Gotzo and Sheikh Uzun Haji, who led the last great Daghestani revolt in 1920–1, the Ishan Madali (the leader of the Andizhan revolt in 1897), and many leaders of the Basmachi revolt in Central Asia (1918–29) were all Naqshbandi murshids or murids. The anti-Russian and anti-Communist movements which broke out in the Chechen territory in 1942, when the German armies were approaching the Northern Caucasus, seem to have been led, or at least inspired by the adepts of the Qadiriya tariqa.

Sufi orders exist in all the Muslim territories of the Soviet Union. In Central Asia the old Naqshbandi order still exercises its influence which seems to force other less influential native tariqa (Kubrawiya, Yasawiya) into the background. In the Volga (both Tatar and Bashkir) territory, where the Naqshbandi penetrated in the eighteenth century, some leaders played a major role in the Tatar intellectual and cultural revival of the late nineteenth and early twentieth centuries. Today, however, Tatar Sufism, if indeed it has survived at all, is greatly reduced in stature.[27] But it is in the Northern Caucasus — their traditional home — that the *tariqa* fared best. According to recent Soviet sources, the number of Sufi adepts in this region is probably higher today than before the Revolution; new branches of old orders were founded during the Soviet period, some of them quite recently (1960s), despite the violent official anti-religious campaign aimed specially at Sufism.

The Sufi orders are not small societies; despite their clandestine or semi-clandestine character, they are mass organisations. For instance, according to Soviet estimates (and Soviet sources have nothing to gain by exaggerating the number of Sufi adepts), ". . . more than half the total number of believers and almost all the clerics in the Northern Caucasus belong to Sufi brotherhoods."[28] This means that in the case of the Chechen-Ingush and Daghestan republics, Sufi brotherhoods have more than 200,000 adepts, a fantastic number for an underground society banned by Soviet law. Furthermore, adepts of Sufi orders are no longer merely mountain peasants or poor artisans as before the Revolution: the proportion of industrial workers and of intellectuals is increasing.

The organisation of today's brotherhoods is a curious blend of the traditional and the new. The innovations which have been introduced are intended to give the brotherhoods greater protection against the Soviet authorities and to root them more deeply within the popular masses. Among the most important of these innovations are the following: first, Sufi orders tend to limit the recruitment of their adepts to specific clans. This policy provides the *tariqa* with a greater degree of secrecy since adepts are bound by the dual loyalties to brotherhood and to clan. Secondly, the Sufi· orders have also begun to accept a large number of women as adepts and indeed as leaders (*sheikhs*). Certain Soviet academic specialists have lamented that the *tariqa* seem to be more effective than the Soviet anti-religious organisations at mobilising Muslim women. Finally, the membership of the *tariqa* has become much younger than ever before and is increasingly drawn from the Soviet intelligentsia.

The *tariqa* are not a passive force detached from the world but are dynamic and aggressive. The adepts are not only interested in advancing spiritually towards God but also in building God's rule on earth. Soviet sources describe them as a "fanatical anti-Soviet, anti-social, reactionary force", but they admit that the emotional and aesthetic aspects of the Sufi ritual appear much more attractive than dull and vulgar official Soviet ceremonies.

"Parallel" Islam is much more dynamic than official Islam. It is beyond the control of the Muslim Spiritual Directorates and therefore of the Soviet authorities as well. Official Islam, unable to satisfy the religious needs of the population, has thus been supplemented and indeed in some cases replaced by the Sufi orders. The adepts perform the necessary religious rites, run their own clandestine religious schools where Arabic is taught, and have their own clandestine mosques which are many times more numerous than the official working mosques.

The activities of the Sufis are often centred around various holy places, the tombs of the mystical or real saints (often Sufi leaders) who died fighting the Russians.[29] The holy places, of which there are hundreds and perhaps thousands, serve as substitutes for the closed mosques and as meeting places where adepts perform the *zikr* and are taught prayers, Arabic and the rudiments of Islamic theology. Simple believers make pilgrimages to these holy places, thus replacing the impossible *hadj* to Mecca. These tombs, therefore, provide a forum of which the Sufi brotherhoods can avail themselves to influence the Muslim masses during religious festivals and other holy events. Most Muslim cemeteries are also established near a holy place, and the guardians of the cemeteries are often adepts of a *tariqa*. Most Muslims (including Communist Party officials) are buried in Muslim cemeteries from which non-Muslims are excluded.

Of particular importance is the constant active counter-propaganda with which the Sufi orders oppose official bureaucratic anti-religious *agitprop*, often successfully. The *tariqa* thus exercise a deep influence on public opinion and are responsible for the high proportion of practicing believers in the Muslim areas of the Soviet Union, especially the Northern Caucasus.

Despite efforts by Soviet authorities, the official Islamic leadership has always refused to condemn parallel Islam as heretical or unorthodox. The few *fetwas* published by the muftis against various Sufi practices (pilgrimage to the holy shrines, collection of the *zakat* by the Sufi brotherhoods, performance of *zikr*) remain moderate and vague and prove the unwillingness of the directorates to consummate a breach with an organisation that personifies the popular aspect of Islam.

6

SOVIET MUSLIMS AND THE FUTURE: PROSPECTS AND PROBLEMS

Demographic shifts[30]

The most striking feature of current Soviet Muslim development is the rapid increase in the size of their respective populations. By themselves, demographic changes among Soviet Muslims promise to put new pressures on Soviet domestic and foreign policy. Till recently, the Slavic populations of the Soviet Union grew collectively at a rate somewhat greater than that of Soviet Muslims. But, as Table 6.1 makes clear, this disparity has been turned on its head. Table 6.2 gives some indication of the relative population shifts. There can be little question that these are worrying trends for Soviet planners, some of whom have estimated the number of Muslims in the Soviet Union by the year 2000 to be as great as 100 million. Today one in every seven Soviet citizens comes from a Muslim people, but by the year 2000 this could be one in three, if Soviet estimates are correct. We believe the estimate of 100 million to be excessive, and prefer that of the American demographer, Murray Feshbach, namely 63–74 million, or one citizen in every four or five.

Table 6.1.   RATE OF POPULATION GROWTH, 1929–79

	1929–59	*1959–70*	*1970–9*
Total Soviet Union	42%	16%	8.4%
Russians	47	13	6.5
Soviet Muslims	41	45	23.2

Table 6.2.   PROPORTION OF MUSLIMS IN SOVIET POPULATION, 1926–2000

	Population of the Soviet Union	*Muslim population of Soviet Union*	*Muslims in total Soviet population (%)*
1926	147,005,000	17,292,000	11.7
1959	208,827,000	24,380,000	11.6
1970	241,720,000	35,357,000	14.6
1979	262,442,000	43,000,000	16.5
2000 (est.)	310,000,000	65–75,000,000	22–25

As noted, comparison of the Soviet censuses of 1959, 1970, and 1979 shows that the demographic gap between Muslims and Russians of the Soviet Union is widening, even if one takes into consideration that the Russians are assimilating several formerly Christian nationalities which either lack a specific historical and cultural tradition, have large diaspora communities outside their national territories, or are foreign communities which the Soviets have deprived of cultural autonomy.*

Between the censuses of 1970 and 1979, the difference in the rhythm of increase of the major Muslim nationalities and that of the Russians was greater than between 1959 and 1970, with two exceptions,† as is shown in Table 6.3. Demographic movement of this magnitude among Soviet Muslims is forcing Soviet planners to face several manpower-related problems of statewide importance. These problems are summarised below.

Labour distribution

Much has been written in the Soviet Union and in the West about the difficulties arising from the lagging birthrate among Slavs, who have traditionally been the bulwark of the Soviet Union's industrial and technological development, and the accelerated birthrate among non-Slavs, particularly Soviet Muslims.[31] While this is a complex issue, in its barest outlines it can be described as follows. Soviet European regions, which house the vast majority of the state's heavy industry, are chronically short of labour, due to the reduced supply of new working-age youth entering the labour pool and the increasing number of older workers who are leaving it, and they are destined to become more so till the late 1990s, when demographic trends could begin to give the Slavs some relief. Soviet Muslim regions, on the other hand, and particularly Soviet Central Asia, are labour-rich, although the great majority of Central Asians engage in agricultural work and thus are lacking in those

---

* Those nationalities lacking a solid cultural and historical background include the eastern Finns and Christian Turks. The small groups enumerated below were converted to Christianity by the Russians between· the fifteenth and eighteenth centuries. Their assimilation by the Russians does not represent a betrayal of their national identity, but simply a promotion to a higher culture. Their population increase between 1970 and 1979 was significantly slower than the average increase of the Russians (6.5%).

† Only two of the important Muslim nationalities showed a marked regression in their rhythm of increase between the two stated periods. The Bashkirs' increase as compared to that of the Russians dropped from 1.92 in 1959–70 to 1.60 in 1970–9, and the Tatars' increase fell from 1.46 times the increase of the Russians to exactly the level of the latter (6.5%).

Table 6.3. GROWTH OF MUSLIM NATIONALITIES 1959-79

Total population	1959 census	1970 census	% increase 1959-70	1979 census	% increase 1970-9
Soviet Union	208,827,000	241,720,000	16	262,085,000	8.4
Russians	114,114,000	129,015,000	13	137,397,000	6.5
Total Muslim population	24,380,000	35,232,000	45	43,397,000	23.2
Uzbeks	6,015,000	9,195,000	53	12,456,000	35.5
Kazakhs	3,622,000	5,299,000	46	6,556,000	23.7
Tatars	4,968,000	5,931,000	19	6,317,000	6.5
Azeris	2,940,000	4,380,000	49	5,477,000	25.0
Tajiks	1,397,000	2,136,000	53	2,898,000	35.7
Turkmen	1,002,000	1,525,000	52	2,028,000	33.0
Kirghiz	969,000	1,452,000	50	1,906,000	31.3
Bashkirs	989,000	1,240,000	25	1,371,000	10.6
Chechens	419,000	613,000	46	756,000	23.3
Ossetians*	413,000	488,000	18	542,000	11.0
Avars	270,000	396,000	47	483,000	22.0
Lezghins	223,000	324,000	45	383,000	18.2
Kabards	204,000	280,000	37	322,000	15.0
Karakalpaks	173,000	236,000	36	303,000	28.4
Darghins	158,000	231,000	46	287,000	24.2
Kumyks	135,000	189,000	40	228,000	20.6
Uighurs	95,000	173,000	82	211,000	22.0
Ingush	106,000	158,000	55	186,000	17.7
Karachais	81,000	113,000	40	131,000	15.9
Kurds	59,000	89,000	51	116,000	30.3
Laks	66,000	86,000	30	100,000	16.3
Adyghes	80,000	100,000	25	109,000	9.0
Turks	—	79,000	—	93,000	17.7
Abkhaz*	65,000	83,000	28	91,000	9.6
Tabasarans	35,000	55,000	57	75,000	36.4
Balkars	42,000	59,000	40	66,000	10.0
Nogais	39,000	52,000	33	60,000	15.4
Dungans	22,000	39,000	77	52,000	33.3
Cherkess	30,000	40,000	33	46,000	15.0
Iranians (Ironis)	21,000	28,000	33	31,000	10.7
Abazas	20,000	25,000	25	29,000	16.0
Tats	11,000	17,000	55	22,000	29.4
Rutuls	7,000	12,000	71	15,000	25.0
Tsakhurs	7,300	11,000	51	14,000	27.3
Aguls	6,700	9,000	34	12,000	36.4
Baluchis	8,000	13,000	62	—	—
Afghans	2,000	4,000	100	—	—

*Partly Muslim.

To the list in Table 6.3 must be added some 200,000–260,000 Muslims who have not been listed in the 1979 census in a way which is readily accessible: Albanians. *c.* 4,000; Afghans, *c.* 4,000 (an old colony in the southern Uzbek SSR); Muslim Georgians, 100,000–150,000; Muslim Armenians, 1,000; and Muslim Tsiganes, up to 100,000. Including these, the total number of Soviet Muslims in 1979 could be estimated as 43,657,000.

skills which the industrial regions of the Soviet Union need most immediately. It would seem a logical, indeed a natural, phenomenon for labour surpluses from the Soviet Muslim regions to seek out and exploit the deficit labour market in the Soviet European regions, but this has not happened. For a variety of reasons Soviet Muslims have not followed what demographers have long recognised as the prevailing pattern of migratory behaviour from surplus area to deficit area.

The Soviet Union needs new labour resources if it is to sustain its current level of development, let alone initiate the new projects that are deemed necessary. In the absence of the hoped-for influx of Central Asian workers to the state's western industrial regions, Soviet planners have toyed with the idea of bringing in ever larger numbers of Bulgarians, Finns, Koreans and, recently, Vietnamese to ease the pinch. Still, these are only stop-gap measures; ultimately, the large labour surpluses of the Soviet Muslim regions must be engaged, and to do this the Soviet authorities would appear to be faced with two main choices. First, they could attempt the forcible relocation of sizeable numbers of Soviet Muslims to the western Soviet Union, but there are obvious reasons why this is unlikely to have a productive outcome. Secondly, industry could be relocated and new industry sited in the Soviet Muslim regions to take advantage of the surplus labour at its source. But this would be a very expensive undertaking which would probably result in, among other things, reduced control by the Russian centre over some of its vital industrial assets. Moreover, the location of industry in Soviet Muslim regions would necessitate expensive training programmes for the indigenous people in the proper industrial and technological skills, as well as in the Russian language. To complicate matters, there is very little migration from the Central Asian countryside to Central Asian cities. Thus the compromise of locating industry in Central Asia near labour resources might be placing it at some distance from available supplies of raw materials and communications.

Filling labour quotas for further Soviet industrial development is only half of the equation. The other half is providing gainful employment for the large and growing labour surpluses in the Soviet Muslim regions, particularly in Central Asia. Eventually the redundant or under-employed labour in these regions could become a serious social problem to the Soviet regime. Most labour surpluses are in rural regions of Central Asia and are located around extensive cotton and vegetable farming complexes. If these surpluses are to be accommodated on the land — assuming that they are not going to migrate away from the countryside to find jobs in the cities or in other regions of the Soviet Union — yet another problem, closely associated with the entire labour question in Central Asia, must be solved: the absence of sufficient water supplies.

For some decades, there has been a series of proposals before the Soviet government to re-route several Siberian rivers into Central Asia to provide water for agriculture and industry.[32] These are grandiose plans, and approval for them can come only after considerable debate. Yet it has not yet come. Central Asian leaders are open in their calls for the decision to be taken and the work begun. All parties agree that agriculture — including the important cotton export crop — cannot be expanded much beyond present limits without more water for irrigation. There is also tacit recognition that the growing rural labour surpluses in the Central Asian region cannot be gainfully occupied until agricultural expansion is undertaken.

Military manpower[33]

The labour pool of young workers supplies not only industry but also the Soviet military. Because of the demographic shifts described earlier, Soviet Muslim populations are becoming "younger" in the sense that a larger and larger share of the population of any given ethnic group can be found within the 18–25 age group. Slavic populations, by comparison, are becoming "older". Even though Muslims are expected to make up between one in every four or five citizens of the Soviet state by the year 2000, young Soviet Muslims, because of the younger age structure of Muslim society, will probably constitute one in every three members of the conscript-eligible labour cohort. This dramatic change in the ethnic composition of the draftable cohort suggests real dislocations in the Soviet armed forces as they are now structured.[34]

First, Soviet leaders, like their Russian counterparts in the empire before them, rely on Russians and other Slavs to man nearly all positions in the armed forces requiring political or technological responsibility. Soviet Muslims have never been used in great numbers — and in some units not at all — in sensitive positions, and any inclination Soviet leaders might have had to reverse this historic trend was damaged severely during the Second World War when several hundred thousand Soviet Muslims fought with Germany against the Soviet state.[35]

Secondly, Soviet Muslims as a group are by far the least proficient in Russian, the language of command. Many arrive for military service without having learned more than a few words or phrases in Russian, if any at all.

Thirdly, the generally lower levels of technological orientation and training among Soviet Muslims limit their utility in any but manual labour support positions.

Fourthly, Soviet Muslims have little predisposition to serve in the Soviet armed forces, unlike other, usually Slavic, nationalities of the Soviet empire, who see the military as a source of prestige and upward mobility. Many factors militate against their serving, including thinly veiled — often blatant — discrimination against Soviet Muslims by non-Muslim soldiers and the officer corps, which is almost exclusively Slavic. Most Soviet Muslims serving their obligatory service terms (usually 2 years) end up in non-combat construction battalions or in support positions in combat units. There are, of course, exceptions, but this would appear to be the pattern of service for the overwhelming majority. Few attend military academies, despite persistent efforts by the regime to enrol a greater number of Soviet Muslims. (Among other things which tend to disqualify Soviet Muslims for academic military training, an examination in Russian language and literature is administered to prospective applicants, most of whom have an insufficient command of the mechanics of the language and little aptitude or desire to discuss the works of Gogol or Gorky in essay form.) Recent studies have suggested that Soviet Muslims, and indeed most non-Slavic nationalities in the Soviet armed forces, leave military service with a heightened sense of their own nationality and not, as Soviet authorities are fond of boasting, with a greater sense of being non-national new Soviet men.[36]

It bears repeating that these imbalances in the Soviet military system are built-in; that is, they are residual policies from the last several hundred years, and are therefore unlikely to be changed quickly or painlessly. It is in this context of reluctant change that the Soviet military manpower dilemma and the Soviet Muslim contribution to it can best be examined.

Although Soviet military planners have some options for dealing with the changing demographic base of the conscriptable labour cohort, none of these options does not involve significant compromises in other directions. For example, assuming that the Soviet military is to remain at approximately its current size the following alternatives are available:
— to place more Soviet Muslims in positions of technological and political responsibility;
— to extend the enlistment term;
— to reduce the size of the armed forces; and
— to engage military construction battalions more fully in the non-military economy.
All these options are expensive. The first, to place more Soviet Muslims in positions of technological and political authority, would diminish Russian control in these areas. To extend the enlistment term would be to rob the already labour-short non-military economy of prime work-age youth. The total size of the armed forces could be reduced, thereby freeing more Slavs for non-military labour, but this in theory would involve the introduction of more labour-saving technology, which is expensive and in short supply. Some combinations of these options — indeed, one can envisage others — might be effective, but none is without costs of some magnitude, whether in capital expenditure or in diminished control over parts of the military system for which Russians have always demanded singular responsibility.

The recent Soviet imbroglio in Afghanistan has underlined the difficulty of implementing changes of the kind noted here by throwing into question the ultimate political loyalty and combat reliability of Soviet Muslim soldiers, many of whom were sent to Afghanistan with the first wave of troops. By nearly all accounts, Soviet Muslim troops performed poorly, fraternised with their Muslim and ethnic kin in Afghanistan, and generally caused their Russian officers grave concern.[37] Most Soviet Muslims — particularly Central Asians — were withdrawn from Afghanistan within the first three months of the conflict and replaced with more reliable and better-trained Slavic troops. This lesson will undoubtedly weigh heavily on any decision by Soviet authorities to integrate Soviet Muslims more fully into the military system as a means of balancing demographic change.

The problem of identity

Demographic gains among Soviet Muslims relative to other nationalities
in the Soviet state, and particularly to Russians and other Slavs, and the
social, economic, and political consequences that are likely to result from
these altered demographic relationships would probably matter little,
other things being equal, if the Soviet Muslim population could be seen
by Soviet planners as bound spiritually to the short- and long-term goals
of Soviet power and the overriding fact of Russian control. To date,
however, there must remain either complete scepticism, or at least
considerable doubt, among Soviet Russian planners that this is the case,
otherwise many of the problems associated with the demographically
dynamic Soviet Muslim population, such as convenient labour surpluses
or ethnically useful troops for projecting Soviet influence into other parts
of the Muslim world, would be treated as assets rather than as problems
requiring solution.

One might argue, as some social scientists have done, that Soviet
Muslims are mostly becoming well integrated economically into the
Soviet system, and that they are developing a stake in that system which
makes dissent unlikely. There can be little doubt that many Soviet
Muslims have prospered under Soviet rule, although it is a false comparison to suggest that they have done better under tight Russian control
than their counterparts just across Soviet borders, most of whom are free
to exercise political and economic choices that are unknown to Soviet
Muslims.[38] A study of the history of the decline of multinational empires
should dictate prudence in accepting that economics is such a powerful
integrator. It is certainly one factor which helps to bind minorities to a
large imperial state, but as experience has shown it is unlikely to be the
main one or even a very important one. Similarly, other measures of
"socialisation", such as linguistic indicators, educational equalisation,
the frequency and ethnic composition of mixed marriages, similarities or
dissimilarities of family habits, and the international composition of the
labour force should be treated with caution as evidence of Soviet Muslim
"integration" or commitment.[39]

The critical issue determining the extent and degree of long-term
commitment of Soviet Muslims to the Soviet Russian state is not
"socio-economics" but identity. Identity among Soviet Muslims is
a complex matter, involving different strata of sympathies, attach-
ments and allegiances — sub-national (tribal or clan), supra-national
(involving a common ethnic awareness) and super-national (involving

allegiance to, e.g., Islam or pan-Turkism).[40] For example, a typical Central Asian might see himself as a Muslim, a Turkestani, or an Uzbek — or perhaps all three simultaneously, although it is our view that in the vast majority of cases Islamic consciousness remains the most consistent, least malleable and most influential.[41] Massive Soviet efforts to eliminate Islamic consciousness and traditional Islamic practices among Soviet Muslims today support this view, as does the persistence, indeed the expansion of "parallel" Islam and Sufi brotherhood activity, described earlier, and the appearance more recently of illegal Islamic "self-published" materials, or *samizdat*.[42] Inasmuch as it is official Soviet policy to eradicate Islamic consciousness in the Soviet Union despite clear evidence that most Soviet Muslims consider Islam to be a critical ingredient in their individual and corporate identity, we find it highly doubtful that, under present conditions, Soviet authorities will be able to feel secure in the allegiance of their Soviet Muslim subjects.

The politics of identity-change among Soviet Muslims can be said to revolve mainly around Russian efforts to break down what Lenin and his immediate successors perceived as the threatening pan-Islamic consciousness of those Muslims who had been reincorporated into the new Soviet empire. They had good reason to see their political problem in this way. Most important pre-revolutionary Muslim leaders of the Russian empire argued that Russian Islam represented one nation which was divided geographically into several groups speaking different languages, but which ultimately belonged to the same historical, cultural and religious traditions. For the first six years of Bolshevik rule, this unity of the Muslim people was accepted implicitly by the new Soviet regime. The term "Muslim" was used officially to designate its nation, its armed forces (the Red Muslim Army), and its central administration (Central Muslim Committee of the People's Commissariat of Nationalities). Moreover, till 1924 the new regime maintained more or less the administrative divisions inherited from the Tsarist empire; these divisions were territorial and historical and took no account of the specific linguistic and ethnic character of the inhabitants. In Central Asia, the Steppe General Government became the Kirghiz (Kazakh) Republic; the Turkestan General Government the Turkestani Autonomous Republic; and the two protected principalities, the Emirate of Bukhara and the Khanate of Khiva, became respectively the People's Republics of Bukhara and of Khorezm.

Thus in the beginning the new regime treated Soviet Muslims as one people, a single nation divided into several states.[43] Muslim Communist leaders were in fact strongly in favour of the concept of one Muslim nation, which could ultimately become one state: the Republic of Turan. The first conflict between the Muslim Communists and the new Soviet leaders occurred in 1919 when Moscow decided to divide the Muslim community of the Middle Volga into a Tatar and a Bashkir state at a time when Muslim leaders were demanding one unified Tatar-Bashkir republic. Following this, Soviet leaders moved to enforce *razmezhevanie*, or the demarcation of the Muslim community of Central Asia. *Razmezhevanie* was designed to replace the sub-national loyalties and awareness (such as those relating to the clan and tribe) with larger loyalties, and to replace supra-national consciousness (religion, pan-Turkism) with more restricted allegiances to modern Soviet nations possessing Stalin's four criteria of nationhood: unity of territory, language, economy and culture. The formation of the new nation-states implied among other considerations the creation of new literary languages and — a still more difficult task — an attempt to discover for each newly-created nation its own culture and its own historical tradition, different from those of its neighbours. Each nation-state was to have its own administrative, economic and political institutions and staff. These creations, it was hoped, would evolve into the foci of a new national consciousness among Soviet Muslims, which in turn would undermine existing allegiances to pan-Turkic and pan-Islamic ideas. But the intended national consciousness was never intended to go beyond its role as a saboteur of other consciousnesses which the new Soviet regime found immediately threatening: it was never intended, especially, to develop and evolve into anything approximating a modern national consciousness of the kind that had already at that time, and with increasing evidence, promised to undermine the fragile multinational structures of other large empires.

Moscow's decision to break up the former Muslim *umma* in this way met with strong opposition from nearly all Muslim Communist leaders. Because of this, Stalin ensured that they were liquidated as "pan-Turkic deviationists".

Before the Revolution, only four Muslim groups in Russia — Volga Tatars, Crimean Tatars, Azeri Turks and Kazakhs — had some rather vague notions of belonging to a separate and distinct nationality. For the most part, Russian Muslims thought of themselves simply as Muslim or, in the case of the sendentary populations, in terms of their place of residence (i.e. as "Bukharaly", "Kazanly", or "Ufaly", for example). In a cultural sense the "Soviet nations" created in the 1920s and 1930s were artificial. No such thing as a specific Uzbek culture or an Uzbek national historical tradition, which could be distinguished from Tajik culture or Turkmen historical tradition, existed. On the contrary, there existed a steadily evolving consciousness among all these peoples — at least among the intelligentsia — of belonging to a common culture and a more or less unified historical tradition based on Islam and a shared Irano-Turkic heritage.

Despite the seemingly enormous obstacles in the path of the inculcation of a sense of national consciousness where none existed before and where existing loyalties, allegiances and identities argued for its rejection, consistent Soviet pressure to force the national identity to undermine and supersede these other identities has borne perhaps unintended fruit. Where there were once tribal and clan groups of Russian Muslim communities, today these communities are notable for their growing attachment to the more exclusive and proprietary notions of modern nationalism. Thus we now find a real Uzbek nation with its own national goals and priorities, which can and occasionally do conflict with objectives that formerly might have been considered as being in the general interest of all Muslims of Central Asia. The Uzbeks are a particularly good example of the potential for hitherto foreign ideas of nationalism to take root in a hostile milieu through artifical insemination. Today the Uzbek nation claims as its own national heroes individuals who were shared by all of those embracing the Islamic Irano-Turkic culture of Russian Central Asia before the Revolution; this is to say that these heroes were never exclusively Uzbek national figures; rather they were common to all. Through this peculiar brand of reverse cultural imperialism the Uzbeks are developing support and legitimacy for their own claim to a national destiny that almost certainly goes far beyond anything the Soviet Russian leadership intended. This new spiritual national awareness combines, augments and is supported by the very real economic and administrative ones; working together and reinforcing each other at various levels, these different kinds of national awareness promise to become a potent political fact in the near future.

While the Uzbeks in Central Asia would seem to have advanced their own national development more than other Muslim nations in the region, the same contributing phenomena are evident to a less but still potent degree among all the larger Soviet Muslim populations, and even among some of the smaller ones. In the context of the Soviet multinational state, as in the more global parlance of national self-determination, the national metaphor can be a very powerful one. The leaders of some Soviet Muslim peoples understand this and have already used national priorities as a tactical instrument to gain concessions from the Russian leadership. When tactics turns to strategy — and often the line between the two is invisible — then it will be possible to say that a true Soviet Muslim nationalist era has begun. Meanwhile, the rapid introduction of native cadres into an increasing number of responsible positions in their own regions — positions traditionally held by Russians — will keep Soviet leaders constantly alert to the fact that dramatic changes are taking place.[44] Friction — nationalist friction — is the likely result.[45]

During the last ten years the Uzbeks in Central Asia, the Volga Tatars in the Middle Volga region, and the Azeris in the Caucasus have become strong poles of attraction for other Muslim national groups. This is not surprising, for Islamic societies are dynastic societies; therefore, it is perhaps a normal development for dynastic leaders to emerge simultaneously with the emergence of Soviet Muslim nations of varying strength. Today all three nations are strong and demonstrate imperialistic tendencies in the sense that they are assimilating other Muslim peoples around them. Their claims to leadership in their respective regions are based on the economic importance of their territories and on their cultural vitality. Not coincidentally, nearly all the historical cultural capitals of Islam are located in their administrative regions: Bukhara, Samarkand, Urgench, Shahrisabz, Kokand, Khiva and Tashkent in Uzbekistan; Baku and Ganja (Kirovabad) in Azerbaijan; and Kazan in the Tatar ASSR.

Borderland dilemmas[46]

The Soviet Union is a borderland empire. For nearly the entirety of its land borders, ethnic groups are divided between it and neighbouring states. Sometimes this division is dramatic, as in Central Asia where ethnic groups are divided among the states of the region all the way down to the tribal level.

Apart from recent demographic gains among Soviet Muslims and the implicit policy problems this growth poses to Soviet planners, the dilemmas raised by the splitting of ethnic populations among several states with different political and economic systems, different alliances, and different views of the political future of the region are perhaps the most worrying to the Soviet leadership. The following states share Muslim populations with the Soviet Union:

CHINA (mostly in Xinjiang province, otherwise eastern Turkestan)[47]

Uighurs. Official sources in the People's Republic of China claim 5.4 million Uighurs within the country, but these estimates, which are extrapolations from demographic work conducted in the 1950s, are probably substantially in error. Assuming that Muslims in the PRC have enjoyed approximately the same birth-rates as those of Soviet Muslims directly across the Central Asian border, it is more likely that Uighurs in the PRC number between 10 and 12 million. This constitutes the bulk of the Uighur population of Central Asia (the Soviet Union had approximately 211,000 Uighurs in 1979).

Kazakhs. PRC authorities claim approximately 900,000 Kazakhs, but if one applies the same assumptions of population growth as above, this figure should probably be nearly doubled to approximately 1.2–1.5 million.
Kirghiz. 113,999.
Uzbeks. 12,453.
Tajiks. 26,503.
Tatars. 4,127.

AFGHANISTAN[48]

Turkmen. Approximately 300,000.
Uzbeks. From 1–3 million.
Tajiks. Probably over 3 million.
Kirghiz. Probably less than 10,000 (approximately 4,000 of these were relocated to Turkey in 1982 as a result of the Soviet invasion of Afghanistan).

IRAN

Turkmen. 300,000–400,000.
Azeris. 4–5 million.
Kurds. Approximately 1 million.

TURKEY

Laz. 400,000.
Kurds. 5–6 million.
Turkmen. Unknown.

IRAQ

Kurds. 1–2 million.
Turkmen. 100,000.

In the context of recent events in the Middle East and in China, these divisions become significant. For example, Islamic militancy arising from the revolution in Iran has been felt among Soviet Muslim populations, although it is difficult to quantify the number of contacts or to make an accurate assessment of their negative impact. It is known, however, that Soviet authorities have become extremely worried about the potentially subversive effects of dynamic Islam on their own rigidly controlled Muslim peoples, and since the early 1980s have moved from a position of support for the Iranian revolution — especially when it assumed its most militant anti-American overtones — to one of condemnation, as it became clear that the impact of Islam in motion could not be confined to Iran itself. Regional and local Soviet media have continuously warned of the inherent dangers of spillover. Unusually candid on this sensitive issue, Soviet media give sufficient evidence to warrant the conclusion that considerable spillover has occurred, and that the Soviet authorities have not yet found adequate measures for limiting the damage.[49]

The Soviet invasion of Afghanistan in December 1979 further encouraged trends set in motion by the ayatollahs in Iran. Breaking with long-standing historical precedent, Soviet authorities authorised the sending of a large number of Soviet Central Asian reservists into Afghanistan in the original invasion force despite the certainty that they would face Muslims of the same nationalities on the Afghan side. For a variety of reasons, including fraternisation, traffic in Qurans, and an unwillingness to engage their Muslim brothers in battle, the vast majority of Soviet Central Asian soldiers were withdrawn within two months. We can assume that they returned to their native Soviet republics with tales of Muslims who were prepared to resist Russians with arms, with first-hand impressions of a vital Islamic state, and with a brief but potent exposure which they would not otherwise have had to members of the same tribes, clans and brotherhoods as they themselves. Moreover, returning Soviet Muslims certainly will have noted that the Afghans are a free people, despite the Soviet invasion.

There can be little question that some Soviet Central Asians welcomed an opportunity to try their hand at the management of a Central Asian state, a task with which many Soviet Central Asian specialists were largely entrusted from the rise of Taraki to the Soviet invasion and perhaps beyond. While this exercise has ostensibly been in the service of Soviet power, it cannot but reinforce the sentiment among thoughtful Soviet Muslim élites that they possess all the tools required to manage a state — either abroad or at home — independent of Russians.

Turkey, which is the home of the largest and most active emigration of Muslims from Central Asia, the Caucasus and the Middle Volga, has recently accepted several thousand Kirghiz refugees from the fighting in Afghanistan.[50]

Of all the Muslim borderland dilemmas, that posed by the People's Republic of China is potentially the most menacing. For years, until the fall of the Gang of Four, the PRC leadership employed what can only be described as a nationality policy on the Soviet model in its own Muslim regions. This included, as it has in all the Soviet Muslim regions, a two-pronged offensive against Islam: official persecution of believers and Islamic institutions, and the inundation of Muslim regions with Han Chinese as a means of ensuring Peking's control while at the same time encouraging the assimilation of natives to Chinese culture. This policy, in all its aspects, has now been admitted openly by Chinese leaders and nationality specialists to have been a dismal failure.

The result of this realisation has been to set in motion significant and, from the Soviet point of view, threatening policy changes in the PRC's most westerly Muslim regions. At the heart of these policy changes lies another realisation: that, unlike the Russians, who constitute less than half the total Soviet population, Han Chinese face no long-term threat from their own minorities, who constitute 6–10 per cent of the total population of the PRC. Moreover, Chinese authorities are beginning to see this relative security from demographic encroachment as a strategic advantage *vis-à-vis* the Soviets.

The new PRC nationality policy towards its Muslims emphasises freedom of religion (thousands of new mosques have been opened in Xinjiang and elsewhere since 1981) and the gradual resettlement of sizeable numbers of Han citizens away from the Muslim areas into which they were settled some years earlier. The latter part of this programme will be difficult to carry out, as many Chinese quickly acknowledge, owing to the many levels of local interest which must be overcome, but in the ongoing Sino-Soviet competition for the allegiance of the mostly Muslim peoples who inhabit the strategic Central Asian border region, this commitment — even if it remains little more than that — could become a potent propaganda instrument for use against the Soviets. The Soviet authorities, for a variety of obvious reasons, certainly cannot match the Chinese declaration with one of their own to remove Russian immigrants from Soviet Central Asia, a handicap with a significance that is unlikely to be lost on the Central Asians themselves.

In addition to articulating a new nationality policy with special provisions for China's Muslims, the PRC leaders appear to have embarked on a stronger Islamic offensive against Soviet influence than at any time in the past. Already the leaders of China's official Islamic establishment have entered the diplomatic competition in the Middle East for the favour of other Islamic societies. The main thrust of their diplomatic efforts has been to condemn Soviet Islamic policy to Muslims abroad. It is too early to understand all the directions of this anti-Soviet Islamic offensive by a bordering *Communist* state professing an alternative and competing Islamic policy; however, it is a challenge the Soviet Union has never had to face in its history, and one it is poorly equipped to deal with.[51]

All these factors are set to make the borderland factor an irritating and potentially damaging one to Russian control of Soviet Muslims in the decades ahead. And it should not be forgotten that beyond the immediate borderland vicinity lies a Muslim world of more than 800 million. It is illogical, we believe, to think that over the long term Soviet Muslims will find Soviet rule a stronger magnet than community with their own, despite the internal squabbles and rifts that divide the larger Muslim world. This is in no sense to suggest that the Soviet Muslim community is about to rebel; while there is evidence of dissent against Russian rule, there is no hint of the Russians being less than prepared to deal with it. For nearly seven decades, Soviet Russian leaders have shown themselves able to manage the ethnic factor in Soviet society by the threat of instant retaliation against any individual or ethnic group daring to challenge Russian control where Russians are not prepared to give it up. It is this threat — both implied and explicit — which underlies other ethnic management techniques, such as providing the occasional safety valve for ethnic unrest or, less frequently, by targeting particular groups with economic incentives and the promise of material advantage. We believe that a variety of forces — from domestic economic stagnation and the impact of demographic shifts to the Soviet Muslim's heightened political awareness and the potential for this awareness to be stimulated from abroad — will make Soviet ethnic management of the Islamic community within its borders more difficult in the years ahead. If for no other reason than this, we should be asking: Who are the Soviet Muslims?

NOTES TO PART ONE

1. A number of recent works discuss the psycho-political implications of Islamic identity among Soviet Muslims. Perhaps the best is Michael Rywkin, _Moscow's Muslim Challenge: Soviet Central Asia_ (London: C. Hurst; Armonk, NY: M.E. Sharpe, 1982), especially ch. 6. See also the special issue of _Central Asian Survey_ (vol. 3, no. 3, 1984), which is devoted to the issue of identity among Soviet Muslims.

2. Several recent books discuss Soviet Muslims within the context of Soviet efforts to maintain a multinational empire. See, for example, Robert Conquest (ed.), _The Last Empire_ (Stanford: Hoover Institution Press, 1985); S. Enders Wimbush (ed.), _Soviet Nationalities in Strategic Perspective_ (London: Croom Helm, 1985); Alexandre Bennigsen and Marie Broxup, _The Islamic Threat to the Soviet State_ (London: Croom Helm, 1983); William O. McCagg, Jr., and Brian D. Silver (eds), _Soviet Asian Ethnic Frontiers_ (New York: Pergamon Press, 1979); and Michael Rywkin, _Moscow's Muslim Challenge_.

3. Albert Wohlstetter, Foreword in Wimbush (ed.), _Soviet Nationalities in Strategic Perspective_, pp. vii–xv.

4. For the history of the spread of Islam on the territory of the present-day Soviet Union, see V.V. Barthold, _Istoriia kul'turnoi zhizni Turkestana_ (Leningrad, 1927), and his _Four Studies on the History of Central Asia_ (New York: Heinemann, 1956–62) in 3 vols. A shorter presentation of this issue is in Alexandre Bennigsen and Chantal Lemercier-Quelquejay, _Les Musulmans oubliés_ (Paris: Maspéro, 1981).

5. For an excellent history of the Crimean Khanate, see Alan W. Fisher, _The Crimean Tatars_ (Stanford: Hoover Institution Press, 1978).

6. For an analysis of the conversion of Muslims (mainly Tatars) to Christianity, see Chantal Lemercier-Quelquejay, "Les Missions orthodoxes en pays musulman de Moyenne et Basse Volga, 1552–1865", _Cahiers du Monde Russe et Soviétique_, vol. 8, no. 3 (July–Sept. 1967, pp. 369–404. For a Soviet view of the question, see V.M. Gorokhov, _Reaktsionnaia shkol'naiia politika tsarizma v otnoshenii Tatar Povolzh'ia_ (Kazan, 1941).

7. Sufism in the Russian empire and the Soviet Union is discussed in Alexandre Bennigsen and S. Enders Wimbush, _Mystics and Commissars: Sufism in the Soviet Union_ (London: C. Hurst, 1986; Berkeley and Los Angeles: Univ. of California Press); Chantal Lemercier-Quelquejay, "Sufi Brotherhoods in the USSR: An Historical Survey", _Central Asian Survey_, vol. 2, no. 4 (Dec. 1983), pp. 1–35; and Alexandre Bennigsen, "Muslim Conservative Opposition to the Soviet Regime: The Sufi Brotherhoods in the North Caucasus", in Jeremy R. Azrael (ed.), _Soviet Nationality Policies and Practices_ (New York: Praeger, 1978), pp. 334–48.

8. For a popular history of the Murid movement, see Leslie Blanch, _The Sabres of Paradise_ (New York: Viking Press, 1960). An excellent scholarly account, including bibliography, is Paul B. Henze's "Fire and Sword in the Caucasus: The 19th Century Resistance of the North Caucasian Mountaineers", _Central Asian Survey_, vol. 2, no. 1 (July 1983), pp. 5–44.

9. See Mehmet Saray, "The Russian Conquest of Central Asia", _Central Asian Survey_, vol. 2/3, Oct. 1982–Jan. 1983, pp. 1–30; and by the same author,

"Russo-Turkmen Relations up to 1874", *Central Asian Survey*, vol. 3, no. 4, 1984.

10. Il'minski's policies are described by Stephen L. Blank, "National Education, Church and State in Tsarist Nationality Policy: The Il'minskii System", *Canadian American Slavic Studies*, vol. 17, no. 4, pp. 466–87; by Isabelle Kreindler, "Ibrahim Altynsarin, Nikolai Il'minskii and the Kazakh National Awakening", *Central Asian Survey*, vol. 2, no. 3 (Nov. 1983), pp. 99–116; and by J. Saussay, "Il'minskij et la politique de russification des Tatars, 1865–1891", *Cahiers du Monde Russe et Soviétique*, vol. 8, no. 3, pp. 404–27. For additional sources, see Isabelle Kreindler, "Non-Russian Education in Central Asia: An Annotated Bibliography", *ibid.*, vol. 1, no. 1 (July 1982), pp. 111–23; and Simon Crisp, "Non-Russian Education in Daghestan: A Bibliographical Note", *ibid.*, vol.2, no. 2 (Sept. 1983), pp. 149–53.

11. The Muslim reform movement is described and analysed by Dzhemaleddin Validov, *Ocherki obrazovannosti i literatury Tatar do revoliutsii 1917 goda* (Moscow, 1933); Galimdzhan Ibragimov, *Tatary v revoliutsii 1905 goda* (Kazan, 1926); and Abdurrahman Saadi, *Tatar Edebiyati Tarihi* (Kazan, 1926). A short presentation of Jadidism is in Alexandre Bennigsen and Chantal Lemercier-Quelquejay, *Les mouvements nationaux chez les Musulmans de Russie: Le Sultangalievisme en Tatarstan* (Paris and The Hague: Mouton, 1960). A recent treatment by a Soviet Tatar scholar is Ya. G. Abdullin, *Tatarskaia prosvetitel'skaia mysl'* (Kazan, 1976).

12. Early Soviet policy toward Islam is described in Alexandre Bennigsen and Chantal Lemercier-Quelquejay, *Islam in the Soviet Union* (London: Pall Mall Press, 1967), esp. pp. 123–53.

13. The best account of this period is given by Soviet scholars themselves. See G. Safarov, *Kolonial'naia revoliutsiia — opyt Turkestana* (Moscow, 1921; reprinted by the Society for Central Asian Studies Reprint Series, no. 5, Oxford, 1985); and T. Ryskulov, *Revoliutsiia i korennoe naselenie Turkestana* (Tashkent, 1925). See also Richard Pipes, *The Formation of the Soviet Union* (Cambridge, Mass.: Harvard University Press, 1964); and G. von Mende, *Der Nationale Kampf der Russland Turken* (Berlin: Weidmann, 1936).

14. Muslim National Communism is described in Alexandre Bennigsen and S. Enders Wimbush, *Muslim National Communism in the Soviet Union: A revolutionary strategy for the colonial world* (University of Chicago Press, 1979).

15. The opening of a number of new mosques in Soviet Muslim territories is reported in *The Central Asian Newsletter*, vol. 2, no. 1 (Feb. 1983).

16. See Chantal Lemercier-Quelquejay, "The USSR and the Middle East", *Central Asian Survey*, vol. 1, no. 1, pp. 43–51; and Alexandre Bennigsen, "Soviet Muslims and the Muslim World" in Wimbush (ed.), *Soviet Nationalities in Strategic Perspective*, pp. 207–26.

17. See Alexandre Bennigsen, "Muslims, Mullahs and Mujahidin", *Problems of Communism*, Nov.–Dec. 1984, pp. 28–44; Yaacov Ro'i, "The Impact of the Islamic Fundamentalist Revival of the Late 1970s on the Soviet View of Islam", in Yaacov Ro'i (ed.), *The USSR and the Muslim World* (London: Geo. Allen & Unwin, 1984), pp. 149–81; and Alexandre Bennigsen, "Soviet Islam since the Invasion of Afghanistan", *Central Asian Survey*, vol. 1, no. 1 (July 1982), pp. 65–78.

18. See Alexandre Bennigsen and Chantal Lemercier-Quelquejay, "Official Islam in the Soviet Union", *Religion in Communist Lands*, vol. 7, no. 3 (Autumn 1979),

pp. 148–60. For recent Soviet analyses of official Islám in the Soviet Union, see (among many others) L.I. Klimovich, _Islam_ (Moscow, 1965); R.R. Mavlintov, _Islam_ (Moscow 1974); N. Ashirov, _Evoliutsiia Islama v SSSR_ (Moscow, 1973); T.S. Saidbaev, _Islam i obshchestvo_ (Moscow, 1978); K.A Merkulov, _Islam v mirovoi politike: mezhdunarodnykh otnosheniiakh_ (Moscow, 1982); Institute of Scientific Atheism, _Islam v SSSR_ (Moscow, 1983); USSR Academy of Science, _Islam — kratkii spravochnik_ (Moscow, 1983); and A. Ahmedov, _Sotsial'naia doktrina Islama_ (Moscow, 1982).

19. op.cit., 6 May 1942.

20. Radio Moscow, 15 April 1979, 1530 GMT; in Arabic.

21. op.cit., 4 May 1979.

22. Personal communication to the authors.

23. _Muslims of the Soviet East_, April 1978, p. 16.

24. On this topic, see Alexandre Bennigsen and Chantal Lemercier-Quelquejay, ''Muslim Religious Dissent in the USSR'', _Religion in Communist Lands_, vol. 6, no. 3, 1978, pp. 155–63.

25. Soviet sources on ''parallel Islam'' are numerous. Among the best are A.D. Yandarov, _Sufizm i ideologiia natsional'no osvoboditel'nogo dvizheniia_ (Alma-Ata, 1975); Kh. B. Mamleev, _Reaktsionnaia sushchnost' muridizma_ (Groznyi, 1966); M.M. Mustafinov, _Zikirizm i ego sotsial'naia sushchnost'_ (Groznyi, 1971); A.M. Tutaev, _Protiv sektanskogo bezzakonia_ (Grozny, 1975); V.N. Basilov, _Kul't sviatykh v Islame_ (Moscow, 1970); S.M. Demidov, _Sufizm v Turkmenii — Evoliutsiia i perezhitki_ (Ashkhabad, 1978); and S. Mambetaliev, _Sufizm zhana anyng Qyurgyz-standagy Agymdary_ (Frunze, 1972).

26. For a description of Sufi practice in the Soviet Union, see Bennigsen and Wimbush, _Mystics and Commissars_, op.cit.

27. See Azade-Ayse Rorlich, ''Sufism in Tatarstan: Deep Roots and New Concerns'', _Central Asian Survey_, vol.2, no. 4 (Dec. 1983), pp. 37–44.

28. V.G. Pivovarov, ''Problemy byta, natsional'nykh traditsii i verovanii v Checheno-Ingushskoi ASSR — sotsiologicheskie issledovaniia'', _Voprosy Nauchnogo Ateizma_ (Moscow, 1975), vol. 17, p. 316.

29. A list (and map) of Soviet Sufi holy places is in Bennigsen and Wimbush, _Mystics and Commissars_, op. cit; see also David Nissman, ''Iran and Soviet Islam: The Azerbaijan and Turkmenistan SSRs'', _Central Asian Survey_, vol. 2, no. 4 (Dec. 1983), pp. 45–60.

30. A great deal has been written on demographic change in the Soviet Union and its Muslim dimension. See, for example, Michael Rywkin, _Moscow's Muslim Challenge_, Ch. 5; Hélène Carrère d'Encausse, _L'Empire éclaté_, Chs 2 and 3; Alexandre Bennigsen and Marie Broxup, _The Islamic Threat to the Soviet State_, pp. 124–35; Murray Feshbach, ''Trends in Soviet Muslim Population: Demographic Aspects'', in Yaacov Ro'i (ed.), _The USSR and the Muslim World_, pp. 63–94; Murray Feshbach and Stephen Rapawy, ''Soviet Population and Manpower Trends and Policies'' in _Soviet Economy in a New Perspective_, Joint Economic Committee, Congress of the United States, 14 Oct. 1976; Godfrey S. Baldwin, _Population Projects by Age and Sex for the Republics and Major Economic Regions of the USSR, 1970 to 2000_, Foreign Demographic Analysis Division, Bureau of the Census, US Dept. of Commerce, International Population Report, series P. 91, no. 26, Sept. 1979; and John F. Besemeres, _Socialist Population Politics: The Political_

Implications of Demographic Trends in the USSR and Eastern Europe (White Plains, NY: M.E. Sharpe, 1980).

31. See Murray Feshbach, "Trends in the Soviet Muslim Population"; S. Enders Wimbush and Dmitry Ponomareff, *Alternatives for Mobilizing Soviet Central Asian Labor: Outmigration or Regional Development*, Santa Monica, California: the Rand Corporation, R-2476-AF, Nov. 1979; Nancy Lubin, *Labour and Nationality in Soviet Central Asia* (London: Macmillan, 1985).

32. See Philip P. Micklin, "Soviet Water Diversion Plans: Implications for Kazakhstan and Central Asia", *Central Asian Survey*, vol. 1, no. 4 (April 1983), pp. 9–43.

33. The best analysis of this problem is Edmund D. Brunner, Jr., "Soviet Demographic Trends and the Ethnic Composition of Draft Age Males — 1980–1995", Santa Monica, California, the Rand Corporation, N-1654-NA, Feb. 1981.

34. For a good historical summary of this problem, see Susan L. Curran and Dmitry Ponomareff, *Managing the Ethnic Factor in the Russian and Soviet Armed Forces: An Historical Overview*, Santa Monica, California: the Rand Corporation, R-2640D1, July 1982.

35. On this problem, see Alex R. Alexiev, "Soviet Nationalities Under Attack: The World War II Experience", in S. Enders Wimbush (ed.), *Soviet Nationalities in Strategic Perspective*, pp. 61–74.

36. For an analysis of continuing problems with Central Asians and other minorities in the Soviet armed forces, see S. Enders Wimbush and Alex Alexiev, *The Ethnic Factor in the Soviet Armed Forces*, Santa Monica, California, the Rand Corporation, R-2787/1, March 1982. For a comparison of Soviet polices and practices as they affect minorities in the military with those of other multinational empires, see S. Enders Wimbush, "Soviet Nationalities in the Soviet Armed Forces", in S. Enders Wimbush, *Soviet Nationalities in Strategic Perspective*, pp. 227–48.

37. S. Enders Wimbush and Alex Alexiev, "Soviet Central Asian Soldiers in Afghanistan", Santa Monica, California, the Rand Corporation, N-1634D1, Jan. 1981.

38. See, for example, the interesting article by Alastair McAuley, "The Soviet Muslim Population: Trends in Living Standards, 1960–75" in Ro'i, *The USSR and the Muslim World*, pp. 95–114.

39. See Michael Rywkin, "The Impact of Socio-Economic Change and Demographic Growth on National Identity and Socialisation", *Central Asian Survey*, vol. 3, no. 3, 1984, pp. 79–98.

40. For a discussion of the three different levels of Central Asian consciousness — sub-national, supra-national, and super-national — see Alexandre Bennigsen, "Several Nations or One People? Ethnic Consciousness among Soviet Central Asians", *Survey*, vol. 24, no. 3(108), Summer 1979, pp. 51–64.

41. *Central Asian Survey*, vol. 3, no. 3, 1985, is devoted to a discussion of the identity problem in Central Asia, particularly its Islamic component.

42. See, for example, H.B. Paksoy, "The Deceivers", *Central Asian Survey*, vol. 3, no. 1, 1984, pp. 123–31; M. Abdyldaev, "Za shirmoi Islama", *Sovetskaia Kirgiziia*, 30 June 1984; A. Dilmukhammedov, *Sovet Uzbekistani*, 24 June 1984; and "Kogda net kontrolia", *Bakinskii Rabochii*, 3 Feb. 1985.

43. For an overview of this issue see S. Enders Wimbush, "The Politics of Identity

Change in Soviet Central Asia'', *Central Asian Survey*, vol. 3, no. 3, 1984, pp. 67–78.

44. On the gradual movement of Soviet Central Asians into positions formerly held by Russians, see the two articles by Michael Rywkin, "The Soviet Nationality Policies and the Communist Party Structure in Uzbekistan", and "Power and Ethnicity: Regional and District Party Staffing in Uzbekistan, 1983–84". Both articles appear in *Central Asian Survey*, vol. 4, no. 1, 1985.

45. On the possibility for conflict between Soviet Muslims and Slavs over positions of authority and jobs, see Steven L. Burg, "Central Asian Political Participation and Soviet Political Development" in Ro'i, *The USSR and the Muslim World*, pp. 40–62.

46. For an overview of this problem, see Daniel C. Matuszewski, "Empire, National-ities, Borders: Soviet Assets and Liabilities" in Wimbush (ed.), *Soviet Nationalities in Strategic Perspective*, pp. 75–100. For specific treatments of individual national-ities, see William O. McCagg and Brian D. Silver (eds), *Soviet Asian Ethnic Frontiers* (New York: Pergamon Press, 1979).

47. The Sino-Russian rivalry over this critical border region is treated by Hans Bräker, "Nationality Dynamics in Sino-Soviet Relations", in Wimbush (ed.), *Soviet Nationalities in Strategic Perspective*, pp. 101–57; Roostam Sadri, "The Islamic Republic of Eastern Turkestan: A Commemorative Review", *Journal, Institute of Muslim Minority Affairs*, vol. 5, no. 2 (July 1984), pp. 294–319.

48. See Audrey C. Shalinsky, "Islam and Ethnicity: The Northern Afghanistan Per-spective", *Central Asian Survey*, vol. 1, nos 2/3 (Nov. 1982), pp. 71—83. Also, by the same author, "Ethnic Reactions to the Current Regime in Afghanistan — A Case Study", *Central Asian Survey* vol. 3, no. 4 (1984).

49. For a discussion of the issue of "spillover", see Alexandre Bennigsen, "Mullahs, Mujahidin and Soviet Muslims", *Problems of Communism*, Nov.–Dec. 1984, pp. 28–44. See the correspondence concerning this article in the following issue of *Problems of Communism*.

50. See Debra Denker, "The Last Migration of the Kirghiz of Afghanistan?", *Central Asian Survey*, vol. 2, no. 3 (Nov. 1983), pp. 89–98.

51. See, for example, Hans Bräker, "Die islamischen Türkvölker Zentralasiens und die Sowjetisch-Chinesischen Beziehunger", *Berichte des Bundesinstituts für ostwissenschaftliche und internationale Studien*, no. 37, 1984; "The Battle of the Hearts and Minds in the Heart of Asia", *Arabia: The Islamic World Review*, vol. 4, no. 40 (Dec. 1984), pp. 36–7; S. Enders Wimbush, "Nationality Research in the People's Republic of China: A Trip Report", Santa Monica, California, the Rand Corpo-ration, N-1713-NA, Aug. 1981; and "From the Editor", *Central Asian Survey*, vol. 2, no. 2 (Sept. 1983), pp. 1–5. For a lengthy discussion of recent changes in Chinese nationality and religion policy and the impact of these changes on the Central Asian region, see Alexandre Bennigsen, Marie McNally-Broxup, Paul B. Henze and S. Enders Wimbush, *Central Asia in the 1980s: Strategic Dynamics in the Decade Ahead*, Foreign Area Research, Kansasville, Wisconsin, 1984.

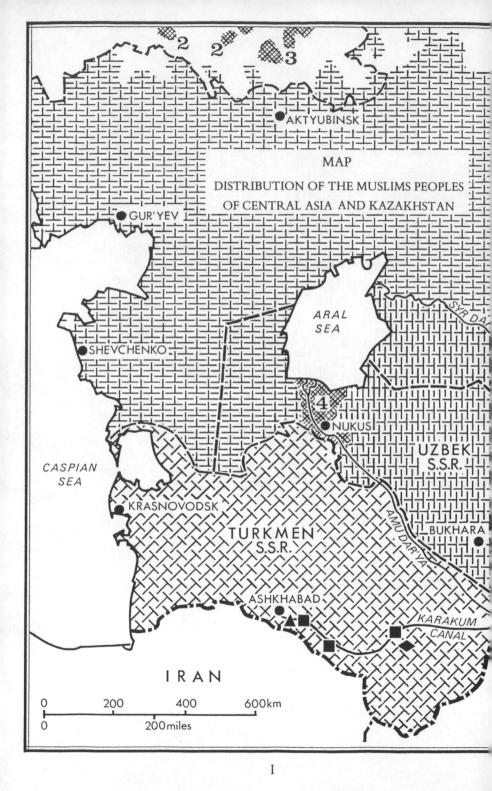

MAP

DISTRIBUTION OF THE MUSLIMS PEOPLES
OF CENTRAL ASIA AND KAZAKHSTAN

I

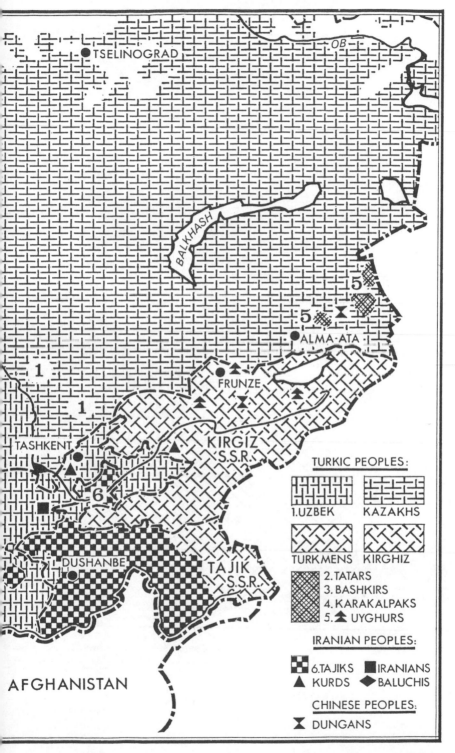

TURKIC PEOPLES:

1. UZBEK KAZAKHS

TURKMENS KIRGHIZ

2. TATARS
3. BASHKIRS
4. KARAKALPAKS
5. ▲ UYGHURS

IRANIAN PEOPLES:

6. TAJIKS ■ IRANIANS
▲ KURDS ◆ BALUCHIS

CHINESE PEOPLES:

✕ DUNGANS

Part Two

7

THE MUSLIMS OF CENTRAL ASIA

In 1979, Central Asia and Kazakhstan had a population of more than 40 million of whom 70% were Muslims. This geographically diversified territory is characterised by a strong historical and cultural unity. Since the earliest centuries of Islam, Central Asia (Turkestan) has been one of the most prestigious territories of the Muslim world. From the seventeenth century until the 1917 Russian Revolution, this great Muslim civilisation declined, but since the Second World War it has entered into an era of revival. Throughout its history till 1924, Central Asia was politically unified or, in its period of decline, divided along geographical lines — never national ones. All Central Asian Muslims have a strong feeling of belonging to the same cultural tradition.

The territory is overwhelmingly dominated by Turks, who in 1970 constituted 90% of the Muslim population. Only minor differences exist between the various Turkic languages (both literary and spoken). A great number of the non-Turkic and Turkic autochthonous population is bilingual, employing both Iranian and Turkic. Sunni Islam is the predominant creed.

Since the Second World War there has been an intense immigration of Russians and other Soviet Europeans (mostly Slavs) to the urban and rural areas of Central Asia. In the steppe areas of Kazakhstan and in Kirghizia this immigration has already turned many of the major cities of the region into Slav bastions at the expense of the local population (see Table 7.1), although this trend would now seem to have been reversed. All the republics of Central Asia and Azerbaijan are becoming more Muslim (see Table 7.2).

The population of Central Asia as a whole has been growing rapidly since the war (see Table 7.3) due both to the immigration of Soviet Europeans and the natural population increase of the natives (see Table 7.4). Central Asia has also received a number of Muslim immigrants from other parts of the Soviet Union (see Table 7.5). A comparison of the 1959 and 1970 censuses suggests that these immigrant groups are not being assimilated by the indigenous Muslims.

Table 7.1.   RUSSIAN AND OTHER NON-MUSLIM IMMIGRANTS IN SOVIET CENTRAL ASIA, 1970 AND 1979 CENSUSES

	Uzbek SSR 1970	Uzbek SSR 1979	Kazakh SSR 1970	Kazakh SSR 1979	Kirghiz SSR 1970	Kirghiz SSR 1979	Tajik SSR 1970	Tajik SSR 1979	Turkmen SSR 1970	Turkmen SSR 1979	Total 1970	Total 1979
Russians	1,473,465	1,665,658	5,521,917	5,991,205	855,939	911,703	344,109	395,089	313,079	349,170	8,508,505	9,312,735
Ukrainians	111,676	113,826	933,461	897,964	120,081	109,324	31,671	35,826	35,398	37,118	1,232,287	1,194,058
Belorussians	16,696	19,073	198,275	181,491	6,868	7,676	4,011	5,412	4,445	5,289	230,590	439,632
Koreans	147,538	163,062	81,598	91,984	9,404	?	8,490	?	3,493	?	250,523	434,972
Germans	—	—	858,077	900,207	89,834	101,057	37,712	38,853	—	?	985,623	1,040,117
Jews	102,855	99,908	27,689	?	7,680	?	14,615	14,667	3,494	?	156,333	?
Armenians	34,174	42,374	12,814	14,022	2,688	3,285	3,787	4,861	23,054	26,605	76,517	91,147
Poles	—	?	61,445	?	—	—	—	—	—	—	61,445	?
Mordvinians	14,176	?	34,371	?	5,390	?	7,025	?	3,488	?	64,450	?
Chuvash	8,869	?	22,871	?	2,092	?	2,254	?	—	?	36,086	?
Moldavians	—	3,152	26,025	30,256	—	1,375	—	580	—	1,561	26,025	36,924
Udmurts	—	—	15,786	?	—	—	—	—	—	—	15,786	?
Lithuanians	—	1,040	14,194	10,964	—	430	—	472	—	224	14,194	13,130
Maris	—	—	9,089	?	—	?	—	—	—	—	9,089	?
Georgians	—	4,088	6,883	7,700	—	1,002	—	808	—	1,047	6,883	14,645
Total Non-Muslims	1,908,722		7,824,495		1,099,972		453,696		386,451		11,674,336	

Table 7.2. MUSLIM AND RUSSIAN POPULATION INCREASES IN MUSLIM REPUBLICS, 1959–79 (%)

	1959		1970		1979	
	Muslims	*Russians*	*Muslims*	*Russians*	*Muslims*	*Russians*
Uzbekistan	79.5	13.5	81.7	12.5	84.2	10.8
Kazakhstan	34.3	42.7	37.5	42.4	41.6	40.8
Azerbaijan	70.2	13.6	76.5	10.0	82.0	7.9
Kirghizia	56.2	30.2	59.8	29.2	64.3	25.9
Tajikistan	71.2	13.3	83.5	11.9	84.3	10.4
Turkmenistan	75.8	17.3	78.8	14.5	82.2	12.6

Table 7.3. POPULATION OF SOVIET CENTRAL ASIA
1959

	Total population	*Muslim population*	*% of Muslims*
Uzbek SSR	8,119,103	6,518,914	80.3
Kazakh SSR	9,294,741	3,231,643	34.7
Tajik SSR	1,980,547	1,616,277	81.6
Kirghiz SSR	2,065,837	1,187,081	57.4
Turkmen SSR	1,516,375	1,174,326	77.4
Total	22,976,603	13,728,241	59.7

1970

	Total population	*Muslim population*	*% of Muslims*
Uzbek SSR	11,799,429	9,740,274	82.5
Kazakh SSR	13,008,726	5,014,757	38.5
Tajik SSR	2,899,602	2,431,815	83.8
Kirghiz SSR	2,932,805	1,803,168	61.5
Turkmen SSR	2,158,880	1,751,671	81.1
Total	33,132,435	20,741,685	62.6

1979

	Total population	*Muslim population (estimate)*	*% of Muslims*
Uzbek SSR	15,389,000	12,965,000	84.2
Kazakh SSR	14,684,000	6,108,000	41.6
Tajik SSR	3,806,000	3,252,000	84.3
Kirghiz SSR	3,523,000	3,265,000	64.3
Turkmen SSR	2,765,000	2,270,000	82.2
Total	40,167,000	26,860,000	66.9

Table 7.4. MUSLIM PEOPLES OF SOVIET CENTRAL ASIA, 1959–79 INCREASE

	1959	1970	% increase	Comments	1979	% increase	Comments
Total population of USSR	208,826,650	241,720,134	16		262,085,000	8.4	
Russians	114,113,579	129,015,140	13		137,397,000	6.5	
Uzbeks	6,015,416	9,195,093	53		12,456,000	35.5	
Kazakhs	3,621,610	5,298,818	46		6,556,000	23.7	
Kirghiz	968,659	1,452,222	50		1,906,000	31.3	
Tajiks	1,396,939	2,135,883	53		2,898,000	35.7	
Turkmen	1,001,585	1,525,284	52		2,028,000	33.0	
Karakalpaks	172,556	236,009	36	Limited assimilation by the Uzbeks	303,000	28.4	
Uighurs	95,208	173,276	82	Recent immigrants and a new awareness of belonging to a distinct group	211,000	22.0	Immigration stopped
Dungans	21,928	38,644	77	As for Uighurs	52,000	33.3	
Tatars	779,840	1,038,078	33	Increase stronger than average for Tatars (19%) due to immigration	1,014,000	11.2	Slight immigration
Azeris	108,169	125,908	16	Increase lower than average for Azeris (49%) due either to moderate assimilation or to migration back to Azerbaijan	Unknown		

Table 7.5.   NON-INDIGENOUS MUSLIM NATIONALITIES IN
SOVIET CENTRAL ASIA, 1970
(complete 1979 figures not yet available)

	Uzbek SSR	Kazakh SSR	Kirghiz SSR	Tajik SSR	Turkmen SSR	Total
Tatars	573,733	287,712	69,373	70,803	36,457	1,038,078
Azeris	38,898	57,699	12,536	—	16,775	125,908
Uighurs	23,942	120,881	24,872	—	—	169,695
Bashkirs	29,761	21,442	3,250	4,842	2,607	52,902
Iranians	15,457	—	—	—	5,068	20,525
Daghestanis	5,892	5,771	3,990	—	8,197	23,850
Dungans	—	17,284	18,910	—	—	36,194
Kurds	—	12,313	7,974	—	2,933	23,220
Ossetians*	—	—	—	5,755	—	5,755
Baluchis	—	—	—	—	12,374	12,374
Afghans	—	—	—	4,148	—	4,148
Total	678,683	523,102	140,905	81,400	84,411	1,512,649

*The Ossetians are only partly Muslim.

Central Asia remains largely a rural area; only Kazakhstan has an urban majority. Moreover, as Table 7.6 shows, the rate of urbanisation has been slow.

Table 7.6.   URBAN AND RURAL POPULATIONS IN SOVIET
CENTRAL ASIA, 1970 AND 1979

1970

	Total	Urban (and %)		Rural
Uzbek SSR	11,799,429	4,321,503	(37)	7,477,826
Kazakh SSR	13,008,726	6,538,652	(50)	6,470,074
Kirghiz SSR	2,932,805	1,097,198	(37)	1,835,307
Tajik SSR	2,899,602	1,076,700	(37)	1,822,902
Turkmen SSR	2,138,880	1,034,199	(48)	1,124,681
Total	32,799,442	14,068,652	(43)	18,730,700

1979

	Total	Urban (and %)		Rural
Uzbek SSR	15,391,000	6,350,000	(41)	9,041,000
Kazakh SSR	14,685,000	7,921,000	(54)	6,764,000
Kirghiz SSR	3,529,000	1,366,000	(39)	2,163,000
Tajik SSR	3,801,000	1,324,000	(35)	2,477,000
Turkmen SSR	2,759,000	1,322,000	(48)	1,437,000
Total	40,165,000	18,283,000	(45)	21,882,000

(i) THE UZBEKS

The Uzbeks are generally Sunni Muslims of the Hanafi school. However, there are small Shi'a colonies in the cities of Samarkand, Bukhara,
and Tashkent.

The republic (SSR) was founded on 27 October 1924, and its territory covers 447,000 square km. (including the Karakalpak ASSR). Its
capital is the city of Tashkent which had a population in 1979 of
1,779,000, compared to 1,384,000 in 1970. Tashkent is the fourth largest
city in the Soviet Union.

Demography. The total Uzbek population in 1979 was 15,391,000,
compared to 11,800,000 in 1970, a rise of 30.4%. The urban population
of the republic was 6,350,000 (41%) in 1979 compared to 36.6% in
1970. In 1970 Muslims constituted 82.6% of the total population of
Uzbekistan, 65.5% of whom were Uzbeks. In 1979 the respective percentages were 84.6% and 68.7%.

The rise in the total number of Uzbeks in the Soviet Union from 1926
to 1979 is as shown by the following figures:

    1926: 3,988,000 (including Uighurs)
    1939: 4,844,000
    1959: 6,015,416
    1970: 9,195,093 (52.8% above 1959)
    1979: 12,456,000 (35.5% above 1970)

Between 1959 and 1970, and again between 1970 and 1979, the
increase of the Uzbeks, equalled only by that of the Tajiks, was the
highest of all the Soviet Muslim nationalities. This increase was due to
their very high fertility rate and also, although to a less degree, to the
assimilation by the Uzbeks of various Turkic nationalities living in their
republic. Now, as in the past, Uzbeks do not emigrate outside Central
Asia. In 1970 99.2% of them were established in various Central Asian
republics (as against 97.2% in 1959) with 84% in Uzbekistan itself. In
1979 99.3% of the Uzbeks were living in Central Asia and 84.8% in
Uzbekistan. Since 1959, therefore, there has been a "consolidation" of
Central Asia (and of Uzbekistan) as "more Turkic" and "more Muslim". Table 7.i.1 shows this trend.

The large increase of Uzbeks in Kazakhstan between 1970 and 1979
was a result of their emigration into the southern regions and cities of
Kazakhstan. The slightly slower increase of the Uzbeks in the other
Central Asian republics may be explained by a limited assimilation of the

Uzbeks by the local nationalities rather than by a return to their own republic. It is a significant fact that between 1959 and 1970 the number of Uzbeks established outside Central Asia decreased by more than half.

In Kazakhstan the Uzbeks constitute a massive rural colony in the Chimkent region: 175,727 Uzbeks, 63.5% of whom are rural dwellers (1970 figures). In the other areas of Kazakhstan, however, they represent the urban element; in the Dzhambul region in 1970 there were 14,337 Uzbeks (79.4% of them city dwellers) and in the Kyzyl Orda region 3,958 (95.2% of them city dwellers).

In 1979, out of the 263,295 Uzbeks living in Kazakhstan, 227,205 (or 86.3%) were in the Chimkent region.

In Tajikistan the Uzbeks constitute a rural population (87.1% rural dwellers) mainly in the Leninabad region (southern part of the Ferghana valley) and in the Gissar valley, southern Tajikistan, around Shartuz, Kolkhozabad and Kurgan Tübe. In Kirghizia, the Uzbeks are also rural dwellers (64%). In 1979, 400,909 Uzbeks (or 94% of the total population) lived in the Osh region (the eastern part of the Ferghana valley). In Turkmenistan the Uzbeks are largely city dwellers: 54.6% urban compared to 45.4% rural. In 1979, out of a total population of 233,730 Uzbeks, 161,480 (or 69%) lived in the Tashauz region (northern Turkmenistan) and 63,448 (or 27%) lived in the Charjow region, along the frontier of Uzbekistan in southeastern Turkmenistan.

Outside Soviet territory, there are about 1,000,000 to 1,500,000 Uzbeks living in northern Afghanistan (in the provinces of Maimanah, Mazar-i Sharif, and Kataghan) and a small group of some 7,500 (mainly city dwellers) in Xinjiang.

Comparison between the censuses of 1959, 1970 and 1979 shows the following trends in the Uzbekistan population:

1. There is a slight assimilation of the foreign Muslim colonies — Tajiks, Kirghiz and Turkmen — by the Uzbeks. Their increase in Uzbekistan is slower than the Soviet average, but this circumstance may also be explained by a slight out-migration of foreign Muslims from Uzbekistan.

2. In the case of the Uighurs, assimilation by the Uzbeks is more pronounced. About 36.9% of the Uighurs living in Uzbekistan in 1970 claimed Uzbek as their first mother-tongue.

3. There was an out-migration of the Azeris from Uzbekistan between 1959 and 1970 but a new wave of immigration to Uzbekistan between 1970 and 1979, mainly of industrial workers.

Table 7.i.1.   POPULATION OF UZBEK SSR, 1959–79

| | Total numbers (and % of total pop.), 1959 | 1970 | | % increase, 1959–70 | % average increase in Soviet Union, 1970 |
		Total numbers (and % of total pop.)	% of urban pop.		
Total population	8,119,103	11,799,429	36.6	43.3	16.0
Uzbeks	5,038,306 (62.1)	7,724,715 (65.5)	23.0	53.3	53.0
Karakalpaks	168,274 (2.1)	230,258 (2.0)	29.8	37.3	37.0
Tatars	445,036 (5.5)	573,733 (4.9)	73.4	28.9	19.0
Kazakhs	342,692 (4.2)	476,310 (4.0)	27.5	39.0	46.0
Tajiks	311,366 (3.8)	448,541 (3.8)	25.2	44.0	53.0
Kirghiz	92,695 (1.1)	110,726 (0.9)	9.8	19.4	50.0
Turkmen	54,804 (0.7)	71,041 (0.6)	12.3	29.6	52.0
Azeris	40,511 (0.5)	38,898 (0.3)	45.9	-4.0	49.0
Uighurs	19,377	23,942	39.0	23.5	82.0
Bashkirs	13,500	20,761	69.5	53.8	25.0
Iranians	—	15,457	—	53.1	—
Tsiganes	7,860	11,362	48.3	44.1	—
Daghestanis	3,283	3,862	65.5	79.5	44.0
Ossetians	8,755	—	—	—	—
Total Muslims	6,546,462 (80.6)	9,751,636 (82.6)	26.5	48.9	—

Russians	1,092,468	(13.5)	1,473,465	(12.5)	89.0	34.9	13.0
Koreans	138,453	(1.7)	147,538	(1.3)	57.9	6.5	13.9
Ukrainians	88,388	(1.1)	111,676	(0.9)	82.8	26.3	9.3
Jews	94,344	(1.2)	102,855	(0.9)	57.0	9.0	5.1
Armenians	27,370	(0.3)	34,174		94.5	24.5	28.0
Belorussians	9,520	(0.1)	16,969		80.4	72.2	14.3
Mordvinians	14,602	(0.2)	14,176		85.9	3.0	1.7
Chuvash	5,226		8,868		74.3	69.7	15.3
Georgians	2,474		—		—	—	—
Other	—		138,071		—	—	—
Total non-Muslims	—		2,047,793	(17.3)	—	—	—

Table 7.i.2.   UZBEK POPULATION IN THE CENTRAL ASIAN REPUBLICS, 1959–79

Uzbek population	1959 (and %)		1970 (and %)		% increase 1959–70	1979 (and %)		% increase 1970–9
Total	6,015,000		9,195,000		52.8	12,455,978		35.5
Uzbek SSR	5,038,306	(83.7)	7,724,715	(84.0)	53.3	10,569,007	(84.8)	36.8
Kazakh SSR	135,932	(2.2)	216,340	(2.3)	59.1	263,295	(2.1)	21.6
Tajik SSR	456,038	(7.5)	665,662	(7.2)	45.3	873,199	(7.0)	31.1
Turkmen SSR	125,231	(2.2)	179,498	(1.9)	43.3	233,730	(1.9)	30.4
Kirghiz SSR	218,640	(2.6)	332,638	(3.6)	52.1	426,194	(3.4)	28.1
Total in Central Asia	5,848,147	(97.2)	9,118,853	(99.2)	55.9	12,365,425	(99.3)	35.6
Outside Central Asia	168,853	(2.7)	76,147 (0.8) in RFSFR		– 54.0	90,553	(0.7)	19.5
			61,588	(0.6)		72,385	(0.6)	17.5
			10,563 in the Ukrainian SSR			9,862	(0.09)	– 6.6

4. Between the three census operations there has been an immigration of Volga Tatars, Crimean Tatars, Kazakhs and Bashkirs to Uzbekistan.

5. As a rule, the foreign Muslim communities living in Uzbekistan are not linguistically assimilated by the Uzbeks (with the exception of the Kirghiz, the Uighurs, the Ossetians — who do not figure in the 1970 census — and the Ironis who do not figure in the 1959 census), as shown in Table 7.i.3

Table 7.i.3.   UZBEK AS A NATIVE LANGUAGE OF
OTHER MUSLIMS, 1959–79

	Population in Uzbekistan			% declaring Uzbek as native tongue		
	1959	1970	1979	1959	1970	1979
Tatars	44,810	573,733	648,764	2.3	1.2	1.3
Kazakhs	335,267	476,310	620,136	1.8	1.5	2.5
Tajiks	·311,375	448,541	594,627	4.4	3.2	5.7
Kirghiz	92,725	110,726	142,182	7.2	8.8	18.7
Turkmen	54,804	71,041	92,285	6.5	3.9	5.4
Azeris	40,511	38,898	59,779	4.0	2.5	3.2
Uighurs	19,377	23,942		37.0	36.9	
Ossetians	8,755			74.2		
Ironis		15,457			79.0	
Bashkirs		20,761			2.2	

6. There has been a steady but not very important urban immigration of Russians, Ukrainians and Belorussians to Uzbekistan.

7. The increase of the Jewish community between 1959 and 1970 may be explained by the relatively high fertility rate of the Central Asian (Bukharian) Jews; it decreased after 1970 through the out-migration of European Jews.

8. The non-Muslim communities are essentially urban. However, Muslims are slowly regaining predominance in the cities, including the capital Tashkent, as shown in Table 7.i.4

The relative importance of the Muslim population (native and immigrant) grew steadily between the 1970 and 1979 censuses in all the regions of Uzbekistan with two exceptions, the *oblast'* of Syr-Darya and Bukhara, where the decrease was respectively from 78.6 to 72.4% and from 85.1 to 84.9%.

The densely populated Ferghana valley (Namangan, Andizhan and

Table 7.i.4.   POPULATION OF TASHKENT, 1959–70
(*1979 figures not yet available*)

	1959	1970
Total population	911,930	1,384,509
Muslims		
Uzbeks	307,879	512,962
Tatars	64,242	98,834
Kazakhs	8,158	15,231
Tajiks	4,585	7,999
Uighurs	—	5,884
Bashkirs	—	3,806
Azeris	—	3,411
Karakalpaks	—	1,488
Total Muslims	384,864	649,715
	(42% of total)	(46.9% of total)
Non-Muslims		
Russians	400,640	564,584
Jews	50,445	55,758
Ukrainians	24,562	40,716
Armenians	10,500	13,364
Belorussians		5,924
Mordvinians		9,343
Others		51,105
Total non-Muslims	486,147	740,794
	(58% of total)	(53.1% of total)

Table 7.i.5.   MUSLIM POPULATION IN UZBEKISTAN
(*by regions, %*)

Regions (oblasts)	1959	1970	
Andizhan	92.9	94.3	+ 1.4
Bukhara	85.1	84.9	– 0.2
Dzhizak	—	89.7	—
Kashka Darya	94.8	94.8	0
Namangan	94.6	95.8	+ 1.2
Samarkand	87.7	89.1	+ 1.4
Surkhan Darya	90.9	93.6	+ 2.7
Syr Darya	78.6	76.2	– 2.4
Tashkent	69.8	72.4	+ 2.6
Ferghana	86.8	88.9	+ 2.1
Khorezm	95.7	96.1	+ 0.4
Karakalpak ASSR	94.2	94.9	+ 0.7

Ferghana *oblasti*), the southern area of the republic (Surkhan Darya and Kashka Darya *oblasti*) and the delta of Amu Darya (Karakalpak ASSR and the Khorezm *oblast'*) have a heavy Muslim majority (above 90%).

Ethnographic data. By a seeming paradox, the Uzbek nation, today the most numerous and most dynamic of all Central Asian nations, is also the one whose consolidation was the most difficult and complicated. In that consolidation, various ethnic groups have not entirely lost their ethnic, social and linguistic peculiarities. The Uzbek nation has been formed of three ethnic layers: the urban population, the descendants of the pre-Shaibanid Turkic tribes, and the descendants of the Shaibanid Uzbek tribes.

The urban population and some old sedentary elements of the Ferghana, the Khorezm and the Angren valleys comprise the first ethnic layer. This group represents the oldest layer and is constituted by the original autochthonous Iranian population of Central Asia who were linguistically turkified. However, before 1917 the population of the cities was (and in some areas still is) bilingual (Iranian and Turkic). Before the Revolution, members of this group were known as Sarts or Tajiks (even if they spoke a Turkic language). Ethnically, members of this group are close to the Tajiks and are very different from the former nomads of a more mongoloid type.

The second ethnic layer is the descendants of the pre-Shaibanid Turkic or Mongol tribes that invaded Central Asia and settled there between the eleventh and fifteenth centuries. Before 1924 members of this group were called *Turks* (the Turkic tribes that had settled in Central Asia between the eleventh and the thirteenth centuries) or *Chagatais* (the Mongol tribes that had come to Central Asia during the Chagatai Khanate in the thirteenth to fourteenth centuries). The most important tribes continue to preserve their identity: the Karluks, the Kypchaks (33,000 in 1926 in the Ferghana valley), the Turks of Samarkand (29,000 in 1917), and the tribes of Mongol origin, such as Jalair, Barlas, Orlat, Kanchin and Mughul. Some tribes (Turks and Kypchaks) were listed in the 1926 census as separate ethnic minorities. Certain of these tribes (Kypchak, Jalair, Barlas) enter also into the composition of other Turkic nations: Nogais, Kazakhs, Karakalpaks, Kirghiz. Ethnically, members of this group are more mongolised than the Sarts.

The descendants of the Shaibanid Uzbek tribes, the last invaders of Central Asia (early sixteenth century), under Mohammed Shaibani Khan, are the third ethnic layer in the Uzbek nation. Before 1917, when they

were nomads who still preserved their tribal structure, they were known
by the name of Uzbeks or Taze Uzbeks (*taze* means pure); when the
tribal structure disappeared (as was the case with sedentaries) they were
called Sart Uzbeks. Ethnically, tribes of this category are more strongly
mongolised and closer to the Kazakhs than to the Sarts.

Some of the most important tribes of Mongol or Turkic origin have
maintained their identity and a strong feeling of tribal kinship up to the
present. This is true of the Lokays of southern Uzbekistan (66,000 in
1929), the Kungrat, the Mangyt, the Kiyat, the Ktay, the Kangly, the
Keneges, the Ming, the Kirk, the Yuz, the Saray, the Kusheht and the
Durman. The Mangyt, the Kungrat, the Kiyat, the Ktay, and the
Keneges enter also into the composition of other Turkic nationalities:
the Kazakhs, the Kirghiz, the Nogais and the Karakalpaks. Members of
such tribes consider themselves as mutually related — as kinsmen.

To this third category belong also some groups of former nomads,
who ethnically and linguistically must be classified halfway between the
Uzbeks and the Kazakhs. Such are the *Kuramas*, "mongrels" of the
Angren valley (50,218 in 1926), listed in the 1926 census as a distinct
national minority, with a specific dialect. These formerly nomadic
Uzbeks — unlike the Kazakhs, the Kirghiz, and the Karakalpaks —
have never been exogamous, but in the past have observed endogamy
within the tribe. At present, endogamous taboos sometimes survive in
the guise of preferential marriages: some tribes before the Revolution
had adopted what was called the dual fratrial system, in which two tribes
were traditionally allied (Kiyat and Kungrat, Kangly and Kanjigaly,
Ktay and Kypchak). Marriage between members of the allied tribes was
— and still is — considered preferable.

The tribal structure of former nomads survives today in the *kolkhoz*
system and in the generalised practice of *mestnichestvo*, often denounced
by Soviet sources. This consists of favouring kinsmen in the selection and
promotion of cadres at all levels. The Uzbek urban population maintains
the system of *jamaat* (in Russian, *obshchina*): a community established in
a particular quarter of the city (*mahalle*), administered by a council of
elders (*aksakal* or "white beards"), possessing its own cemetery and
often its own house of prayer. All Soviet surveys acknowledge the
ignorance of the authorities concerning the inner life of the *mahalle*
which — when undisturbed — represents a closed world, governed by
its own rules and deeply impregnated by Islam. It seems that the Sufi
orders and the traditional Muslim guilds are rooted in the *mahalle*
system.

Language and the problem of assimilation. The spoken Uzbek language consists of two groups of dialects. The first is the dialect of middle Uzbekistan (Tashkent, Samarkand, Bukhara, Andizhan, Kokand, Karshi, Dzhizak and Katta-Kurgan) which, contrary to all other Turkic languages, possesses no euphonic harmony. The second group consists of the northern dialects (along the Kazakhstan border, Chimkent, Turkistan, and in Kashka-Darya south of Bukhara) which have preserved the euphonic harmony.

The literary language, before the Revolution, was Chagatai or old Uzbek, which had reached its apogee in the fifteenth century. It was in common use among all the Turkic-speaking peoples of Central Asia (and, up to the middle of the nineteenth century, even among the Tatars of the Volga). After the Revolution, the Uzbek language was consolidated, although the dialectal and cultural differences between the sedentary Sarts and the nomadic Uzbeks made this difficult. Consolidation has been achieved gradually through the new literary Uzbek language, which replaced Chagatai in 1923, and was facilitated by the sedentarisation of the nomads. The choice of the Uzbek literary language and the changes that occurred several times in Soviet official linguistic policy reveal the difficulties that the literary language encountered in this domain.

The new Uzbek language, transcribed in a modified Arabic alphabet, was adopted in 1923. It was based on the phonetic principles of the strongly Iranised urban dialects which had lost Turkic vowel euphonic harmony and were very different from the dialects spoken in the countryside. In 1927, when the Uzbek languages were endowed with the Latin alphabet, the basis of the literary language was changed; it was then made to correspond to the spoken language of the town of Turkistan in northern Uzbekistan (now part of Kazakhstan) and, as regards grammar, to the Tashkent dialect. Because of its strictly Turkic euphony, it was barely intelligible to the urban population of Uzbekistan.

This language was discarded in 1937 in favour of a third literary tongue based on a more Iranised Tashkent dialect (without the euphonic harmony and founded on the grammar of the Ferghana speech). In 1940–1 the Latin alphabet was replaced by the Cyrillic, but the basis of the literary language remain unchanged. Despite the transformation of their literary script in favour of the Cyrillic alphabet and Russian import-words, the Uzbeks remain among the least russified of all Soviet Turks. In 1959 approximately 98.4% of them claimed Uzbek as their first mother-tongue. This percentage had barely changed in 1970, when it reached 98.6%.

Religious data. In the Soviet Union Uzbekistan occupies a central position in relation to Islam. The only two working *medressehs* (Mir-i Arab of Bukhara and Imam Ismail al-Bukhari of Tashkent) and the most important Muslim Spiritual Board (Tashkent) are within its territory. The only religious Muslim periodical (*Muslims of the Soviet East*) is published in Tashkent. There is probably a greater number of working mosques in Uzbekistan than in the four other Central Asian republics. Finally, the Mufti of Tashkent behaves as the official leader of Soviet Islam both in the Soviet Union, *vis-à-vis* the Soviet government, and abroad. As a rule, the foreign Muslim delegations visiting the Soviet Union are received by the Tashkent mufti. Islamic international congresses are generally held in Tashkent, Samarkand, or Bukhara.

The great majority of Uzbeks are Sunni Muslims of the Hanafi rite. There are small groups of Shi'a (Twelvers) in the cities of Samarkand and Bukhara, whose relations with the Sunni Muslims are friendly and whose mosques are sometimes used for the celebration of the two rites.

Official Islam is particularly well organised and influential in Uzbekistan. There are probably about 150 working cathedral mosques, and in Tashkent in 1979 Soviet sources listed 12 cathedral mosques and a "a hundred small mosques" (Mufti Zia ud-Din Babakhanov, Radio Moscow, 1 April 1979, in Arabic). Of the twelve mosques the names of nine are known, namely Tilla-Sheikh, Navas, Chapan-Ata, Mirza Yusuf, Sheikh Zeinutai, Yakka Saray, Barak Khan, Allan, and Hoja Alambardor. A thirteenth mosque, Navruz, was under construction in July 1979. In Bukhara there are three mosques: Tagban-Bavta, Hoja Zeinutdin, and Hoja Tabbat. In Samarkand there are also three mosques: Hoja Zeinmurad, Imam al-Bukhari (at Hartang) and Hoja Ahrar, along with some small mosques (according to Mufti Zia ud-Din Babakhanov, as cited above).

Most of the other working mosques are in the Ferghana valley. Andizhan has three mosques: Devaney, Mohammad Khan Töre and the Uighur mosque. Namangan has two: Sheikh Imam and Mahdum Ishan. There is at least one mosque in each of the following cities: Margelan, Ferghana, Kokand, Gök Angak (Andizhan region), Khavast (Ferghana region, built in 1974), Akhunbabaev (district of Jala Kuduk, Andizhan region), Kuteiba ibn Muslim in Kurgan Tepe (Andizhan region),

Girhduvan (Supi Chayan), Sharisabz (Hazrat-i Imam), and Karshi (Gök Gumboz).

Another concentration of mosques is in the region of Dzhizak and Syr Darya. There is one mosque in each of the following towns: Gallaaral Ak-Kurgan (built 1979), Bakht (district of Gulistan, Syr Darya region, a new mosque built 1979), Zaamin (built 1978), and Dzhizak (a new mosque built 1978). In the northwestern part of the republic (Khorezm) we have located two working mosques in Urgench (Said Aba and Saidniaz Shamkar) and one in Khiva. In southern Uzbekistan we have found only one working mosque, at Termez (Murch Baba).

Probably there is at least one official working mosque in every town of the republic, except maybe in the southern part of the republic (the region of Surkhan Darya and Kashka Darya) where the population of former nomads has always been less deeply Islamised than that of the cities. According to recent Soviet surveys, it would seem also that each urban *mahalle* has a non-official house of prayer with a non-registered (often self-appointed) mullah.

Non-official Islam is represented in Uzbekistan by the following Sufi orders:

— Naqshbandiya, a fourteenth-century *tariqa*, its centre in Bukhara (silent *zikr*), with adepts in all of Uzbekistan;

— Kubrawiya, a twelfth-century *tariqa*, its centre in Khorezm (loud *zikr*), with adepts in the Khorezm region, the Karakalpak ASSR, and the Tashauz region of Turkmenistan.

— Yasawiya, a twelfth-century mystical *tariqa*, its centre in southern Kazakhstan (loud *zikr*). It was modernised during the last years (women are now accepted in the *zikr*); its adepts are mainly in northern Uzbekistan.

— Qadiriya, a twelfth-century *tariqa*, renovated after the Second World War by deported Chechens and Ingush. It is the most popular of Sufi brotherhoods today (loud *zikr*) with adepts in all of Uzbekistan.

— Kalendariya, an itinerant order (no *zikr*) with adepts throughout Uzbekistan; it was founded by Sheikh Safa of Samarkand in the sixteenth or seventeenth century.

Holy places of pilgrimage are numerous in Uzbekistan, but the part they play — as well as that of the Sufi orders in general — in the revival of Islam is less significant in Uzbekistan than in other territories of Central Asia where the tribal structures remain strong. Some of the most famous holy places are placed under the control of the Muslim

Spiritual Board of Tashkent. Such are the tombs of Hoja Ahrar, the Naqshbandi saint, and of Imam Ismail al-Bukhari in Samarkand.*

The Sufi orders control the surviving Muslim guilds, which have been observed by Soviet specialists in the main cities of Uzbekistan, Tashkent included. Some new occupations are organised on the model of traditional guilds, as is the case, for instance, of the Tashkent taxi-drivers, whose patron saint is the Prophet Daud (David).

According to recent Soviet surveys, the Uzbeks — especially the city dwellers — are the most religious of all Central Asian Muslims. Also, Uzbekistan is an area where various religious customs are the most strictly observed because of the total confusion between religious and national characteristics. Such customs as circumcision, religious marriage, payment of *kalym*, burial at a Muslim cemetery and early marriages of young girls are maintained by believers and non-believers alike because they are considered national, popular traditions. Contrary to what is found in the former nomadic territories of Uzbekistan, the survival of Islam as a religion, as a corpus of customs and as a way of life is due not so much to the activity of the Sufi orders as to the strong influence exercised by official Islam on the urban population.

Despite the excellent relations between the official Muslim establishment and local Soviet authorities, anti-religious campaigns have been particularly intense in Uzbekistan. Between 1948 and 1975, at least 177 anti-Islamic books and pamphlets were published in the Uzbek language, a fact which makes the Uzbeks the most heavily propagandised of all Muslim nationalities. The Daghestanis are second with 140 titles and the Kazakhs third with 126. In 1935 the Uzbek Association for the Diffusion of Scientific and Political Knowledge organised 66,000 antireligious lectures in Uzbekistan. In 1959 this number had risen to 146,500.

---

* Other famous shrines were transformed into anti-religious museums during Khrushchev's antireligious campaign, but according to Soviet sources, the shrines still attract pilgrims. Such is the case of the tomb (*mazar*) of Qusam ibn Abbas (better known as Shah-i Zenda) in Samarkand; the tomb of Bahautdin Naqshband, founder of the Naqshbandi order in Bukhara; the tomb of Palvan Pir in Khiva (a museum since 1960); the tomb of Hojami Kabri in the city of Namangan (a museum since 1965); the mythical tomb of Caliph Ali Shah-i Mardan in the Ferghana region.

(ii) THE KAZAKHS

The Kazakhs are Sunni Muslims of the Hanafi school; there are no non-Muslim Kazakhs. The Soviet Socialist Republic of Kazakhstan was created as an Autonomous Republic on 26 August 1920 under the name of the Kirghiz ASSR. It was renamed the Kazakh ASSR and became a Union Republic (SSR) on 5 December 1936. Its territory covers 2,717,300 square km and its capital is Alma Ata (population in 1979 910,000; 729,000 in 1970). The total population of the republic in 1979 was 14,685,000, of which the urban population numbered 7,921,000 or 54% (50% in 1970). Till the 1920s, Russian literature referred to the Kazakhs as Kirghiz.

Demography. The total number of Kazakhs in the Soviet Union at different times has been as follows:

    1926: (together with the Kirghiz) 4,285,000
    1939: 3,098,800
    1959: 3,622,000
    1970: 5,299,000 (increase from 1959: 46%)
    1979: 6,556,000 (increase from 1970: 23.7%)

Of the Kazakhs in 1970, 79.9% lived in Kazakhstan and 90.8% in Central Asia, as compared to 76.9% and 87.3% respectively in 1959. In 1979 80.7% of the total Kazakh population lived in Kazakhstan and 91.9% in Central Asia. Between the three census operations we observe a concentration of Kazakhs in their national territory, due to either immigration into Kazakhstan of those formerly living abroad or — which is less probable — to their assimilation by other Turks outside Kazakhstan.

Beyond Kazakhstan the Kazakhs represent essentially border colonies. In Uzbekistan, they form rural colonies; only 27.5% are established in cities. The main concentration of Kazakhs is in the northern region of the republic, as shown by these figures from the 1970 and 1979 censuses:

	1970	1979 (incomplete)
Karakalpak ASSR	186,038	243,926
Tashkent region	164,349	208,002
Bukhara region	51,408	70,242
Syr Darya region	386,811	*
Khorezm region	8,391	*
Samarkand region	6,099	*
Tashkent (city)	15,231	*

*No figures published.

The Kazakh colonies in Uzbekistan seem comparatively stable; their increase between 1959 and 1970 (39%) is only slightly lower than the average of the Kazakh SSR (46%). They are neither submitting to assimilation by the Uzbeks nor emigrating from Uzbekistan. Between 1970 and 1979 the increase of the Kazakh community in Uzbekistan was more rapid than their average increase.

In Turkmenistan, Kirghizia and Tajikistan, in 1970, the Kazakhs were distributed equally between urban and rural colonies. The proportion of urban Kazakhs in these three republics was 58.2, 40.1 and 41% respectively. The marked decrease of Kazakhs in Turkmenistan and Tajikistan was probably due to the out-migration of Kazakhs returning to Kazakhstan.

In the RSFSR the important Kazakh community (518,000 in 1979) is not composed of immigrants but of the border rural colonies. Urban Kazakhs constitute only 22.5% of this community (1970 figures). The main Kazakh colonies are in western and central Siberia and the lower Volga. There were 4,195 Kazakhs living in the city of Moscow in 1970.

Table 7.ii.1.   KAZAKH POPULATION, 1970–9

	1970	1979 (incomplete)	Increase or decrease (%)
A. WESTERN AND CENTRAL SIBERIA			
Altay *krai*	19,689	19,457	decrease
Khabarovsk *oblast'*	1,743		
Kurgan *oblast'*	12,581	14,040	+ 11.6
Novosibirsk *oblast'*	12,184		
Omsk *oblast'*	52,703	61,157	+ 16.0
Orenburg *oblast'*	93,214	98,612	+ 5.8
Sverdlovsk *oblast'*	4,210		
Tiumen' *oblast'*	8,868		
Cheliabinsk *oblast'*	27,559		
Chita *oblast'*	1,586		
B. LOWER AND MIDDLE VOLGA			
Astrakhan *oblast'*	96,661	106,954	+ 10.6
Volgograd *oblast'*	31,548	34,872	+ 10.5
Kuibyshev *oblast'*	10,392		
Saratov *oblast'*	57,369	63,345	+ 10.4
Kalmyk ASSR	7,095		

Table 7.ii.2. INCREASE OF KAZAKH POPULATION, 1959–79

	1959	% of total	1970	% of total	% increase 1959–70	1979	% of total	% increase 1970–9
No. of Kazakhs								
in Kazakh SSR	2,787,309	76.9	4,234,166	79.9	51	5,289,349	80.7	24.9
in Uzbek SSR	342,692	12.3	476,310	9.0	39	620,136	9.5	30.2
in Turkmen SSR	69,552	1.9	68,519	1.3	−1.5	79,539	1.2	16.7
in Kirghiz SSR	20,067	0.5	21,998	0.4	9.6	4,442	0.4	22.7
in Tajik SSR	12,555	0.3	8,306	0.2	−33.6	9,606	0.1	20.4
in Central Asia	3,162,629	87.3	4,809,299	90.8	52.1	6,023,072	91.9	25.2
outside Central Asia	459,371	12.7	489,509	9.2	6.5	533,370	8.1	8.3
in RSFSR	—	—	477,820	9.0	—	518,060	7.9	8.4
in Ukrainian SSR	—	—	7,555	0.1	—	7,171	0.1	—
Total	3,622,000	—	5,298,818	—	46	6,556,442	—	23.7

The modest increase (6.5 and 8.3%) of the Kazakhs in the RSFSR between the three census operations is probably due to an out-migration rather than to their assimilation by the Russians.

In Kazakhstan itself the Kazakhs constitute a minority: 30% of the total population in 1959, 32.6% in 1970 and 36.0% in 1979. Even with the addition of the other Muslims (Tatars, Uzbeks), Muslims as a whole are still a minority: 42.1% compared to 57.9% of various non-Muslims. Of the non-Muslims the Russians represent 40.8% of the total population and are numerically the largest community of the republic. However, since 1959 the Muslims are steadily regaining the upper hand in Kazakhstan. Soviet Europeans steadily emigrated to Kazakhstan between the census of 1959 and that of 1970, but the inflow of non-Muslims was counterbalanced by the natural population increase of Muslims. The exceptionally marked increase of the Uzbeks, Tatars and Uighurs is also partly due to their immigration (in the case of Uighurs from Xinjiang). Muslims constitute the majority in the southern and western regions of Kazakhstan while the Europeans predominate in the northern, eastern, and central areas. Table 2 illustrates the total population composition of Kazakhstan.

Muslim communities in Kazakhstan are predominantly rural, with the exception of the Tatars (70.6% urban), the Bashkirs (61.2% urban), and — to a less degree — the Uzbeks (40.3% urban). In Kazakhstan the Muslim urban population in 1970 was composed of Kazakhs (26.3%), Uighurs (24.5%), Azeris (30.2%), Tajiks (25%) and Dungans (14.5%).

European communities in Kazakhstan in 1970 were primarily urban: Russians (69.1%), Ukrainians (53.7%) and Jews (95.3%). Some European colonies, however, constitute an exception and are mostly rural; this was true in 1970 of Belorussians (51.8%), Poles (64.1%) and Udmurts (61.2%).

In 1970 the Kazakhs were an absolute majority in two regions only: Gur'ev (west) and Kyzyl-Orda (south). Together with other Muslim groups, they were in a majority in six regions out of eighteen: Kyzyl-Orda (72.4%), Chimkent (66.3%), Gur'ev (65.5%), Ural'sk (51.8%), Alma-Ata (50.5%) and Aktiubinsk (50.2%). In three other regions, where the majority of the population were Europeans, the Kazakhs were the leading community in 1970: Dzhambul (40.7%), Semipalatinsk (43.6%) and Taldy-Kurgan (41.3%).

In 1979 the Kazakhs were in an absolute majority in five regions: Aktiubinsk, Gur'ev, Kyzyl-Orda, Ural'sk and Chimkent. With other

Muslim groups they had the majority in nine regions: Aktiubinsk (54.6%), Alma-Ata (51.6%), Chimkent (70.4%), Gur'ev (77.4%), Dzhambul (50.9%), Kyzyl Orda (77.2%), Semipalatinsk (50.4%), Taldy-Kurgan (51.3%) and Turgay (53.7%). Kazakhstan is steadily acquiring a more pronounced "Muslim" and "Turkic" character.

Table 7.ii.3. POPULATION OF THE KAZAKH SSR, 1959–79

	1959	1970	% increase 1959–70	1979	% increase 1970–9
Total population	9,294,741	13,008,726	39.9	14,684,000	12.9
Kazakhs	2,787,309	4,234,166	51.9	5,289,000	24.9
Tatars	191,680	287,712	50.1	313,000	8.8
Uzbeks	135,932	216,340	59.1	263,000	21.6
Uighurs	59,840	120,881	102.0	148,000	22.4
Dungans	9,980	7,284	73.2	22,000	202.0
Azeris	—	57,699	—	73,000	26.5
Bashkirs	—	21,442	—	—	—
Tajiks	—	15,981	Unknown	Unknown	—
Kurds	—	12,313	—	—	—
Kirghiz	—	9,612	—	—	—
Daghestanis	—	5,771	—	—	—
Total Muslims	—	4,999,201	—	6,178,000(?)	23.6
Russians	3,972,042	5,521,917	39.0	5,991,000	8.5
Ukrainians	761,432	933,461	22.6	898,000	– 35,461*
Germans	658,698	858,077	30.3	?	
Belorussians	107,348	198,275	84.7	181,000	– 17,275*
Koreans	74,019	81,598	10.0	92,000	12.7
Poles	—	61,445	—	—	—
Mordvinians	—	34,371	—	—	—
Jews	—	27,689	—	—	—
Moldavians	—	26,025	—	—	—
Chuvash	—	22,871	—	—	—
Udmurts	—	15,786	—	—	—
Lithuanians	—	14,194	—	—	—
Armenians	—	12,814	—	—	—
Maris	—	9,089	—	—	—
Georgians	—	6,883	—	—	—
Others	—	177,255	—	—	—
Total non-Muslims	5,573,539	8,001,750		7,162,000(?)	

* Numbers of persons.

Table 7.ii.4.   KAZAKHSTAN MUSLIM POPULATION, 1970–9
(by oblast')

	Total population (and % of Muslim)	Total population (and % of Muslims)	Muslim pop. % increase
Aktiubinsk	550,582 (50.2)	630,383 (54.6)	4.4
Alma-Ata	712,148 (50.5)	850,218 (51.6)	1.1
Chimkent	1,287,431 (66.4)	1,564,957 (70.4)	4.0
East Kazakhstan	845,251 (24.2)	878,881 (26.4)	2.2
Gur'ev	499,577 (65.5)	369,996 (77.4)	11.9
Dzhambul	794,320 (47.9)	931,204 (50.9)	3.0
Karaganda	1,552,056 (22.3)	1,454,764 (17.8)	− 4.5
Kokchetav	589,204 (24.5)	616,106 (26.4)	1.9
Kustanay	889,621 (17.9)	942,938 (18.7)	0.8
Kyzyl Orda	491,780 (72.4)	562,191 (77.2)	4.8
North Kazakhstan	555,836 (17.6)	572,709 (19.3)	1.7
Pavlodar	697,947 (27.4)	807,224 (28.9)	1.5
Semipalatinsk	713,827 (47.1)	773,489 (50.4)	3.3
Taldy-Kurgan	610,046 (46.6)	662,799 (51.3)	4.7
Tselinograd	754,955 (21.6)	809,369 (23.1)	1.5
Turgay	221,441 (36.5)	270,185 (40.0)	3.5
Ural'sk	513,077 (51.8)	585,501 (53.7)	1.9
Dzhezkazgan		449,153 (43.3)	
Mangyshlak		252,552 (49.5)	

Ethnographic data. The Kazakh nation is unique among the Central Asian Muslims. Before the Revolution the Kazakhs were mostly nomads. In the 1930s they were subjected to a very brutal sedentarisation programme, but tribal organisation survived and is still perceived by the population as a reality.

The Kazakh nation was formed of different layers of nomadic tribes of various origins which arrived in the Kazakh steppes between the tenth and sixteenth centuries and have since preserved their original names. In the tenth and eleventh centuries the Turkic tribes (Usun, Kypchak, Karluk) arrived; in the twelfth century, a Mongol tribe (Kara Kitay or Ktay); in the thirteenth century, more Mongol tribes (Nayman, Ming, Mangyt, Tangut and Dulat); and in the fifteenth and sixteenth centuries, turkified Mongol tribes (Kangly and Argyn). These same tribes enter into the composition of other Turkic nations — the

Uzbeks, Karakalpaks, Kirghiz, Nogais, Bashkirs and Crimean Tatars. Kinship between members of these tribes has been preserved.

In the fifteenth and sixteenth centuries the Kazakh tribes were regrouped into three loose state formations or hordes (*zhuz*): the Great, the Middle and the Lesser. In the early nineteenth century the Lesser gave birth to a fourth, the *Bukey* (or Inner) Horde. The Kazakh hordes have never been politically unified and the *zhuz* represented the only form of political activity till the Russian conquest.

The Great *Zhuz (Ulu Zhuz)* in eastern and southeastern Kazakhstan is divided into 12 tribes: Kangly, Sary Usun, Shanshkyly, Ysty, Dulat and Jalair (the two most numerous and politically important tribes), Alban, Suan, Bes-Tangbaly, Oshakty, Sizgeli and Shaprashty. The Great *Zhuz* remained nominally under a Chinese protectorate until the eighteenth century. From then until the middle of the nineteenth century, it was dominated by the *khans* of Kokand. It was the last of the hordes to be annexed by Russia in the late nineteenth century.

The Middle *Zhuz (Orta Zhuz)* was west and north of the Great *Zhuz* in the central, northern and southern areas of Kazakhstan. Numerically the most important of the three hordes, it is divided into five great tribes: Argyn, Nayman, Kypchak, Kungrat and Kerey.

The Lesser *Zhuz (Kishi Zhuz)*, in western Kazakhstan, is divided into three tribes: Bay Uly, Zhet Ru (seven clans) and Alim Uly. The Middle and the Lesser *Zhuz* accepted a Russian protectorate in 1741.

The tribes are divided into clans (*ru*) and then into sub-clanic formations (*taip*). Popular consciousness continues to recognise as realities both the clans and the sub-clans. The *kolkhoz* often corresponds to a *taip*. In Kazakhstan, more than in any other Central Asian republic, the selection and the promotion of various cadres (party, government and economic) depends closely, if unofficially, on the tribal and clanic relations system. Exogamic rules were observed very strictly before the revolution. Thus marriages were forbidden within the *taip* and discouraged within the *ru*. Exogamy is today still observed in some areas, though it is gradually disappearing.

Religious data. Islam had penetrated into the sedentary or semi-sedentary southern regions of Kazakhstan (regions of Kzyl-Orda, Dzhambul, and Chimkent) by the ninth century. This area is today the most religious of all Kazakhstan, and most of the working mosques are located there, in the cities of Dzhambul, Kzyl-Orda, Turkistan, Chimkent and Alma-Ata.

In the steppe territory of western, central and northern Kazakhstan,

Islam was definitely implanted much later — in the early fourteenth century. It remained superficial, with its practice limited to the feudal ruling aristocracy only, while the nomadic masses remained more or less faithful to the traditional shamanism. There was a new wave of Islamisation in the fifteenth and sixteenth centuries due to the Sufi missionaries of the Yasawiya and later of the Naqshbandiya brotherhoods. However, it was only after the establishment of the Russian protectorate in the late eighteenth century that Islam really took root among the masses. This was brought about by Volga Tatar merchants, who built mosques and founded Quranic schools under the protection of the Russian authorities.

In the late nineteenth century a third wave of Muslim expansion touched southern Kazakhstan. This time Islam was brought from Bukhara and Kokand by Uzbek merchants. However, the nineteenth-century Kazakh renaissance, sponsored by the progressive elements of the nomadic aristocracy (Chokan Vali Khanov, Abay Kunanbaev, Ibray Altynsaryn), had a marked secular character. On the eve of the Revolution, the great majority of Muslim clerics in the Kazakh territory were aliens — Volga Tatars or Uzbeks — while the leading élite (of aristocratic nomadic origin) remained the most westernised of all the Muslim élites of Russia.

Paradoxically, it has been during the Soviet period that Islam has gained a new impulse, so that at present it is more firmly implanted within the masses and better supported by the native élite than before the Revolution. Several phenomena are responsible for this evolution:

— the uprising of the tribes in 1916 and the slaughter of the nomads which followed it;

— the denomadisation policy of the 1930s, when one-third of the Kazakhs died of hunger;

— the arrival after the Second World War of the deported Chechens and Ingush who introduced a new and extremely well-organised Sufi brotherhood (Qadiriya).

Official Islam is today represented in Kazakhstan by 30-40 working mosques. We have located the following twenty "cathedral mosques": Alma-Ata, Turkistan (at the tomb of Ahmed Yasawi, one of the most venerated holy places of pilgrimage of all Central Asia), Semipalatinsk, Dzhambul, Kzyl-Orda, Kazalinsk, Aktiubinsk, Kargaly, Karaganda, Novokazalinsk, Cheltar, Kentan, Tselinograd, Gur'ev, Ural'sk, Petropavlovsk, Mergen, Abay, Chimkent and Pavlodar. Parallel Islam is represented mainly in southern Kazakhstan in the following Sufi orders: Yasawiya, Naqshbandiya and Qadiriya (in its Kunta Haji form and only since the Second World War).

The level of religiosity is very different in the regions where the Kazakhs, or Muslims in general, are in the majority (south and west) from those in which the Kazakhs have been reduced to the rank of a minority (north, central). In the first case, the social traditions sanctified by customary law that is supposed (erroneously) to be of religious origin (*adat*) are still alive, and the early marriage of girls (*kalym*), levirate and sororate (*amengerstvo*), extreme respect for elders (*aksakalizm*), circumcision, religious marriage and religious burials are complied with by a large majority, under the pressure of what recent Soviet sources call "conservative public opinion". However, in regions where Kazakhs are greatly outnumbered, these traditional customs are rapidly disappearing. The anti-religious campaign is intense: between 1948 and 1975 126 anti-Islamic books were published in Kazakhstan in the Kazakh language. In this respect, the Kazakhs come immediately after the Uzbeks (177 titles) and the Daghestanis (140 titles).

Language and the problem of assimilation. Like the Karakalpak, the Kazakh language belongs to the Nogai-Kypchak sub-group of the Kypchak or northeastern group of Turkic tongues. The spoken language has few dialects, which are not very different from each other. The literary language was fixed in the middle of the nineteenth century and has been enhanced since then by a rich and diversified literature with an abundant press. The Kazakh literary language is one of the least russified Turkic tongues.

In the 1979 census, the proportion of Kazakhs who declared Kazakh as their native language was 97.5% (98.4% in 1959) and 98% in 1970. There is therefore a very slight linguistic assimilation of the Kazakhs living in the RSFSR by the Russians, and in Uzbekistan by the Uzbeks or by the Karakalpaks. In 1979 the percentage of Kazakhs who claimed Russian as their native language was 2%, which constitutes the highest proportion among Central Asian Muslims. In the RSFSR, out of 518,060 Kazakhs, 44,190 (8.5%) claimed Russian as their first mother-tongue — a rather high proportion. This linguistic russification is facilitated by the fact that there are no Kazakh schools and no Kazakh press in the RSFSR.

In Uzbekistan in 1979, 96.7% of the Kazakhs claimed Kazakh as their native language, 1.5% claimed Uzbek, and 1.8% claimed Karakalpak, Tajik, and Russian. The assimilation of the Kazakhs living in Uzbekistan is less advanced because Kazakh schools and a Kazakh press exist in three regions of Uzbekistan (Bukhara, Syr Darya, and Tashkent).

National awareness and nationalism. A triple identity exists among the Kazakhs. First, there is a very intense sub-national identity. A Kazakh defines himself first by his *zhuz* and then by his tribe. In the case of international tribes entering into the composition of other Turkic nations (Mangyt, Nayman or Ktay) the bond of kinship is still strongly felt.

Secondly, there is an equally strong national awareness. The Kazakhs were the first of all the Central Asian Muslims to acquire a national, purely Kazakh consciousness; this was established by the middle of the nineteenth century. This consciousness is a result of several factors: pride and a feeling of superiority over the sedentaries on the part of the nomads; a long tradition of power, going back to the Mongol empire; and the existence of an authentic purely Kazakh culture, with a brilliant literature and a numerous and highly-qualified Kazakh élite.

A growing supra-national awareness is the third identity. It includes a Turkestani awareness which appeared before the Revolution and is symbolised by the desire of some Kazakh progressive leaders to join the pan-Turkestani political movement. This trend was represented in the camp of the Bolsheviks' adversaries by Mustafa Chokay, the leader of those centred in Kokand who sought autonomy, and in the Bolshevik camp by Turar Ryskulov. Supra-national awareness also takes the form of a pan-Islamic awareness. Weak before the Second World War, it has been developing since 1945.

Kazakh nationalism is more complicated than the nationalism of other Central Asian Muslims. Before the Revolution, the Kazakh élite (the nineteenth-century reformers and the early twentieth-century political leaders) was secularist, modernist, westernised and moderately pro-Russian. The xenophobia of the popular masses was directed first against the Russians (because of the European rural immigration) and also against the Volga Tatar merchants and the Uzbek sedentaries encroaching upon their lands.

Since the Revolution, the anti-Russian trend has been greatly intensified and continues to grow because of the 1916–17 repressions, the tragic denomadisation of the 1930s, and the overwhelming inflow of Russian and other European immigrants since 1950. The "Russians, go home" feeling is characteristic of the general Kazakh attitude. An anti-Chinese xenophobia has also been growing since 1950.

The Kazakh intellectual élite is numerous, sophisticated and of a high intellectual level. *Mirasizm* (rediscovery of the national past) is typical of its present attitude. A new sense of solidarity with other Central Asian Turks (especially Uzbeks) is steadily progressing. There is no defensive "cultural" nationalism. Neither the Russians nor the Uzbeks are threatening Kazakh culture. Since 1970 and the release of census data showing that despite the continued immigration of Europeans to Kazakhstan, the Kazakhs (because of their high fertility rate) are steadily regaining their position as the leading community in their republic; both the elite and the masses are acquiring a renewed confidence in the future.

(iii) THE KIRGHIZ

The Kirghiz are Sunni Muslims of the Hanafi School, and their administrative unit is the Kirghiz Soviet Socialist Republic, founded on 14 October 1924, under the name of Kara Kirghiz Autonomous Region. On 25 May 1925, it was renamed the Kirghiz Autonomous Region (part of the RSFSR); it became the Kirghiz Autonomous Republic on 1 February 1926 and finally the Kirghiz SSR on 5 December 1936. Its total territory covers 198,500 square km. The capital is Frunze, whose population was 533,000 in 1979 and 430,618 in 1970. The total population of Kirghizia in 1979 was 3,529,000, of which the urban population accounted for 1,366,000 or 39% (37.5% in 1970).

Demography. Like Kazakhstan and unlike the other Central Asian republics, Kirghizia has received, since the Second World War, an important flow of European immigrants, both urban and rural. Between 1939 and 1959 the proportion of the Kirghiz in their own republic decreased from 52% to 40.5%, but despite the continuing immigration of Europeans after 1959, the relative numerical importance of the Muslim population of Kirghizia grew steadily between 1959 and 1979 because of the large natural increase of the Kirghiz and the Uzbeks. Tables 7.iii.1 and 7.iii.2 show population statistics for Muslims and non-Muslims (by ethnic group) in 1959, 1970 and 1979.

Table 7.iii.1. MUSLIM POPULATION IN THE KIRGHIZ SSR, 1959–79

	1959 (and % of total)	1970 (and % of total)	% increase 1959–70	Comments	1979 (and % of total)	% increase 1970–9
Total	2,065,837	2,932,805	42.0		3,522,832	
Kirghiz	836,832 (40.5)	1,284,773 (43.8)	53.5	Normal increase and assimilation of Kazakhs	1,687,382 (47.9)	31.3
Uzbeks	218,640 (10.6)	332,638 (11.4)	52.1	Normal increase	426,194 (12.1)	28.1
Tatars	56,266 (2.7)	68,373 (2.5)	23.3	Continuing immigration of Tatars from the Volga	72,018 (2.0)	3.8
Uighurs	12,757 (0.7)	24,872 (0.8)	59.0	New immigration from Xinjiang	29,817 (0.8)	20.6
Kazakhs	20,067 (1.0)	21,998 (0.7)	9.6	Assimilation by the Kirghiz and out-migration	27,442 (0.7)	22.7
Tajiks	15,221 (0.7)	21,929 (0.7)	44.0	—	23,209 (0.7)	4.9
Dungans	11,088	19,837 (0.7)	79.0	New immigration from Xinjiang	26,661 (0.7)	—
Azeris	10,428	12,536 (0.4)	20.3	—	17,207 (0.5)	—
Kurds	4,783	7,974 (0.3)	66.7	Small immigration from the Caucasus	?	—
Daghestanis	3,180	3,990 (0.1)	25.5	—	?	—
Bashkirs	2,595	3,250 (0.1)	25.2	—	?	—
Total Muslims	1,192,856 (57.7)	1,803,168 (61.5)	51.2		2,309,930 (65.6)	24.4

Table 7.iii.2. NON-MUSLIM POPULATION IN THE KIRGHIZ SSR, 1959–79
(incomplete figures)

	1959 (and % of total)	1970 (and % of total)	% increase 1959–79	Comments	1979 (and % of total)	% increase 1970–9	Comments
Russians	623,562 (30.2)	855,935 (29.2)	37.3	Continuing immigration from European Russia	911,703 (25.9)	6.5	Immigration from European Russia slowed down
Ukrainians	137,031 (6.6)	120,081 (4.0)	–12.4	Assimilation by the Russians	109,324 (3.1)	–10,757 people	Assimilation by the Russians
Germans	39,915 (1.9)	89,834 (3.1)	125.0	Immigration from Siberia, essentially a rural population (62.5%)	101,057 (2.9)	12.5	Immigration from Siberia
Koreans	3,622 (0.1)	9,404 (0.3)	159.5	New immigration	?	—	
Jews	8,610 (0.3)	7,680 (0.3)	–10.8	Out-migration and assimilation by the Russians	?	—	
Belorussians	4,613 (0.2)	6,868 (0.2)	16.8	—	7,676	11.7	
Mordvinians	5,617 (0.2)	5,390 (0.2)	–4.0	Assimilation by the Russians	?	—	
Armenians	1,919 (0.1)	2,688 (0.1)	40.0	—	3,285	22.2	
Chuvash	1,220 (0.1)	2,092 (0.1)	71.5	—	?	—	
Total non-Muslims	826,109 (39.9)	1,099,272 (37.5)	33.0	—	1,213,000 (34.4)	0.3	
Others	—	16,733	—		—	—	

The Europeans — especially the Russians — constitute the majority of the urban population. In 1970 the Europeans represented 62% of the city dwellers and of those the Russians represented 51.4%. In the capital, Frunze, Muslims in 1970 constituted 20.3% of the total population and Kirghiz only 12.3%. In the rural areas, the Europeans are concentrated almost exclusively in the Issyk-Kul *oblast'*, around Lake Issyk-Kul and in the valleys of Chu and Talas. The mountainous region (Naryn *oblast'*) and the Ferghana valley (Osh *oblast'*) have important Muslim majorities: 96% and 86.2% respectively in 1970, 96.1% and 86.7% in 1979.

The Muslim population of Kirghizia is essentially rural, except for the Volga Tatars, the Bashkirs and, to a less degree, the Uighurs and the Kazakhs. The Uzbeks and the Tajiks are border colonies living in the Ferghana valley (Osh *oblast'*); the Kazakhs are city dwellers (in Frunze) and have a small rural border colony in the Talas valley. All other Muslims are recent immigrants. Table 7.iii.3 outlines the Muslim rural and urban populations by ethnic group.

Table 7.iii.3. MUSLIM URBAN AND RURAL POPULATIONS, 1970
(*1979 figures not yet available*)

	% urban	% rural
Kirghiz	14.5	85.5
Uzbeks	36.0	64.0
Tatars	80.3	19.7
Uighurs	46.4	53.6
Kazakhs	40.2	59.8
Tajiks	28.3	71.7
Dungans	26.1	73.9
Azeris	23.0	77.0
Kurds	21.7	78.3
Daghestanis	24.8	75.2
Bashkirs	71.2	28.8

There is practically no linguistic assimilation of the immigrant Muslims by the Kirghiz. In 1979 the proportion of "Kirghizified" was 0.5% for the Uzbeks, 1.0% for the Tajiks, 3.6% for the Uighurs and 12.6% for the Kazakhs.

The total number of Kirghiz in the Soviet Union has been increasing rapidly especially since the Second World War. In 1926 there were 762,700 individuals; in 1939, 884,300; in 1959, 968,700; and in 1970,

1,452,222. That is an increase of 49.9% between 1959 and 1970, one of the highest among Soviet Muslim nationalities. In 1979, there was a population of 1,906,000, an increase of 31.3% from 1970 (again one of the highest).

In 1970, out of this total population, 1,234,773 (or 88.5%) lived in the Kirghiz SSR. There are Kirghiz border colonies in Uzbekistan where 110,726 or 7.6% of the Kirghiz population lives in the western part of the Ferghana valley, and in Tajikistan where 33,485 (or 2.4%) live in the southern part of the Ferghana valley and in the eastern Pamirs. There are also colonies in Kazakhstan (9,612 or 0.7%) and Turkmenistan (354 or .02%). In 1979, out of a total population of 1,906,000 Kirghiz, 1,687,382 (88.5%) lived in Kirghizia, 142,182 (7.4%) in Uzbekistan, 58,576 (2.5%) in Tajikistan, 9,352 (0.5%) in Kazakhstan and only 272 in Turkmenistan. Thus, out of the 1,906,271 Kirghiz, 1,887,564 or 99% lived in Central Asia.

In 1970 only 15,011 (.8%) lived in the RSFSR. Of those in the RSFSR 797 were in Moscow (1970 figure) of whom only 82 were russified linguistically, and 2,370 (.1%) lived in the Ukrainian SSR. Of all Central Asians the Kirghiz are the least migratory Muslim nationality. Those Kirghiz living in Uzbekistan are moderately assimilated by the Uzbeks: between 1959 and 1970 the Kirghiz community increased only by 19.4% (from 92,695 to 110,726 individuals), whereas the general increase of the Kirghiz during this period was 49.9%.

Outside the Soviet Union, Kirghiz communities exist in China. An estimated 97,000 Kirghiz lived there in 1980, mainly in the Kyzyl Su autonomous region. There are also communities in Afghanistan, estimated at less than 10,000 in Wakhan, many of whom are currently being resettled in Turkey. There are also Kirghiz in the Mongolian borderlands: around 2,000 Khotons (a Turkic tribe close to the Kirghiz) and some hundreds of Kalmak-Kirghiz or mongolised Kirghiz.

Ethnographic data. The Kirghiz have preserved up till the present many elements of their traditional society. The basic cell of the community is the extended family (*bir atanyng baldary* or "children of the same father") constituting a group of 5–15 small families descending from the same ancestor, 6–7 generations removed. Exogamy is still observed within this unit. Members of such a family consider themselves as close relatives.

Above the extended family is the village community (*jema'at*) formed by 5–7 enlarged families. The Kirghiz *kolkhoz* are generally based on one or two village communities. Above the village communities there are clans and tribes, which remain geographical and psychological realities. A Kirghiz — and this is true also of the intellectual class — defines himself in terms of his tribal and clan origin; the selection of cadres (government or party) is often based on tribal kinship. Members of the same clan consider themselves as kinsmen.

Kirghiz tribes are divided into two great federations. The first is the federation of Otuz Uul ("30 Sons"), which is again divided into two wings (*kanat*). The "Right Wing" (Ong Kanat) is located in northern Kirghizia and also in southern and western Kirghizia, and we shall first describe its composition.

In northern Kirghizia (Issyk-Kul *oblast'*) and the eastern part of the Naryn *oblast'*, there is the Tagay tribe, the most important numerically and politically of all Kirghizia. The political (government or party apparatus) and intellectual leadership of the Kirghiz nation is exercised by members of the Tagay tribe. It is composed of the following thirteen clans:

— *Bugu*, established south and east of Lake Issyk-Kul, along the Chinese border (the most numerous of all Kirghiz clans);

— *Sary Bagysh*, west of Lake Issyk-Kul;

— *Bagysh*, in the Tien Shan mountains, south of Talas and north of the Ferghana valley, near Yangi-Yol and south of Yangi Bazar;

— *Mongoldor*, in the upper Naryn valley and north of the Ferghana valley;

— *Tynym Seyit*, in the Aksoy valley, along the Chinese border and south of Issyk-Kul;

— *Sayak*, north and west of Issyk-Kul;

— *Salto*, in northern Kirghizia, west of Frunze, along the Kazakh border (the second most numerous of Kirghiz clans);

— *Azyk*, west of Issyk-Kul, south of Tokmak;

— *Cherkir Sayak*, in central Kirghizia, west of Lake Son-Kul;

— *Sun Nurun*, northern Kirghizia, east of Frunze;

— *Cherik*, in the Aksoy and Kara-Su valleys, along the Chinese border;

— *Zhetiger*, lower Naryn valley; and

— *Baaryn*, south of Tokmak.

In southern and western Kirghizia (Osh and part of the Naryn *oblast'*) are the following: first, there is the Adigine tribe, divided into six small clans in the eastern part of the Ferghana valley (districts of Uzgen, Kyzyl-Jar, Sufi-Kurgan). The Kungrat clan (which exists also in Uzbekistan, Kazakhstan, and Karakalpakistan) belongs to the Adigine tribe, but is established near Przheval'sk, east of Issyk-Kul, separate from the other clans. There is also the Mungush tribe, divided into two clans in the southeastern Ferghana valley (Kok-su valley) and around Osh.

The "Left Wing" (Sol Kanat) of the "30 Sons" federation is subdivided into eight clans, scattered in western and central Kirghizia:
— *Kushchu*, north of the Ferghana valley, near Yangi-Yol;
— *Saruu*, north of the Ferghana valley, in the lower Naryn valley;
— *Munduz*, in eastern Ferghana, around Jelalabad;
— *Zhetigen*, in northern Kirghizia, in the Talas valley;
— *Ktay*, in western Kirghizia, lower Talas valley, and Chatal valley;
— *Basyz* and *Toboy*, in central Kirghizia, upper Naryn valley; and
— *Ching Bagysh*, northern part of the Ferghana valley, near Jelalabad.

The second great federation of Kirghiz tribes is that of Ich Kilik with ten important tribes in southern Kirghizia (southern part of the Ferghana valley) and in the eastern Pamirs (Tajikistan), as follows:
— *Kypchak*, west of the Sokh valley;
— *Nayman*, Ferghana valley, all southern Ferghana and the Kyzyl Su valley, in the southeastern Ferghana valley;
— *Teyyit*, north of the Nayman;
— *Kesek*, southwestern Ferghana, south of Solukta;
— *Ihoo Kesek*, east of Sokh;
— *Kandy*, southwest of Ravat;
— *Boston*, southeast of Sokh; and
— *Noygut*, upper Sokh valley.

Some Kirghiz clans of the "Left Wing" and of the Ich Kilik federation — Nayman (of Mongol origin), Ktay (of Mongol origin), Teyyit (of Mongol origin), Kesek (of Mongol origin), Kungrat, Boston and Kypchak — enter into the composition of other Turkic nations: Uzbeks, Karakalpaks, Kazakhs, Nogais, Bashkirs, Crimean Tatars, Karachais, and Kumyks. Members of these tribes continue to consider themselves as kinsmen.

Besides the tribes of Kirghiz origin there are in Kirghizia some ethnic groups of Mongol or Kazakh origin, that are not yet completely assimilated by the Kirghiz. The most important are the Sart Kalmyks, Oirot Mongols who migrated into the Issyk-Kul area in the 1860s and were converted to Islam. They live near Przheval'sk (east of Lake Issyk-Kul). In 1955, they numbered 2,400 (2,796 in 1926), of whom some 600 still speak a Mongol dialect. Another group is the Chala Kazakhs ("incomplete Kazakhs"), a Kazakh clan of several hundred who are partly assimilated by the Kirghiz near Frunze.

Various social traditions still observed by the Kirghiz (both rural and urban) help to maintain the traditional structure of the Kirghiz community and protect it from close contact with the non-Muslim immigrants. Among such traditions are the levirate and sororate, marriage by exchange, and the payment of *kalym* (bride price).

Religious data. There are no non-Muslim Kirghiz in the Soviet Union; all Kirghiz are Muslims. Islam penetrated the territory of present-day Kirghizia in the late sixteenth and early seventeenth centuries through the Ferghana valley. Central and northern Kirghizia became Muslim lands only in the early eighteenth century. The Sufi orders were almost entirely responsible for the Islamisation of the Kirghiz, the missionary activity of the *tariqa* being facilitated by the existence of a strong clan system. Sufism in Kirghizia today is distinguished by its conspiratorial and secret character (abandoning the loud *zikr* for the silent one) and its rustic, deeply popular character.

Four traditional Sufi orders were — and still are — active in Kirghizia. First is the Naqshbandiya, an old Bukharan order, powerfully organised and especially popular in Kirghizia. It directed the Holy War against the Buddhist Oirots. Next is the Qadiriya, an old *tariqa*, which was already established in the Ferghana valley in the late eighteenth century and was revitalised after the Second World War by the inflow of North Caucasian deportees. The third order is the Yasawiya, another old *tariqa* originating from southern Kazakhstan, and the fourth order is the Kubrawiya, an old *tariqa* imported from Khorezm.

Two more Sufi groups cropped up recently and seem to play an active role today in the religious life of the Kirghiz:

The Order of Lachi is a dissident, almost heretical splinter group of the Yasawiya, which appeared in the Ferghana valley (Osh, Margelan, Kokand) in the late nineteenth century. Persecuted by the pre-revolutionary Islamic establishment, the Lachi welcomed the advent of the Bolsheviks, an attitude similar to that of the Vaisites (*see* Volga Tatars), but they were rapidly disillusioned, broke with Soviet rule and formed a clandestine secret society, which was rediscovered by the Soviet authorities only in the 1950s. The adepts of this *tariqa* form some purely Lachi settlements in Osh *oblast'*: the villages of Sai, Rabat, Gaz, Kshtut, Raut-Kant (district of Batkent), Sur, Ormogh, Syrt and Yarkutan (district of Frunze).

The Order of the Hairy Ishans (*Chachtuu Ishander*) is another offspring of the old mystical Yasawiya, which appeared in the Ferghana valley in the 1920s, after the end of the Civil War in Kirghizia (in the areas of Osh, Jelalabad, Arslanbad and Kyzyl-Kiya). The order is accused by the Soviet authorities of being extremely conservative and fanatically anti-Soviet. The Hairy Ishans introduced many innovations into the practice of Sufism. In particular women are admitted to the *zikr* and are even allowed to form their own, purely female groups. The order is a secret society, and despite the two waves of persecution, in 1935-6 and 1952-3 (when some of its leaders were executed), it still survives.

As regards religious practice, Kirghizia is divided into two completely different zones. First is the north central and the eastern mountainous regions of Kirghizia (Issyk-Kul *oblast'* and the eastern part of the Naryn), inhabited by the clans of the "Right Wing" of the Otuz Uul tribal federations; these are superficially Islamised, and various shamanistic and totemistic beliefs and practices remain alive. There are only a few working mosques. However, Sufi brotherhoods have recently penetrated this territory and the Islamisation of northern Kirghizia seems to have been in progress since the 1960s. We have located only four working mosques in this area: at Frunze, Panfilov, Cholpan-Ata (Issyk-Kul) and Przheval'sk. This last is a Dungan mosque.

The second zone is southern Kirghizia — Osh *oblast'* and the western part of the Naryn *oblast'* (Ferghana valley). These are old Islamic territories; the local populations, Kirghiz and Uzbeks, were thoroughly Islamised in the sixteenth century through the influence of Kokand. The city of Osh, capital of southern Kirghizia (with four working mosques), is one of the religious centres of Central Asia. Official Islam is represented by a relatively small number of working mosques. We have located at least twenty: Osh (four), Kochkor-Ata (Naryn), Suzak (Osh), Alexandrovsk, At-Bashy (Naryn *oblast'*), Bazar Kurgan (Osh), Ala-Búka (Osh), Jelalabad (Osh), Palas (Naryn), Kazarman (Naryn), Iski-Naukat (Osh), Uzgun (Osh), Yangi Bazar (Naryn), Sulukta (Osh), Alai-Gulcha (Osh), Raboche-Dekhanskoe (Osh), Kushrab (Osh).

Parallel Islam, represented by the Sufi brotherhoods, controls numerous holy places, situated mainly in the Ferghana valley. Some of them are among the most venerated of all Central Asia. The most important are:

— The Throne of Süleyman (Solomon) (Süleyman Dagi, Takht-i Süleyman), in the vicinity of the city of Osh. The most popular pilgrimage place of all Central Asia and called the "Second Mecca", it attracted in the 1950s some 50,000 pilgrims at the festival of Kurban Bairam. It was closed in the 1960s, but is still visited by pilgrims (2,000 in the late

1960s). In 1959 the Mufti of Tashkent published a special *fetwa* against pilgrimages to the Throne of Süleyman.

— A group of Karakhanid tombs in the city of Uzgen (district of Yangi-Yol, Osh *oblast'*), reputed to have been built by the Prophet Daud (David).

— The tomb of Sheikh Aldiyar, Mount Aldiyar, Osh *oblast'*.

— The tomb of Kirghiz-Ata (a mythical saint: "the father of the Kirghiz"), near Naukat, Osh *oblast'*.

— Apshir-Ata, the tomb of the Sufi Sheikh Ismanali, near Naukat.

— Ala Buki, the tomb of the Shah Fazil, in the district of Yangi-Yol, Osh *oblast'*.

— The tomb of Hoja Alamdar, district of Yangi-Yol, Osh *oblast'*.

— The tomb of Idris Peyghamber (the Prophet Enoch), near the village of Yangi Bazar, Osh *oblast'*.

— Arslanbab, the tomb of the mythical saint Arslan Baba, in the district of Bazar Kurgan. One of the most popular Kirghiz holy places, second only to the "Throne of Süleyman". Although it was closed by the authorities in the 1960s, pilgrimages continue.

— The tomb of Sheikh Ak Taylak Ata, near Bazar Kurgan, Osh *oblast'*. Although it was closed in the 1960s pilgrims are still coming from Uzbekistan and Tajikistan.

— The tomb and the holy spring of Hazrat-i Ayub (the Prophet Job), in Jelalabad (Osh *oblast'*). It was closed in 1959 but pilgrimages go on.

— The tomb of Yunus Peyghamber (the Prophet Jonas) in Osh.

The total number of holy places in Kirghizia seems to be much larger than elsewhere in Central Asia (some Soviet sources mention 100–200). They serve as unregistered places of worship and often have a clandestine religious school. Muslim cemeteries are, as a rule, built in the immediate vicinity of a holy place. As a Kirghiz *mullah* said in 1978: "You may pretend to be an atheist, yet like everybody else you will finish in a Muslim cemetery".

Thanks to the combined efforts of official and parallel Islam (Sufi adepts), the Kirghiz part of the Ferghana valley is at present one of the most religious territories of Central Asia. But the Kirghiz attachment to Islam is sometimes more of a social than of a spiritual character. A typical example was quoted in 1967 by a Soviet author, Arstanbekov: a militant atheist, member of the Communist Party and president of a Kirghiz *kolkhoz*, had struggled all his life against religious "survivals" and had closed the *kolkhoz* mosque. After his retirement, he became a devout Muslim scrupulously observing Friday prayers, the Ramadan fast, and all the other prescriptions of Islam because "as an atheist he would have been completely isolated. So, without becoming a real believer, he turns Muslim for the sake of social decorum."

Recent Soviet specialists have classified the southern Kirghiz into the following three categories:

— the fanatics, a minority group of Sufi adepts and some registered *mullahs*, who indulge in missionary work and are intolerant towards non-believers;

— the orthodox believers who observe all the basic prescriptions of Islam but do not attempt to force their views on the non-believers; and

— the irreligious who nevertheless observe some prescriptions of Islam, under neighbourhood pressure, for the sake of social conventions.

The vitality of Islam in southern Kirghizia explains the intensity of anti-religious propaganda, more intense in Kirghizia than in other Central Asian republics with the exception of Uzbekistan. Between 1948 and 1975 sixty-nine anti-Islamic books were published in Frunze. In 1955 the Society for the Propagation of Scientific and Political Knowledge (specialising in anti-religious propaganda) delivered 17,200 anti-religious lectures in Kirghizia, and in 1975 the number of these lectures had risen to 45,000 (in Tajikistan for the same years there were 13,800 and 40,500 lectures, respectively).

A new impulse was given to anti-Islamic propaganda after 1962 by the organising of five- and eight-month seminars for scientific atheists. A high school with 100 students training as anti-religious propagandists was created in 1964. Also created in 1964 was the Council for Scientific Atheism attached to the republican Ministry of Culture. The Council for Scientific Atheism was attached to the Central Committee of the Communist Party of Kirghizia, and a special council for atheism was attached to the presidium of the Kirghiz trade union (Profsoyuz). In 1962, special "schools of Communist work and life" (*trud i byt*) were started; there were then 153 schools with a student body numbering 6,564; but in 1963–4 the number of these schools increased to 874 with a total of 22,000 students. The activity of the Znanie (knowledge) Society also increased: in 1962 there were 64,146 lectures, in 1963, 79,742 lectures (3,427 directed against Islam), and in 1964, 97,118 lectures (6,722 directed against Islam). There are speical anti-religious motor clubs, equipped to reach distant mountainous areas. Anti-religious propaganda is also conducted by radio broadcasts, theatre, opera and even ballet.

National awareness and nationalism. The Kirghiz have preserved a strong sub-national identity which is clanic rather than tribal, but at the same time their awareness of belonging to a Soviet Kirghiz nation is intense and steadily developing. One can safely say that of all the Central Asian nationalities the Kirghiz form the one which has the keenest conscious-ness of forming a distinct modern nation. This consciousness is a result of several factors: their geographical and linguistic remoteness from other Central Asian Turks, the relative unimportance of Islamic influence in northern Kirghizia, the traditional hostility of the Kirghiz against the Uzbeks of the Kokand Khanate; another factor is the originality of the Kirghiz oral literature (Kirghiz epic songs such as *Manas, Sementey, Seytek, Er-Töshtuk*) which has no parallel among other Central Asian Turks. The last factor is the emergence, after the Revolution, of an authentic, brilliant and purely Kirghiz literature, enhanced by two outstanding writers — the poet Aaly Tokombaev and the novelist Chingiz Aytmatov — thanks to whom Soviet Kirghiz culture has become a reality. As a consequence the supra-national identity, the awareness of belonging to a "Turkestani" nation, to an "Islamic *millet*", is weaker among the Kirghiz than among other Central Asian Muslims.

However, its comparatively numerous mosques, its holy places of pilgrimage and of legal and illegal worship, and its clandestine religious schools have led to southern Kirghizia gaining a special reputation for religious education in the *Dar ul-Islam*. The constant contact with Muslim brethren from abroad (Uzbeks, Tajiks) who come to worship at its shrines and holy places, the ready response of the rural population to the teachings of popular Sufism, and the "Islam before all else" principle of the Muslim religion constitute unifying poles of attraction. These forces might well develop — now or in the not too distant future — into a strong Islamic supra-national consciousness despite the memories of an ever-receding past and the clumsy and ineffectual, although massive, efforts of anti-religious "foreign" (i.e. Russian) propaganda.

Defensive *cultural nationalism* is relatively weak. The Kirghiz nation is not threatened by linguistic or biological assimilation by any other Central Asian nation and even less so by the Russians. Between 1959 and 1970 the percentage of the population claiming Kirghiz as its native language rose fractionally from 98.7 to 98.8% — one of the highest percentages among the Soviet Turks. In this respect an exception is represented by the Kirghiz living in Uzbekistan, who are moderately assimilated linguistically by the dominant nationality: the percentage of Kirghiz in Uzbekistan claiming Kirghiz as their first mother-tongue dropped from 92.3% in 1959 to 90.6% in 1970. In Tajikistan, on the contrary, this percentage rose from 95.5 to 97.6% during the same period.

Historical nationalism in Kirghizia is directed principally against the Uzbeks. Before the Russian conquest of Kirghizia (in the 1870s), the Khanate of Kokand dominated southern Kirghizia, and its ruthless rule left a solid heritage of anti-Uzbek xenophobia (anti-Kokand uprisings of the Kirghiz clans in 1845, 1857, 1858 and 1873). There is no hostility towards the Kazakhs, with whom the Kirghiz share a common history.

The anti-Russian tradition has its solid roots in the following events. First, the Russians massacred the Kirghiz in 1916 after the great revolt of the Kazakh and the Kirghiz tribes. Some 150,000 Kirghiz then escaped to China. Anti-Russian feeling is present in the Ferghana valley which was the main centre of Basmachi activity. The brutal Russian collectivisation and sedentarisation policies, with consequences that were almost as tragic as in Kazakhstan, also fostered anti-Russian traditions. Last, the purges of 1936–8 were particularly heavy in Kirghizia, where the not too numerous intelligentsia was practically liquidated.

Administrative nationalism — that is, the competition for jobs — pits the Kirghiz against the Russians but also against Tatars and Uzbeks. In their own republic the Kirghiz constitute the rural community, while the Russians, the Tatars, and to some extent the Uzbeks dominate the cities. In 1970 the distribution of the urban population was 14.5% Kirghiz; 36.1% Uzbeks living in Kirghizia; 66% Russians; and 80.3% Tatars.

(iv) THE TAJIKS

The Tajiks are mostly Sunni Muslims of the Hanafi school. However, there are an unknown number of Shi'a (Twelvers) in the cities of Leninabad and Dushanbe (10,000 to 30,000); and Ismailis of the Nizarit rite (followers of the Aga Khan) in the Gorno-Badakshan Autonomous *Oblast'* (see Pamirian peoples).

Tajikistan was an Autonomous Republic (ASSR) founded on 14 October 1924 and attached to the Uzbek Republic. It became a Union Republic (SSR) on 5 October 1929. Its territory covers 143,000 square km. and its capital is Dushanbe, with a population in 1979 of 493,000. The total Tajikistan population in 1979 was 3,801,000.

Demography. The total number of Tajiks in the Soviet Union (including the Pamirians) was as follows: 1926, 980,000; 1939, 1,229,000; 1959, 1,397,000; 1970, 2,136,000 (1959–70, an increase of 52.9%); 1979, 2,898,000 (1970–9, an increase of 35.7%). Between 1959 and 1970 and between 1970 and 1979, the Tajiks scored the largest increase of all the major Muslim nationalities in the Soviet Union. This development is almost exclusively due to their very high fertility rate.

Tajiks do not migrate outside their territory. In 1979, 77.2% lived in their national republic and 21% in the neighbouring territories of Uzbekistan (20%) and Kirghizia (1%). More than 99% live in Central Asia, and there are only insignificant colonies in the RSFSR (0.7%) and the Ukraine (0.1%).

Table 7.iv.1.   POPULATION COMPOSITION IN THE
TAJIK SSR, 1959–79

	1959 (and %)		1970 (and %)		1979 (and %)		% increase 1970–9
Tajiks	1,051,173	(53.1)	1,629,920	(56.2)	2,237,047	(58.8)	37.2
Uzbeks	455,038	(23.0)	665,662	(23.0)	873,199	(22.9)	31.1
Tatars	56,893	(2.6)	70,803	(2.4)	79,529	(2.1)	13.0
Kirghiz	25,665	(1.3)	35,485	(1.2)	48,376	(1.3)	35.3
Turkmen	7,115	(0.4)	11,043	(0.4)	13,991	(0.4)	26.8
Kazakhs	12,555	(0.6)	8,306	(0.3)	9,606		15.6
Total Muslims	1,608,439	(81.2)	2,421,219	(83.5)	3,261,749	(85.7)	34.7
Russians	262,611	(13.3)	344,109	(11.9)	395,089	(10.4)	14.8
Germans	32,588	(1.6)	37,712	(1.3)	38,853	(1.0)	3.0
Ukrainians	26,921	(1.4)	31,671	(1.1)	35,806	(0.9)	13.6
Jews	12,415	(0.6)	14,615	(0.5)	14,667	(0.4)	2.6
Others	37,573		50,276		108,000	(2.8)	—
Total	1,980,547		2,899,602		3,806,220		31.2

In Uzbekistan, Tajik colonies exist in the following regions (1979 census); Andizhan *oblast'* 37,793 (16,031 in 1970); Bukhara 19,728 (19,585 in 1970), Dzhizak 7,752, Ferghana 87,306 (66,056 in 1970), Kashka Darya 55,054 (40,666 in 1970), Namangan 95,275 (71,801 in 1970), Samarkand 86,557 (62,826), Surkhan Darya 113,032 (83,271 in 1970), Syr Darya 32,085 (27,026 in 1970), Tashkent 67,465 (53,066 in 1970).

Table 7.iv.2.   TAJIK POPULATION DISTRIBUTION IN THE SOVIET UNION, 1959–79

	Population in 1959 (and %)	Population in 1970 (and %)	% increase 1959–70	Population in 1979 (and %)	% increase 1970–9
Tajik SSR	1,051,173 (75.2)	1,629,920 (76.3)	55.0	2,237,048 (77.2)	37.2
Uzbek SSR	311,366 (22.3)	448,541 (21.1)	44.0	594,607 (20.5)	32.6
Kirghiz SSR	15,221 (1.1)	21,927 (1.0)	44.0	23,209 (0.8)	4.9
Kazakh SSR	—	15,981 (0.7)	—	19,293 (0.7)	20.7
Turkmen SSR	—	1,271 (0.1)	—	1,255 (0.04)	−1.3
Total in Central Asia	Unknown	2,117,640 (99.1)	—	2,875,432 (99.2)	35.7
Outside Central Asia	—	18,360 (0.9)	—	23,265 (0.8)	26.7
Including RSFSR	—	14,108 (0.7)	—	—	—
Including Ukraine	—	2,473 (0.1)	—	2,415 (0.08)	−2.4
Total in Soviet Union	1,397,000 (75.2)	2,136,000	52.9	2,898,097	35.7

7,999 Tajiks lived in the city of Tashkent in 1970. Tajiks living in Uzbekistan have not been linguistically assimilated by the Uzbeks, although in the areas inhabited by them there are no Tajik newspapers and very few Tajik schools. Table 7.iv.3 lists the number of Tajiks in Uzbekistan and their spoken languages. Outside the Soviet Union, Tajiks live in Afghanistan, where they are the most numerous community (3–4 million). There are small groups in northern Pakistan and in China (Pamirian peoples, Sarykolis and Vakhis).

Table 7.iv.3.   TAJIKS IN UZBEKISTAN

	Population in 1959 (and %)	Population in 1970 (and %)
Total Tajiks	311,375	448,541
Speaking Tajik	295,534(94.9)	431,194(96.1)
Speaking Uzbek	13,833 (4.4)	14,024 (3.2)
Speaking Russian	1,636 (0.5)	3,003 (0.6)

In 1979, Muslims constituted 85.7% of the population of the Tajik SSR. Of these 58.8% were Tajiks and the rest from various Turkic nationalities: Uzbeks, Tatars and Kirghiz. The non-Muslim population represented in 1979 only 14.3% (compared to 18.9% in 1959 and 16.1% in 1970) of the total population of Tajikistan (Russians account for 10.4%). In spite of the immigration of the Europeans to Tajikistan between 1959 and 1979, the republic is steadily acquiring a more pronounced Muslim indigenous character.

There is no linguistic assimilation of the Turks living in Tajikistan by the dominating Iranian Tajiks: in 1970, only 0.6% of the Uzbeks, 0.5% of the Kirghiz and 0.1% of the Turkmen, Tatars and Kazakhs living in Tajikistan claimed Tajik as their first mother-tongue. But the relatively low increase of the Uzbeks living in Tajikistan (23% between 1959 and 1970, the average increase of the Uzbeks being 53%) may be explained by the fact that in 1970 a certain number of Uzbeks claimed to be Tajiks.

The majority of the population is rural, and Tajikistan is the only Muslim republic where the percentage of urban population in relation to the total decreased between 1970 and 1979. However, Muslims are steadily regaining the majority in the population of Dushanbe, the capital of the republic. In 1959 the Tajiks represented 35.3% of the capital's population (79,114 within the total population of 224,242). In 1970 this percentage rose to 42.8% (160,097 compared to the total population of 373,885). The 1979 figures are still not available.

Table 7.iv.4.   URBAN POPULATION IN TAJIKISTAN, 1959–79

	Total population	Urban population	% of urban population
1959	1,980,547	646,178	32.6
1970	2,899,602	1,076,700	37.1
1979	3,801,000	1,324,000	34.8

Ethnographic data. The Tajiks are an old sedentary nation. With a few minor exceptions, they have completely lost tribal clanic structures; in Tajikistan the largest social unit in which the members consider themselves kinsmen is the extended family *(kawm, toifa)*, which as a rule corresponds to a village. Endogamy is still partly practiced by the Tajiks, but is limited to the extended family. Traditional customs, such as the *kalym*, the early marriage of girls, the levirate and the sororate, preference of marriage between cousins, sexual segregation, "aksakalism" and even polygamy are observed by the Tajiks more generally than by any other Muslim nationality of Central Asia.

Nevertheless, the Tajik nation is not completely consolidated. There still remain some ethnic groups differing from other Tajiks by their language, social structure or material culture. These include:

— *The Pamirian peoples* (see below, p. 121), in the western part of the Autonomous Region of Gorno-Badakshan. They differ from the Tajiks by their language and their religious background (they are Ismailis).

— *Mountain Tajiks*, inhabitants of the higher mountains. They have dialects of their own and a specific material culture.

— *The Yagnobis*, a small group of some 3,000–5,000 people (in 1926 there were 3,000 of whom 2,500 spoke the Yagnobi language) established in the valley of Yagnob, affluent of Fan Darya (an affluent of Zerafshan) and in the higher valley of Varzob. The Yagnobis speak a language that is completely different from that spoken by the Tajiks, and is supposed to be derived from the old Sogdian language. The Yagnobis are Sunni Muslims, and their assimilation by the Tajiks is more advanced than that of the Pamirians.

— *The Chagatais*, a curious group of Turkic origin, or perhaps Turkicised Mongols, listed as Tajiks in the last two Soviet censuses (1959 and 1970). They are, however, gradually losing their Turkic language and adopting Tajik, although some of them still speak in Uzbek. In 1926 the Chagatai group numbered some 70,000 individuals in the Surkhan Darya region of Uzbekistan and in the Kurgan Tübe region of southern

Tajikistan: 64,000 of them were Tajik-Chagatai (speaking Tajik) and 6,000 were Uzbek-Chagatais (speaking Uzbek).

— *The Harduris*, an Iranian-speaking group established in the Surkhan Darya region of Uzbekistan, different from other Tajiks in that they have preserved a semi-nomadic way of life. They accounted for 8,400 people in 1926.

Language and the problem of assimilation. The Tajiks share the literary language of the Iranians and the Afghans, which moreover has been used for centuries by Muslims in India and all Central Asia (since the later ninth century). Transliterated in Cyrillic script since 1939, it has absorbed a number of Russian words which distinguish it from literary Persian.

The Tajiks also have in common with the Iranians and the Afghans the same brilliant classical literature, which belongs as well to the Uzbeks. For example, the poet-philosopher Ibn Sina (Avicenna), who wrote in Arabic and in Persian, is claimed by the Uzbeks because he was a native of Khorezm, at present part of Uzbekistan.

The Tajiks are one of the least russified Muslim nationalities of the Soviet Union. In 1970 only 13,288 Tajiks out of a total of 2,135,883 (or 0.6%) declared Russian as their native language, whereas the remaining 98.4% claimed Tajik. In 1979, out of a total of 2,897,697 Tajiks, 22,666 (or 0.7%) claimed Russian as their "first native language" and 1.5% Uzbek; the remaining 97.8% claimed Tajik.

Religious data. According to all the recent Soviet surveys, the Tajiks are among the most religious of Central Asian nationalities, and traditional customs constituting the Muslim way of life are most tenacious in their territory.

In 1963 there were 18 working mosques in Tajikistan with 68 registered *imams*. In 1964 the number of registered clerics was reduced to 39, and it is probable that the number of working mosques has also decreased. There are four mosques in Dushanbe: Karamirishkor, Hoja Yakub, Sarisiya and Mawlana Yakub Charhi in a suburban village (Gissar). The last-named mosque contains the tomb of a Sufi saint and is the most venerated shrine in all Tajikistan.

In Leninabad (formerly Khojent) there are two working mosques: Sheikh Maslahetdin and Tugbabakhan. There is one in each of the following cities: Kanibadam, Isfara, Ura-Tübe, Regar, Pandjikent, Kurgan Tübe, Kuliab and Shahrinaw.

Parallel Islam is represented in Tajikistan by the adepts of some Sufi

brotherhoods (mainly of the Naqshbandiya) which are more structured than in the other Central Asian republics. There are also numerous non-registered *mullahs*, some of whom are former *imams* whose mosques have been closed; others are members of the itinerant *tariqa* (Kalendariya). A special category of half-Sufi and half-shaman also exists. The representatives of parallel Islam control numerous holy places which, in the absence of working mosques, tend to become the real centres of religious life. The following shrines (*mazar*) of historically real or mythical saints are the most popular centres of pilgrimage in Tajikistan:
— the *mazars* of Hoja Yakub Charhi and of Molla Junayd in the village of Gissar, near Dushanbe;
— the *mazar* of Imam Zainulabeddin in the district of Shartuz, Kurgan-Tübe region;
— Ballagardan, near Regar (valley of Varzob, west of Dushanbe);
— Hoja Abi Garm, in the district of Lenin, near Dushanbe (turned into a sanatorium in 1962);
— the *mazar* of Hoja Takkabard, in the district of 'Kanibadam, Leninabad region;
— the *mazar* of Amir Hamadani in Kuliab;
— the *mazar* of Hoja Sabzpush and Mawlana Ali Mohammed in the district of Aini, Leninabad region;
— the *mazar* of Hoja Tajeddin, in the district of Dangara, Kuliab region;
— the *mazar* of Hoja Mahmud Bashow in the city of Pandjikent (it was turned into a sanatorium in 1962, but pilgrimages were still continuing in 1964–5).

Soviet anti-religious activity is particularly fierce in Tajikistan and is directed first against the traditional way of life and secondly against holy places and parallel Islam. Universities of atheism exist in Dushanbe and Leninabad, and there is a Museum of Atheism in Leninabad. In 1966–7, forty special seminars for training anti-religious propagandists were organised in Tajikistan. In 1955 the Association for the Propagation of Scientific and Political Knowledge organised 13,800 lectures on anti-Islamic themes. In 1959 the number of lectures reached 40,500. Between 1948 and 1975, seventy anti-Islamic books and pamphlets were published in Tajikistan.

Nationalism and national awareness. After the downfall of the Samanid (Iranian) kingdom and the arrival of the first Turkic invaders in Central Asia in the eleventh century, Central Asia was ruled by the Turkic or

Mongol dynasties whose official language, however, was literary Persian. Since the fifteenth century urban communites of Central Asia have shared a common culture, employing two literary languages (Persian and Turkic) with an obvious predominance of the Persian, which remained the main literary language of the area till the Russian Revolution. There was not — and there could not be — any ethnic discrimination against Tajiks, and the linguistic differences between Turks and Iranians were of little importance. Before the Revolution, the term Tajik was practically synonymous with the term *Sart*; it served to designate the entire sedentary population of Central Asia speaking a Turkic or Iranian language, as opposed to the nomadic Turks.

Before the Revolution, the Tajiks were not conscious of forming a nation different from the Uzbeks, or of belonging to a specific Iranian culture. All pre-revolutionary intellectuals were bilingual (Chagatai and Persian). At present bilingualism is still generalised among the city-dwellers in both Uzbekistan and Tajikistan. Mixed marriages between Tajiks and Uzbeks are very frequent. As a rule there is no linguistic, cultural or historical basis for nationalism among the Tajiks, except for the marginal resentment of some Tajiks that the hallowed cities of Central Asian culture — Samarkand, Bukhara and Khiva — which many of their intellectuals consider to be purely Tajik cultural centres, are in Uzbekistan.

The words "Turkestani" for intellectuals and "Muslim" for the rural masses symbolised the pre-revolutionary national awareness, which today is still closely bound up with religion. However, since the Second World War new trends have appeared in the nation's evolution, which may favour the birth of a strictly Tajik nationalism. Two of them are particularly significant.

The first of these is the growing awareness in the Tajik intelligentsia of their Iranianism, which implies a new feeling of kinship with the Tajiks of Afghanistan and even with the Shi'a Iranians, and has as a corollary a growing sense of being different from the Uzbeks. This trend is especially marked among the young intellectuals who are nationalist but indifferent to Islam and reject the idea of a Central Asian unity around a common religion or a common historical pan-Turkestani tradition. The recent evolution of the two Iranian countries across the border — Afghanistan and Iran — and a closer contact with Afghan Tajiks may give a new impulse to this recent form of Tajik nationalism. Recent attacks launched by Soviet authorities against pan-Iranism reveal its progress and its political danger.

The second trend is a growing and aggressive Uzbek imperialism. Because of their numerical, economic, cultural, and political importance, the Uzbeks tend more and more to play the part of the Central Asian big brother. The Tajiks are most threatened and may also be the first of the Central Asians to react against this new Uzbek ascendancy. The Uzbeks already enjoy in Tajikistan a certain cultural autonomy. In 1970, out of 55 central and local newspapers published in Tajikistan, 13 were in both the Uzbek and Tajik languages, and three were in Uzbek exclusively (one was in Kirghiz). Moreover, Uzbek schools exist in certain areas. The Tajiks are denied reciprocal privileges for their colonies in Uzbekistan. Only one Tajik newspaper is published outside Tajikistan (a central republic-level newspaper appearing in Tashkent). However, at present, the only points at issue between the two communities concern the problem of Uzbek cadres in Tajikistan, who are too numerous for the Tajiks' liking.

A Russian presence is little felt in Tajikistan (except in Dushanbe), but according to the most recent surveys, anti-European xenophobia, while less openly expressed than in Uzbekistan, is nevertheless growing in intensity. There are no traditions of anti-Russian uprisings (except the Basmachi movement which in Tajikistan lasted until 1931), and no specific Tajik history or culture distinct from the traditions and customs common to all Central Asian Muslims.

(v) THE TURKMEN

The Turkmen are Sunni Muslims of the Hanafi school. The Turkmenistan Republic (SSR) was founded on 27 October 1924, and its territory covers 488,100 square km. Its capital is Ashkhabad which in 1979 had a population of 312,000. The total population of Turkmenistan in 1979 was 2,759,000.

Demography. The total number of Turkmen in the Soviet Union was 766,000 in 1926, 811,800 in 1939, 1,002,000 in 1959, 1,525,000 in 1970 (52.2% more than 1959), and 2,028,000 in 1979 (33% more than 1970). Between 1939 and 1979 the population increase of the Turkmen was one of the highest among the Soviet Muslim nationalities, just behind the Uzbeks and the Tajiks. This increase was due mainly to the high fertility rate of the Turkmen and to some degree to the assimilation of some smaller Muslim groups living in Turkmenistan (Baluchis, Kazakhs,

Karakalpaks, Arabs, Hazaras, Jamshids). The Turkmen do not migrate outside their territory; most live in Turkmenistan (93.3%) and in the border areas of Uzbekistan (4.5%). Table 7.v.1 illustrates the Turkmen population distribution.

Table 7.v.1.   TURKMEN POPULATION DISTRIBUTION, 1959–79

	1959 (and %)	1970 (and %)	1970 (and %)
Turkmenistan	923,724 (92.2)	1,416,700 (92.9)	1,891,695 (93.3)
Uzbekistan	54,804 (5.5)	71,041 (4.7)	92,285 (4.5)
Tajikistan	7,115 (0.7)	11,043 (0.7)	13,991 (0.7)
Kazakhstan	—	3,265 (0.2)	2,241 (0.1)
Kirghizia	—	352 (0.02)	607 (0.03)
All Central Asia	—	1,492,401 (97.8)	2,000,819 (96.6)
All outside Central Asia	—	32,883 (2.2)	27,094 (−1.4)
All Soviet Union	1,002,000	1,525,284	2,027,913

In Uzbekistan, Turkmen colonies are located mainly in the western regions. In the Karakalpak ASSR, there are 48,655 (1979), in Surkhan-Darya *oblast'* 13,685 and in Kashka-Darya *oblast'* 12,469 (both in 1979). The assimilation of the Turkmen living in Uzbekistan by the Uzbeks is relatively advanced. Between 1959 and 1970, the Turkmen community in Uzbekistan increased by only 29.6% (whereas for the same period the overall increase there was 52.2%). However, in 1970 94.8% of the Turkmen in Uzbekistan declared Turkmen to be their first mother tongue and only 4% claimed Uzbek.

The Turkmen colony in Tajikistan has a better resistance to assimilation, as is shown by its large increase between 1959 and 1970: from 7,115 in 1959 to 11,043 in 1970 (55.2%) and 13,991 in 1979 (26.7%). Also, a high percentage of Turkmen in Tajikistan declare Turkmen to be their first mother tongue (98%).

Outside Central Asia, small Turkmen groups exist in Armenia (515 in 1979), in Azerbaijan (598) and in Georgia (672), and there is a relatively important colony in the northern Caucasus (about 20,000, of whom in 1970 8,313 were in the Stavropol' *krai* and some 6,000 to 7,000 in northern Daghestan and in the Astrakhan *oblast'*). These immigrants — called *Trukhmen* in the northern Caucasus — descend from the Turkmen tribes of the Mangyshlak area that were driven into the Caucasus by the Kalmyk invaders of the eighteenth century. The

Stavropol' Turkmen — an entirely rural community (96.5% of them are peasants) — have resisted assimilation despite their small number and their isolation. In 1970, 98% among them spoke Turkmen, but their language is strongly influenced by that of the Nogais.

Outside the Soviet Union, Turkmen groups exist in the northwest of Afghanistan (about 300,000); in Iranian Khorassan (about 400,000); in eastern Turkey; and in northern Iraq (about 200,000).

The Turkmen are essentially a rural nation. In 1970 only 31% were city-dwellers and 69% were rural (in 1959 the proportion was 25.4% and 74.6%). In 1979, Turkmen constituted 68.4% of the population of their own republic, in which the Muslim community amounted to 83.2% of the total. Table 7.v.2 shows the various nationalities living in Turkmenistan.

A comparison between the three censuses shows five trends. First, there was an out-migration of Kazakhs from Turkmenistan between 1959 and 1970. Secondly, there was a relatively important immigration of Volga Tatars and Daghestanis into Turkmenistan, but between 1970 and 1979 the Tatar immigration has either been stopped, or the Tatars are being assimilated by the Turkmen. Thirdly, the Turkmen Republic is acquiring a more Turkmen and a more Muslim character. The non-Muslim population of Turkmenistan is essentially urban: 95.6% of the Russians and 83.3% of the Ukrainians in 1970. However, the Muslims are regaining supremacy in the cities. Thus in 1959 the non-Muslims represented 60.3% of the population of Ashkhabad while in 1970 the proportion had been reduced to 53.1%. Fourthly, there has been a slight Russian immigration into Turkmenistan between the three censuses. The Russian community had increased in 1970 by 19.2% (instead of the average increase of 13%). In 1979 the increase was 11.5% (average 6.5%), but the relative importance of the Russians decreased between the three censuses from 17.3% in 1959 to 14.5% in 1970 and 12.6% in 1979. Fifth and last, there is no linguistic assimilation by the Turkmen of various Turkic colonies in Turkmenistan (see Table 7.v.3).

Ethnographic data. The Turkmen nation created in 1924 has a unique position among the Soviet Muslims. It constitutes at present a tribal confederation rather than a modern nation. Before 1917, in the absence of a unified Turkmen state or of a coherent tribal confederation, the tribe was the highest form of territorial power. Since 1924 the tribes have been steadily losing their economic autonomy; nevertheless the tribal system is still not a simple survival but a territorial, social and

Table 7.v.2.   MUSLIM POPULATION IN TURKMEN SSR 1959–79

	Pop. in 1959 (and % of total)		Pop. in 1970 (and % of total)		Increase (%) 1959–70	Pop. in 1979 (and % of total)		Increase (%) 1970–9
Total population	1,516,373		2,158,880		42.3	2,764,748		28.1
Turkmen	973,724	(64.2)	1,416,700	(65.6)	53.3	1,891,605	(68.4)	33.6
Uzbeks	125,231	(8.3)	179,498	(8.3)	43.3	233,730	(8.5)	30.4
Kazakhs	69,552	(4.6)	68,519	(3.2)	–1.6	79,539	(2.9)	16.7
Tatars	29,946	(2.0)	36,457	(1.7)	21.8	40,439	(1.5)	9.7
Azeris	12,868	(0.85)	16,775	(0.78)	30.4	23,548	(0.9)	43.1
Baluchis	7,626	(0.5)	12,975	(0.6)	62.3	18,584	(0.6)	43.2
Dagestanis	5,379	(0.35)	8,197	(0.38)	52.4	11,555	(0.4)	40.9
Iranians	—		5,068	(0.23)	29.6	—		—
Kurds	2,263	(0.15)	2,933	(0.14)	—	—		—
Karakalpaks	2,548	(0.17)	2,542	(0.12)	—	—		—
Tajiks	—		1,271	(0.06)	—	—		—
Total Muslims	1,179,137	(77.8)	1,751,670	(81.1)	48.5	2,300,000	(83.2)	31.3

Russians	262,701	(17.3)	313,079	(14.5)	19.2	349,170 (12.6)	11.5
Ukrainians	20,955	(1.4)	35,398	(1.6)	68.9	37,118 (1.3)	4.5
Armenians	19,696	(1.3)	32,054	(1.1)	17.0	26,605 (1.0)	17.1
Belorussians	3,198	(0.2)	4,445	(0.2)	39.0 (new immigration)	5,289 (0.2)	18.9
Jews	4,078	(0.27)	3,494	(0.16)	− 14.3 (out-migration)	—	—
Koreans	1,919	(0.13)	3,493	(0.16)	82.0	—	—
Mordvinians	4,128	(0.27)	3,488	(0.16)	− 15.5 (assimilation by Russians)	—	—
Other non-Muslims	—		20,759	(1.1)	—	—	—

Table 7.v.3. TURKMEN AS "FIRST MOTHER LANGUAGE",
1959–79

Immigrant colonies	% speaking Turkmen in 1959	% speaking Turkmen in 1970	% speaking Turkmen in 1979
Uzbeks	2.2	1.9	2.6
Kazakhs	0.7	0.6	0.7
Azeris	1.6	1.0 (17.3% speaking Russian*)	1.2 (18.7% speaking Russian*)
Tatars	2.1	1.2 (15.8% speaking Russian*)	1.1 (19.8% speaking Russian*)

* i.e. The percentage of this nationality claiming Russian as a first language. Thus Russian has a stronger attraction to those non-indigenous nationalities than Turkmen.

psychological reality. Not only does the *kolkhoz* conform as a rule to the clanic tribal structure, but tribal loyalties continue to exercise a deep influence on the promotion of political cadres, both of the government and of the party. Thus the Turkmen Communist Party is traditionally dominated by the Tekke tribe, as is the selection of university members.

Each tribe has its own territory, and its members are bound by a strong sense of kinship. The tribal identity is reinforced by the still observed rules of endogamy and the persistence of tribal dialects. The Turkmen are divided into seven major and 24 small tribes. The figures given below are from the last census to observe these distinctions (1926) and, therefore, cannot be considered even as approximate; there has probably been at least a doubling of each. The 1926 figures are given solely to suggest the proper quantitative rank ordering of the tribes:

MAJOR TRIBES

— *Tekke*: 500,000 people in central Turkmenistan (Murghab and Tejen valleys);

— *Ersary*: 300,000 people in southeastern Turkmenistan (Amu Darya valley, south of Charjow; also in northwest Afghanistan);

— *Yomud*: 200,000 people in western Turkmenistan, Caspian Sea shore south of Mangyshlak and the western part of the Khorassan oasis; also in northern Iran;

— *Göklen*: 120,000 people in southwestern Turkmenistan: Sumbar and Chandyr valleys (district of Kara-Kala), also in northern Iran;

— *Salor*: 70,000 people in eastern Turkmenistan, around Charjow and in the upper Tejen valley (district of Serakh); also in northern Iran;

— *Saryk*: 70,000 people in southern Turkmenistan, Murghab valley (district of Iolatan, Takhta Bazar and Kushka); also in northeastern Iran and northwestern Afghanistan;
— *Chowdor*: 50,000 people in northern Turkmenistan: Khorezm oasis, north of Mangyshlak, and in Stavropol' *krai*.

SMALLER TRIBES

These vary in size from some hundreds to about 30,000 individuals. We list those which, because of their number or because of a special prestige attached to their origin, are the most important:
— *Ali Eli*: southern Turkmenistan, eastern part of the Kopet Dagh, also in northeastern Iran and northwestern Afghanistan;
— *Bayat*: in eastern Turkmenistan, upper Amu Darya valley;
— *Chandyr*: in northeastern Turkmenistan, Khorezm oasis;
— *Karadashly*: in northeastern Turkmenistan and the western part of the Khorezm oasis;
— *Nokhurli*: in southern Turkmenistan, Sumbar valley; a small group in Tajikistan;
— *Emreli*: in northeastern Turkmenistan, Khorezm oasis, also in northern Iran;
— *Sayat*: in eastern Turkmenistan, Amu Darya valley, near Charjow;
— *Mukry* and *Alam*: in southeastern Turkmenistan, Amu Darya valley, near Kerki;
— *Marchaly*: in southern Turkmenistan, Baharden district;
— *Ata*: in eastern Turkmenistan, Amu Darya valley and Charjow;
— *Hoja*: in western Turkmenistan, north of Krasnovodsk, and in southern Turkmenistan, near Kyzyl Arvat;
— *Seyid*: in western Turkmenistan, south of the Kara Bogaz gulf;
— *Shikh*: in western Turkmenistan, south of the Kara Bogaz gulf and also north of Krasnovodsk.

The last four tribes — called holy tribes (*Ovlad-Awliya*) — enjoy a special prestige although they are numerically small. They are supposed to be of Arab origin, and their members are deemed to descend from one of the first four Khalifs.

The tribes are divided into various sub-tribal formations (*tire, urug, kawm*); these in turn divide into clans, and the clans are subdivided into small monogamous or extended families (from 10 to 20 members). Endogamy limited to the clan is preferred. Turkmen *kolkhozy* are generally restricted to one or two clans. Each clan has its own cemetery near the tomb of a common ancestor. There are thus well-knit social units.

Turkmen society differs from other Muslims of Central Asia by the vitality of various social customs and traditions: sex discrimination; the persistence of polygamy and various traditional marital customs, such as the early marriage of girls, *kalym*, marriage by abduction, levirate, *karshylyk* marriage (a sister and a brother married to a brother and a sister); frequent religious marriages, and refusal to let Turkmen girls marry outside the tribe. Other customs included the psychological persistence of the division of Turkmen society into three pre-revolutionary classes — nobles (*iq*), former slaves (*kul*), and a middle class of noble or slave origin (*yarym*) — and extreme respect paid to the members of the holy tribes of the Hojas, Seyids, Atas, and Shikhs.

Language and the problem of assimilation. The Turkmen language, which is divided into many dialects, belongs to the Oghuz group of Turkic languages. It is therefore closer to Azeri, Crimean Tatar and Turkish than to Uzbek or Kazakh. A literary language (half Turkmen, half Chagatai) appeared in the eighteenth century and was the medium for a brilliant panoply of poets (Mahtum Kuli, Devlet Mahmud, Azadi, Molla Nepes, and Kemine). A new Soviet literary Turkmen language, based on the Yomud and the Tekke dialects, was created in the early 1920s; it was transcribed in Arabic characters, then in Latin, and from 1939 in Cyrillic.

Linguistically, the Turkmen are among the least russified. In 1979, 98.7% of them claimed Turkmen as their native tongue, compared to 0.9% who declared Russian. The majority of these russified Turkmen live in the RSFSR or are city dwellers (11,537 out of 12,319). A small number of Turkmen (4,487 or 3%) are in the process of being assimilated by the Uzbeks and the Tajiks.

The Turkmen oral literature is common to all Oghuz Turks, such as *Ker Oglu* and *Korkut Ata*, as are epic songs and romantic poems: *Tahir and Zohra, Leila and Mejnun, Shahsenem and Garib*. Soviet Turkmen literature is poor compared to the prestigious traditional oral literature and the remarkable poetic works written in the eighteenth century. The corpus has not been enhanced by any outstanding writer who could be compared to the Kirghiz Chingiz Aytmatov.

Religious data. All Turkmen are Sunni Muslims. Shi'ism is represented in Turkmenistan by Azeri immigrants. Among the Turkmen — formerly a nomadic people — Islam has a profile which differs from that prevailing in other areas of Central Asia. This is primarily because the Islamisation

of Turkmen tribes, which took place between the twelfth and fourteenth centuries, was due to the efforts of the Sufi orders, especially the
two Turkestani *tariqa*: the Yasawiya, founded by Ahmed Yasawi, who
died in 1166 and whose tomb is in the city of Turkistan in southern
Kazakhstan, and the Kubrawiya, founded by Najmuddin Kubra
(1145–1221) whose tomb is near Kunia-Urgench, in western Khorezm,
Tashauz *oblast'*, in the Turkmen SSR. The third great Sufi order, the
Naqshbandiya, with its centre in Bukhara, appeared in the Turkmen
country only in the nineteenth century.

Before the Russian conquest Turkmen Islam presented a curious
blend of orthodox Islam, Sufi mysticism, the cult of ancestors (especially
strong among the nomadic aristocracy) and various shamanistic practices. Russian conquest of the Turkmen territory resulted in a temporary
decline of Sufism and, as its corollary, in a rapid renaissance of orthodox
Islam brought from Bukhara. The number of Sufi *ishans* dropped spectacularly from 105 in 1899 to only 47 in 1900, while the number of
mosques increased from 161 in 1896 to 481 in 1911.

In 1928 Soviet authorities launched an anti-religious drive aimed at
the complete destruction of Islam among the Turkmen. The campaign
was the harshest and the most violent of all anti-Islamic attacks in
Central Asia. It lasted until 1941, but after a short respite during the
war, the anti-religious offensive was resumed in 1948, and it still continues. Its consequence was the weakening of the official establishment
and the revival of parallel, popular Islam.

Official Islam has been reduced practically to a void, and there are less
than 30 registered clerics in Turkmenistan; in 1979 there were only four
working mosques left: two are in the Mary *oblast'* (southern
Turkmenistan) and one is the mosque of Hoja Yusuf Baba Hamadani, in
the village of Bairam Ali. Incidentally, this tomb, situated near the
mosque of the saint Yusuf Hamadani, teacher of Ahmed Yasawi, is one
of the most famous holy places of Central Asia. The other is the mosque
of Talkhatan Baba, in the village of Iolatan. Two more mosques are in
the Tashauz *oblast'* (northern Turkmenistan): the mosque of Shalikar in
the city of Tashauz and the mosque of Bilal Baba in the city of Iliaty.

However, the level of religious practice is independent of the number
of mosques and is high throughout the country. Many religious rites are
observed by official unbelievers, including intellectuals. According to
the most recent Soviet surveys, the persistence of religious feeling is due
to the following five factors:

— The increased activity of Sufi orders.

— The confusion between religious and national characteristics: religious customs (e.g. the Kurban Bairam festival) are deemed to be part of the Turkmen tradition; the terms "Muslim" and "Turkmen" are practically synonymous.
— The pressure of conservative public opinion.
— The influence of Uzbekistan. A Soviet survey revealed, for instance, that in the district of Deynaw (Charjow *oblast'*) the number of people who "under the influence of Uzbek clerics" fasted during the month of Ramadan in 1961 "was double what it had been in the preceding year".
— The influence of Iranian propaganda, especially via the broadcasts formerly made in Turkmen by Radio Gorgan, accused by Soviet specialists of stirring up the religious feelings of the population.

According to recent surveys (done in 1977, 1978 and 1979), circumcision, religious burials and the celebration of the great religious festival (Kurban Bairam) are observed by "almost 100%" of the population of the Tashauz and Charjow *oblasts* (northern and eastern Turkmenistan). In 1978, in the *kolkhoz* of Kara Kala, district of Baharden, Ashkhabad *oblast'*, circumcision was performed on 100% of males, the fast of Ramadan was observed by 50%, and the five daily prayers by 30%. The same year, in the *kolkhoz* Moskva, district of Kunia-Urgench, Tashauz *oblast'*, Kurban Bairam was celebrated by 96.2% of the population, the fast of Ramadan was observed by 27%, and 25% of the *kolkhozniks* visited various holy places of pilgrimage. In 1970 a survey of the *kolkhoz* Kizly Yuldyz (district of Kunia-Urgench, Tashauz *oblast'*) revealed that 85.6% of the *kolkhozniks* considered circumcision necessary, 50% for "hygienic reasons" and 35.5% because "it is the mark of Islam". The remaining 14.4% considered it "desirable".

The Sufi orders are still active in Turkmenistan: the Yasawiya, Kubrawiya (closely connected with the traditional Muslim guilds) and the Naqshbandiya (especially strong in eastern Turkmenistan). The first two practice the loud *zikr*, the last the silent *zikr*.

In Turkmenistan more than in any other territory of Central Asia, the Sufi orders are closely bound with the tribal structure of the nation. The leadership of the *tariqa* is always hereditary and is limited to the four holy tribes (the *Awlad*) — the Ata, Hoja, Seyid and Shikh — whose members, as mentioned above, are deemed to descend from one of the four Medina Khalifs, and are thus accorded great prestige by the people. All the members of these tribes bear the title of *ishan*. In 1978 a survey in the *kolkhoz* Karl Marx, district of Lenin, Tashauz *oblast'*, revealed that

66.6% of the population believed in the holiness of the *ishans*. A parallel survey in the district of Baharden (Ashkhabad *oblast'*) showed that 46% of the population believed that the *ishans* had superhuman powers, 24% did not believe in their holiness, 15% hesitated and 15% refused to answer.

The activity of parallel Islam is centred around the holy places which are found all over the Turkmen territory but especially in the north (Tashauz *oblast'*) and in the west (Krasnovodsk *oblast'*). According to a recent Soviet survey, 62 holy places were active in 1978 and attracted thousands of pilgrims. There was also an unknown but certainly large number of unregistered houses of prayer, run by the adepts of the Sufi brotherhoods. In 1965, at the time of Kurban Bairam, hundreds of pilgrims visited the tomb of Najmuddin Kubra near Kunia-Urgench. The following year the same holy place was visited during Kurban Bairam "by 25 to 30 pilgrims every hour", some of them coming from Uzbekistan and even Tajikistan.

The holy places of pilgrimage may be classified into four main categories.

— Places connected with mythical personages, often pre-Islamic places of worship. Such are the *mazars* (tombs) of Divan-Burkh (a pre-Islamic deity) at Kunia-Urgench (Tashauz *oblast'*) and of Baba Gamber (a supposed follower of Khalif Ali) in the Kopet Dagh (Ashkhabad *oblast'*); another tomb of the same Baba Gamber on the bank of the Murghab river (district of Iolatan, Mary *oblast'*); and the tombs of Ashyk Aydam, a mythical protector of poets; of Nalad Baba, a protector of irrigation; of Zengi-Baba, a pre-Islamic deity, protector of cattle.

— The tombs of the former rulers, Khorezm shahs and Seljuk sultans, such as the *mazar* of Sultan Sanjar near Bairam Ali (Mary *oblast'*), or the tomb of the Khorezm shah, Atsyz Il-Arslan (Kunia-Urgench).

— The tombs of tribal ancestors, such as the *mazar* of Saly Gazan, ancestor of the Salor tribe, in the district of Serakh (Ashkhabad *oblast'*). Also included is the *mazar* of Molla Kakka, ancestor of the Saryk tribe, in the district of Kyzyl Atrek, Krasnovodsk *oblast'*; the *mazar* of Ersary Baba, ancestor of the Ersary tribe, in the Balakhany mountains, Krasnovodsk *oblast'*, and the *mazar* of Atuali Baba, ancestor of the Sovrali clan of the Goklen tribe, in the district of Kara-Kala, Krasnovodsk *oblast'*.

— The most venerated tombs are those of the Sufi saints, some of whom are at the same time the ancestors of the holy tribes (*Awlad*). To this category belong the following:

- the *mazar* of Hoja Yusuf Hamadani, in Bairam Ali, Mary *oblast'*. This tomb and that of Najmuddin Kubra are the two most venerated shrines of Turkmenistan.
- The *mazar* of Gözli Ata, a fourteenth-century Yasawi ishan, ancestor of the Ata tribe, in the Great Balakhany mountains, Krasnovodsk *oblast'*.
- The *mazar* of Ak Ishan, another saint of the Yasawi order, ancestor of the Bokusdat clan of the Tekke tribe, in the village of Archman, district of Kyzyl Arvat, Krasnovodsk *oblast'*.
- The *mazar* of Pakyr Sheikh, also a Yasawi saint, ancestor of the Shikh tribe, in the village of Bendesen — district of Kyzyl Arvat, Krasnovodsk *oblast'*.
- The *mazar* of Kara Akhun Ishan, near Nebit Dagh, Krasnovodsk *oblast'*.
- The *mazar* of Ovezjan Hoja, near the city of Charjow.
- The *mazar* of Kurban Murat Ishan, a Sufi saint, the spiritual leader of the resistance of the Tekke tribe against the Russians in 1881, in the city of Gök Tepe, Ashkhabad *oblast'*. This is one of the most venerated holy places in Turkmenistan. In 1972, 600 pilgrims visited the *mazar* during the feast of Kurban Bairam.
- The two *mazars* of Dana Ata, a Yasawi saint, in western Turkmenistan: one in the village of Ajiguiyi in the Great Balakhany mountains, Krasnovodsk *oblast'*, and the second in the Karen Dagh, 35 km. south-west of Kazanjik, Krasnovodsk *oblast'*.
- The *mazar* of Chopan Ata (yet another Yasawi saint), one of the most venerated in western Turkmenistan, in the Mangyshlak peninsula, Krasnovodsk *oblast'*.
- The *mazar* of Seyid Nejefi, ancestor of the Turkmen Hoja in the village of Hoja Kala, on the Sumbar river, Ashkhabad *oblast'*.
- The *mazar* of Sheikh Sherep, another ancestor of the Turkmen Hoja, near the village of Nokhur, district of Baharden, Ashkhabad *oblast'*.
- The *mazar* of Saragt Baba (the Sufi Saint Abul Fazl), one of the most venerated shrines of southern Turkmenistan, district of Serakh, Ashkhabad *oblast'*.
- The *mazar* of Ismamut Ata, a Sufi saint, in the district of Takhta, Tashauz *oblast'*. In 1972, hundreds of pilgrims visited it during Kurban Bairam.
- The *mazar* of Astana Baba, in the district of Kerki, Charjow *oblast'*.
- The *mazar* of Mashad Ata, in the village of Madan, district of Kyzyl Atrek, Krasnovodsk *oblast'*.

Turkmen Sufism is marked by the persistence of purely shamanistic practices, condemned by the orthodox Islamic establishment but deeply rooted in popular beliefs. By a curious process of inter-penetration, the shamanistic practices, rites, and rituals have acquired during the Soviet period an external appearance of Islam, while the Sufi adepts, especially those of the Kubrawiya *tariqa*, often behave like shamans. The anti-religious propaganda (44 anti-religious books between 1948 and 1975) is almost entirely directed against Sufism and various traditional social customs. The satirical monthly journal *Tokmak* ("Spanking"), published in Ashkhabad, specialises in anti-Sufi propaganda.

Nationalism and national awareness. It is sub-national, tribal and clan consciousness that predominates in Turkmenistan. Turkmen still define themselves by their tribal and clan origin, and tribal loyalties are stronger than in any other Muslim area of the Soviet Union. The persistence of tribal or clan loyalties is both an asset and a liability for the Soviet authorities. It allows them to fight Turkmen nationalism by opposing one tribe against another, but at the same time it isolates the Turkmen in their closed world and represents an obstacle to rapprochement with the Russians.

The supra-national, Islamic or Turkestani consciousness is weaker here than among other Central Asian nationalities, which differentiates the Turkmen from other Central Asian Turks. This is due to several factors. First, the Turkmen belong to the Oghuz group and are histori-cally and culturally closer to the western Turkic peoples (Ottomans, Azeris, Crimean Tatars) than to the Central Asian Turks. The second factor is the immense superiority complex of the Turkmen: they are a warlike, aristocratic nation, strikingly different even in physical charac-teristics from other Turks. This feature is reflected in their attitude towards other Central Asian Muslims. Parallel Islam, more powerful than official Islam and closely connected to the tribal structure of Turk-men society, is the third factor. Such ties do not foster the emergence of a pan-Islamic identity.

Despite the persistence of sub-national loyalties and the fact that Turkmen tribes have never been able to form a national state, and were often divided among different powers (Iranian empire, Bukhara, Khiva), and despite tribal rivalries and conflicts, the Turkmen are conscious of a certain unity. It may be said that their modern national awareness can be distinguished from that of other Muslim Central Asian nationalities because its roots strike deep into history. It is based on several factors.

One is the century-long struggle of the Turkmen tribes against the Shi'a Iranians and the Khanate of Khiva. Another is the existence of a common Turkmen culture, a brilliant Turkmen poetic art, and a specific Turkmen way of life. Finally, there is the long tradition of wars against the Russians: the victorious defence of Gök Tepe in 1879 by the Tekke tribe; the destruction of the same fortress in 1881 by the Russians and the massacre of its population; the participation of the Turkmen tribes in the Basmachi movement (Junayd Khan in the Khorezm oasis, 1918-24); the anti-Soviet uprisings in 1927 and 1931; and the numerous Soviet purges of Turkmen cadres for the offence of nationalism.

Turkmen nationalism is of the most pronounced anti-Russian character. The Turkmen consider themselves different from and superior to the other Central Asian Turks, their neighbours (Kazakhs, Karakalpaks, Uzbeks) and other lesser groups living in their territory (Baluchis and Arabs). There is no competition with the Uzbeks and other Turks for official positions; no external danger is threatening the Turkmen language or culture. There are no anti-Uzbek or anti-Kazakh trends in Turkmen nationalism.

(vi) THE DUNGANS

The Dungans are Sunni Muslims of the Hanafi school, an immigrant community in the Soviet Union enjoying extraterritorial cultural autonomy. They came from China and Central Asia in two waves, in 1877-8 and in 1881-4, after the defeat of the great Muslim uprising against the Manchu dynasty. Their origin is unclear; they could be either Chinese converted to Islam in the Middle Ages or immigrant Muslims — Arabs, Iranians, and Turks — who became completely Chinese. The majority of Dungans (Hwei-Hui in Chinese) live in China, and in 1953 numbered 3,500,000 according to a census of that year. Since October 1958 they have been endowed with the Ningsia-Hui Autonomous *Oblast'* in the People's Republic of China. In the Soviet Union they live in Kazakhstan, Kirghizia, and Uzbekistan (see Table 7.vi.1). The strong increase of the Soviet Dungans between 1959 and 1970 is a result of a limited immigration from China in the early 1960s and natural increase.

The Dungans are essentially a rural nationality. They live in closed communities, forming their own Dungan villages and their own quarters in cities. As a rule their *kolkhozy* are either purely Dungan or composed of a Dungan majority.

Table 7.vi.1.   DUNGAN POPULATION IN THE SOVIET UNION,
1959–79

	1959	1970	% increase 1959–70	1979	% increase 1970–9
Total in the Soviet Union	21,928	38,644	76.2	51,694	34.6
In Kazakhstan	10,000	17,284	72.8	22,491	27.3
In Kirghizia	11,100	19,837	78.7	26,661	34.4
In Uzbekistan	600	1,400			

In Kazakhstan the Dungans live in the city of Alma-Ata (1,303 in 1970) and in the *oblast'* of Alma-Ata (1,834 in 1970). They also live in the *oblast'* of Dzhambul (12,743 in 1970, 17,512 in 1979) in the cities of Dzhambul and Panfilov; and in the villages of Chilik, Dzhalpak-Tübe, Karakunuz and Shor Tübe. Purely Dungan *kolkhozy* or those where they form the majority are "Krasnyi Oktiabr' " (Dzhambul), "Kommintern" and "Kommunisticheskii" (both in the Kurday district).

In Kirghizia Dungans live in the city of Frunze (1,575 in 1970), in Chunlley (15,377 around Frunze), in the city of Tokmak, and in the villages of Khunchi, Milianfan, Milantan and Alexandrovka. There is a Dungan *kolkhoz*, "Druzhba". They also live in the Moskovskii district, in the Issyk-Kul *oblast'* (1,840 in the city of Przheval'sk), in the village of Yrdyk (near Przheval'sk), in a Dungan *kolkhoz* "Dnishin" (district of Jety Oghuz), and in Osh *oblast'* (585 in the *kolkhoz* "Kyzyl Shorti", Kara-Su district). In Uzbekistan small Dungan groups are in Tashkent and in the Ferghana valley.

The Dungans speak various dialects of Chinese. Those of Kirghizia use the Kansu dialect; those of Kazakhstan the Shensi dialect. The Kansu dialect is the basis of the Soviet literary language created in the later 1920s and transcribed in Cyrillic script since 1954. A Dungan newspaper *Shywedi Chi* ("Flag of October") is published in Frunze. The Dungans of Uzbekistan are losing the use of Chinese and being rapidly Uzbekified; those of Kazakhstan and Kirghizia maintain the use of Chinese but are as a rule bilingual and often tri-lingual (Chinese, Kirghiz or Kazakh, and Russian). In 1959 Chinese was declared their native language by 95.5% of the Dungans, in 1970 by 94.3% and in 1979 by 94.8%.

The Dungans are strongly religious. Before the Russian Revolution in one Dungan village (Kara Kunuz) there were 47 mosques and in the city of Pishpek there were seven. At present we have located two working Dungan mosques, in the cities of Przheval'sk (Kirghizia, district of Issyk-Kul) and Panfilov (Kazakhstan, Dzhambul *oblast'*), both built in the style of a Chinese pagoda. The high level of Dungan religious feeling explains the intensity of the anti-religious propaganda directed against them. Since the 1960s special anti-religious broadcasting has taken place in Dungan (Radio Frunze). Between 1948 and 1975 two anti-Islamic books in Dungan were published in Frunze.

Like the Uighurs, the Dungan community has been and is still treated favourably by the Soviet authorities. Dungans enjoy an authentic extra-territorial cultural autonomy. A Dungan press exists in Kirghizia and Kazakhstan, and a "Section of Dungan Culture" functions at the Academy of Science of the Kirghiz SSR. However, the use of the Dungan community as a possible reservoir of propagandists and political cadres against China is limited by the fact that the Dungans remain essentially a *kolkhoznik* community.

The national identity of the Dungans is essentially religious. They identify themselves first as Muslims, but also as Chinese Muslims. The memory of their original homeland remains alive. The Dungans would identify themselves as "from Kansu" (*Kansaluk*), "from Shensi" (*Shensili*), or, in the same vein, as "*Yarkandi*" and "*Kashgarlyk*" ("one who comes from this place"). Chinese national costumes and most Chinese foods are still common among them.

The Dungans of Kirghizia and Kazakhstan do not mix with the autochthonous Turkic population (except the Uighurs). The social structure of their communities is still partly territorial, and this helps them to remain separate from the other Muslims. Endogamy within the community is still observed, and mixed marriages with Turks are extremely rare. Extended families (up to thirty members living together and sharing their income) are still common.

(vii) THE KARAKALPAKS

The Karakalpaks are Sunni Muslims of the Hanafi school. The Karakalpak ASSR (part of the Uzbek SSR) covers a territory of 165,000 square km. It is in the eastern part of the Amu Darya delta and the Khorezm oasis; its western and eastern border areas are part of the Ust Urt and Kyzyl Kum deserts. The capital is Nukus with 109,000 inhabitants (1979). The total population is 904,000 (1979).

Before the Revolution, the Karakalpak area was the Amu Darya *oblast'* of the Turkestan General Government. On 16 February 1925 it became the Karakalpak Autonomous Region of the Turkestan ASSR. In May 1925 the Karakalpak Autonomous Region became part of the Kazakh ASSR, and 20 March 1932 part of the RSFSR. In 1936 the region was the Karakalpak ASSR, part of the Kazakh SSR, and finally, on 5 December 1936, it became part of the Uzbek SSR.

Demography. The total number of Karakalpaks in the Soviet Union may be shown as follows:
1926: 126,000
1939: 186,000 (an increase of 47.6% from 1926)
1959: 172,000 (a decrease of 6.5% from 1939 due to assimilation by the Uzbeks)
1970: 236,000 (an increase of 36% from 1959)
1979: 303,000 (an increase of 28.4% from 1970)
Between 1959 and 1970, the increase of the Karakalpaks was the lowest of all Central Asian Turks (Kazakhs 46%, Turkmen 52%, Uzbeks 53%, Kirghiz 50%), probably because a certain number of Karakalpaks declared themselves Uzbeks.

The bulk of the Karakalpaks live in their national territory. There are only a few groups of them living outside their republic in old colonies. In 1979, 298,000 Karakalpaks (98.3%) lived in the Uzbek SSR (Table 7.vii.1).

Table 7.vii.1. KARAKALPAK POPULATION DISTRIBUTION, 1959–70

	Total population	In the Karakalpak ASSR	% in the ASSR	Outside the Karakalpak ASSR	% outside
1959	172,556	155,999	90.4	16,557	9.6
1970	236,009	217,505	92.2	18,504	7.8
1979	303,324	281,809	92.9	21,515	7.1

In 1970, 12,275 Karakalpaks lived in the Uzbek SSR (outside their own ASSR). Of these 8,668 lived in the Bukhara region (district of Kemineh), 1,428 in the city of Tashkent, 732 in the Ferghana valley, 1,447 in the Zerafshan valley (Samarkand region), 2,542 in the Tashauz region of the Turkmen SSR and 2,267 in the RSFSR (mainly in the city of Moscow). Smaller groups (1,420) lived in Kazakhstan and Kirghizia, and some 2,000 Karakalpaks lived in northern Afghanistan. In 1979, 15,979 lived in the Uzbek SSR outside their republic.

The Karakalpaks living in Turkmenistan are not assimilated by the Turkmen: 95.4% of them spoke the Karakalpak language in 1970. As to those living in Uzbekistan, those of Zerafshan and Ferghana are being rapidly assimilated by the Uzbeks. Those of Bukhara maintain their customs and their ethnic identity but are losing the use of their language: of the 8,668 Karakalpaks of Bukhara only 42% spoke Karakalpak in 1970, while 14.6% spoke Uzbek and 42.3% spoke Tajik.

The population of the Karakalpak ASSR is mainly rural, but the rate of urbanisation is more rapid than in Uzbekistan as a whole or in Kirghizia and Tajikistan: the proportion of urban dwellers was 27% in 1939, 35.5% in 1970, and 42% in 1979. In 1979 the Karakalpaks represented a minority in their own national republic, 31% of the total population. Muslims represented 94.9% in 1970 (compared to 92.5% in 1959 and 94.2% in 1970). The Karakalpak Republic is the most Muslim and the most Turkic of all Soviet administrative units. Russian influence is hardly felt at all. The southern part of the republic is mainly Uzbek. Kazakhs predominate in the eastern and western districts close to the borders, and represent an important urban element (41.3% of the Kazakhs live in the cities compared to 30% of Karakalpaks and Uzbeks). Kazakhs represent 31% of all city dwellers (the Karakalpaks only 26.2%). Tatars (mostly from the Volga) are also city dwellers (82.7%).

Table 7.vii.2.   POPULATION OF THE KARAKALPAK ASSR, 1979

Karakalpaks	281,809	(31.1%)
Uzbeks	285,400	(31.5)
Kazakhs	243,926	(26.9)
Turkmen	48,655	(5.4)
Total Muslims	859,790	(94.9)
Russians	21,187	(2.3)
Others (*Muslims*: Daghestanis, Tatars;		
non-Muslims: Ukrainians, Koreans)	24,423	
Total	905,500	

Koreans and Russians make up a small part of the population in the Karakalpak ASSR. The Koreans are mainly city dwellers (82%). Some rural Koreans live along the left bank of the Amu Darya, south of

Chimbay (a Korean rice-growing *kolkhoz*). The Russians represent a small colony which is steadily losing its importance. Mainly urban (88%), the Russians in the Karakalpak ASSR are largely descendants of Ural Cossacks (Old Believers) who settled in the delta of the Amu Darya as fishermen in 1875. Between 1959 and 1970, the Russian community increased by 2,199 individuals or 9.5%, instead of the average growth of 13%. It would seem that in the late 1960s, there was a small out-migration of Russians from the Karakalpak ASSR. The Korean colony, too, has lost some 1,000 individuals through out-migration.

Ethnographic data. The Karakalpak nation was created in the 1920s. The Karakalpaks descend from various tribes of Mongol and Turkic origin which in the fifteenth and sixteenth centuries belonged to the Great Nogai Horde established north of the Caspian Sea, and which in the seventeenth and eighteenth centuries moved eastward and settled south of the Aral Sea. Until the 1917 Russian Revolution, they represented a loose confederation of semi-nomadic tribes, divided into two federations (*arys*). The first federation is the Kongrat Arys, mainly of Turkic origin, which in turn is divided into two smaller groups: the Shulluk, subdivided into eight tribes including the important Kiyat, of Mongol origin, and the Zhaungirs, subdivided into seven clans. The second federation is the On Tort Urun Arys ("The Federation of 14 Clans"), divided into four great tribes: the Ktay and Keneges (Mongol origin) and the Kypchak and Mangyt (Turkic origin).

The Karakalpak tribes — in particular the Kongrat, the Ktay, the Kypchak, the Keneges and the Mangyt — are splinters of the great tribes of the same names which go to make up the other Turkic nations: Crimean Tatars, Bashkirs, Nogais, Uzbeks and Kazakhs. Before the Revolution, these tribes possessed their own territory and their own economic unity. The Kongrat still occupy the right bank of Amu Darya, and the "Federation of the 14 Clans" occupies mainly the left bank. Today the tribes have lost their economic specificity but survive as ethnographic groups of the Karakalpak nation. The awareness of belonging to a tribe as well as the feeling of kinship with members of the same tribe in other Turkic areas of the Soviet Union is still vivid.

The tribes are subdivided into clans (*uru*) and these into a sub-clanic formation called *koshe*, or a group of families descending from a common ancestor over four to five generations. The Karakalpak *koshe* is still a psychological reality. A *koshe* has its own territory, and its members are linked by a strong sense of close kinship. As a rule, a Karakalpak *kolkhoz* corresponds to a clan (*uru*) with a limited number of *koshe*. Within the *koshe* the Karakalpak family presents a traditional type. Exogamous taboos are still observed (marriage outside the clan), as well as the levirate and the payment of *kalym*. Ethnically the Karakalpaks are closer to the Kazakhs than to the Uzbeks.

Language and the problem of assimilation. The Karakalpak language belongs to the Kypchak-Nogai group of Turkic languages, as do Kazakh and Nogai. It is divided into two dialects: the northeastern, which is closer to Kazakh, and the southwestern, which is closer to Uzbek. Karakalpak remained a non-literary language until 1930, when it was endowed with a Latin alphabet (after an unsuccessful attempt to transliterate it in Arabic characters). In 1940 it received a Cyrillic alphabet.

Karakalpak is still a semi-literary language. Soviet Karakalpak written literature is insignificant; the traditional oral literature is identical to the Kazakh (*Koblandy batyr*), to the Crimean Tatar (*Er Shora*), to the Uzbek (*Alpamysh, Kyrk Kyz*) and to the Nogai (*Edighe*) epic cycles. The *Alpamysh* and *Kyrk Kyz* belong to the Kongrat tradition, and the *Edighe* and *Er Shora* to the Mangyt tradition.

In spite of the absence of authentic Karakalpak literature, there is no linguistic assimilation of the Karakalpaks by the more developed Uzbeks. In 1959, 95% of the Karakalpaks declared their national language as their native one; in 1970, 96.6% did so. The Russian language has made little progress; in 1970 only 878 Karakalpaks (less than 0.4%) declared it to be their first language. In 1979, 95.8% of the Karakalpaks declared Karakalpak as their native language. The number of "russified" Karakalpaks was 1,470 (0.5%).

Religious data. The Karakalpak ASSR is one of the more religious territories of the Soviet Union. In 1914 there were 553 mosques in the territory of the present-day republic. Official Islam is controlled by the Muslim Spiritual Directorate of Tashkent. The number of working mosques today is impossible to determine, but it is probable that there are less than ten. We have located five working mosques in the cities of Nukus, Turtkul, Khojeili and Chimbay.

Unofficial or parallel Islam is especially strong and active among the Karakalpaks and is more influential than official Islam. The Karakalpak ASSR, especially its northern, purely Karakalpak part, is one of the main centres of Central Asian Sufism. The following four *tariqa* are represented: the Naqshbandiya (silent *zikr*); the Kubrawiya (loud *zikr*; centre in Khorezm); the Yasawiya (loud *zikr*; centre in southern Kazakhstan); and the Kalendariya, an itinerant order especially strong among the Karakalpaks. The leadership of the Sufi orders is hereditary, and often the recruitment of the *tariqa* is limited to certain clans.

The main holy places of pilgrimage run by Sufi adepts (generally the tomb of a Sufi *murshid* surrounded by a working cemetery) are situated in the northern part of the republic. They include Ishan Kala near Khalkabad; Tokmak Ata near Muynak; Sultan-Baba in the mountains of Sultan Oweis Dagh, district of Biruni; Shamun Nabi and Mazlum-Slu in the district of Khojeili; Narimjan-Baba in the district of Turtkul; and Daud-Ata in the district of Kongrat. Religious rites and customs are better observed by the Karakalpaks than by any other Muslim national-ity of Central Asia. Circumcision is practiced as a national tradition by nearly all. "Only some few individuals among the Karakalpaks do not perform the rite of circumcision" (Bazarbaev, p. 113).

The level of religiousness of the Karakalpaks has been analysed recently by Bazarbaev (1973). He classifies Karakalpak society as follows:
— *Firm believers*, "intolerant fanatics", average 11.4%;
— *Believers* by tradition, average 14.4%;
— *Hesitant*, interested in the external aspect of Islam and performing its rites as part of the national tradition, average 13.6%;
— *Indifferent*, observing certain prescriptions of Islam such as circumci-sion, prayers and fasting; average 39.1%;
— *Atheists*, average 21.5%.
The proportion of atheists is higher among the younger generation aged 18–30 (47.8% compared with only 13.2% among those aged 42–54 years old, and 6.8% above 54 years), among intellectuals (89% among gra-duates from higher educational institutions, compared with only 4.3% among the non-educated) and among men (23.4% compared with 20.3% of women). However, even the majority of atheists have their male children circumcised and are buried religiously in Muslim cemeteries.

The anti-religious campaign in the Karakalpak ASSR is somewhat more intense than in other territories of Central Asia. Between 1948 and 1975 there were 11 anti-religious books, directed especially against Islam, published in the Karakalpak language (for a total population of 236,000 in 1970). The rate of anti-religious books per 1,000 individuals is 1:21 (compared to 1:30 for the Tajiks, 1:34 for the Turkmen, and 1:51 for the Uzbeks). In 1970, 2,605 anti-religious public conferences were organised in Karakalpakistan, and in 1971 there were 3,726.

National awareness. Of all Central Asian Muslim peoples, the Karakalpaks are probably the least aware of belonging to a modern Karakalpak nation. Their consciousness of belonging to a *koshe* (sub-clan) or to a specific tribe is still very keen, and their loyalties are generally limited to these two formations. Because of the persistence of reli-giousness, their awareness of being part of the Muslim *Umma* is equally strong. Finally, the fact of tribal kinship with other Turkic ethnic groups (Bashkirs, Nogais, Crimean Tatars, Kazakhs, Uzbeks) gives to the Karakalpaks a pan-Turkic sense of brotherhood with other former nomadic nations.

On the other hand, the Karakalpak nation lacks historical traditions of its own. The Karakalpaks share their epic songs and their great ancestors — generally the leaders of the Mangyt or the Kongrat tribes — with the Nogais, the Crimean Tatars, the Bashkirs and the Kazakhs. The more recent chapters of Karakalpak history are also shared with other Turkic nations, especially the Kazakhs and the Turkmen. The Karakalpaks took an active part in the great uprising of the Kazakh tribes against Russian rule in 1916, and in 1918–20 their territory was one of the main centres of Basmachi activity. The Turkmen leader, Junayd Khan, had many Karakalpaks among his guerrilla fighters.

Nationalism. Historical nationalism does not exist for the reasons explained above, and cultural nationalism remains exceedingly weak.

Administrative and political nationalism is equally weak. The Uzbeks living in the Karakalpak ASSR have the same economic and professional standard of living and are not considered by the Karakalpaks as aliens or oppressors. There is even a certain linguistic and cultural assimilation of the Uzbeks and of the Kazakhs living in the Karakalpak ASSR by the Karakalpaks (Table 7.vii.3). The political, economic, and intellectual cadres of the Karakalpak ASSR are more or less proportionate to the numerical importance of the Karakalpak and Uzbek communities

Table 7.vii.3.   UZBEKS AND KAZAKHS SPEAKING
KARAKALPAK, 1959–79

	1959 (and %)	1970 (and %)	1979 (and %)
Uzbeks	1,452 (1.0)	2,796 (1.3)	10,005 (3.5)
Kazakhs	2,516 (1.9)	3,688 (2.0)	9,334 (3.8)

within the republic. Thus there is no hostility between the two communities. The Russians in the republic are too few to represent a threat and moreover the majority are of the "poor white" type who are not considered by the native Muslims as colonial masters.

(viii) THE UIGHURS

The Uighurs are Sunni Muslims of the Hanafi school. There is no national Uighur territory in the Soviet Union. The Soviet Uighurs are recent (nineteenth-century) immigrants from Xinjiang in China, who were settled in Kazakhstan, Uzbekistan, Kirghizia .and, in smaller groups, Tajikistan and Turkmenistan. In China (province of Xinjiang) the total number of Uighurs is estimated by the authorities at 5.5 million, but it is likely to be closer to 10-12 million.

Contrary to Stalin's theory of nationalities, the Uighurs (as well as the Dungans and the Kurds), deprived of a national administrative entity, have nevertheless the status of a nationality and enjoy a kind of extraterritorial cultural autonomy in the Soviet Union. The appelation "Uighur" was adopted only recently at the All-Uighur Congress in Tashkent in 1921. Before that, they used names derived from their place of origin in Xinjiang: Kashgarlyk (from Kashgar), Aksuluk, Yarkandlik (from Yarkand), and Turfanlik (from Turfan). The northern (Kazakhstan) Uighurs bore a name derived from their social and economic position: Taranchis or peasants. This is often still the case. In Central Asia, other Turks generally call the Uighurs "Kashgarlyks".

Demography. The total number of Uighurs in the Soviet Union was 108,570 in 1926; 95,208 in 1959; 173,276 in 1970 (an increase from 1959 of 82%); and 210,602 in 1979 (an increase of 21.8% from 1970). The numerical regression of the Uighurs between 1926 and 1959 is due to the assimilation of those living in Uzbekistan by Uzbeks. Between the 1939 and 1970 censuses, the Uighurs increased by 82%: the highest percentage among all Central Asian Muslims. This exceptional growth is due to two different factors. First is the immigration of Uighurs from Xinjiang to Kazakhstan (around 60,000 Uighurs are said to have migrated from Xinjiang to the Soviet Union between 1959 and 1966 — maybe an exaggerated figure). The second factor is the favourable policy of the Soviet government, inspiring the Soviet Uighurs with a greater awareness of belonging to a specific nationality, different from other Turkic nationalities in Central Asia. It is likely that in 1970 a number of Uighurs, previously assimilated by the Uzbeks or the Kazakhs, were encouraged to consider themselves once more as Uighurs. The Soviet Union's favourable treatment of its Uighurs reflects the fierce competition between it and China to influence each other's border minorities.

There are two groups of Uighurs: southern and northern. The southern group — the Uighurs of Ferghana ("Kashgarlyks"), originally from the Kashgar and Yarkand area of Xinjiang — migrated in the middle of the nineteenth century to Central Asia. These small groups of families were settled by the Russian authorities in the Ferghana valley amid the local Uzbek and Kirghiz population. Their ultimate destination was to be assimilated by the Uzbeks. In 1970 this group numbered some 50,000. In Uzbekistan there were 23,942 Uighurs in 1970, 39% urban and 61% rural (1979 figures not yet available). There were 5,884 Uighurs living in the city of Tashkent, 5,157 in the Tashkent *oblast'*, and 11,054 in the Andizhan *oblast'* (districts of Pahtaabad, Izbaskent and Lenin). In Kirghizia there were 23,872 in 1970 (46% urban and 54% rural). There were 6,686 in the Frunze *oblast'* and 8,031 in the Osh *oblast'* (districts of Aravan and Karakul); 2,765 in the Issyk-Kul *oblast'*; and 571 in the Naryn *oblast'* (1970 figures). Smaller groups of southern Uighurs are settled in Turkmenistan (district of Bairam Ali) and in Tajikistan.

The northern group, the Uighurs of Semirechie, or *Taranchis*, originating mainly from the Ili valley in Xinjiang, migrated to Central Asia in the late nineteenth century. Some of them arrived *en masse* after the defeat of the great Muslim revolt of 1881-3 against the Manchus (45,373 Ili Uighurs migrated to Semirechie during this short period). A third wave of migrants from Xinjiang arrived in the late 1950s and early 1960s. The Ili Uighurs came in large groups and were settled by Russian authorities in areas of sparse population. They do not mix with the local Kazakh population, and are likely to survive as a nationality.

In 1970, this group — an essentially peasant one — represented 120,881 individuals of whom 24% were urban and 75% rural — one of the highest proportions of countryside dwellers in Central Asia. In 1970 there were 19,105 Uighurs in the city of Alma-Ata (particularly in the "Sultan Korghan" quarter) and 72,692 in the Alma-Ata *oblast'* (88,556 in 1979) where they represent the majority of the population of the Uighur district (centre Chunja) and about half the population in the Enbekshi Tatar district (centre Issyk). They are also numerous in the districts of Chilik (centre Chilik), and form smaller colonies in the districts of Naryn and Ili. There are also 24,791 Uighurs in the Taldy-

Kurgan *oblast'* (1979 figures), particularly in the district of Panfilov (centre Panfilov, formerly Yarkand, the Uighur political centre). There were 2,441 Uighurs in the Chimkent *oblast'* and 1,389 in the Semipalatinsk *oblast'* (1970 figures). There are no Uighur colonies outside Central Asia. Table 7.viii.1 shows the population distribution of Uighurs in the Soviet Union. In 1979 the census listed 147,943 Uighurs in Kazakhstan (an increase of 24.4%) and 29,817 Uighurs in Kirghizia (an increase of 20.6%). The number of Uighurs in Uzbekistan was not indicated.

Table 7.viii.1. UIGHUR POPULATION DISTRIBUTION IN THE SOVIET UNION, 1959–70

	1959	*1970*	*% increase 1959–70*	*Urban (and %) 1970*
Total in Soviet Union	95,208	173,276	82.0	53,355(31)
In Uzbekistan		23,942	23.5	9,353(39)
In Kirghizia	13,800	24,872	109.0	11,548(46)
In Kazakhstan	59,800	120,881	102.0	29,618(24)
Elsewhere (Tajikistan-Turkmenistan)	2,231	3,581	60.5	

Ethnographic data. The Uighurs are an old sedentary nation. All clan and tribal divisions disappeared long ago. However, the Uighur nationality in Soviet Central Asia is lacking in ethnic unity. In the northern (Kazakh) group, the ethnic and cultural influence of the Chinese (and, to a less extent, of the Mongols) is clearly apparent. The Uighurs speak the northern dialect, known as the *Kulja* or *Taranchi*, which has been elected by the Soviet authorities to serve as the basis of the Uighur (or rather the neo-Uighur) literary language. The Uighur of Ferghana are more marked by Iranian influence, and their dialect — the *Yarkand-Kashgari* — is far removed from the northern one and thus from the literary language. Only the northern Uighurs are expected to survive as a distinct nationality, for those of the Ferghana valley in Uzbekistan and Kirghizia seem destined to become assimilated by the Uzbeks.

In 1979, 95.7% of the Uighurs in Kazakhstan spoke their own language; 2.3% spoke Russian and only 1.3% spoke Kazakh. There is no linguistic and cultural assimilation by the Kazakh environment. This

may be explained by the protection which the Soviet authorities grant
to the Uighurs but also by the isolation of their rural communities from
the Kazakhs. Among the countryside-dwellers the proportion of
Uighur-speaking people is higher (98.3% in 1970) than among the city
dwellers (91.1% compared to 7.3% Russian-speaking and only 1%
Kazakh-speaking).

In Uzbekistan the proportion of Uighurs who declared Uighur to be
their native language in 1970 was only 59.2%, and the proportion of
Uzbek-speaking Uighurs was 36.9%. Among the city-dwellers —
because of the influence of the intellectuals — the proportion of
Uighur-speakers is strikingly higher: 74.6%, with only 16.6% speaking
Uzbek and 7.7% Russian (1970 figures). Among the rural element, the
linguistic assimilation is already far advanced: 49.7% of the Uighurs
declared Uzbek as their native language in 1970.

This phenomenon is due to three factors. First, the Ferghana Uighurs
form small isolated groups closely connected to a dense Uzbek population. Secondly, the southern Uighurs share with the Uzbeks their way
of life, their customs, and their social-familiar structure; mixed marriages are frequent. The southern dialect (*Yarkand-Kashgari*) is very close
to literary Uzbek. The switch from Uighur to Uzbek represents an
almost imperceptible process. The third factor is that in Kirghizia the
assimilation of the Uighurs is slower than in Uzbekistan, and it is
noteworthy that the Uighurs are not being assimilated by the Kirghiz
but by the Uzbeks. In 1979, 75.2% of the Uighurs declared Uighur as
their native language, 3.6% spoke Kirghiz, 4.0% Russian and 17.1%
Uzbek. Among city-dwellers the Uighur-speaking percentage reached
86.4% in 1970 (compared to 6.9% speaking Uzbek, 4% speaking Russian and only 2.6% speaking Kirghiz). Among the Uighur peasants,
assimilation is more advanced: 73.2% are speaking Uighur compared to
21% speaking Uzbek and only 4.3% speaking Kirghiz (1970 figures).

More than any other Muslim group in Central Asia, the Uighurs have
preserved certain social traditions. Endogamy within their community is
observed among the northern Uighurs (and constitutes another obstacle
to their assimilation by the Kazakhs); and polygamy is more frequent
than among other Central Asians, as well as the use of the *paranja* by
Uighur women. The payment of *kalym* is unknown among the
Uighurs.

Language and the problem of assimilation. In the Soviet Union the neo-
Uighur literary language was created on the basis of the northern

Taranchi dialect. Until 1939 it was transcribed in Arabic characters, from 1939 to 1946 in Latin characters, and since then in Cyrillic. The literary language of the Uighurs of China, based on the southern dialect, was written in Arabic characters up to 1956. Then it was announced by the Chinese authorities that Uighurs would adopt a Cyrillic alphabet, but in 1958 this decision was cancelled and a special Latin alphabet was introduced, replaced recently by the Arabic.

The Uighurs of Kazakhstan enjoy full cultural extraterritorial autonomy. They have their own press; two republican newspapers, *Kommunizm tughi* in Alma-Ata (in Cyrillic script), and *Yanghi Hayat*, are printed in an adjusted Arabic script and intended primarily for those Uighurs who studied their language in Arabic script in Xinjiang and subsequently moved to the Soviet Union. Both these newspapers are distributed in other Central Asian republics.

There are no special Uighur mosques, except one built in the Chinese style at the turn of the last century in Yarkand (the present Panfilov) and one in Andizhan. We have no evidence that the first is still in use. The anti-religious propaganda designed especially for the Uighurs is relatively important. Between 1948 and 1975 five anti-religious books were published in the Uighur language, and the rate of anti-religious books per 1,000 individuals is 1:34 (compared to 1:42 for the Kazakhs and 1:52 for the Uzbeks).

National awareness. Soviet Uighurs are recent immigrants whose ties with their motherland — Xinjiang — are not completely severed. They belong to an old sedentary nation with a high and ancient culture, the second in importance of all inner Asian Turks (after the Uzbeks). The awareness of belonging to the Uighur nation varies with the different groups, southern or northern.

In the case of the southern Uighurs, who, as we have seen, are rapidly losing their identity and are in the midst of assimilation by the Uzbeks, national awareness is more Islamic, Turkic or Turkestani than Uighur. The intellectuals of the northern groups, by contrast, have a strong consciousness of belonging to one great Uighur nation. Soviet authorities endeavoured in the past to oppose these awarenesses but since 1977 they have, up to a point, encouraged among the Uighurs of Kazakhstan the sense of unity with their brethren of China. Nevertheless, it must be remembered that the northern Uighur group is predominantly a peasant community whose consciousness does not go beyond a limited *geographical* awareness, and that the number of Uighur intellectuals is still very low.

Nationalism. There is no Uighur cultural nationalism: the Uighurs share with the Uzbeks the same traditional oral literature poems of *Ker Oglu, Tahir and Zohra, Ahmed and Yusuf*. Moreover, the modern neo-Uighur literary language is the closest of all Turkic languages to the classical Chagatai — the traditional literary language of Central Asia. The so-called classical old Uzbek literature (especially the works of the greatest "Uzbek" poet Ali Shir Navai) is more accessible to the Uighurs than to the Uzbeks.

The historical nationalism of the Uighurs presents a more complex problem. Its origins go back to the revolt of Xinjiang Muslims against the Manchus in the middle of the nineteenth century, and in the beginning it had a strong anti-Chinese character. This was reinforced more recently (in the 1950s and 1960s) by the exodus of a large number of Chinese Uighurs to Kazakhstan. However, an anti-Russian tradition in Uighur nationalism must not be neglected. In 1916, the northern Uighurs took an active part in the great uprising of the Kazakh tribes against Russian administration, and after the defeat of the rebellion a certain number of Russian Uighurs escaped to China. Another exodus to China of northern Uighurs fleeing collectivisation took place at the end of the 1920s and in the early 1930s.

(ix) THE BALUCHI

The Baluchi are partly Sunni Muslims of the Hanafi school and partly Shi'a of the Ja'farite rite. An immigrant community, they came to Central Asia in three main migratory waves from Afghanistan (district of Chahansur in Afghan Seistan) and from Iranian Seistan. The first group arrived in the late nineteenth century; the second between 1917 and 1920; and the last and most important one between 1923 and 1928, propelled by economic reasons.

In 1959 the Baluchi community numbered 7,842, in 1970 12,582 and in 1979 18,997. The marked increase between the three is due partly to the natural fertility of the Baluchi community.

The Baluchi live in the Mary *oblast'* of the Turkmen SSR (18,488 individuals in 1979): in the district of Iolatan (*kolkhoz* "Zhdanov", 63% Baluchi, *kolkhoz* "Kalinin", and the *sovkhoz* "Zehmet"); in the district of Turkmen-Kala (*kolkhoz* "Kuybyshev"); and in the district of Bairam-Ali. Small groups of Baluchi in Tajikistan (district of Parkhar and Kolkhozabad) are being assimilated rapidly by the Tajiks and have already lost the use of their language.

Soviet Baluchi speak the Khorassan (western) dialect. Small groups of Brahuis still preserved in the 1960s the use of their own Dravidian language, but the Iranian-speaking Baluchi are rapidly assimilating them. The loyalty of the Baluchi of Turkmenistan to their native tongue is exceptionally strong: in 1959, 94.9% of them claimed it as their first language; in 1970 and 1979 the figure was 98.1%. However, Baluchi remains a non-literary tongue, and the community is using Turkmen for this purpose. In 1979, 53.8% of the Baluchi had a good knowledge of Turkmen (compared to only 4.1% who knew Russian — one of the lowest percentages in the Soviet Union).

The Baluchi of Turkmenistan represent a purely rural community (only 9% of them are urban) and are not being assimilated by the Turkmen. They maintain their tribal division in ten tribes. The Dravidian Baluchi (Brahuis) consider themselves the Baluchi of the Brahui tribe. It seems that the Soviet authorities favour the survival of the Baluchi community in Turkmenistan, and there have recently been some attempts (with inconclusive results so far) to endow the Baluchi with a literary language of their own.

(x) THE PAMIRIAN PEOPLES

This appelation designates a certain number of national and ethnic groups linked by the territory on which they are officially established and, for the most part, a common religious allegiance. They are also called "Mountain" or "Pamirian" Tajiks (*Gornye, Pripamirskie*) or "Galcha" peoples. The majority of the Pamirian peoples are Ismailis of the Nizarit rite (followers of the Aga Khan). The Yazgulems and the Vanchis are Sunni Muslims of the Hanafi school. The vast majority of the Pamirian peoples are rural dwellers. The proportion of urban population in 1970 was 13%.

Demography. The Pamirian peoples live in the western part of the Gorno-Badakhshan Autonomous *Oblast'* (Pamir) founded on 2 January 1925 as part of the Tajik ASSR. The eastern part of the Autonomous Region is sparsely populated by the Kirghiz. Total territory covers 63,700 square km. The population was 119,000 in 1970 and 127,709 in 1979. Of this total 115,484 were "Tajiks" (this term covering the real Tajiks as well as the "Pamirians"), 8,503 were Kirghiz (in the eastern part of the Pamirs) and 1,779 Russians (1.4%). The capital is Khorog. The Pamirian peoples speak languages belonging to the East Iranian group, very different from that of the Tajiks. Tajik is used as the literary language (an unsuccessful attempt was made in 1931 to turn Shugni into a literary language).

The Pamirian peoples are divided into the following groups: the Yazgulems, in the valley of the river Yazgulem; the Rushans, in the valley of the Pyanzh, between the rivers Yazgulem and Bartang; the Bartangs, in the valley of the river Bartang; the Vanchi, who live near the Tajiks and have been almost wholly assimilated by them; the Shugnans, most numerous of the Pamirian peoples, in the middle valley of the Pyanzh, south of the Rushans and in the valleys of its tributaries, Gunt and Shah-Dara; the Ishkashimis, in the southernmost part of the Pamirs, south of the Shugnans, and the Vakhis, in the high valley of Pandj and of its tributary, the river Pamir.

In the census of 1939 the Pamirian peoples in the Soviet Union totalled 37,960 (a minimum). In 1959 they were listed as Tajiks but claimed their national languages as their native ones; at that time they numbered 42,400. This increase is due to natural causes and proves that linguistic assimilation of the Pamirians by the Tajiks is slight. Today the Pamirians probably number 60,000 to 100,000.

Outside the Soviet Union, Pamirian peoples are found in Afghanistan. In 1966 their number was estimated at about 15,000 (6,000 Shugnans, 2,000 Ishkashimis, 3,000 Rushans and 3,500 Vakhis). Small groups of Sarykolis — an ethnic group related to the Shugnans — live in China and even smaller groups of Vanchis in Pakistan.

Religious data and national awareness. The national consciousness of the Pamirian peoples is based on religion. Since the eleventh century they have belonged to the Ismaili sect, a result of the missionary activity of the great mystic poet Nasir-i Khosrow (1004–72). The Yazgulems are the exception; they were converted to Sunnism in the nineteenth century and in consequence are being assimilated by the Tajiks; they have preserved the use of their language but have adopted the Tajik culture. Another Pamirian group, the Vanchis, who live in the valley of the river Vanch and adopted Sunni Islam a little before the Yazgulems, have lost their language and have been almost entirely assimilated by the Tajiks.

The Ismaili Pamirians isolate themselves not only from the Tajiks and the Kirghiz but also from those Pamirians who have adopted Sunni Islam. There are practically no mixed marriages between the Ismailis and the Sunnis.

The Ismaili religion, with its old tradition of clandestinity, has survived as a kind of secret society; there are no Ismaili mosques and no official clerics, but private houses of prayers and itinerant clerics are still numerous. At least up till the Second World War, contacts were regularly maintained with the Ismaili centres in India. Anti-religious propaganda, especially directed against Ismailism, is relatively active. Several pamphlets were published in the 1960s: e.g. Kh. Dodikhudoev, *Mazhabi Ismailiya ve Mohiyat-i Ichtimoy-i On* ("Modern Ismailism and its Reactionary Essence"), Dushanbe, 1967. In 1978 a special seminar to train anti-Ismaili propagandists was held in Khorog.

(xi) THE IRONIS

The Ironis are Shi'a Muslims of the Ja'farite ("Twelvers") rite. This appelation covers a community of people springing from different origins but unified by a common Shi'a faith. Most of the Ironis are descendants of Iranian slaves and prisoners taken in the area of Mary by the Emir Shah Murad of Bukhara in 1785; others are members of merchant colonies originating from Iran or Afghanistan. This group includes some Baluchi and even local Shi'a, a circumstance which goes to show that religious consciousness in this particular case is stronger than the national one.

Before the Revolution the Ironis numbered 55,000, about 30,000 of whom were descendants of former slaves or old immigrants and 25,000 were new immigrants, some of them still Iranian citizens. Before 1910 the Central Asian Shi'a were closely integrated into the Sunni community, but after the Shi'a-Sunni mutual massacres of 1910 in Bukhara, the Ironi community isolated itself, and mixed marriages were ruled out.

The Ironis are mainly city-dwellers. In 1970, 52.6% of them lived in Central Asian cities, mainly Bukhara, speaking Persian, while those of Samarkand were turkified and spoke Uzbek. In 1959, according to the census figures, the number of Ironis had fallen to 20,766, of whom 44.7% spoke Persian. By 1970 their number (as per the census) had risen to 27,501, i.e. by 34.4%. This increase shows that the assimilation of the Shi'a community by the Uzbeks had not yet gone very far. Of that

number 10,160 spoke Persian, 2,850 declared Russian to be their native
language and 14,516 spoke a Turkic language — Uzbek or Turkmen.
In the 1979 census the Ironis were listed as "Persians" (*Persy*). Their
number was 31,313, an increase of 12.7%.

In 1970 there were 14,472 Ironis in Uzbekistan (53.1% in the cities)
and 12,044 in other Central Asian republics, mainly Turkmenistan. The
majority of the Ironis living in Uzbekistan spoke Uzbek (12,302); only
1,984 spoke Persian, and 735 spoke Russian. In 1979, 30.7% of the
Ironis spoke Persian, 9.8% spoke Russian and 60.5% various Turkic
languages.

To our knowledge there are no special Shi'a mosques in the cities of
Central Asia. Theoretically the Shi'a of Central Asia are placed under the
religious jurisdiction of the Muslim Spiritual Board of Baku (not of
Tashkent).

(xii) THE CENTRAL ASIAN TSIGANES (GYPSIES)

The Central Asian Tsiganes (self-denomination: *Mugi* or "Fire Worshippers") numbered officially 7,600 persons in 1959, but it is probable
that they were actually more numerous. 6,020 claimed Tajik as their
native tongue and the others Uzbek. In 1970 11,362 Tsiganes (including
a certain proportion of European non-Muslim Tsiganes) lived in
Uzbekistan, in the regions of Samarkand, Kashka Darya and Bukhara.
Of these 1,138 claimed Uzbek and 4,324 Tajik as their native language.
The 1970 census does not mention the total number of Central Asian
Tsiganes, but it is probable that some 5,000 lived in Tajikistan and
Turkmenistan.

The Central Asian Tsiganes are divided into two separate, ethnically
different groups: the Luli (Uzbek) or Jugi (Tajik), and the Mazangs.
Members of the two groups isolate themselves from the native population of Central Asia, and do not intermarry with them.

The Tsiganes are only superficially Muslims (Sunni of the Hanafi
school) and preserve many pre-Islamic rites and beliefs. They are bilingual (Tajik and Uzbek), but the majority consider Tajik their native
language. They also use a secret language: *lavz-i mugat*, with a special
vocabulary (mainly Iranian).

(*Note*: The total number of Tsiganes in the Soviet Union in 1979 was
209,000, compared to 175,000 in 1970. According to some not very
reliable reports, about 50% of this total may be considered superficially
as Muslims.)

(xiii) THE CENTRAL ASIAN ARABS

The Central Asian Arabs are Sunni Muslims of the Hanafi school. They did not appear in 1970 census registrations, but in 1959 they were listed as a separate nationality, and numbered 7,987 persons of whom only 2,727 spoke Arabic, 143 Russian, 2,776 Tajik, and 2,240 Uzbek. They were a purely rural community. In 1959 only 945 Arabs lived in cities (4.8% of the community).

The circumstances of the arrival of Arabs in Central Asia are debatable. It is probable that they came to this area in several waves and settled there at different periods. The oldest layer is probably represented by the descendants of the conquerors of the eighth century, while the most recent one consists of the descendants of Arab tribes of northern Afghanistan (areas of Balkh, Andhoy), resettled in Central Asia by Ubaydullah Khan, the Shaibanid ruler of Bukhara in the sixteenth century. It is also possible that some Arabs were brought to the region of Samarkand by Timur in the fifteenth century.

The Central Asian Arabs live mainly in the middle and lower Zerafshan valley, between Samarkand and the Karakul lake (Samarkand region). There is one large cattle-raising Arab *kolkhoz*, "Kalinin", in the district of Past Dargon, in the Samarkand region. Smaller groups are to be found in the lower valleys of Kashka Darya and Surkhan Darya (Uzbekistan), in the valley of Vakhsh in Tajikistan, and in eastern Ferghana. Small urban colonies exist in the cities of Bukhara, Karshi, Katta-Kurgan (Uzbekistan), Leninabad and Kuliab (Tajikistan). The Arabs live as a rule in isolated villages and do not mix with the native population. Endogamy is still observed within the Arab community and the dead are buried in purely Arab cemeteries.

The language spoken by Central Asian Arabs is close to the Iraqi dialect. It remains a vernacular tongue, and Arabs use Uzbek or Tajik as the literary language. The linguistic assimilation of the Soviet Arabs by the native population of Central Asia is well advanced.

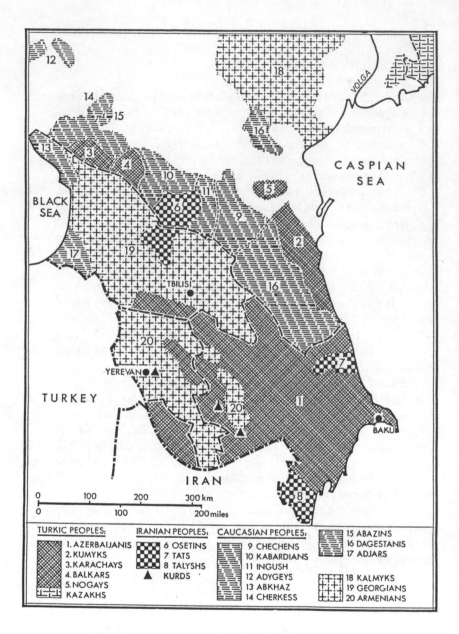

THE MUSLIM PEOPLES OF THE CAUCASUS

8

THE MUSLIMS OF TRANSCAUCASIA AND THE NORTH CAUCASUS

The territory situated between the southern slopes of the Great Caucasian range and the Turkish and Iranian frontiers is divided between three
Transcaucasian republics, Georgia, Armenia, and Azerbaijan, and is only
partly Muslim. It was in this area that Islam encountered the strongest
resistance. After an initial rapid expansion in what is now Azerbaijan in
the seventh and eighth centuries, its progress was obstructed and finally
completely blocked by two strong bastions of Christian culture: Orthodox Georgia and Monophysite Armenia. The process of the Islamisation
of eastern Transcaucasia remains incomplete. We still find in Azerbaijan
small groups of autochthonous Christians (5,492 Udins in 1970) and
Jews (in 1959, 12,960 Azerbaijani Jews declared Tati to be their first
language). Often conquered and occupied by Muslim invaders (Arabs,
Seljuks, Iranians), Georgia and Armenia succeeded for hundreds of
years — at least until the seventeenth century — in avoiding a massive
conversion of their population to Islam. Only isolated individuals, generally belonging to the highest level of feudal nobility, decided to change
their faith and become Muslims. Already in the eighth century the
eastern borderline between Islam and Christianity coincided more or less
with the present-day frontiers between Georgia and Armenia on one side
and Azerbaijan on the other.

Islam resumed its progress in western Transcaucasia only in the seventeenth century as a result of the efforts of the Ottoman Turks and the
Crimean Tatars. It was in the seventeenth and eighteenth centuries that
part of the Abkhaz and an important group of the Gurians adopted
Islam. Their descendants, the Adjars (about 150,000 in 1979), still live
in the southwestern corner of Georgia. In the eighteenth century Islam
also made limited progress in eastern Georgia: a small group of a few
thousand Georgians of eastern Kakhetia were converted to Islam. Their
descendants (the Ingilois) still live in northwestern Azerbaijan. In the
early twentieth century the number of Muslims in Transcaucasia
increased with the immigration into Armenia and Georgia of Kurds
from eastern Anatolia and the arrival of Volga Tatars in Azerbaijan.

Azerbaijan, as we have seen, is one of the three federal republics
(SSRs) that share the territory of Transcaucasia. It was created on 28

April 1920, and became part of the Transcaucasian Federative Socialist Republic on 12 March 1922. In December 1922 it became part of the Transcaucasian Federation, and in December 1936 a Republic of the Soviet Union. Its territory covers 86,000 square km. (including Nakhichevan ASSR and Nagorno-Karabakh AO). The Azerbaijan population was 6,028,000 in 1979 (17.8% more than in 1970). The urban population in 1979 was 3,200,000 or 53% (50% in 1970). The capital is Baku, with a population in 1979 of 1,550,000 (22.5% more than in 1970). Baku is the fifth largest city in the Soviet Union.

The Azerbaijan SSR has two autonomous areas. The first is the Nakhichevan ASSR, founded on 9 February 1924 with a territory of 5,500 square km. Its population was 239,000 in 1979 (18.2% more than in 1970); its urban population was 63,000 (26%, compared to 24.5% in 1970). Its capital is Nakhichevan. The second autonomous area is Nagorno-Karabakh, founded on 7 July 1923, with a territory of 4,400 square km. Its population was 161,000 in 1979 (6.6% more than in 1970). Urban dwellers numbered 71,000 (44%, compared to 38% in 1970). Its capital is Stepanakert.

The second federal republic in Transcaucasia is Georgia (Georgian SSR), founded on 25 February 1921. It became part of the Transcaucasian Socialist Republic on 12 March 1922, part of the Soviet Union (as comprised in the Transcaucasian Federation) on 30 December 1922, and finally part of the Soviet Union proper on 5 December 1936. Its territory covers 69,700 square km., including the Abkhaz and Adjar ASSRs, and the South Ossetian AO. Its population in 1979 was 5,016,000 (7% more than in 1970). Its urban population was 2,601,000 (or 52%, compared to 48% in 1970). The capital is Tbilisi, with a population of 1,066,000 in 1979, 19.9% more than in 1970.

The Georgian SSR has three autonomous areas. First is the Abkhaz ASSR, founded on 4 March 1921, with a territory of 8,600 square km. Its population was 506,000 in 1979 (3.9% up on 1970). Its urban population was 238,000 (47%, compared to 44% in 1970). The capital is Sukhumi, with a population in 1979 of 114,000.

The second autonomous region is the Adjar ASSR, founded on 16 July 1921, with a territory of 3,000 square km. Its population was 355,000 in 1979 (14.6% up on 1970). The urban population was 161,000 (45%, compared to 44% in 1970). The capital is Batumi, which had a population in 1979 of 124,000.

The South Ossetian AR is the third autonomous areas. Founded on 20 April 1922, it has a territory of 3,900 square km. Its population was

98,000 in 1979 (a *decrease* from 1970 in absolute numbers by 1,421 or 1.4%). Urban dwellers numbered 41,000 (42%, compared to 36% in 1970). The capital is Tskhinvali (formerly Staliniri).

The third federal republic in Transcaucasia is the Armenian SSR, founded on 29 November 1920. It became part of the Transcaucasian Federative Socialist Republic on 12 March 1922, and part of the Soviet Union (as comprised in the Transcaucasian Federation) on 30 December 1922. It finally became a Union Republic on 5 December 1936. Its population was 3,031,000 in 1979 (21.6% more than in 1970). The urban population numbered 1,993,000 (66%, compared to 59% in 1979). The capital is Erevan, which had a population of 1,019,000 in 1979 (33% more than in 1970).

Table 8.1.   POPULATION OF TRANSCAUCASIA, 1959–79

	1959	1970	% increase 1959–70	1979	% increase 1970–9
Total	9,504,810	12,295,312	29.3	14,056,956	14.3
Georgia	4,044,045	4,686,358	15.9	4,993,182	6.5
Azerbaijan	3,697,717	5,117,081	38.4	6,026,515	17.7
Armenia	1,763,048	2,491,873	41.3	3,037,259	21.8

Demography

The Muslim population of Transcaucasia numbers around 5,662,000 and is composed of the following groups: Azeris, Daghestanis, Kurds, and Tatars. Although the 1979 census data are incomplete, they showed the following population distribution of those groups. Of the Azeris 4,708,832 are in Azerbaijan, 256,678 in Georgia and 160,841 in Armenia. There are 205,127 Daghestanis and 31,350 Tatars in Azerbaijan. Of the Kurds 25,688 are in Georgia, 51,000 in Armenia and an unknown number in Azerbaijan.

To these thoroughly Islamised groups, it is necessary to add a certain number of Muslims belonging to nationalities that are mainly non-Muslim and are not listed in the census. There are Georgian Muslims (Adjars and Ingilois) in Georgia numbering about 150,000. Probably less than 10% of the Ossetians living in the South Ossetian AO of Georgia are Muslims; the majority of Ossetians living in Azerbaijan (about 15,000) are Muslim. Probably 50% of the Abkhaz are Muslims (91,000 Abkhaz in 1979). There is also the Tat community, who are Jewish,

Table 8.2.   MUSLIM POPULATION OF TRANSCAUCASIA, 1959–79
(*1979 figures not yet available in detail*)

	1959	% of total	1970	% of total	% increase 1959–70	1979 (estimate)	% of total	% increase 1970–9
Total	3,098,000	32.6	4,600,000	40.0	48.2	5,662,000	40.3	23.0
Armenian SSR	135,000	7.6	186,000	7.5	39.2	212,000	7.0	14.0
Georgian SSR	310,000	7.6	414,000	8.8	31.4	490,000	9.7	17.6
Azerbaijan SSR	2,653,000	71.7	4,000,000	78.1	50.6	4,960,000	82.3	24.0

Muslim (the majority) and Christian. We may assume that in Azerbaijan, out of the 8,848 Tats in 1979, some 5,000 were Muslims. There are also Armenian Muslims (Khemshins), numbering about 1,000. The 1970 census does not mention the existence of the Meskhetian Turks, but the 1979 census lists 92,689 ''Turks'' (*Turki*) partly in Transcaucasia.

The general increase of the Muslim population was considerably higher than the average of the total population of the territory between 1970 and 1979: 48.2% against 14.5%. Table 8.2 shows the Muslim population distribution.

Between the three censuses (1959, 1970, 1979), the general demographic process in the three Transcaucasian republics consisted of national consolidation through the assimilation of smaller national groups and also through the process of immigration and out-migration of various native and foreign groups. This process is marked by the out-migration of the Russians and the Armenians from Azerbaijan and from Georgia: between 1959 and 1970 these two communities increased in Azerbaijan by only 1.7% and 9.4%, respectively (compared with the general increase of 13% and 27.7%). Between 1970 and 1979 they decreased in absolute numbers: the Russians from 510,059 to 475,000 and the Armenians from 483,520 to 475,000. As there is no assimilation of these communities by the Muslim Azeris, there probably is a steady out-migration of Russian and Armenian cadres from Azerbaijan for economic, social or psychological reasons. The process of out-migration is even more spectacular in Georgia, as shown by Table 8.3.

Table 8.3.   OUT-MIGRATION FROM GEORGIA

	Population *1959*	*Population* *1970*	*Increase* *1959–70* *(and %)*	*Population* *1979*	*Increase* *1970–9* *(and %)*
Russians	407,886	396,694	− 11,192 (2.7)	371,608	− 25,086 (0.06)
Ukrainians	52,236	49,622	− 2,614 (5.5)	45,036	− 4,586 (0.1)
Armenians	442,916	452,309	9,393 (2.1)	448,000	− 4,309 (0.09)

The Muslim population of Azerbaijan, Armenia and Georgia is, by contrast, relatively stable. The increase of the Azeris in these three republics in 1959–70 was, respectively, 51.4%, 37.5% and 41.7%, which probably indicates a slightly lower fertility rate for Azeris in Georgia and Armenia, although some out-migration is also possible. In 1970-9, the respective increase of the Azeris in the three republics was 24.7, 8.6% and 17.6%.

Armenians leaving Azerbaijan are moving into Armenia. The increase of their community in Armenia between 1959 and 1970 is significantly higher than their general increase in the Soviet Union as a whole: 42.3% as against 27.7%. Between 1970 and 1979 the corresponding increases were 23.4% (in Armenia) and 16.6% (in the Soviet Union).

Transcaucasia is the only Soviet Muslim territory where Sunni Islam is in a minority; the majority of the Muslims belong to Shi'a Islam. Some 75% of the Azeris and all the Muslim Tats belong to the Shi'a Jafarite or Ithna Ashariya ("Twelvers") rite. The remaining 25% — consisting of the Azeris, the Muslim Abkhaz, the Adjars, the Ingilois, the majority of the Kurds, the immigrant Volga Tatars, and the Meskhetian Turks — belong to the Hanafi school of Sunni Islam. The Daghestanis are Sunni of the Shafei school. At present the main difference between the Sunnis and the Shi'a is cultural and political rather than theological. The Sunnis are traditionally more inclined toward the Turkic world (Ottoman empire, Turkey, Volga Tatars) and also toward Daghestan; the Shi'a are inclined towards Iran.

A minority of the Kurds in Armenia and Azerbaijan and the Turkic Karapapakh tribe in Azerbaijan belong to the heretical, semi-clandestine, syncretistic sect of Ali Illahis ("Those who divinise Ali"), the self-denominated Ahl-i Hakk ("People of the Truth"), totalling 5,000. The Bahais (not recognised by other Muslims as such) are represented by some colonies (numbers unknown) mainly in Azerbaijan. A group of Kurds in Armenia (14,000 in 1926) are Yezidis ("Devil Worshippers"). They are not recognised by other Muslims as belonging to Islam. The Ali-Ilahis, the Bahais and the Yezidis have no recognised religious administration. Deprived of clerics and a regular cult, their faith survives rather as folklore.

The Muslims of Transcaucasia — unlike those of Central Asia — are subject to many different influences: Russian of course, but also Turkish, Iranian, Tatar and Daghestani. Models for political radicalism and mass mobilisation around a "revolutionary" ideology may come from Moscow, as well as from Iran and even from Daghestan or Turkey.

All three Transcaucasian nations have an old, brilliant and sophisticated culture; as a consequence there is virtually no linguistic or cultural assimilation of one nationality by another. This is especially true of the Muslim Azeris. By contrast, the Kurds are being linguistically assimilated not only by the Azeris but also by the Christians. Table 8.4 shows the assimilation of the Azeris, Armenians, Georgians, and Kurds.

Table 8.4.   ASSIMILATION OF NATIONALITIES, 1970–9

1970	Azerbaijan SSR		Georgian SSR		Armenian SSR	
	Total pop.	Total assimilated (and %)	Total pop.	Total assimilated (and %)	Total pop.	Total assimilated (and %)
Azeris	—	—	217,758	2,436 (1.1)	148,189	277 (0.2)
Armenians	483,500	700 (0.1)	452,309	32,246 (7.1)	—	—
Georgians	13,595	127 (0.9)	—	—	1,439	87 (6.0)
Kurds	5,488	1,222(22.3)	20,690	1,569 (7.6)	37,486	2,661 (7.1)

1979	Azerbaijan SSR		Georgian SSR		Armenian SSR	
	Total pop.	Total assimilated (and %)	Total pop.	Total assimilated (and %)	Total pop.	Total assimilated (and %)
Azeris	—	—	255,678	5,015 (1.9)	160,841	374 (0.2)
Armenians	475,486	107,116(22.5)	488,000	74,975(16.7)	—	—
Georgians	11,412	?	—	—	1,314	?
Kurds	?	—	25,688	6,367(24.8)	50,822	7,140(14.0)

(i) THE AZERI TURKS

Of the Azeri Turks 75% are Shi'a (Ithna Ashariya), and 25% are Sunni Muslims of the Hanafi school. There are no non-Muslim Azeris. Their territory is a federal republic created on 28 April 1920 after the liquidation by the Red Army of the independent Republic of Azerbaijan. The geographical area covers 86,600 square km, including the ASSR of Nakhichevan and the AO of Nagorno-Karabakh. The population in 1979 was 6,028,000, an increase of 17.8% over 1970. The urban population was 3,200,000 (or 53%, compared to 50% in 1970). Its capital is Baku, population in 1979 1,550,000, an increase of 22.5% over 1970.

The total Azeri population in 1939 was 2,274,800; in 1959, 2,939,728; in 1970, 4,379,937 (an increase from 1959 of 49%); and in 1979, 5,477,000 (an increase from 1970 of 25.0%). In 1979, 4,708,832 (86.0%) of the Azeris lived in their national republic, 255,678 in Georgia and 160,841 in Armenia, making altogether 5,125,351 in Transcaucasia. In Georgia and Armenia, the Azeris represent rural border colonies. In these two republics, the urban Azeris constituted in 1970 18.2% and 9.8% of their respective communites. In the Daghestan ASSR there were 64,514 Azeris in 1979, constituting 41% of the urban population. The total number of Azeris living in the Caucasus was 5,189,865 (94.7% of all Azeris) in 1979.

Table 8.i.1.   POPULATION OF THE AZERBAIJAN SSR

	1959 population (and % of total)	1970 population (and % of total)	% increase 1959–70	1979 population (and % of total)	% increase 1970–9
Azeris	2,494,381(67.5)	3,776,778(73.8)	51.4	4,708,832(78.1)	24.7
Daghestanis	121,442 (3.3)	177,165 (3.4)	45.9	205,127 (3.4)	15.7
Tatars	29,552 (0.8)	31,787 (0.6)	7.5	31,350 (0.5)	0
Georgians (partly Muslim Ingilois)	9,526	13,595	42.7	?	—
Kurds	—	5,488	—	—	—
Tats	—	7,769	—	8,848	13.9
Ossetians (partly Muslims)	—	2,315	—	—	—
Russians	501,282(13.5)	510,059 (9.9)	1.7	475,486 (7.9)	-7.2
Armenians	442,089(11.9)	483,520 (9.4)	9.4	475,255 (7.9)	-1.7
Jews	40,204 (1.1)	41,288 (0.8)	2.7	35,497 (0.5)	-16.3
Ukrainians	24,778 (0.7)	29,160 (0.5)	13.1	26,402 (0.4)	-10.4
Udins	3,202	5,492	71.5	5,841	6.2
Belorussians	4,284	4,929	15.0	4,782	-3.1
Moldavians	1,501	1,549	3.2	1,397	-10.9
Poles	1,483	1,264	-17.0	—	—
Assyrians	1,367	1,231	-10.0	—	—
Mordvinians	—	1,150	—	—	—
Others	—	23,692	—	—	—
Total	3,697,717	5,117,081	38.4	6,026,515	17.8

In 1979 some 176,032 Azeris (3.2%) formed émigré colonies in Central Asia: in Kazakhstan (73,345 compared with 57,699 in 1970); in Uzbekistan (59,779–38,898 in 1970); in Turkmenistan (23,548–16,775 in 1970); in Kirghizia (17,207 — 12,536 in 1970); and in Tadzhikistan (2,153–1,553 in 1970). The Azeri colony in Turkmenistan is almost entirely urban (oil specialists); in 1970 the urban element represented 96.7% of their community. In the other republics the community is divided between rural settlers and city-dwellers (technicians, engineers); the proportion of city-dwellers are: Kazakhstan 30%, Uzbekistan 46% and Kirghizia 23%. Between 1959 and 1970 the number of Azeris living in Central Asia decreased by 25,292; they have returned to Azerbaijan.

Table 8.i.2.   POPULATION OF BAKU, 1959–70

	1959 population (and % of total)	1970 population (and % of total)	% increase 1959–70
Azeris	372,676 (37.7)	586,052 (46.3)	+ 57.3
Russians	337,835 (34.2)	351,290 (27.7)	+ 3.9
Armenians	170,086 (17.2)	207,464 (16.4)	+ 22.0
Jews	29,204 (2.9)	29,716 (2.3)	I 1.7
Tatars	25,169 (2.5)	26,481 (2.1)	+ 5.2
Ukrainians	13,995 (1.4)	14,406 (1.1)	+ 2.9
Daghestanis	17,426 (1.8)	25,636 (2.1)	+ 47.1
Tats	5,698 (0.6)	7,524 (0.6)	+ 32.0
Georgians	2,994 (0.3)	3,283 (0.2)	+ 9.6
Belorussians	—	2,383 (0.2)	—
Others	—	11,480 (0.9)	—
Total	987,228	1,265,515	+ 28.2

Besides the Azeri colonies in the Caucasus and in Central Asia, there are a few others in some non-Muslim territories of the Soviet Union. In 1970 there were 41,286 in the RSFSR (Daghestan ASSR excluded), and in Moscow 4,889; in the Ukraine there were 10,769 and in Belorussia 1,335. The Azeris rank among the least migratory of the Soviet Muslim Turks. They give the impression of being especially reluctant to move to territories outside *Dar ul-Islam*. Beyond the boundaries of the Soviet Union, the Azeris are to be found in northwestern Iran (Iranian or southern Azerbaijan). Their number is estimated there at between 4,500,000 and 6,000,000.

Non-Muslim communities in Azerbaijan have been rapidly shrinking,

spectacularly so in the case of Russians and Armenians. Between the
three censuses (1959–79), there has been a steady out-migration of these
two nationalities from Azerbaijan, where they are mainly city-dwellers.
In 1970, 470,191 Russians (92.2% of the community) and 344,577
Armenians (71.3% of the community) lived in the cities. Of the 138,943
Armenians living in the countryside, 76,748 (55.2%) were in the
Nagorno-Karabakh Autonomous *Oblast'*, a territory where in 1970, the
Armenians represented 80.5% (121,068) of the total population
(150,313).

The evolution of the Baku population between the 1959 and 1970
censuses illustrates the growing numerical importance of the Muslim
community. In 1970, with 50.8% of the Muslims, Baku was the first
capital of all the Muslim republics to attain a Muslim majority.

In the two autonomous territories of the Azerbaijan Republic, the
same process of Azeri consolidation went on between 1939 and 1970.
Table 8.i.3. illustrates this trend.

Table 8.i.3.   POPULATION DISTRIBUTION, NAKHICHEVAN
ASSR AND NAGORNO-KARABAKH AO˙

	1959	1970	% increase	1979	% increase
Nakhichevan ASSR					
Azeris	127,508	189,679	48.7	229,968	21.2
Russians	3,161	3,919	23.9	3,807	– 0.03
Armenians	9,519	5,828	– 38.8	3,406	– 58.4
Total	141,351	202,187	43.0	240,459	18.9
Nagorno-Karabakh Autonomous Oblast'					
Azeris	17,995	27,179	51.0	37,264	37.1
Armenians	110,053	121,068	10.1	123,076	1.6
Russians	1,790	1,310	– 26.8	1,265	– 3.56
Total	130,406	150,313	15.2	162,181	7.9

Ethnographic data. The Azeris are an old sedentary nation which, with
some rare exceptions, has preserved none of its tribal or clan traditions.
However, they are not yet completely "consolidated" as a nation. The
exceptions to the lack of tribal structures are represented by four ethnic
groups, which were nomadic or semi-nomadic before 1917. These
groups have retained a certain memory of their tribal origin, and
members consider themselves as kinsmen: the Airums in western Azer-

baijan; the Padars in eastern Azerbaijan; and the Shah Sevens in southern Azerbaijan, along the Iranian border. There three tribes exist also in Iranian Azerbaijan and in Khorassan, where they are still nomads. The Shah Sevens in particular constitute in Iran a numerous and powerful group.

A fourth tribe, more differentiated from the mass of Azeris, is the Karapapakhs (estimated at 39,000 in 1926), of Turkmen origin. Part of the Karapapakhs are to be found in the area of Kirovabad, and part are in the Adjar ASSR. A certain number of the Karapapakhs are Ali Ilahis, which somewhat hinders their assimilation by the Azeris. Another group, the Talysh (77,000 in 1926), established in southeastern Azerbaijan, has been listed officially as Azeri since the 1939 census. However, they have preserved their ethnic identity and the use of their Iranian dialect and are not assimilated by the Azeris.

Language and the problem of assimilation. The Azeri-Turkic tongue belongs to the southwestern (Oghuz) group of Turkic languages. It is subdivided into four groups of dialects not very different from each other. There is the eastern group (dialects of Kuba, Baku, Shemakha, Mughan and Lenkoran) and the western group (dialects of Kazakh, Genje, Karabakh, of the Airums). There is also the northern group (dialects of Nukha and Zakataly-Kakh) and the southern group (dialects of Nakhichevan, Ordubad, Tabriz and Erevan).

Azeri-Turkic is an old literary language close to the Osmanli-Turkish. It started to develop in the fourteenth century, flourished from the fifteenth to the eighteenth, and was enhanced in the nineteenth century by a brilliant group of modernist writers. On the eve of the Revolution, it was the *lingua franca* of most of the Turkic, Iranian and Ibero-Caucasian Muslims of the Northern Caucasus and Transcaucasia.

During the first years of the Soviet régime (till 1928), the Soviet authorities seemed anxious to promote the linguistic (and therefore political) influence of the Azeris on other Muslim peoples of the northeastern Caucasus, above all in Daghestan. Throughout the first decade of Soviet rule, Daghestan was subjected to a rapid "turkification". This process was welcomed by all Daghestani Communist leaders. Najmuddin Samurskiy, first secretary of the Central Committee of the Communist Party of Daghestan, wrote in 1928: "It is in the interest of the world revolution that teaching in Daghestan should be in Azeri Turkic and not in Russian. . . . Daghestan should thus serve as a bond of union between the USSR and the East."

In 1923 Azeri became the only official school language of Daghestan (replacing Arabic) and kept this position till 1928, when the campaign against pan-Turkism started throughout the Soviet Union. It then lost its monopoly in teaching, and in 1930 it ceased to be the language of inter-ethnic relations in Daghestan, except in the south, where people of the Samurian group were still using it after the Second World War as their second language. The elimination of the Azeri tongue was completed only after 1953, when the Samurian group of peoples (Tsakhurs, Rutuls and Aguls), who till then possessed no written language and were using Azeri and Lezghin as such, replaced them with Russian, which was then awarded a teaching monopoly.

The Azeri rank among the least russified of all Muslim Turkic peoples of the Soviet Union. Between 1959 and 1970 the percentage of those who claimed Azeri as their first language grew from 97.6% to 98.2%; in 1979 it fell slightly to 97.9%. In 1970, 57,513 (1.3%) of the Azeris considered Russian their first language. The following percentages show the Azeris living in different parts of the Soviet Union who used their language as their native tongue (1979 figures): in Azerbaijan 98.7%; in Georgia 98.0%; in Armenia 99.3%; in Daghestan 97.2%; and in Kazakhstan 90.8% (russified 7.9%). In 1970 there were 4,347,087 individuals whose mother-tongue was Azeri, i.e. a slightly higher number than the total of Azeris who declared Azeri to be their mother-tongue. The difference (45,790) consists of various smaller ethnic groups: Daghestanis (6.6% assimilated by the Azeris), Tats, Kurds (22.3% assimilated by the Azeris), and Muslim Georgians living in Azerbaijan.

The Azeri language, literary since the fourteenth century, is the least russified of all Turkic languages. Since 1970 it has been cautiously but steadily purged of Russian words, which have been replaced by Turkic, Arabic, or Persian ones. The Azeris have also introduced certain Latin letters (h, j) in the Cyrillic alphabet, in use since 1939, thus making the Turkish of Turkey more accessible to them. The vitality of the Azeri literary language is illustrated by a rich and diversified literature, by the growing use of Azeri in the curricula of the University and the Academy of Science, and also by the existence of an Azeri press outside the Republic. There are five Azeri newspapers published in Georgia (one at the republican level in Tbilisi, four at the district level, mixed Georgian and Azeri, in Bolnisi, Gardabani, Dmanasi and Marneuli). There are seven newspapers published in Armenia (one republican in Erevan and six district: Amasiya, Vardanis, Kafan, Masis, Krasnosel'sk and Echmiadzin). There is also an Azeri newspaper in Daghestan (district level in Derbent).

Religious data. Azerbaijan was conquered and occupied by the Arabs in the middle of the seventh century and extensively but not completely Islamised. Of the pre-conquest Christian and Jewish population there remain the Udins and the native Jews. The Udins are descendants of the autochthonous Christians belonging to the Church of Arran (Albanian of the Caucasus); formerly Orthodox, they joined in the eighth century the Armeno-Gregorian (Monophysite) Church. The Udins numbered 2,500 in 1926; 3,700 in 1959; 5,492 in 1970. The majority, who live in the district of Kutkashen (Azerbaijan), are Monophysite, and a minority living in the village of Oktomberi (Georgia) are Orthodox of the Georgian Church. The native Jews are Jewish Tats. The Soviet census of 1970 does not distinguish among the different groups of Caucasian Jews (41,288 Jews in Azerbaijan), but in 1959, 8,357 Azerbaijani Jews claimed Tati as their first mother tongue.

With these two exceptions and excluding the Armenians and Georgians of Azerbaijan, the rest of the autochthonous population of the republic are Muslim. In the late fifteenth to sixteenth centuries, Azerbaijan had become the centre of the Safavi power (Ardabil in Iranian Azerbaijan) with its predominant creed, Shiism. There are no precise statistics concerning the religious situation in this region, but according to recent estimates the composition of the population is 70–75% Shi'a, 25–30% Sunni (Hanafi school), with small groups of Ali Illahis and Bahais. It may be estimated that in 1970 the Shi'a totalled 2,700,000 Azeris and about 5,000 Muslim Tats, and the Sunnis over 1,000,000 Azeris, 177,000 Daghestanis, 32,000 Tatars, and 5,000 — the majority — Kurds.

Shi'a Islam is predominant in southwestern Azerbaijan (Nakhichevan ASSR) and in all the districts of southern Azerbaijan along the Iranian border: Zangelan, Jebrail, Fizuli, Ishimli, Astrakhan-Bazar, Saliany, Lerik, Lenkoran, Astara, Yardimli. Shi'as are also in the Apsheron peninsula and the city of Baku, and in Kirovabad, Ujar, Gökchay, Kazakh, Taus, Aydam and Berda'a. Sunni Islam dominates the northern part of the republic, in the districts of Nukha, Zakataly, Kakh, Balakhany, Gusar, Khachmas, Shemakha and Kuba. Both the Shi'as and the Sunnis are present in western and central Azerbaijan, with a marked predominance of the Shi'as.

The Ali Illahis live in the area of Kirovabad, and there are small Bahai colonies (*ca* 1,000 members in 1927) in the cities of Baku (700 in 1927), Kuba, Kirovabad, Saliany and Balakhany.

The Muslims of Transcaucasia are administered by the Muslim

Spiritual Board of Transcaucasia, with its centre in Baku. It is a mixed body (Shi'a and Sunni) with the Shi'a *Sheikh ul-Islam* Mir Kazanfer Akbar oglu as chairman, born in 1904 and elected in 1978 to replace Ali Aga Suleyman Zade, who had been the *Sheikh ul-Islam* since 1969 and died at the age of 92. In 1980 Mir Kazanfar Akbar oglu was replaced by Alla-Shukur Pashaiev, his former Deputy-Chairman. The two deputy chairmen are the Sunni mufti, Haji Ismail Ahmedov, who has first place, and the Shi'a Haji Alla-Shukur Pashayev (till 1980, when he became *Sheikh ul-Islam*). In 1978 the board created a special Department of International Relations (Director, Sabri Hasanov). The authority of the board extends over all Shi'a of the Soviet Union: Azeris, Tats, Talysh, Central Asian Ironis, and some Kurds; and the Sunnis of Transcaucasia, Sunni Azeris, Adjars, Ingilois, Muslim Abkhaz, Kurds and Meskhetian Turks.

Before the Revolution there were 2,000 mosques and 786 Quranic schools in Azerbaijan alone, and in 1928 there still remained 969 Shi'a and 400 Sunni mosques. The number of working mosques now under the board's control is reduced to sixteen: 14 Shi'a and 2 Sunni. We have located the following. In Baku there are two, Taze Pir and Adarbek, and in the neighbourhood of Baku, in the village of Mashtaga, there is a third. In Kirovabad (formerly Ganja) there are two: Shah Abbas and Kazaklar. There are also working mosques in Khachmas, Sabirabad, Saliany, Kuba, Astara, Gökchay, Sheki, Nakhichevan, the village of Mechet-Aga near Sumgait, the village of Buzovna (40 km. from Baku) and Zakataly, and the village of Gök Imam (near Kirovabad). The number of registered clerics can be estimated at 50-70. There are at least two Sunni working mosques in Georgia (Tbilisi and Batumi) and a single Shi'a one in Armenia (Erevan).

Almost all mosques are now mixed, serving both the Sunnis and the Shi'as. Because of the shortage of registered clerics, it may happen that the same mullah performs the Sunni and the Shi'a rites, a unique example of Sunni-Shi'a mutual tolerance. The cemeteries, however, remain separate. There are no Muslim educational institutions in the Caucasus, and Shi'a clerics are trained in the two *medressehs* of Bukhara and Tashkent.

The skeleton structure of official Islam is insufficient for even the rudimentary religious needs of the Muslim population, and Islam in Transcaucasia would have been reduced to the level of a cultural vestige of the past without the activity of parallel Islam. According to recent (1970s) Soviet sources, parallel Islam has under its control about 1,000 clandestine houses of prayer and some 300 major holy places of pilgrimage. The most important are as follows:

— Pir Said *mazar*, village of Marzdaran, district of Mashtaga (Apsheron);
— At Aga *ziarat*, village of Shuvalan, district Azizbekov (Apsheron);
— the imprint of Ali's foot, in the village of Buzovna, district of Mashtaga (Apsheron);
— Imam Zade *ziarat*, village of Nehrau, near Berda'a;
— Asaf Kef *pir*, in the mountain of Asaf Kef (Nakhichevan);
— Nüsnüs *pir*, district of Ordubad (Nakhichevan);
— Aldede *mazar*, village of Agdam, district of Tauz;
— Dedegünesh *pir*, village of Dedegünesh, district of Shemakha;
— Hay Imam *ziarat*, near Kirovabad, the most popular of the holy places of Azerbaijan;
— Mammed Efendi or the "Great Ziarat", district of Nukha;
— Haji Efendi *pir*, village of Aslanbeyli, district of Kazakh;
— Dalag *pir*, village of Muju, district of Ismaily;
— Shahbab *pir*, in the Karabagh;
— the tomb of Haji Murat, companion of Shamil, in the village of Kypchak.

The holy places of Azerbaijan enjoy a greater prestige than those of other Muslim territories, particularly Central Asia, and are attended by larger masses of believers, probably because of the more mystical, popular and picturesque aspects of Shiism. These places of pilgrimage are real centres of religious life, more significant in this respect than the few working mosques.

Parallel Islam is represented in Azerbaijan by two different establishments. In the Shi'a areas it is represented by what the Soviet sources call the living saints — the *Seyids* (descendants of the Prophet) — who still enjoy the prestige which their origin confers on them. In the absence of the regular registered clerics, they perform the necessary religious rites. Parallel Islam is also represented in the Sunni areas, especially the northern districts of Kazakh, Kirovabad, Zakataly, Nukha, Kuba and Shemakha, by the adepts of the Naqshbandiya brotherhood, closely connected with the Naqshbandi groups in Daghestan.

Soviet sources provide abundant information on the religious level of the Azeris. Unfortunately much of it is contradictory, which is due partly to the special climate surrounding religious matters in the Shi'a territories, an extreme example of which is the traditional right of Shi'a adepts to disown their faith and deny their affiliation to it (*takiya, ketman*). Such a course of action, bordering on apostasy, but which is legal as far as Shiism is concerned, helps to create an atmosphere of secrecy and ambiguity.

The Shi'a have been completely cut off since 1928 from their great religious centres in Iraq and Iran. Since Stalin's death contacts have not been re-established, except for some rare visits of Soviet Shi'a leaders to Iran in the late 1940s.

Being a structured, hierarchically organised establishment, Shi'a Islam is more sensitive to external pressure and has suffered more than the highly decentralised Sunni Islam. At present, official Azeri Shi'a clerics seem more submissive to the Soviet regime than are Sunni clerics. There is no Transcaucasian equivalent of the Iranian ayatollahs, no attempt to imitate their dynamism and their claim to national leadership — which would in any case be impossible under local political circumstances. Nevertheless, Shiism, endowed with an intense emotional appeal and built around the cult of sacrifice and the theme of martyrdom accepted by Imam Husain, has a more stirring, more romantic character than Sunnism. Moreover the Shiite principle whereby death in the defence of true faith is the best fate that can befall a believer — inasmuch as it opens wide to him the gates of paradise — constitutes a powerful and unyielding lever of spiritual and, in case of need, political force. All Soviet surveys stress that the "level of religiosity" is higher in the southern districts and around Baku, i.e. in the purely Shi'a regions. Recent Soviet surveys also show that the religious level is higher in the cities, especially Baku, than in the countryside, and in the lowlands than in the highlands.

Official Sunni Islam in Azerbaijan, reduced to a skeleton administration, is completely submissive to the regime. But parallel Sufi Islam remains conservative and vigorous, a result of the influence of Sufi adepts from Daghestan.

In order to resist the pressure exercised by the Soviet regime in the religious domain more effectively, the two rites, Sunni and Shi'a, have elaborated since the Revolution a *modus vivendi* and established a genuine cooperation; as we have seen, they use the same mosques. Although our information in this respect is incomplete, it would seem that there is a current of mutual influence between the two branches of Islam. Thus parallel Shi'a Islam is modelled on the underground structure and the clandestine activity of the Sunni *tariqa*, while the Sunni Sufi brotherhoods have adopted the rule of Shi'a secrecy. The tendency to consider the Ja'farite rite of Shiism ("Twelvers") as the fifth legal school (*mazhab*) of Islam, which existed before the Revolution, has gained considerable ground since the Second World War. In northern Azerbaijan, where Sunni Islam predominates, the opposition between Sunnism and Shiism is sometimes more apparent. Thus mixed marriages are rare. The difference between the two rites is also stressed by the use among the Shi'a population of Shi'a names: Ali, Husain, Hasan, Zeinal (for Zein ul-Abdin), Jafar, Sadik and Reza.

The great religious festivals, especialy the *Ashura* (commemorating on the 10th of the month of Muharrem the death of Imam Husain), remain extremely popular and are attended by large masses of both believers and non-believers. Sacred dramas staging the death of the Imam Husain are sometimes performed. These festivals are deemed to be the expression of a national and not a strictly religious tradition. The confusion between the religious and the national is probably stronger in Shi'a Islam than among the Sunnis: "One who is not circumcised cannot be a Muslim, a non-Muslim cannot be an Azeri." This confusion is reinforced by the presence of an important Christian (Armenian) community, reputed to be the "enemy" of the Muslims.

Anti-religious propaganda of Russian inspiration is intense and is directed mainly at the Shi'a rite. Between 1948 and 1975 96 anti-Islamic books and pamphlets were published in Azeri. In this special contest the Azeris occupy fourth rank — after the Uzbeks, the Daghestanis and the Kazakhs — as targets for Russian atheist propaganda. There are atheist universities in Kirovabad and Nakhichevan, and about 15,000 anti-religious lectures are delivered each year.

National awareness. Within the Soviet Union, the Azeris are a Muslim minority, isolated from their brethren by international frontiers or by interposed strong Christian communities. As a result their national awareness and nationalism are conditioned, more than in any other Soviet Muslim territory, not only by domestic but also by external factors. Sub-national (tribal and clan) awareness survives intensely only among the Iranian-speaking Talysh. Among the Ayrums, the Padars, the Shah-Sevens and the Karapapakhs it is disappearing.

Traditionally the Azeris had different ways of defining themselves. Four definitions existed before 1917 which continue in our time. First is the religious, purely Shi'a identity, implying a solidarity with Iran, which before the Revolution represented the dominant ideology of the deeply religious rural masses and of the conservative urban elements, who expected spiritual guidance from Iran (which never came). At present, because of the isolation of northern Azerbaijan from Iran and because of the differences between Sunni and Shi'a, the strictly Shi'a identity has diminished. It is still too early to assess the possible impact of the Iranian revolution on the Shi'a identity of the Azeris. The feeling of pan-Islamic solidarity with the Islamic world in general, including Sunni Islam, fares better, mainly because of the impact of the fundamentalist revival in the North Caucasus.

Second is the limited national, historical and purely Azeri identity. This feeling of kinship and solidarity with the southern Azeris was little developed before the Revolution; the interest aroused in Russian Azerbaijan by the Tabriz Revolution of 1908-11 was of a social rather than a national character. No serious irredentist claims have been advanced since 1920 by Soviet Azeris, and today their interest in the southern Azeris is more rhetorical than real. From time to time, there is talk in Baku of the "oppressed brothers" of the south, but it is neither an expression of a deep popular feeling (comparable to the claims of Soviet Armenians on eastern Anatolia) nor — for the time being at least — an outline of an official strategy. Up till now the only hint of irredentist claims originates not from northern but from southern (Iranian) Azeris.

The Turkish identity is the third Azeri option. It implies a certain distance from other Soviet Turks but a sense of kinship and solidarity with the Turks of Turkey. This was the position before 1920 of the more radical, progressive, para-revolutionary, non-religious Azeri intelligentsia, opposed to both Iran and Russia, who thought that the solution of the Azeri problem was in political union with Turkey. It seems that this Turkic identity still survives, at least among the Azeri intellectuals. The passionate but platonic interest of the Azeri élite in Turkey, and the somewhat weaker interest in Iranian affairs, reflect this situation.

The fourth possibility is a pan-Turkic identity. Before the Revolution, the liberal-moderate intelligentsia was little interested in religious matters, hostile to Iran, and opposed to the Turkish orientation of the radical-progressives. They joined the great pan-Islamic and pan-Turkic movement, led by the Volga Tatars, and played a major part in the political life of pre-revolutionary Muslims of Russia. The general weakening of religious feeling (and of the differentiation between Sunnis and Shi'a), the isolation of Soviet Azerbaijan both from Iran and Turkey, and the more frequent contacts with other Soviet Turks favour the emergence of this identity.

Azeri nationalism. Azeri nationalism is conditioned by the following factors: demographic vitality, the proximity of the Armenians, the relatively weak influence of Russia, and the foreign influence of Turkey, Iran and Daghestan. Demographic vitality is shown by the fertility rate of the Azeris, one of the highest among the Soviet Muslims (17.5% in 1970). They were third after the Tajiks (20.75%) and the Uzbeks (19.5%). Since 1959 the non-Muslims (Russians and Armenians) have been steadily moving out of the country, and by 1970, for the first time since 1917, they had again become the majority of the city of Baku. This movement gives to Azeri nationalists the feeling that "we" (the Muslims) are stronger than "they" (the aliens) and that "time is working for us".

The Armenian presence is strongly felt by Azeris; traditionally, the Azeri élite have regarded the Armenians as rivals. Before and during the Revolution this anti-Armenianism was the basis of Azeri nationalism, and under the Soviet regime Armenians remain the scapegoats who are responsible for every failure. Russians, whose presence has always been limited except in Baku, occupy only second place in the ranks of the "hated aliens".

Foreign influence is also important. An old cultural centre and an integral part of the Muslim world, Azerbaijan is subject to the same forces urging a return to radical fundamentalism which we observe in other Muslim countries: Iran, Turkey or the North Caucasus. No direct foreign influence is needed to fuel this trend; however, the Azeris have always looked abroad for models. Daghestan used to provide a model of active resistance (holy war); Iran might give an example of struggle against imperialism (in this case, Russian). Turkey is increasingly offering Azeris an attractive alternative both to Soviet life and to the extremism of the Iranian ayatollahs. If Turkey continues to expand economically and to entertain an awareness of its role as leader of the large Turkic world, Soviet Azeris could be among those most dramatically affected. Turkish broadcasts are widely listened to in Baku as elsewhere, and a Turkish "world-view" is being cultivated among many parts of the Azeri intellectual élite.

Azeri nationalism (especially the relationship with the Russians) bears the stamp of Shi'a *takiya*. It is more advanced than in other Muslim territories, but at the same time it is more cautious. There have been relatively few purges and few acute "nationalist" conflicts in Azerbaijan, but there is a steady, cautious, constant and generally successful opposition of the Azeri intellectuals to the official Soviet policy of rapprochement. Resistance to linguistic and cultural assimilation has been especially successful, and Azeri cadres are steadily gaining control of the party and Soviet hierarchies and — what may be even more important — of the Academies of Science and universities. Azerbaijan gives the impression that it has reached a stage which the Central Asian republics will only attain some years hence. It may be that Soviet Azeris will show the other Soviet Muslims how to fight for autonomy without open conflict with Moscow.

Bibliography. The Azeri language is easily accessible to those who know Turkish and Russian, and this very ease, paradoxically, explains why there are so few specialists on Azerbaijan. The Azeri language and literature are not taught in any Western university, and indeed there are few western specialists on Soviet Azerbaijan. Among the best known are Audrey Altstadt-Mirhadi, Azade-Ayse Rorlich and Tadeusz Swieto-chowski. The work by the last-named, *Russian Azerbayjan: The Shaping of National Identity in a Muslim Community* (Cambridge University Press, 1985), is well researched and well written. Soviet sources on the subject are numerous and exceptionally rich. Two Soviet specialists are especially important:

— Nugman Ashirov, the best Soviet specialist of Islam in general, but being an Azeri he places emphasis on Azeribaijan. Especially notable are his major works: *Evoliutsiya Islama v SSSR* (The Evolution of Islam in the USSR), Moscow, 1973; *Islam i Natsii* (Islam and the Nation), Moscow, 1975; *Nravstennye poucheniia sovremennogo Islama* (The Moral Preachings of Contemporary Islam), Moscow, 1971; and *Musul'manskaya propoved'* (Muslim Preaching), Moscow, 1978.

— Magsad Sattarov, an Azeri specialist who published the best work on Islam in Azerbaijan (in Azeri), *Islam dini galyglary* (Islamic Religious Survivals), Baku, 1967.

(ii) MUSLIMS OF THE NORTH CAUCASUS

The territory of the North Caucasus surveyed here extends over the entire Caucasian mountain range from the Black Sea and the Sea of Azov in the west to the Caspian Sea in the east. In the north it is limited by the purely Russian territories of Krasnodar and the Stavropol' *krai*, and in the south by the republics of Georgia and Azerbaijan.

During the Russian Revolution — early in 1918 — a United Mountain Republic comprising almost the whole of the Northern Caucasus, and including some purely Russian territories, was proclaimed by

Muslim nationalist leaders. It was incorporated into Soviet Russia and replaced on 20 January 1920 by the Mountain (Gorskaia) Autonomous Republic. A year later Daghestan was separated from the Mountain Republic. On 1 September 1921 Kabarda was established as a separate autonomous *oblast'* (AO). In 1922 the Mountain Republic was still further dissected with the creation of the Karachai-Cherkess AO (30 November) and the Balkar national district (*okrug*) on 16 January. The Mountain Republic was from this time limited to the Chechen, Ingush and Ossetian territories. In 1924, with the formation of the Ingush AO and the North Ossetian AO (July 7), the Mountain Republic ceased to exist.

At present the Northern Caucasus is divided into the following indigenous administrative units (from west to east). In the west is the Adyghe Autonomous *Oblast'* established on 27 July 1922, under the name of Adyghe-Cherkess AO and renamed in 1936 the Adyghe AO. Its capital is Maikop.

Next is the Karachai-Cherkess Autonomous *Oblast'* (capital, Cherkessk), created on 12 January 1922; it was separated on 26 April 1926 into the Karachai AO and the Cherkess National *Okrug*. On 30 April 1928 the latter was changed into the Cherkess Autonomous Region (*Oblast'*). In 1944 the Karachais were deported and the region was renamed the Cherkess AO. With the return of the Karachais the Karachai-Cherkess AO was reestablished on 9 January 1957.

East of that area is the Kabardino-Balkar Autonomous Republic (ASSR), established on 1 September 1921 under the name of the Kabard AO. It became the Kabardino-Balkar Autonomous *Oblast'* on 16 January 1922 and then the Kabardino-Balkar ASSR on 5 December 1936. With the deportation of the Balkars in 1944, the territory was renamed Kabardinian ASSR and important changes were made in the frontier delimitations. It became once more the Kabardino-Balkar ASSR when the Balkars were rehabilitated and allowed to return to their homeland on 9 January 1957. Its capital is Nal'chik.

Next is the North Ossetian ASSR, established originally as the North Ossetian AO. It was changed to the North Ossetian ASSR on 5 December 1936. Its capital is Ordzhonikidze.

The Chechen-Ingush ASSR was established as the Chechen AO on 30 November 1922. The Ingush AO was created on 7 July 1924, and the two territories were united on 15 January 1934 under the name of Chechen-Ingush AO, which became an ASSR on 5 December 1936. The republic was liquidated on 7 March 1944 with the deportation of the two peoples and reestablished under the same name when they returned on 8 January 1957. Its capital is Groznyi.

Last is the Daghestan ASSR, created on 20 January 1921. Its capital is Makhach-Qala.

The native population of the Northern Caucasus region is not entirely Muslim; the process of Islamisation, which started in the eighth century in Daghestan to the east of the territory, has never been finished, and the Ossetian territory around the pass of Daryal is still mostly Christian. With the exception of the Tats, all the autochthonous North Caucasian Muslims are Sunni — of the Shafe'i school in Daghestan and of the Hanafi school elsewhere. The Azeris and the Tats of Daghestan are Shi'a of the Ja'farite rite. The total Muslim population native to the Northern Caucasus, and established in the Caucasus as well as abroad, amounted in 1979 to about 3,450,000.

The Muslim native population is divided into three linguistic groups: Turkic, Iranian and the autochthonous Ibero-Caucasian. The Turks in 1970 numbered 413,000 and in 1979, 485,000. This population also included Kumyks (189,000 in 1970 and 228,000 in 1979); Karachais (113,000 in 1970 and 131,000 in 1979); Balkars (59,000 in 1970 and 66,000 in 1979); and Nogais (52,000 in 1970 and 60,000 in 1979). There is also a small group of Turkmen, living in the Stavropol' territory, called *Trukhmen* (8,313 in 1970). They are remnants of a Turkmen tribe defeated in the early eighteenth century by Kalmyk invaders and brought to the Northern Caucasus.

The second Muslim linguistic group is Iranian, probably about 150,000 Muslims in 1979. Within the Iranian group are Ossetians, with a total population of 488,000 in 1970 and 542,000 in 1979. However, only the Digor tribe is entirely Muslim; the majority, represented by the Iron and the Tual tribes, are Orthodox Christians. Also within the Iranian linguistic groups are the Tats, of whom there were 17,109 in 1970 and 22,000 in 1979, with 6,440 living in Daghestan and 7,769 in Azerbaijan in 1970. The Tats represent a curious hetero-religious community; some are Muslim, others are Jewish (often listed with the Jews), and fewer are Christian of Armeno-Gregorian faith. They have in common their Iranian tongue, but only the Jewish-Tati dialect is a literary language.

The third linguistic group, the Ibero-Caucasians, numbered 2,339,000 in 1970 and 2,817,000 in 1979. Table 8.ii.1 shows the various ethnic groups within the Ibero-Caucasians.

The percentage of urbanised North Caucasian Muslims remains low.

Table 8.ii.1.   ETHNIC GROUPS SPEAKING AN IBERO-CAUCASIAN
LANGUAGE, 1970–9

Ethnic group	Region	1970	1979
Chechens	Chechen-Ingush ASSR	613,000	756,000
Avars*	Daghestan ASSR	396,000	483,000
Lezghins	Daghestan ASSR	324,000	383,000
Kabardians	Kabardino-Balkar ASSR	280,000	322,000
Darghins†	Daghestan ASSR	231,000	287,000
Ingush	Chechen-Ingush ASSR	158,000	186,000
Adyghes	Adyghe AO	100,000	109,000
Laks	Daghestan ASSR	85,000	100,000
Tabasarans	Daghestan ASSR	55,000	75,000
Cherkess	Karachai-Cherkess AO	40,000	46,000
Abazas	Karachai-Cherkess AO	25,000	29,000
Rutuls	Daghestan ASSR	12,000	15,000
Tsakhurs	Daghestan ASSR	11,000	14,000
Aguls	Daghestan ASSR	9,000	12,000

*Including the Andi and the Dido.
†Including the Archis, the Kaytaks and the Kubachis.

In 1970 the North Caucasian Muslim community was still basically a
rural society of peasants and cattle breeders. There were only a few
industrial workers among the Ossetians, the Ingush, the Chechens
(Groznyi oilfields), the Kumyks and the Lezghins (Baku industrial
centre, Derbent, and Makhach-Qala). As a rule these workers were
engaged, temporarily or permanently, in industrial work in urban
centres situated either outside their national units or in the Turkic
(Kumyk) lowlands. There are no important cities in the mountains.
Table 8.ii.2 shows the percentages of urbanised North Caucasians.

Despite the linguistic differences, the Northern Caucasus area presents a real psychological unit. All the mountaineers (*Gortsy* or *Tawlu*)
have the same way of life, code of honour, folklore, epic songs, dances
and even costume. They also have the same feeling of superiority to other
Muslims (and *a fortiori* the non-Muslims).

The heavily populated North Caucasian mountains cannot provide
for the needs of a fast-growing rural population. Nevertheless, until
1970 at least, there was no important out-migration of the native population. Outside the Northern Caucasus we find large groups of North
Caucasians in two areas: in Transcaucasia (Table 8.ii.3) and Central Asia
(Table 8.ii.4).

Table 8.ii.2.   URBANISED NORTH CAUSASIANS, 1926–70

	% 1926	% 1970
Ossetians (partly Muslim)	7.9	53.3
Kumyks	7.5	40.3
Ingush	3.5	38.7
Lezghins	7.3	30.5
Balkars	1.2	28.4
Kabardians	—	23.9
Darghins	0.8	22.7
Chechens	1.0	21.8
Adyghes	—	21.6
Cherkess	—	21.1
Avars	1.1	18.7
Abazas	0.6	17.6
Karachais	3.2	16.4
Nogais	0.4	16.2
Tabasarans	0.1	16.2
Laks	3.1	12.7
Tsakhurs	1.1	11.7
Aguls	0.0	3.6
Rutuls	0.0	1.4

Table 8.ii.3.   NORTH CAUCASIANS IN TRANSCAUCASIA
(AZERBAIJAN SSR, GEORGIAN SSR, ARMENIAN SSR), 1970

	Population
Ossetians	152,500
	(mainly Christian)
Lezghins	140,900
Avars	30,735
Tsakhurs	6,208
Balkars	1,167
Laks	1,451
Darghins	863
Tabasarans	279
Rutuls	111
Aguls	32
Total (approx.)	334,246

Table 8.ii.4.   NORTH CAUCASIANS IN CENTRAL ASIA, 1970

Chechens	40,454
Ingush	20,225
Ossetians	15,136
Lezghins	10,006
Laks	5,087
Darghins	4,991
Balkars	4,941
Karachais	3,000
Avars	959
Tabasarans	626
Kumyks	554
Nogais	306
Tsakhurs	104
Total (approx.)	106,389

The Ossetians (in the South Ossetian AO of Georgia), Lezghins, Avars and Tsakhurs in Azerbaijan are rural border colonies. The other groups of these nationalities consist mainly of workers who have migrated to the industrial areas in Georgia and Azerbaijan.

Chechen, Ingush, Karachai and Balkar colonies in Central Asia make up the remainder of the 1944 deportees who were left in more or less permanent exile in this area. The other communities form urban colonies, mainly of industrial workers. The average rate of urbanisation among North Caucasians in Central Asia is 50-80%. The 1970 census listed some 10,000 North Caucasian industrial workers living in the Ukraine.

The national profile of the Muslim population of the Northern Caucasus is constantly changing (Table 8.ii.6). Many factors condition the demographic trends: natural fertility, assimilation of smaller or simply less dynamic communities by larger or more energetic ones, the attraction of Azerbaijan, and assimilation by the Russians. The growth of the more important groups between 1926 and 1970 is presented in Table 8.ii.5.

Between 1970 and 1979 the average increase of the North Caucasians (21.4% for the Daghestanis and 23.4% for the Chechens) must be compared with the very small increase of the Slavs (Russians, 6.5%; Ukrainians, 3.9%; Belorussians, 4.25%) and the higher increase of the Central Asians (Uzbeks, 35.5%; Tajiks, 35.7%; Turkmen, 33.0%) and of the Azeris (25.0%). It is significant that the Ossetians — the only North Caucasian community with a Christian majority — have

Table 8.ii.5.   GROWTH OF THE NATIVE POPULATION IN THE NORTH CAUCASUS, 1926–79

	1926	1959	% increase 1926–59	1970	% increase 1959–70	1979	% increase 1970–9
Ibero-Caucasians							
Adyghes	205,195 {	79,631		99,855	25.3	109,000	9.15
Cherkess		30,453	52.8	39,785	30.6	116,000	15.6
Kabardians	—	203,620	—	279,928	37.4	322,000	15.0
Abazas	13,825	19,591	41.7	24,448	29.9	29,000	13.9
Ingush	74,097	105,980	43.0	157,605	48.7	186,000	18.0
Chechens	318,522	418,756	31.4	612,674	46.3	756,000	23.4
Avars	197,392	270,394	37.0	396,297	46.5	483,000	21.5
Darghins	125,764	158,149	25.7	230,932	46.1	287,000	24.3
Laks	40,380	63,529	57.3	85,822	35.1	100,000	16.5
Lezghins	134,529	223,129	65.8	323,829	45.1	383,000	18.3
Tabasarans	31,983	34,700	8.5	51,188	47.5	75,000	46.5
Rutuls	13,000	6,732	48.0	12,071	79.3	15,000	24.3
Tsakhurs	3,000	7,321	121.0	11,103	51.6	14,000	26.1
Aguls	—	6,709	—	8,831	31.6	12,000	35.9
Turks							
Balkars	33,307	42,408	37.3	59,901	41.2	66,000	10.2
Karachais	55,123	81,403	47.6	112,741	38.5	131,000	16.2
Kumyks	94,549	134,967	42.7	188,792	39.9	228,000	20.8
Nogais	36,274	38,583	6.4	51,784	34.2	60,000	15.9
Iranians							
Ossetians	272,272	412,592	51.5	488,039	18.3	542,000	11.0
Tats	29,000	11,000	– 62.0	17,109	55.5	22,000	28.6

Table 8.ii.6.   MUSLIMS AND NON-MUSLIMS IN THE
NORTH CAUCASUS 1970-9

	Population (and %)	
	1970	*1979*
Adyghe AO		
Total	385,644	404,390
Muslim	83,632(22)	86,388(21.4)
Non-Muslim	303,012(78)	318,002(78.6)
Karachai-Cherkess AO		
Total	344,651	367,111
Muslim	164,618(48)	180,752(52.4)
Non-Muslim	180,033(52)	163,899(47.6)
Kabardino-Balkar ASSR		
Total	588,203	666,546
Muslim	320,891(54.5)	363,314(54.5)
Non-Muslim .	267,372(45.5)	303,232(45.5)
North Ossetian ASSR		
Total	582,581	592,002
Ossetians	269,326	299,022(50.5*)
Other Muslims	31,494 (5.7)	33,320 (5.6)
Other non-Muslims	251,761(45.5)	259,660(43.9)
Chechen-Ingush ASSR		
Total	1,064,471	1,155,805
Muslim	650,471(61.1)	768,172(66.5)
Non-Muslim	414,001(38.9)	387,633(33.5)
Daghestan ASSR		
Total	1,428,540	1,628,159
Muslim	1,167,393(81.7)	1,388,230(85.3)
Non-Muslim	264,147(18.3)	239,929(14.7)

*Partly Muslim (100,000–150,000)

the lowest increase rate; also that nationalities deported in 1944 (Chechens, Ingush, Karachais, Balkars, part of the Avars, and the Muslim Ossetians), whose increase between 1926 and 1959 was slower than that of other communities, have recovered spectacularly after 1959 and display very high fertility rates.

To the native Caucasian Muslim population we must add some 75,000 foreign Muslims, mainly Azeris, Volga Tatars and Bashkirs. The Tatars — merchants, teachers and clerics — migrated into this area during the nineteenth century. Tatar colonies exist in all the administrative units of the Northern Caucasus (1970). In the Adyghe AO there were 2,154 Tatars; in the Karachai-Cherkess AO 1,668; in the Daghestan ASSR 5,770; in the Kabardino-Balkar ASSR 2,664; in the North Ossetian ASSR 1,658; and in the Chechen-Ingush ASSR 5,771. The Azeris represent an urban element in Daghestan and have rural colonies in the Samur valley in southern Daghestan. In 1970 they numbered 54,403.

In 1970 the total population of the North Caucasian ASSRs and regions (excluding the purely Russian areas of Krasnodar and Stavropol') numbered some 4,364,000. With the exception of about 286,000 Ossetians, whose religious background is difficult to ascertain, this population was composed of Muslims (2,417,000 or 59.2%) and of various non-Muslims (1,947,000 or 40.8%). The area can be divided into three parts. In the west, after the massive exodus of the Cherkess tribes to Turkey in the 1860s, the Muslim population was reduced to a small minority. In the central Caucasus the Ossetian territory remains a non-Muslim bastion. And in the eastern Caucasus Muslims dominate completely; the relative importance of their community has been steadily growing since 1959 (see Tables 8.ii.6 and 8.ii.7).

A comparison of the increase of the Muslim communities between 1959 and 1979 would be as follows: from 53.4% to 54.5% in the Kabardino-Balkar ASSR; from 43.5% to 66.5% in the Chechen-Ingush ASSR; and from 74.1% to 85.3% in the Daghestan ASSR. In the Chechen-Ingush ASSR and in Daghestan, between 1970 and 1979 the non-Muslim community decreased in absolute numbers. It lost 26,368 members in Chechnia and 24,218 members in Daghestan through out-migration.

The predominance of non-Muslims (Russians and Ukrainians) is especially striking in the cities. Russians represent: 84.2% of the urban population of the Adyghe AO; 73.2%, Karachai-Cherkess AO; 60.1%, Kabardino-Balkar ASSR; 45.2%, North Ossetian ASSR; 60.8%, Chechen-Ingush ASSR; and only 31.6%, Daghestan ASSR (1970 figures).

Linguistic data. Before the Russian Revolution four literary languages (five if we count Russian) were used in the Northern Caucasus: Ottoman Turkish in the west, Volga Tatar, Azeri Turkic and Arabic. In the late nineteenth century, the local Ibero-Caucasian or Iranian languages were either non-literary or semi-literary. When the Northern

Table 8.ii.7.   NON-MUSLIM COMMUNITIES IN THE NORTH
CAUCASUS, 1970–9

| | 1970 | | | |
	Russians	*Ukrainians*	*Belorussians*	*Armenians*
Adyghe AO	276,537	11,214	2,088	5,217
Karachai-Cherkess AO	162,442	4,819	1,015	—
Kabardino-Balkar ASSR	218,595	10,362	—	2,033
North Ossetian ASSR	202,367	9,250	1,406	13,355
Chechen-Ingush ASSR	366,959	12,676	2,312	14,543
Daghestan ASSR	209,570	8,996	—	6,615
Total	1,436,470	57,317	6,821	41,763

	Greeks	*Georgians*	*Jews*	*Germans*	*Koreans*
Adyghe AO	—	—	—	—	—
Karachai-Cherkess AO	1,744	—	—	—	—
Kabardino-Balkar ASSR	—	1,993	5,578	5,262	3,773
North Ossetian ASSR	2,957	10,323	2,044	2,099	2,521
Chechen-Ingush ASSR	—	—	5,045	—	—
Daghestan ASSR	—	2,059	22,149	—	—
Total	4,701	14,375	34,815	7,361	6,294

| | 1979 (incomplete) | | | | |
	Russians	*Ukrainians*	*Armenians*	*Georgians*	*Germans*
Adyghe AO	285,626	12,078	6,359	—	—
Karachai-Cherkess AO	165,451	—	—	—	—
Kabardino-Balkar ASSR	234,137	12,139	—	—	9,905
North Ossetian ASSR	200,692	10,574	12,912	11,347	—
Chechen-Ingush ASSR	336,044	12,021	14,621	—	—
Daghestan ASSR	189,474	—	—	—	—
Total	1,411,424 (*decrease of* 25,046)	?	?	?	?

Caucasus was conquered by the Red Army in 1920, efforts were made to introduce Arabic officially as the main literary language, but the attempt was rapidly abandoned and Arabic was condemned as the language of the clerical class. However, it was still impossible to promote the use of local languages. Until 1928 Azeri Turkic was favoured and then abandoned, but after that year the newly-created local languages were favoured as the official languages of the administration, press and education. At first the majority of North Caucasian literary languages were transliterated in the Arabic script; then they were changed between 1923 and 1928 to the Latin alphabet, and finally in 1938 to the Cyrillic (Table 8.ii.8).

Table 8.ii.8.   LITERARY LANGUAGES IN THE NORTH CAUCASUS

	First established	Original alphabet	Latinised	Cyrillised
Abaza	1932	Latin	—	1938
Kabardino-Cherkess	mid-19th C.[1]	Arabic & Cyrillic	1923–4	1938
Adyghe	1927[2]	Latin	—	1938
Karachai-Balkar	1924	Latin	—	1939
Ossetian				
Iron (Christian)	18th C.[3]	Georgian & Cyrillic	1923	1938
Digor (Muslim)	—	Arabic	1923[4]	—
Chechen	mid-19th C.	Cyrillic & Arabic	1923	1938
Ingush	1923	Latin	—	1938
Avar	mid-19th C.	Arabic	1928	1938
Darghin	19th C.	Arabic	1928	1938
Lak	19th C.	Arabic	1928	1938
Lezghin	1928	Latin	1928	1938
Kumyk	late 19th C.	Arabic	1927	1938
Nogai				
Aq Nogai	1928	Latin	—	1938
Qara Nogai	1928	Latin	—[5]	—
Tat[6]	?	Hebrew	1928	1939
Tabasaran	1936	Latin	—	1939

[1]By the late nineteenth century the Cyrillic was abandoned in favour of Arabic.
[2]Up to that time, all Circassians used the same literary language; in 1927 a separate Adyghe literary language was created.
[3]In the nineteenth century the Cyrillic alphabet was used exclusively.
[4]Digor Ossetian was abolished as a literary language in 1939.
[5]Qara Nogai was abolished as a literary language in 1938.
[6]Only the dialect of the Jewish Tats, the vocabulary of which is strongly influenced by Hebrew, is a literary language. The dialect of the Muslim Tats has not received an alphabet.

After having eliminated the two languages which could have achieved the linguistic unity of the area — Arabic and Azeri Turkic — the Soviet authorities tried to impose Russian as the only common tongue and also as the main vehicle for inter-tribal and international relations. This effort had but limited success, as the 1970 census demonstrated. At present bilingualism (Russian and a native language) or polylingualism (Russian, Azeri and one or two Caucasian languages) is a generalised practice, but loyalty to the native tongue has been preserved. In some cases (Cherkess, Kabardians, Karachais, Avars, Kumyks, Darghins and Lezghins), the percentage of linguistically russified North Caucasians has even decreased between 1959 and 1970 (Tables 8.ii.9 and 8.ii.10).

Table 8.ii.9.   LANGUAGE MAINTENANCE AMONG NORTH CAUCASIANS INSIDE AND OUTSIDE THEIR NATIONAL TERRITORIES, 1959–79

	1959		1970		1979*
	Inside	Outside	Inside	Outside	Inside
Adyghes	99.0	85.9	99.1	84.9	98.7
Cherkess	99.3	53.2	98.7	67.6	98.6
Abazas	96.1	78.3	97.8	41.5	97.7
Kabardians	99.2	78.9	99.1	79.2	98.8
Karachais	99.6	83.1	99.5	89.3	99.3
Balkars	98.9	89.3	98.8	86.8	98.6
Ossetians†	98.1	70.4	98.5	66.9	98.2
Ingush	99.4	96.6	99.3	92.4	98.9
Chechens	99.7	97.7	99.6	94.5	99.7
Avars	99.3	80.6	99.3	81.6	99.2
Kumyks	99.0	89.4	99.3	91.0	99.1
Nogais	86.7	95.3	86.6	95.2	83.4
Laks	98.3	82.2	98.3	80.9	98.3
Darghins	99.2	90.5	99.1	92.5	99.0
Tabasarans	99.5	89.6	99.5	83.4	98.2
Lezghins	98.1	87.5	98.8	88.9	98.3

*Incomplete figures.
†Includes Ossetians of both the North Ossetian ASSR and the South Ossetian AO.

Religious data. Islam penetrated into Daghestan in the seventh century, but its progress was slow. Up to now, the central part (Ossetian territory) remains non-Muslim. Official Islam is represented by the Muslim Spiritual Board of Daghestan and the Northern Caucasus, founded in 1945 and with its seat at Makhach-Qala (before 1974 in Buynaksk, Daghestan ASSR). Its authority covers all the autonomous areas with the exception of the Abkhaz ASSR and South Ossetian AO (ruled by the Baku board) and the territories (*krais*) of Krasnodar and Stavropol'. The chairman of the Board is Mufti Mahmud Gekkiev, elected in September 1978 to replace Mufti Abdul al-Hafiz Omarov (elected 1976), who resigned perhaps in opposition to the policies of the Great Mufti of Central Asia, Zia ud-Din Babakhanov.

Table 8.ii.10.   NORTH CAUCASIANS CLAIMING RUSSIAN AS
THEIR NATIVE LANGUAGE (%)

	1959	1970	1979
Daghestanis	1.6	1.9	2.3
Avars	0.8	1.0	1.3
Darghins	0.9	1.2	1.4
Lezghins	3.0	3.7	4.7
Kumyks	1.4	1.2	1.5
Laks	3.2	3.7	4.1
Tabasarans	0.5	0.1	1.5
Nogais	1.9	1.8	2.4
Rutuls	0.07	0.03	0.6
Aguls	0.4	0.04	1.2
Tsakhurs	0.01	0.08	0.4
Chechens	1.0	1.2	1.3
Ingushes	1.9	2.4	2.5
Ossetians	4.9	5.4	6.6
Kabardians	1.9	1.8	2.0
Balkars	2.2	2.3	2.7
Cherkess	6.7	5.4	5.9
Abazas	1.8	2.5	3.4
Karachais	1.5	1.6	2.0
Adyghes	3.2	3.4	4.2

The new mufti is a Balkar, born in 1935, who graduated from the
medresseh Mir-i Arab in 1965 and was formerly — from 1975 — deputy
chairman of the Muslim Spiritual Board of the Northern Caucasus. The
deputy chairman is Ahmed Dakaev, who also graduated from Mir-i
Arab, as did the chairman of the Department of International Relations,
Abdul-Hasan Elderkhanov. The number of working mosques controlled
by the Spiritual Board of Makhach-Qala is small, probably fewer than 50
(27 in the Daghestan ASSR, 7 in the Chechen-Ingush ASSR, and about
10 in the other territories).

"Unofficial" Islam is represented by two Sufi brotherhoods — the
Naqshbandiya and the Qadiriya. The Naqshbandiya was introduced first
from northern Daghestan and Chechnia in 1783 (Imam Mansur) and,
for the second time, from Shirvan — southern Daghestan — in the
1820s. The Naqshbandi led the resistance of the mountaineers to the
Russian conquest from 1824 to 1856, and the great revolt of Daghestan-
Chechnia in 1920-2. The brotherhood is very much alive, especially in
Daghestan and in eastern Chechnia. The Qadiriya, which was introduced

into Chechnia in the 1850s from Baghdad under the name of the Kunta Haji brotherhood, is divided today into five sub-orders (*wird*): the Kunta Haji proper in Daghestan and Chechnia; the Bammat Giray, mainly in Chechnia; the Batal Haji, a conspiratorial order accused by Soviet sources of practicing terrorism, mainly in the Ingush territory; the Chim Mirza in Chechnia and the Ingush territory; and the Vis Haji, a new order founded in the 1950s during the deportation of the Chechens and Ingush to the Kazakh SSR. This last order is secret, and active in Chechen-Ingush country, northern Daghestan, Muslim Ossetia, and even Kabarda.

Sufism in the Northern Caucasus has always been and still is a revivalist, radical and even revolutionary force. As such, both the Naqshbandiya and the Qadiriya have always been anti-Russian and anti-Communist. The Naqshbandiya is more intellectual and aristocratic, and practises the silent *zikr*. The Qadiriya is more popular and more conspiratorial, and better fitted to underground activity. It practises the loud *zikr* with songs and dances. The recruitment of the Sufi brotherhoods is, as a rule, limited to certain clans. The direction of some of them is hereditary: for example, the Mitaev family (Chechen) for Bammat Giray Haji, the Belhoroev family (Ingush) for Batal Haji, and the Zagiev family (Chechen) for Vis Haji.

From the religious point of view, the Northern Caucasus may be divided into two parts. The eastern part (Daghestan ASSR and the Chechen-Ingush ASSR) is a bastion of Muslim conservatism, the most religious territory of all Soviet Islam. On the other hand, the central and western parts (the North Ossetian ASSR, the Kabardino-Balkar ASSR, the Karachai-Cherkess AO and the Adyghe AO) have few working mosques and had no Sufi activity, at least until the Second World War.

The political attitudes of the North Caucasian Muslims are still somewhat conditioned by their traditional clan structure. Some descend from "democratic" classless societies such as those found among the Chechens, the Ingushes, the majority of the Daghestanis, the Adyghe tribes, the Balkars and the Karachais. The awareness of belonging to a clan (or, less often, to a tribe) is still alive among some of these groups. Others descend from "aristocratic" feudal societies, divided before the Revolution into social classes. These included the Kabardians, some Daghestanis (Kumyks, some of the Avars), Muslim Ossetians (Digors), and some eastern Cherkess. Before the Revolution, the Russian authorities succeeded in coopting some elements of the feudal nobility, and today the former aristocratic societies seem more willing to cooperate with the Soviet authorities than with their democratic cousins. Sufi brotherhoods have less hold on these societies.

In the Northern Caucasus more than in any other Muslim territory, anti-Russian xenophobia has a logical economic basis. In the nineteenth century the mountaineers were deprived of their best lands in the foot-hills and forced into the mountains, where at present a demographic explosion is taking place. The desire to recover their lands and expel the Russian intruders is still one of the elements fanning the general xeno-phobia. This desire is the basis of North Caucasian nationalism, reinforced by the memories of a struggle stretching over almost two centuries against Tsarist and Soviet authorities.

The national awareness in the Northern Caucasus presents a compli-cated picture of intermingled sub-national clan loyalties and supra-national (Islamic or mountaineer) identities. As a rule, the modern Soviet national identities are still very weak. Chechen, Avar or Karachai are geographic or linguistic identities, not national ones.

The existence of an important, active and well organised North Caucasian emigration in Turkey, Syria, Jordan, Egypt and the United States may be a factor in the political development of the North Caucasus Muslim nationalities. This emigration has mainly been composed of the western Cherkess Adyghe tribes (Circassians), the Muslim Abkhaz, and to a less degree the Kabardians, the Muslim Ossetians, the Karachai-Balkars, the Chechens and the Daghestanis. The first emigration was in 1865, and the most recent that of Second World War prisoners who remained in the West. The emigrants use a *lingua franca* (a composite Cherkess language), share the same traditions, eat the same food and have the same folklore. The Caucasian emigration is deeply religious — more so than any other Soviet Muslim émigré group. It is united around a new identity — the mountaineer (*gortsy*) or "Cherkess" — and it endeavours to maintain personal ties with the former homeland in the Northern Caucasus. Many Syrians, Turks or Jordanians visiting the Soviet Union are descendants of the North Caucasians and speak the local languages.

(iii) THE DAGHESTANIS

The Daghestanis are Sunni Muslims of the Shafe'i school. There are some Shi'a (Ja'afarite rite) among the Azeris of southern Daghestan, among the Tats and in one Lezghin village. The Daghestan ASSR was founded on 21 January 1921, and its territory covers 50,300 square km. Its population (1979) was 1,627,000, 13.9% more than in 1970. Its urban population was 639,000 (39%) in 1979, compared to 35.3% in 1970. The rural population was 988,000 (61%) in 1979, compared to 64.7% in 1970. Its capital is Makhach-Qala, with a population (1979) of 250,000.

Demography. Daghestani is a collective denomination covering about two dozen ethnic-linguistic groups of whom only ten were considered nationalities and listed in the 1959, 1970 and 1979 censuses. The others are considered ethnographic groups and were not listed separately in the census operations. Some of the latter have, however, a linguistic, social and cultural specificity and have not yet been assimilated by the more important national groups. Out of the ten Daghestani nationalities, two are Turkic (Kumyks and Nogais) and eight are Ibero-Caucasian (Avars, Darghins, Lezghins, Laks, Tabasarans, Rutuls, Aguls, and Tsakhurs), of which three (the Rutuls, Aguls, and Tsakhurs) have no literary language. In addition to the ten autochthonous Muslim nationalities, there exist foreign Muslim groups, either border colonies (Azeris, Tats, Chechens), or immigrant city-dwellers, Tatars and Ossetians. Table 8.iii.1 shows the composition of the Daghestani populations in 1959, 1970 and 1979.

Table 8.iii.1. DAGHESTANI PEOPLES OF THE SOVIET UNION

	1959	1970	Increase 1959–70	1979	Increase 1970–9	% living in the Daghestan ASSR		
						1959	1970	1979
Avars	270,394	396,297	46.6	483,844	22.0	88.5	88.1	86.7
Lezghins	223,129	323,829	45.1	382,611	18.2	48.7	49.8	49.3
Darghins	158,149	230,932	46.0	287,282	24.2	93.7	89.9	85.9
Kumyks	134,967	188,792	39.9	228,418	20.6	89.5	89.5	88.5
Laks	63,529	85,822	35.1	100,148	16.3	84.1	84.2	83.3
Tabasarans	34,700	55,188	59.0	75,239	36.4	96.7	96.5	95.3
Nogais	38,583	51,784	34.2	59,546	15.4	38.7	42.0	41.9
Rutuls	5,732	12,071	79.3	15,032	25.0	97.5	97.7	95.0
Tsakhurs	7,321	11,103	51.6	13,478	27.3	58.4	38.8	33.8
Aguls	6,709	8,831	31.6	12,078	36.4	95.1	97.9	94.9

The discrepancies in the increases of the different peoples between 1970 and 1979 reflect the complexity of the national-demographic process. Strong increases among the Avars, Darghins and Kumyks correspond to the leading position of these three nationalities, due to their historical and cultural prestige. The even stronger increase of the Samurian group (southern nationalities: Tabasarans, Rutuls, Tsakhurs and Aguls) is due not so much to their higher fertility rate as to the fact that in 1959 and 1970 many members of these nationalities declared that they belonged to another national group (perhaps Azeri or Lezghin). The relatively slow increase of the Lezghins, Laks and Nogais may be

Table 8.iii.2.   DAGHESTANI PEOPLES OUTSIDE
THE DAGHESTAN ASSR

Avars	*46,993 (11.9% of total Avars)*
	20,735 in Azerbaijan (border colony)
	4,337 in Chechen-Ingush ASSR (border colony)
	1,323 in Stavropol' *krai*
	959 in Kazakh SSR
	6,740 in RSFSR
	2,988 in Central Asia and Transcaucasia
Lezghins	*161,108 (49.8% of total Lezghins)*
	137,250 in Azerbaijan (border colony)
	3,650 in Georgian SSR (border colony)
	4,243 in Turkmen SSR (immigrants)
	2,570 in Kazakh SSR (immigrants)
	1,708 in Ukrainian SSR (immigrants)
	1,599 in Kirghiz SSR (immigrants)
	1,585 in Uzbek SSR (immigrants)
	7,773 in RSFSR
Darghins	*23,156 (10.1% of total Darghins)*
	6,752 in Stavropol' *krai*
	4,961 in Kalmyk ASSR
	1,026 in Chechen-Ingush ASSR
	1,599 in Turkmen SSR
	1,419 in Kirghiz SSR
	1,337 in Uzbek SSR
	863 in Azerbaijan SSR
	636 in Kazakh SSR
	634 in Ukrainian SSR
	3,657 in RSFSR
Kumyks	*19,773 (10.5% of total Kumyks)*
	7,218 in Chechen-Ingush ASSR
	6,363 in North Ossetian ASSR
	1,157 in Stavropol' *krai*
	554 in Kazakh SSR
	2,933 in RSFSR
	1,548 in Central Asia and Transcaucasia

Laks   13,497 (15.8% of total Laks)
    1,090 in Chechen-Ingush ASSR
    1,035 in Stavropol' krai
      997 in Kabardino-Balkar ASSR
      509 in North Ossetian ASSR
      388 in Moscow city
      375 in Krasnodar krai
      218 in Rostov oblast'
    1,762 in Uzbek SSR
    1,590 in Turkmen SSR
    1,205 in Azerbaijan SSR
      861 in Tajik SSR
      617 in Kazakh SSR
      257 in Kirghiz SSR
      574 in Ukrainian SSR
      246 in Georgian SSR
    1,773 in RSFSR

Tabasarans   1,935 (3.5% of total Tabasarans)
    279 in Azerbaijan SSR
    225 in Kazakh SSR
    224 in Uzbek SSR
    177 in Turkmen SSR
    794 in RSFSR
    236 elsewhere (perhaps Transcaucasia)

Nogais   30,034 (58% of total Nogais)
   22,402 in Stavropol' krai
    5,534 in Chechen-Ingush ASSR
      380 in Kabardino-Balkar ASSR
      155 in Kazakh SSR
      151 in Uzbek SSR
    1,093 in Karachai-Cherkess Autonomous Oblast'
      320 in Transcaucasia

Rutus   272 (2.3% of total Rutuls)
    111 in Azerbaijan SSR
    105 in RSFSR
     56 in Central Asia

Tsakhurs   6,794 (55% of total Tsakhurs)
    109 in Tatar ASSR
     48 in Bashkir ASSR
     73 in Uzbek SSR
    264 in RSFSR
   6,239 elsewhere in Transcaucasia

Aguls   187 (2.1% of total Aguls)
    32 in Azerbaijan SSR
   115 elsewhere in Transcaucasia

explained, at least in part, by the fact that they had been assimilated respectively by the Azeris (this is the case of the important Lezghin community in northern Azerbaijan), the Kumyks, and the Darghins.

Some Daghestani peoples form important border colonies in Azerbaijan, Georgia and the Chechen-Ingush ASSR (Lezghins, Avars, Tsakhurs). The Nogais, formerly a nomadic group, are equally distributed between the Daghestan ASSR and the Stavropol' *krai*. There is, since the Second World War, a limited migration of the Daghestanis to Central Asia. Table 8.iii.2 shows those Daghestanis outside the Daghestan ASSR.

The Daghestani peoples are basically a rural community, but the percentage of city and rural dwellers varies greatly, depending on the different nationalities. The Daghestani immigrant colonies in Central Asia are mostly industrial workers, with the sole exception of those in Kirghizia.

Table 8.iii.3.   DAGHESTANI POPULATION ABROAD, 1970
(1979 figures not yet available)

	Total population	Urban	%	Rural	%
Total in USSR	1,364,649	359,735	26.3	1,004,914	73.7
In Daghestan	1,060,815	252,338	23.8	808,477	76.2
In Azerbaijan SSR	177,165	54,078	0.5	123,087	69.5
In Stavropol' *krai*	32,981	4,230	12.8	28,751	87.2
In Chechen-Ingush ASSR	19,674	3,741	19.0	15,933	81.0
In Turkmen SSR	8,197	7,457	91.0	740	9.0
In North Ossetian ASSR	7,879	1,715	21.7	6,164	78.3
In Kalmyk ASSR	6,660	470	7.0	6,190	93.0
In Uzbek SSR	5,892	3,862	65.5	2,030	34.5
In Kazakh SSR	5,771	4,670	80.9	1,101	19.1
In Georgian SSR	4,649	1,555	33.4	3,094	66.6
In Kirghiz SSR	3,990	991	25.0	2,999	75.0
In Kabardino-Balkar ASSR	2,196	1,356	61.7	840	38.3

The decrease in 1970 and 1979 in absolute numbers of the Russian community in Daghestan (mainly an urban community — 76.2%) and the slow increase of the Jewish community in 1979 may be explained by various economic reasons, but also by the psychological climate and particularly the undisguised hostility of the Muslims toward them.

Table 8.iii.4. URBAN DWELLERS AMONG DAGHESTANIS, 1970
(1979 figures not available)

	% of urban dwellers (total USSR)
Avars	18.7
Lezghins	30.5
Darghins	22.7
Kumyks	40.3*
Laks	47.8*
Tabasarans	16.2
Nogais	12.6
Rutuls	1.4
Tsakhurs	11.7
Aguls	3.6

*Workers in Caspian ports.

Table 8.iii.5. POPULATION OF THE DAGHESTAN ASSR, 1959–70

	1959 total population (and % of republic pop.)		1970 total population (and % of republic pop.)		% increase 1959–70
Total population	1,062,472		1,428,540		34.4
Daghestanis, including	736,201	(69.3)	1,060,815	(74.2)	44.1
Avars	239,373	(22.5)	349,304	(24.5)	45.9
Darghins	148,194	(13.9)	207,776	(14.5)	40.2
Kumyks	120,859	(11.4)	169,019	(11.8)	39.8
Lezghins	108,615	(10.2)	162,721	(11.4)	49.8
Laks	53,451	(5.0)	72,240	(5.1)	35.1
Tabasarans	33,548	(3.2)	53,253	(3.7)	68.7
Nogais	14,939	(1.4)	21,750	(1.5)	45.6
Rutuls	6,566	(0.6)	11,799	(0.8)	79.7
Aguls	6,378	(0.6)	8,644	(0.6)	35.5
Tsakhurs	4,278	(0.4)	4,309	(0.3)	0.7
Azeris	38,224	(3.6)	54,403	(3.8)	42.3
Chechens	12,798	(1.2)	39,965	(2.8)	212.3
Tats	—		6,440	(0.4)	—
Tatars	—		5,770	(0.4)	—
Ossetians	—		1,633	(0.1)	—
Total Muslims	—		1,169,026	(81.8)	—
Russians	213,754	(20.1)	209,570	(14.7)	– 1.9
Jews	21,427	(2.0)	22,149	(1.6)	3.3
Ukrainians	—		8,996		—
Armenians	—		6,615		—
Georgians	—		2,059		—

Ethnographic data. The Daghestanis are not consolidated into one nation nor are the official ten groups listed in the 1970 and 1979 censuses consolidated as distinct nationalities: each is divided into tribes, clans, free societies and village communities. The importance of these sub-groups is often recognised as greater than that of any over-arching concept of nationality. The clan, tribal and village loyalties — the very awareness of belonging to a clan or to a tribe — are more effective, even today, than the loyalties and awareness of belonging to an Avar or to a Tabasaran nationality. Moreover, some nationalities (Avars, Darghins and Nogais) include several smaller ethnic groups speaking a different language which is generally not understood by other groups. In some cases (that of the Avars, for instance) each valley has its own dialect. There follows a brief description of the various Daghestani ethnic groups.

AVARS. The Avars are the most important Daghestani nationality; for-merly the most warlike (the Avars took part in the Murid movement in the nineteenth century and in the 1920 uprising), they therefore enjoy the greatest prestige among Daghestanis. The Avars live in the follow-ing districts in the western part of the Daghestan ASSR; Khunzakh, Gunib, Kakhib, Gergebil, Gumbetov, Charoda, Tliarata, Botlikh, Tsumada, Tsunta, Akhvakh and Kazbek, i.e. in the highest mountain-ous area of the republic. There are also some Avar groups in the districts of Buinaksk and Levashi, inhabited mainly by the Kumyks and the Darghins, respectively. Outside Daghestan, the Avars can be found in the districts of Zakataly and Belokany of the Azerbaijan SSR. The Avar country, as well as the Darghin and Lak territories, continue to rank today among the least sovietised and least russified areas of the Soviet Union, where the traditional institutions are still strong.

As already mentioned, the Avar nation is not yet consolidated. Four-teen ethnic groups are divided into three main linguistic groups, distrib-uted among the highest valleys of Avaristan; some 50,000 individuals are listed officially as Avars, but each group maintains its specific identity and the use of its language, very different from Avar proper and from each other.

The basic cell of Avar society remains the village community (*sel'skaya obshchina*), corresponding to one, two or, unusually, more *auls* and divided into sub-clan formations (*tukhum* — or ''people of the same house'': 60–70 members descending from the same ancestor). Members of the *tukhum* are economically interdependent. Before 1917 they partici-

Table 8.iii.6.   AVAR ETHNIC GROUPS

Andi Group (7 small groups), total pop. in 1954 (est.): 50,000

Andi proper	1926 (census)	7,953
	1954 (est.)	10,000
Akhvakh	1926 (census)	3,720
	1933 (est.)	4,610
Bagulal	1926 (est.)	3,301
	1950 (est.)	5,000
Botlikh	1926 (census)	3,370
	1933 (est.)	1,864
Godoberi	1926 (census)	2,000
Chamalal	1954 (est.)	6,500
Karata	1954 (est.)	7,000
Tindi	1933 (est.)	4,700

Dido Group (or Tsunta) (4 small groups), total pop. in 1954 (est.): 18,000

Dido proper	1933 (est.)	7,200
Bezheta	1926 (census)	2,500
Khvarshi	1933 (est.)	1,600
Khunzal	1933 (est.)	600
Archis	1926 (census)	854
	1933 (est.)	1,930

pated in endless vendettas among themselves.

The village community, still very much alive and generally corresponding to one or more *kolkhoz*, is administered by traditional bodies:
the village assembly (*jema'at*) and the council of elders. Before the
Revolution, endogamy was strictly observed within the *tukhum*. Marriage within the village community is still considered preferable. The
Sufi *tariqa* have superimposed their own territorial organisations on the
system of village communities and of the *tukhum*, reinforcing both the
communities and the *tariqa* themselves.

The Avar language possesses many dialects, one for each valley. A
written language appeared in the eighteenth century, based on the
composite language of the army (*bolmatz*), in Arabic script. It was
changed to Latin script in 1928 and to Cyrillic in 1938.

LAKS. The Laks are a relatively small nationality but possess greater
cohesion than the other Daghestani groups. They have no ethnographic
subdivisions and are endowed with a common historical tradition (all
Laks were part of the former Kazi Kumukh Khanate). The Lak territory, and more especially the *aul* of Kazi-Kumukh, was the centre of

Islam in Daghestan, and the Laks enjoy among the Daghestanis a unique position of cultural and religious prestige.

The Laks live in middle Daghestan between the Darghin and the Avar territories. They form the majority of the population in the districts of Lak, Kuli and Novo-Lakskoe (this part isolated in the Kumyk area), forming an immigrant colony of 19,446. They also form isolated villages in the districts of Dakhadaev (*aul* Shadni), Kurakh (*aul* Burshi-Maka) and Charoda (*aul* Shadi). The first written work in Lak appeared in 1734 in Arabic script. A Lak journal appeared in Petrograd in 1922 (Arabic script); a Lak newspaper in Arabic script was published in Daghestan in 1923. Latin script was introduced in 1928 and Cyrillic in 1938.

LEZGHINS. Second numerically among the Daghestani nationalities, the Lezghins are without the cultural or political prestige of the Avars or the Laks (they did not participate in the Shamil movement). They dominate southern Daghestan, and theirs is the second spoken language of the peoples of the Samurian group (Tabasaran, Rutul, Tsakhur, Agul and the Shah-Dagh peoples in northern Azerbaijan — the Samur valley and the mountains bordering it). Living in a more open country, more accessible to external (Azeri) influence, the Lezghins have not preserved the traditional structure of their society as well as the other Daghestanis.

In Daghestan, the Lezghins live in the districts of Kurakh, Kasum-kent, Magaramkent, Dokuzpara and Akhty (where they constitute the majority of the population). They also form part of the population of the districts of Rutul and Khiv. In Azerbaijan they live in the districts of Kuba and Kusar.

Before the Revolution, the village community was — as in other areas of Daghestan — the basis of the Lezghin society, but it constituted a weaker social body than its Avar or Lak equivalents. The clan and sub-clan systems have almost entirely disappeared, as well as the large extended families; endogamy is seldom observed. The Lezghins have a higher proportion of industrial workers (in the Baku area) than the other Daghestanis.

No written language existed before 1917. There were some unsuccessful attempts to transcribe Lezghin in Arabic script in the 1920s. Latin script was introduced in 1928 and Cyrillic in 1938.

TABASARANS. The Tabasarans belong to the southern (Samurian) group of Daghestani peoples, and inhabit a territory north of the Samur valley, part mountainous and part lowland (districts of Tabasaran and Khiv). Ethnically the Tabasarans present a strong unity. The clan system is well preserved; customs such as the *tukhum* vendettas and the *kalym* are observed; endogamic taboos have been weakened. The Lezghin cultural and linguistic influence is strong. No literary language existed before 1932. They began using Latin script in 1932 and Cyrillic in 1938.

AGULS. The Aguls are a small group without a written language, belonging to the Samurian (southern) group of Daghestani peoples who live in a high mountainous territory north of the Samur valley. They form the population of 21 villages of the Agul district (centre: Tpig). Isolated from the rest of the world, the Aguls have preserved their traditional structure. The *tukhum* — a large extended family of 20–40 families — is the basis of the Agul society. Endogamy is strictly observed within the *tukhum*. The Aguls are culturally influenced by the Lezghins, and Lezghin is used as the official language of the district.

RUTULS. This is a small group with no written language, belonging to the Samurian (southern) branch of the Daghestani peoples. The Rutuls live in 22 villages — 20 in the Rutul district of Daghestan ASSR (18 in the Samur valley, 2 in the Akhty Chay valley) and 2 in the Azerbaijan SSR (*auls* of Shin and Kainar in the Nukha district). The area populated by them is of relatively easy access. The traditional structure (*tukhum*) is weaker than among their neighbours; endogamy is not strictly observed. The cultural influence of Azerbaijan is rather strong; the Rutuls use Azeri as their official language.

TSAKHURS. The Tsakhurs are a small Samurian group, with no written language, living in the highest part of the Samur valley, an almost completely isolated area of high mountains. They inhabit the district of Rutul (13 villages); small groups also live in the districts of Zakataly, Kakh, and Belokany in Azerbaijan. The traditional structure is well preserved, including village communities, *tukhum*, endogamy and vendetta. The Tsakhurs use Azeri as their official language.

KUMYKS. The Kumyks are the major Turkic nationality of Daghestan, descendants of the Kypchaks (Polovtsy), established in the lowlands of northern and northeastern Daghestan. They represent the majority in seven districts — Khasavyurt, Babayurt, Kizilyurt, Buinaksk, Karabudakhkent, Kaiakent and Kaitak — covering the lowlands of Daghestan, except for Kaiakent and Kaitag which are in the medium-altitude central Daghestan mountain zone. The Kumyks are also found in all important cities of the republic: Makhach-Qala, Buinaksk,

Khasavyurt, Izberbash, and Derbent. Small groups live in the Chechen-Ingush and North Ossetian ASSRs.

The Kumyks remain divided into three groups as they have been in the past. The first is that of the northern Kumyks, located in the districts of Khasavyurt, Babayurt and, in part, Kizilyurt. Then there are the central Kumyks, their most important group, who formed the Shamkhalat of Tarku, which was the most powerful of all Daghestani feudal principalities (in the districts of Buinaksk, Karabudakhkent and Kizilyurt). The third group are the southern (mountain) Kumyks, who before the Russian conquest belonged to the principality of the Utsmi of Kaitag (district of Kaiakent and Kaitak).

The northern Kumyks took part in the Shamil movement while the central Kumyks sided with the Russians; the southern Kumyks remained more or less neutral. Living in an open country, the Kumyks are more accessible to external influences (such as Russian and Azeri). They have a high proportion of city-dwellers, including a relatively important number of industrial workers in the Caspian ports. The traditional structure of their society has almost disappeared. The *tukhums* remain only as a memory, and endogamy is no longer observed. However, the village community remains a living body, and religious influences are still strong. They have possessed a literary language (with Arabic script) since the late nineteenth century, adopting Latin script in 1928 and Cyrillic in 1938.

NOGAIS. The Nogais are the second Turkic nationality of Daghestan, although less than half of them actually live there. The Nogai nationality is divided into two groups: the Qara ("Black") Nogais of Daghestan, former nomadic cattle breeders, and the Aq ("White") Nogais of the Stavropol' *krai*, former sedentary farmers. This division corresponds to the historical distinction between the eastern Greater Nogai Horde (Qara Nogais) and the western Lesser Nogai Horde (Aq Nogais). The Qara and Aq Nogais speak different languages, not merely different dialects.

In Daghestan the bulk of the Nogais live in the Nogai steppe between the Terek and the Kuma rivers (district of Qara-Nogai). Smaller groups live in the Kizlar, Babayurt and Khasavyurt districts. In the Stavropol' *krai*, the Nogais live mainly in the district of Achi Kulak. Lesser groups are to be found in the districts of Kochubey (*aul* Karamurzin) and of Mineral'nye Vody (*aul* Kangly). Nogai villages exist also in the Chechen-Ingush ASSR (seven *auls* and Kargaly, Turomov and Shelkov) and in the Karachai-Cherkess AO (seven *auls* and Erkenyurt, Adil-Khalk, Okon-Khalk, Kizilyurt, Kurban-Khalk and Kizil Togay). The Nogais of the southern Volga area and of Crimea were assimilated by the Tatars by the nineteenth century.

The Nogais are divided into four major tribes — the Bujak, Edisan, Jambulak, and Edishkul — and five lesser ones — the Mansur, Kypchak, Karamurza, Tokhtam and Novruz. The feeling of kinship within these nine tribes is still stronger than the awareness of belonging to a Nogai nation. Since the sixteenth century, various attempts have been made, without great success, to endow the Nogai with a written language (Arabic script). In 1928 two different literary languages (Aq Nogai and Qara Nogai) were introduced with Latin script; they were replaced in 1938 by a single Nogai literary language (based on the Aq Nogai language) with Cyrillic script.

DARGHINS. The Darghins occupy middle Daghestan, which is more easily accessible than the Avar country, in the medium-altitude mountainous area between the Caspian plain and higher Daghestan, which is populated by the Avars and the Laks. Almost as numerous as the Avars but with a less warlike past (they did not join collectively in the Shamil movement or participate in the 1920–1 uprising), the Darghins do not enjoy the Avars' historical prestige.

The Darghin nationality is not completely consolidated. The Darghins proper are divided into several groups possessing distinct dialects. They live in the districts of Sergo-Kala, Dakhadaev (centre in Urkarakh), Levashi and Akusha. Isolated Darghin villages are scattered in the Kumyk district of Buinaksk (villages of Kadar, Karamakh and Jankurbi); in the Avar district of Gunib (village of Megab); and in the Agul district (villages of Amukh and Chirakh). Besides the Darghins proper, we find among them two non-assimilated ethnic groups, speaking *sui generis* languages different from Darghin: the Kaitaks (14,430 in 1926) and the Kubachis or Zirehgarans (2,371 in 1926). The Kaitaks are the majority in the district of Kaitak (centre: village of Majala) where they live alongside the Darghins and the Kumyks, and in the village of Itsari in the district of Levashi (where the majority are Darghin). The Kubachis, a nation of one village, live in the village of Kubachi and ply the trade of silversmith.

As with the Avars, the village community is the basis of Darghin society. It is an active social body covering one or two (seldom more) villages and numbering between 200 and 1,000 members; it is administered by a *jema'at* (assembly) and a council of elders. It is divided into *tukhums* (large extended families of 60–80 members) and *jins* (smaller extended families). Before 1917 members of the *tukhum* practised vendetta and were bound by economic interdependence. Endogamy was observed within the *tukhum*. The sense of kinship and marriage within the village community still survive. Written language (in Arabic script) appeared in the nineteenth century but remained semi-literary; Latin script was introduced in 1928, to be replaced by the Cyrillic in 1938.

Languages and assimilation. Daghestan was called by the Arabs "the mountain of languages". The population speaks some 30 different languages and as many different dialects which are incomprehensible outside each particular group that uses them. Thus the linguistic problem in Daghestan is basically political: no political unity of the area is possible without a minimum linguistic unity. Various attempts have been made in this direction since the early nineteenth century.

In the mid-nineteenth century, during the time of the pre-eminence of the Naqshbandiya in the North Caucasus, classical Arabic was the official written language of Shamil's Imamate and the inter-ethnic spoken *lingua franca* of northern and central Daghestan, and maintained its position till the 1917 Revolution. The first Daghestani newspaper *Jaridat al-Daghestan*, published in St Petersburg in 1908, used Arabic. Today Arabic remains the official language of the Muslim Spiritual Board of the Northern Caucasus (Makhach-Qala) and is still used by intellectuals of the older generation and also by some younger ones. By 1928, however, Arabic had definitely lost its position as a spoken inter-ethic *lingua franca*; it was partly replaced in southern Daghestan by Azeri Turkic, which served until the Second World War as the second spoken language of the Lezghins, the Tabasarans, the Rutuls, the Aguls and the Tsakhurs, and to a certain extent is still used so today. In northern Daghestan the Kumyk language played the same role but on a much smaller scale. Today Russian serves as the language of inter-ethnic communication for the whole territory. Tables 8.iii.7 and 8.iii.8 show the language differences in Daghestan, and enable the following observations to be made:

1. Only the Nogais are losing their linguistic identity and are being assimilated by the Kumyks.

2. The Kumyk influence is comparatively strong in northern and central Daghestan among the Avars and the Darghins but is non-existent in the south.

3. The Azeri influence is strong in the south and among the Avars living near the border of Azerbaijan but not in northern Daghestan.

Table 8.iii.7. LINGUISTIC DATA OF DAGHESTAN ASSR
(*Native languages per 1979 census*)

	Population	Claiming their own language as native	%	Number claiming another language		
				Russian	A Daghestani language	Other languages (mainly Azeri)
Avars	418,634	415,387	99.2	2,390	731*	126
Darghins	246,854	244,352	99.0	1,794	643*	65
Kumyks	202,297	200,572	99.1	1,516	101	108
Lezghins	188,804	185,563	98.3	1,922	190	129
Laks	83,457	82,065	98.3	1,186	144*	62
Tabasarans	71,722	70,398	98.2	531	105	688
Nogais	24,977	20,823	83.4	100	4,030†	24
Rutuls	14,288	14,212	99.5	56	15	5
Aguls	11,459	11,376	99.3	49	33	1
Tsakhurs	4,560	4,543	99.6	14	1	2
Russians	189,474	189,405	99.9		49	20
Azeris	64,514	62,769	97.3	1,340	144	261 (?)

*Mainly Kumyk
†Kumyk

Table 8.iii.8. KNOWLEDGE OF A SECOND LANGUAGE IN
DAGHESTAN ASSR, 1979

	Population	Claiming second languages		
		Russian	Daghestani	Another language (mainly Azeri)
Avars	418,634	265,047	2,704	993
Darghins	246,854	156,447	4,411	499
Kumyks	202,297	146,569	569	366
Lezghins	188,804	121,486	489	2,803
Laks	83,457	61,328	842	459
Tabasarans	71,722	42,013	2,220	3,348
Nogais	24,977	18,482	96	12
Rutuls	14,288	7,344	288	1,499
Aguls	11,459	7,180	837	89
Tsakhurs	4,560	2,028	9	842
Russians	189,474	—	1,516	1,102
Azeris	64,514	46,057	375	94

4. Lezghin is used as the second language by the Tabasarans, the Aguls and the Rutuls.

5. Avar influence is steadily spreading in central Daghestan among the Darghins and the Laks.

6. All Daghestanis practice what may be called "vertical polylingualism": the ethnic groups living in the highest valleys speak the language of the group living below them in the middle and the lower parts of the valley, while the latter group, in turn, speaks the language of the nationality living in the lowlands. Thus the Andi and the Dido groups speak Avar, the Tsakhurs and the Tabasarans speak Lezghin; the Avars speak Kumyk; and the Lezghins speak Azeri. This polylingualism is only partly included in the census data.

The absence of linguistic unity is even more spectacular when we consider the problem of the written languages. Before the 1917 Revolution, among the Ibero-Caucasian languages, only Avar, Lezghin and Lak had written characters (in Arabic script), but they remained semi-literary. Even Kumyk — written since the end of the nineteenth century — did not become a real literary language. Arabic was still used as the written language of northern and central Daghestan, and Azeri Turkic was used in the eastern and southern part of the territory. Arabic was officially banned after 1920 as "clerical" and "reactionary", and a linguistic unification around a Turkic language — Azeri or Kumyk — was attempted by the Daghestani Communist leaders in 1923. This policy of the "turkification" of Daghestan was justified by three arguments: the hatred of the Muslims for the Russian language; that a Turkic language was the only one that might oust Arabic; and the uselessness of giving a written form to the local Ibero-Caucasian languages (see Samurskiy, *Daghestan*, Moscow, 1924, pp. 116–18).

The policy of "turkification" was pursued until 1928, after which it was gradually set aside, and beginning in 1933 the "de-turkification" of the territory began. In 1933, of the 12 newspapers published in Daghestan, 9 were in Turkic (7 in Kumyk, 1 in Azeri, 1 in Nogai), one in Tati, and only two in Ibero-Caucasian languages (one in Darghin and one in Lezghin). Kumyk was then the second language of all Daghestani peoples and the language of inter-tribal relations. It was also in the process of becoming the main written language of Daghestan. In 1933–4, the proportion of Turkic newspapers fell from 75% to 68%: 10 Turkic (8 Kumyk, 1 Azeri, 1 Nogai), against 3 Ibero-Caucasian (1 Avar, 1 Darghin, 1 Lezghin) and 1 Tati. By 1935 the 10 Turkic newspapers constituted only 30% of all those published in Daghestan (7 in Kumyk, 2 in Azeri, 1 in Nogai), against 19 Ibero-Caucasian (7 Avar, 3 Darghin, 1 Lak, 6 Lezghin, 2 Chechen) and 1 Tati. In 1936 only 8 Turkic newspapers were left (out of the 33 published in Daghestan) and in 1938 only 5 (out of 24). In 1956 Kumyk had definitely been deprived of its character as a unifying language: there were at the time 6 Kumyk newspapers, 2 Azeri, 14 Avar, 8 Darghin, 6 Lezghin, 3 Lak, 2 Tabasaran and 1 Tati.

Thus the Arabic and Turkic languages were discarded as possible means to solve the linguistic problem, and Daghestan was condemned, against the desire of the first Muslim Communist leaders, to linguistic division. In 1930, 11 languages were proclaimed as official languages of the republic: Russian, Kumyk, Azeri, Avar, Lak, Darghin, Lezghin, Tabasaran, Chechen, Tati and Nogai. In 1936 a twelfth official language was temporarily added: Akhvakh (a language of the Andi group which again lost its official status in the same year). Chechen ceased to be an official language in Daghestan in 1944 and Nogai in 1938; finally, Tati disappeared in the 1960. Today, besides Russian and Azeri, six indigenous Daghestani languages are official (Avar, Darghin, Lak, Lezghin, Tabasaran and Kumyk) and are used for scholarly purposes. It seems that only four of them are more or less stable and might eventually serve as modest poles of consolidation, namely Avar, Darghin, Lezghin and Kumyk: these languages are used at the University of Makhach-Qala. But Russian remains (together with Azeri) the only *real* literary language of Daghestan.

The distribution of Daghestani newspapers provides an indication of the relative cultural importance of each national group, as shown in Table 8.iii.8.

The present-day linguistic situation may be summarised as follows:

1. There is no linguistic russification of the Daghestani population.

2. All the nationalities, even those deprived of a written language, remain remarkably loyal to their spoken tongues.

3. Bi- or even tri-linguism is not a factor facilitating ethnic assimilation. Nor is the weakness of the Ibero-Caucasian languages a factor that facilitates the assimilation of the natives by the Russians.

4. The "turkification" of Daghestan has been stopped.

5. Judging from the development of their press in 1970, the Avars are in the processs of becoming the dominant nationality of Daghestan.

The linguistic situation of the Daghestani nationalities outside the

Table 8.iii.8.   LANGUAGE OF DAGHESTANI NEWSPAPERS, 1970

Total no. of newspapers: 51

In Russian	2 republic-level (Makhach-Qala)
	3 city-level (Derbent, Izberbash, Kizlar)
	6 district-level (Agul, Buinaksk, Rutul, Tarumovka, Khasavyurt)
	11
In Avar	1 republic-level (Makhach-Qala)
	14 district-level (Karata, Botlikh, Gergebil, Mekhal'ta, Gunib, Dylym, Levashi, Sovetskoe, Tlarata, Untsukul, Khunzakh, Agvali, Bezheta, Tzurib)
	15
In Lezghin	1 republic level (Makhach-Qala)
	5 district-level (Akhty, Kurakh, Khiv, Magaramkent, Kasumkent)
	6
In Darghin	1 republic level (Makhach-Qala)
	5 district-level (Akusha, Urkarakh, Majalis, Levashi, Sergo-Qala)
	6
In Kumyk	1 republic-level (Makhach-Qala)
	4 district-level (Babayurt, Buinaksk, Novokaiakent, Karabudakhkent)
	5
In Lak	3 district-level (Vachi, Kumukh, Novolakskoe)
In Tabasaran	2 district-level (Khuchi, Khiv)
In Azeri	1 Derbent
In Nogai	1 Terekli Mektebe
In Chechen	1 Khasavyurt

Daghestan ASSR is strikingly different. While in their national territory the loyalty to the national tongue is remarkable even in the case of nationalities whose languages have no written form (Aguls, Rutuls, Tsakhurs), the same Daghestanis living outside their national republic are submitting to a steady process of linguistic assimilation. Thus in Azerbaijan the proportion of Lezghins in 1970 claiming Lezghin as their native language was 91.2% (98.2% in Daghestan); of Avars 82.6%

(99.2% in Daghestan); of Tsakhurs 95.1% (99.9% in Daghestan); and of Laks 80.9% (98.3% in Daghestan). In Uzbekistan, the proportion is even smaller: only 76.7% of Lezghins and 87.5% of Laks claimed their national language as their native one.

Religious data. The majority of Daghestanis are Sunni of the Shafe'i school. The Nogais, the immigrant Volga Tatars and the Chechens are Sunni of the Hanafi school. The majority of the Azeris living in and around Derbent and the Tats are Shi'a "Twelvers", as well as the Lezghins of the *aul* Miskinji (district of Dokuzpara). The total number of the Shi'as in 1970 was around 50,000.

Daghestan, together with the Chechen-Ingush ASSR, is the most solid bastion of conservative Islam. Converted by the Arabs already in the eighth to ninth centuries, the Daghestanis' Islamisation was completed and deepened after the end of the eighteenth century by the systematic activity of the Sufi brotherhoods. It was also reinforced by a century-long holy war waged against the Russian invader. In 1925 Najmuddin Samurskiy-Efendiev, first secretary of the Daghestan *obkom* of the RCP(b) (*Daghestan*, Moscow, 1925, pp. 129–30) wrote:

Daghestan has been for centuries the seat of Arabic culture. . . . The sheikhs, *imams* and *ulema* whom we meet in each Daghestani *aul* are well versed in Arabic and have a thorough knowledge of the ancient Arabic culture, science, and philosophy, and of the subtleties of the Muslim religion. Many of them are famous Arabists, celebrated throughout the entire Muslim world. Thousand of disciples from all over the Muslim lands of Russia, Turkey and Iran used to visit them. They were surrounded by the glamorous halo of their deep learning and their words were considered as law. . . .

In 1919, another Communist leader, Ulubiy Buinakski, wrote: "The Daghestanis accept or reject everything according to the prescriptions of (*shari'at*) law."

Before the Revolution there were in Daghestan 2,656 mosques (as well as 22 Orthodox churches and 26 synagogues), some 800 Quranic schools (*medressehs* and *mektebs*), and over 40,000 clerics (called "Arabists" in Daghestan). Official Islam is now represented by the Muslim Spiritual Board of the Northern Caucasus, in Makhach-Qala. In 1977 (when there were in Daghestan 5 Orthodox churches and 3 synagogues), it controlled 27 working mosques with around 50 clerics. We have located the following working mosques: Makhach-Qala, Buinaksk (Kumyk territory), Derbent (mixed Sunni-Shi'a), Levashi (Darghin-Avar territory), Botlikh (Andi territory), Khasavyurt (Kumyk territory),

Khajal Makhi near Levashi (Darghin-Avar territory), Turshunay (district of Babayurt, Kumyk territory), Urkarakh (Darghin territory), Akusha (Darghin territory), and Gubden, Kakashur and Ulubii *aul* in the Leninskii district. It is probable that other working mosques are situated in the Avar territory (Untsukul, Khunzakh, Gunib, Tlarata, Tindi), but in the southern part of Daghestan (the Lezghin, Tabasaran, Rutul, Agul, Tsakhur areas) and in the Lak territory there were none left in 1978. There are no official Quranic schools and no religious publications.

Parallel Islam is represented by the Naqshbandiya and to a less degree by the Qadiriya *tariqa*. The Sufi orders are especially strong in northern and western Daghestan (Avar and Kumyk territories), and indeed Daghestan and the Chechen-Ingush Republic are today the strongest bastion of Sufism in the Soviet Union. The activity of the *tariqa* is centred around the holy places of pilgrimage (*mazars*: tombs of the Sufi ancestors who died fighting the Russians, less often holy springs and caves). In 1970 there were some 100 important holy places and several hundred lesser ones in Daghestan and Chechnia. They are periodically closed by the Soviet authorities, only to be opened again by the believers. The most important holy places still in use are as follows:

— The tomb of Sheikh Abdurrahman of Sogratl, a Naqshbandi sheikh, in the *aul* of Kazanishchi, near Buinaksk in the Kumyk territory;

— The tomb of the Sheikh Mohammed of Belokany (a Naqshbandi sheikh killed by the Bolsheviks in 1922), *aul* of Gergebil in the Avar territory;

— The tomb of Sheikh Suleyman, *aul* of Ukhul, district of Akhty in southern Daghestan (Lezghin territory);

— The tomb of Sheikh Shalbuz in the same district of Akhty;

— The tomb of Sheikh Dirib Haji, *aul* Rucha, district of Charoda (Avar territory);

— The tomb of Sheikh Haji Ramazan, *aul* Shtul, district of Kurakh, Lezghin territory;

— The tomb of the forty martyrs (Kirklar) killed by the Russians in 1877–8;

— The village of Akhul'go (in the Avar territory) where many of Shamil's *murids* were killed by the Russians;

— The tomb of Sheikh Bashir (a Naqshbandi *murshid*) and of his successors, the Sheikh Abdi Arab and Abdul Wahhab Haji Dydimov, in the *aul* Aksoy, district of Khasavyurt in the Kumyk territory;

— The tomb of Vali Kyz (a mythical woman saint) in the *aul* of Agach, district of Karabudakhkent (Kumyk territory).

Other less renowned holy places were recently in use in the *auls* of Utamysh (district of Kaiakent, Kumyk territory); Dzhengutay (Kumyk territory); Irakay (near Tsudakhar); Paraul (district of Buinaksk, Kumyk territory); Nizhnie Kazanishchi (district of Buinaksk, Kumyk territory); Lutkyn (district of Charoda, Avar territory); Nakazukh (district of Gumib, Avar territory); Tlukh (district of Charoda, Avar territory); Levashi (Darghin-Avar territory); Ashilta (Avar territory); and Yarkany (district of Untsukul, Avar territory). The holy places are scattered all over Daghestan, including the southern area where their activity compensates for the lack of official mosques.

According to the most recent Soviet sources (especially the monthly *Sovietskiy Daghestan*), the Sufi orders are responsible for the activity of the underground Quranic schools and countless houses of prayer and therefore for the high level of religious observance in this area. All Soviet sources testify that the Daghestanis (together with the Chechens and the Ingush) are the most religious of all Soviet Muslims; however, the level of religiosity is uneven. The Nogais, formerly nomads, are only superficially Muslim; the southern Daghestanis (especially Lezghins) are less religious than the Avars and the Laks; the Darghins and the Kumyks are in-between.

In Daghestan Islam is closely bound to various social customs, and the confusion between religious and national customs is more complete than in any other Soviet Muslim territory. According to a survey conducted in 1974, out of 1,584 people interviewed, 1,077 (68%) declared themselves to be believers (about 50% were firm or "fanatical" believers); 97 were hesitant (6%); and 410 were non-believers (26%) (A. Makatov, *Islam, veruiushchiy, sovremennost'*, Makhach-Qala, 1974). A survey organised in 1966–7 among the Komsomol revealed that 19.5% of the Young Communists aged 14–30 declared they were believers. Moreover (according to A. Makatov), the level of religiosity has been increasing during the last years as is proved by the attendance of believers at various official and unofficial ceremonies (*zikr*) and the payment of *sadaqa* (voluntary contribution for the mosques and the holy places).

Anti-religious propaganda aimed at parallel Islam is especially violent. Between 1948 and 1975, 140 anti-Islamic books and pamphlets were published in Daghestan in various languages. This region is therefore second in this respect, between Uzbekistan (with 107 titles) and Kazakhstan (with 126 titles).

Nationalism and national awareness. Nationalism is a complex issue among Daghestanis because of the lack of ethnic, cultural and historical unity. There are several main considerations.

First is the existence of a strong sub-national (clan) awareness. In the mountainous areas the *tukhum* (large extended family) and the village community remain the basic cells of native society. Endogamy, obligation to participate in vendettas, and a very strong feeling of kinship are observed within the *tukhum* and the village community. The *tukhums* and the village communities have preserved their traditional institutions (such as *jema'at*, or assembly, council of elders, village community courts). They also serve as the basis for the Sufi brotherhoods. The clan and religious identities are often blended and reinforce each other.

Second is the absence of any historical national awareness: "Daghestan" is a geographical and not a historical concept. The various historical formations which have existed in Daghestan during the period between the Arab and the Russian conquests (principalities of the Shamkhals of Tarku, Khanate of Avaristan, Khanate of Kazi-Kumukh, Utsmi of Kaytag, Ma'sum of Tabasaran, Khanate of Kurin) were too weak to leave behind any cultural or political heritage. Moreover, all three principalities were hetero-ethnic.

The third main point is the absence or weakness of modern national Soviet identity. "Avar", "Lak" or "Agul" are geographical and administrative rather than national or ethnic designations. The absence of linguistic unity, the survival of numerous non-written languages (Andi, Dido, Kaitak) and innumerable dialects, often very different from each other, corresponding to each official and written language slow down the emergence of modern Soviet nationalities.

The fourth factor is the existence of a powerful supra-national identity. It has a double character: the mountaineer and the Muslim. The mountaineer identity unifies all North Caucasian mountaineers around the same way of life, culture and destiny, and a common feeling of immense superiority over "bad Muslims" of the lowlands and, even more, over the *"Kafirs"*. The religious, purely Muslim, identity is the conservative, rigorous, fighting Islam, strengthened by a tradition of holy war stretching over much more than a century (1783–1922). The political and cultural prestige of various Daghestani peoples is based even today on the part which they played in the holy war. In this respect the Avars occupy the first rank (Shamil was an Avar).

The absence of psychological, political or cultural russification (with the exception of the use of Russian as the inter-tribal language of communication) is the fifth factor. As regards xenophobia among the

Soviet Muslims, the Daghestani community stands second only to the Chechen-Ingush who occupy first place.

The sixth point is that since the Second World War a new trend has made a cautious appearance: a slow unification of various Daghestani peoples around the Avars, the most prestigious of all Daghestanis. This unification is still more psychological than formal, yet the growing importance of the Avars is reflected in the figures of the 1979 census.

The seventh and last point is that Daghestani nationalism has a negative rather than a positive, constructive character — its xenophobia has already been referred to. It is an opposition of Muslims versus *Kafirs*, and is based almost exclusively on religion. It seems that nothing remains today of the Daghestani national Communism of the 1920s and early 1930s as represented by its leader Najmuddin Samurskiy-Efendiev (liquidated by Stalin in the 1930s) whose ideology consisted of a curious blend of pan-Islamism and Marxism.

(iv) THE CHECHEN-INGUSH

The Chechens and Ingush are two Muslim nationalities — Sunnis of the Hanafi school — speaking closely related languages, yet each with a different historical background. The Chechen-Ingush Autonomous *Oblast'* (AO) was established on 15 January 1934, on the basis of the Chechen AO created in November 1922 and the Ingush AO established in July 1924. On 5 December 1936 it became an Autonomous Republic (ASSR); this was liquidated on 3 March 1944 and the populations were deported to Soviet Asia. The Muslim populations were allowed to resettle in their homeland after 1968. The Chechen-Ingush territory in 1977 was 19,300 square km. Its population in 1979 was 1,155,805, and in 1970 1,064,471 (an increase of 8.4%). The urban population was 491,000 or 43% in 1979 (41.7% in 1970). The capital is Groznyi, which had a population of 375,000 in 1979.

Demography

Chechens	1926	318,000
	1959	418,756
	1970	612,674 (46.3% more than in 1959)
	1979	755,782 (23.4% more than in 1970)
Ingush	1926	74,000
	1959	105,000
	1970	157,605 (48.7% more than in 1959)
	1979	186,198 (18.0% more than in 1970)

The Chechens and the Ingush have recovered from the genocide attempted against them in 1943–4 and scored the highest fertility rate and also one of the highest increase rates of all North Caucasian Muslims between 1959 and 1970 and between 1970 and 1979. The resettlement of the deported nationalities took place mainly after 1968. In 1959 only 243,974 Chechens (58.3%) out of 418,756 were living in the Chechen-Ingush ASSR. (The 1959 census gives no indication of their location outside the Chechen-Ingush ASSR; probably Central Asia and Siberia.) In 1970, 508,898 (83.1%) Chechens were living in their national republic, and in 1979 this figure was 611,405 (80.9%).

For the Ingush the figures are even more significant. In 1959, 48,273 individuals (45.5%) out of the total of 105,980 were living in the national territory; in 1970, the figure for Ingush living there was 113,675 (72.1%), and in 1979, 134,744 (72.4%) out of a total of 186,198 Ingush.

Outside the Chechen-Ingush ASSR, the Chechens and the Ingush live in the following areas (1970 census figures). In that year, of the Chechens 39,965 were in the Daghestan ASSR, a border population in the district of Khasavyurt; 4,791 were in the Kalmyk ASSR; 1,402 were in the North Ossetian ASSR; 4,403 were in the *krai* of Stavropol'; 2,527 were in the *oblast'* of Rostov; 10,234 were in other areas of the RSFSR; and there were probably 40,545 in Central Asia. Of the Ingush 18,387

Table 8.iv.1.   MUSLIMS AND NON-MUSLIMS IN THE
CHECHEN-INGUSH ASSR, 1979
(incomplete figures)

Muslims	Population (and % of total)		Non-Muslims	Population (and % of total)	
Chechens	611,405	(52.9)	Russians	336,044	(29.1)
Ingush	134,744	(11.7)	Armenians	14,621	(1.3)
Daghestanis, including	22,023	(1.9)	Ukrainians	12,021	(1.0)
Kumyks	8,087				
Nogais	6,093				
Avars	4,970				
Darghins	1,249				
Laks	1,058				
Total population of the republic	1,155,805				
Total Muslim	768,172	(66.5)	*Total*		
"Others" (unknown)	24,947	(2.1)	*non-Muslims*	362,686	(31.4)

were in the North Ossetian ASSR, a border population; 5,318 were in
other areas of the RSFSR; and there were probably 20,225 in Central
Asia.

The Chechens and the Ingush live essentially in rural communities. Of
the Chechens in 1970, 133,628 or 21.8% were urban dwellers, as against
479,046 rural dwellers. Of the Ingush in 1970, 60,931 or 38.6% were
urban, against 96,674 rural. In the Chechen-Ingush ASSR, the Muslims represent 61.1% of the population. Table 8.iv.1 shows the distribution of Muslim and non-Muslim communities, and Tables 8.iv.2 and
8.iv.3 show the ethnic distributions of urban and rural communities.

Table 8.iv.2.   URBAN COMMUNITIES IN THE
CHECHEN-INGUSH ASSR, 1970

Total urban population: 444,062 (45.7% of total)

	Communities	*% of nationality*	*% of total urban population*
Chechens	90,805	17.8	20.4
Ingush	35,612	31.3	8.0
Russians	269,947	73.6	60.8
Daghestanis	3,741	19.0	3.1
Ukrainians	9,735	76.8	2.2
Tatars	4,335	77.8	1.0
Jews	4,855	96.2	1.2
Ossetians	1,446	54.5	0.3
Belorussians	1,700	73.5	0.4
Others	8,219	65.9	1.8

The comparison between the 1959, 1970 and 1979 censuses in Table
8.iv.1 shows that in the Chechen-Ingush Republic the relative importance of the Muslim community has been rapidly increasing. In 1959 the
Chechens represented only 34.3% of the total population of the republic, but this rose to 47.8% in 1970 and 52.9% in 1979; the Ingush for
their part, made up 6.8% of the population, rising to 10.7% in 1970 and
11.7% in 1979. Together with the Daghestanis, the Chechens and the
Ingush formed 43.5% of the population in 1959, rising to 60.3% in
1970 and 66.5% in 1979.

The relative numerical importance of the Russians in the republic
declined dramatically from 49% in 1959 to 34.5% in 1970 and 29.1% in
1979. The actual size of the Russian community was 348,343 in 1959,
366,959 in 1970, and 336,044 in 1979. The increase of the Armenian
community was also slow (78 individuals only between 1970 and 1979)

Table 8.iv.3.   RURAL COMMUNITIES IN THE
CHECHEN-INGUSH ASSR, 1970

Total rural population: 620,409 (58.3% of total)

	Communities	% of nationality	% of total urban population
Chechens	418,093	82.2	67.4
Ingush	78,063	68.7	12.0
Russians	97,012	26.4	15.6
Daghestanis	15,933	8.1	2.5
Armenians	876	6.1	0.2
Ukrainians	2,941	23.2	0.5
Tatars	1,263	22.2	0.2
Jews	190	3.8	0.03
Ossetians	1,206	45.5	0.2
Belorussians	612	26.5	0.1
Others	4,247	34.1	0.7

while the Ukrainian community decreased by 1,689 between 1959 and 1979 through out-migration or assimilation by the Russians. Probably the climate of religious and political hatred which characterises the relations between the Russians and the native Muslims is the main reason for the gradual departure of the Russians and other Europeans from the Chechen-Ingush country.

Ethnographic data. Neither the Chechens nor the Ingush have ever passed through the feudal stage of development. The clan and tribal relations — the basis of their society — are still in full force. The basic cell of Chechen society is the *taip*, a clanic, exogamous, patronymic formation, with members descending from a common ancestor (twelve generations as a rule). A *taip* corresponds generally to two or three (seldom more) villages, with an average of 200 families per village. The most important Chechen *taip* are the Benoy, Tsontaroy, Dyshni, Kurchaley, Aleroy, Belgetoy, Arsenoy, Shatoy and Belkhoy. Other *taip* are of foreign origin: Tarku (Kumyk), Jay (Avar), and Kubchi (Darghin).

Before the Revolution, the Chechen *taip* was based on common economic interests. This bond has since disappeared, but the *taip* nevertheless remain political and psychological realities. Each has its own cemetery, is ruled by an assembly of elders, and has its unofficial clanic court (*taipanan Kkhel*). The *taip* are divided into smaller, sub-clanic formations (*nek'e* or *gar*), comprising a group of 10–50 families bound by certain strict obligations (hospitality and, in the past, participation in vendettas) and ruled by a council of elders. In general, these clanic and sub-clanic formations serve as a basis for Sufi brotherhoods.

In the mountainous areas of southern Chechnia, the *taip* are grouped in tribes (*tukhum*). The most important are the Malkho, Galay, Nakhchimakhoy, Chanto and Chaberloy. Before the Revolution, the Chechen *tukhum* corresponded to a political unit, and each formed a free society. They have lost this status *de jure*, but remain nevertheless a *de facto* and psychological reality. As a rule, each *tukhum* still has its own dialect. Traditional customs, such as polygamy, the payment of *kalym*, and the exogamic (and not endogamic) taboos, are still observed. The "obnoxious survivals" of the *taip* traditions are often denounced by Soviet sources.

Taip organisation is roughly the same among the Ingush, but in their case the *taip* are smaller. Exogamic taboos, as well as other traditional customs (*kalym*, polygamy, levirate) are more strictly observed. Above the *taip*, the Ingush tribes or societies (corresponding to the Chechen *tukhum*) also have a well-preserved psychological existence. The five most important tribes are the Jerakh, Fepin (Kistin), Galgay (the most powerful), Tsori and Metskhal. Each *tukhum* corresponds to an area and has its own dialect. As in the Chechen territory (and maybe even more so), the Ingush clans are used by the Sufi orders as a basis for recruitment.

Language and assimilation. The Chechens and the Ingush speak languages of the same North Caucasian or Ibero-Caucasian group. They understand each other more or less easily, and the numerous dialects are not very different from each other. Neither of the languages had a written form before the October Revolution. Ingush became a written language in 1923, in Latin script, and Chechen in 1925 (based on a lowland dialect). In 1938 both languages were endowed with the Cyrillic script.

Despite the 15–20 years spent in deportation in Siberia or Kazakhstan, where they were deprived of their national schools and press, the Chechens and the Ingush have preserved the use of their native tongue remarkably well. In 1959 and 1970, the proportion of natives claiming respectively Chechen and Ingush as their native language remained more or less stable. Of the Chechens 98.8% claimed Chechen as their native language in 1959, 98.7% in 1970, and 98.6% in 1979. Of the Ingush 97.9% claimed Ingush as their native language in 1959, 97.4% in 1970 and 97.4% in 1979. In 1970 the number of Chechens who declared Russian to be their native language was 7,375 (1.2%); the corresponding number of Ingush was 3,814 (2.4%). In 1979 the corresponding figures were

9,708 (1.3%) Chechens and 4,644 (2.5%) Ingush. In their own national republic the proportion of those who claimed their national language as their native language was even higher. Of the Chechens in 1970, 99.5% (97.8% urban and 99.9% rural) claimed Chechen as their first language; the corresponding figures for the Ingush was 99.3% (98.2% urban and 99.8% rural).

The distribution of the national press does not correspond to the vitality of the native languages. In 1970 there were three republican newspapers in the Chechen-Ingush ASSR published in Groznyi: in Russian with 90,000 copies, in Chechen with 16,000, and in Ingush with 4,300. There were also two city-level newspapers, both in Russian, in Gudermes and Malgobek. There were also eleven district-level newspapers: four in Russian (Groznyi, Nazran, Naurskaia, Ordzhonikidzevs-kaia); six mixed (Russian and Chechen in Akhty-Nartan, Znamenskoe, Nozhay-Yurt, Sovetskoe, Urus-Martan, and Shali); and one in Chechen (Vedeno). There are no district newspapers in Ingush.

There was no linguistic assimilation of the deported Chechens and Ingush by the Russians or by any other nationality during the deportation to Central Asia or Siberia. Nor are the weaker Ingush assimilated linguistically or biologically by the more numerous Chechens. The clan and tribal loyalties remain as strong as ever and form an obstacle to the biological symbiosis of these two closely related groups. Although the Ingush have a relatively high proportion of city dwellers, their fertility rate is among the highest of the entire Caucasus.

Religious data. Together with North Ossetia, the Chechen-Ingush territory was the last area of the Northern Caucasus to receive Islam. Brought by the Kumyks and the Avars, it penetrated into Chechnia from Daghestan in the sixteenth century, but its progress was very slow. Only in the late seventeenth century did all traces of Christianity (in its Gregorian form) and paganism disappear from the Chechen territory. The Ingush area was converted to Islam by the Sufi Qadiri missionaries only in the late nineteenth century. The last non-Muslim *aul*, Algety, in high Ingushetia, was converted in 1862.

According to all Soviet sources, the Chechens and the Ingush are "the most religious" of all Soviet Muslims. This is due to a long histori-cal tradition of holy war: from the insurrection in 1783 led by Imam Mansur, a Naqshbandi sheikh, to the numerous anti-Soviet uprisings (1920–2, 1940–3). Their religious-militant spirit was fostered above all and more recently by the deportation of the Chechens and the Ingush to Soviet Central Asia and Siberia in the 1940s. Islam in its most conservative form, as represented by various Sufi *tariqa*, became the very basis of Chechen-Ingush identity during the exile of these populations in Siberia and Kazakhstan.

After the deportation of the native Muslims in 1943, a unique experiment — the total destruction of Islam through the suppression of its official organisation — was tried in the Chechen-Ingush territory. In 1943 all mosques were closed (there were 806 and 427 *medressehs* in this area in 1917), and they were not reopened when the mountaineers were allowed to return to their homeland in the 1960s. Soviet sources are forced to admit that this radical measure did not achieve any positive result: the Chechens and the Ingush are more religious than ever. As a matter of fact, those who were already members of Sufi *tariqa* had no need of mosques; and this lack of mosques and of an official establishment of sorts could only contribute to the development of clandestine brotherhoods in the territory. They increased the number of their adepts by recruits who might otherwise have remained within the ranks of the moderate and conciliatory official Islam. Thus the restrictive measures taken by the Soviet authorities promoted the missionary work of the *tariqa*.

In 1978, thirty-five years after the mosques were closed, two new ones were opened: in the *auls* of Prigorodnoe, near Groznyi (Chechen area) and Surhohi (Ingush area). In 1979–80 five new "cathedral" mosques were opened in the following villages: Novye Atagi, Dubay-yurt, Achkhay-Martan, Znamenskoe and Urus-Martan. There are probably fewer than thirty official clerics nominated by the Spiritual Board of Makhach-Qala.

Parallel Islam is represented by two *tariqa*, the Naqshbandiya and the Qadiriya. After a first attempt made in the late eighteenth century by Imam Mansur to introduce the Naqshbandi order into the region from Bukhara, it was finally brought there in the middle of the nineteenth century from Daghestan (Avar country) by a *naib* of Shamil: Tasho Haji. A third group of Naqshbandis came to the Chechen territory in the late nineteenth century from the Kumyk area of Daghestan (the so-called Aksay dynasty).

In Soviet literature the Qadiris are called "zikrists". This *tariqa* was introduced into the territory in the late nineteenth century by a Kumyk, Kunta Haji, who died in a Russian prison in 1867, and in the 1870s was sub-divided into sub-*tariqa* (*wird*). The first was Bammat Giray Haji, whose founder was Bammat Giray Mitaev of the *aul* of Avtura, district of Shali. Limited at first to the Chechen *taip* Gunoy, it was later extended to the whole of Chechnia and to northern Daghestan. Its leadership is hereditary in the Mitaev family. The second sub-*tariqa*, founded by Batal Haji Belhoroev of Surhohi, Nazran district, has the name Batal Haji. Limited mainly to the Ingush territory, it is the most puritan and fanatical of all Soviet Sufi orders. The leadership is hereditary in the Belhoroev family. The next *wird* is Chim Mirza (also called "The Drummers"), founded by Chim Mirza of Mairtup, Shali district, in the Chechen territory. A fourth *wird*, Vis Haji (also called "The White Caps"), was founded in the late 1940s in Kazakhstan by Vis Haji Zagiev, a Chechen, and is today the most popular of all Qadiri orders from Kabarda to northern and central Daghestan; it is also the most modernist in its methods and the most conservative in its doctrine.

Sufi orders are closed, semi-secret societies, but their recruitment is very extensive. In 1926 Soviet sources counted some 60,000 adepts among the Chechens and 10,000 among the Ingush. In 1975 the Soviet sociologist Pivovarov estimated that "half of all Muslim believers in the Chechen-Ingush ASSR are members of a *tariqa*," which would raise their number to 150,000–200,000 adepts. Chechen-Ingush Sufism has the following characteristics:

1. A complete symbiosis of the very decentralised Sufi organisation and the clanic structure. Sufi groups of 30–50 members often comprise all the members of an extended family (*gar*). Each group is headed by a sheikh.

2. An absolute confusion between religious, clan and national loyalties.

3. Their underground, clandestine, actively militant anti-Soviet (anti-Russian and anti-Communist) character.

4. An excellent organisation. The orders have their own criminal courts and treasury; they collect the *zakat*. Some of them (Batal Haji) impose heavy fines in the case of transgressions and even pronounce death penalties (for apostasy). Discipline is exceptionally strict.

5. A great modernism in missionary work: women are accepted (even as sheikhs); children participate in the *zikr*; transistor radios and recorders are used. The *tariqa* control a great number of clandestine houses of prayer and Quranic schools, situated as a rule in the vicinity of holy places of pilgrimage.

6. Endogamy within the *tariqa* practiced by the most conservative orders: Batal Haji and Vis Haji.

The activity of the Sufi orders is centred around the holy places of pilgrimage, generally the tombs of Sufi sheikhs. Naqshbandi centres (the most important) include the tombs of these sheikhs: Abdul Aziz Sheptukaev, near Groznyi; Solsa Haji Yandarov (executed in 1929) at Urus-Martan; Baybatyr Haji and his son Ysup Haji Baybatyrov, in the *aul* of Nozhay-Yurt; Ummal Haji (a *naib* of Shamil) near the *aul* Shali (one of the most important); Uzun Haji (one of the leaders of the 1920–2 rebellion), *aul* of Vedeno (the most important); Tasho Haji ("The Great Haji"), *aul* Soyasan near Nozhay-Yurt; and Mohammed Haji Karataev), *aul* Bachi-Yurt, district of Kurchaloy. Qadiri centres include: Mount Khetcha-Korma, near the *aul* of Tsentoroy, district of Nozhay-Yurt; the tomb of the mother of Kunta Haji, *aul* of Guni, district of Vedeno; the tomb of Bammat Giray Mitaev, *aul* of Avtura, district of Shali; and the tomb of Batal Haji Belhoroev, *aul* of Surhohi, district of Nazran.

According to 1970 figures (Pivovarov), the level of religious feeling in the Chechen-Ingush Republic is expressed in the following figures. Believers include 53% of the Chechens, 43% of the Ingush, and 12% of the Russians (averages only). Official atheists include (averages) 21.5% of the Chechens, 30% of the Ingush, and 69.1% of the Russians. Chechen believers are classified as follows: 39.3% by conviction ("fanatics"), 54.7% due to tradition, and 6% for other reasons. A survey taken in 1972 among the members of a Sufi order revealed that 32.2% became adepts following a spiritual call; 36.2% because their relatives belonged to a *tariqa*; and 10.1% lied and pretended that they did not belong to the *tariqa*. The remaining 22.5% refused to answer.

National awareness. Closely related by their language, way of life and religion, the Chechens and the Ingush are separated and even opposed to each other because of their different historical backgrounds. The Ingush did not participate either in the Shamil movement in the nineteenth century or in the great rebellion of 1920–2. The purely Soviet national awareness of belonging to a modern Chechen or Ingush nation is still extremely weak, probably even non-existent. The sub-national clan or tribal (*taipa* and *tukhum*) awareness is strong. However, since the deportation of the 1940s, it is the supra-national awareness of belonging to the Muslim *Umma* which predominates. Nationalism, based on the holy war tradition and on undisguised hatred of the Russians, is extremely xenophobic.

(v) THE CHERKESS TRIBES

Before the Russian conquest of the western and central Caucasus, the area between the Black Sea and Ossetian territory was the domain of the Cherkess tribes, also known as Circassians. This was a large group of some 1,500,000, divided into many tribes and speaking several dialects but belonging to the same historical, religious, social and cultural background. After the Russian conquest, most of the western Cherkess tribes and some eastern Cherkess (Kabardians) emigrated to the Ottoman Empire. There remained in the Caucasus only scattered and disrupted remnants of the former mighty Cherkess nation, and the territory was thickly populated by Russian immigrants.

Soviet statistics distinguish three Cherkess groups. First are the Adyghes, in the extreme western part of the Northern Caucasus, in the lower valleys of the Kuban and Laba rivers, where they form the Adyghe Autonomous *Oblast'*. Second come the Cherkess proper, living along the middle part of the Kuban river valley and its affluents, the Greater and the Lesser Zelenchuk, where they form the Karachai-Cherkess Autonomous *Oblast'*. These so-called "Cherkess" are former Kabardian tribes who migrated to the Kuban flatlands from the Kabarda mountains in the early 1800s. The third group consists of the Kabardians or eastern Cherkess in the central part of the Northern Caucasus, along the valleys of the Malka, Baksan and Terek and their tributaries. This area is divided between the lowlands, the foothills and the higher mountains. It forms the Kabardino-Balkar Autonomous Republic. In fact, all three Cherkess groups belong to the same nation, speaking closely related dialects and using two literary languages. The common self-denomination is Adyghe ("Cherkess" is a Turkish name, and "Kabard" or "Kebertey" is a local geographical designation, while Circassian is the common designation in English).

The Cherkess tribes are split between three national territories. First is the Adyghe Autonomous *Oblast'* (AO), which is part of the Krasnodar *krai*. Founded on 27 July 1922 under the name of Adyghe-Cherkess AO and renamed the Adyghe AO in 1936, its territory in 1977 covered 7,600 square km. Its population in 1979 was 404,000, an increase of 4.7% on 1970. Its urban population in 1979 was 193,000 or 48% (39.6% in 1970). Its capital is Maikop, which in 1979 had a population of 128,000, mainly Russians.

The second national territory is the Karachai-Cherkess AO, part of the Stavropol' *krai*. It was founded on 12 January 1922 and split on

26 April 1926 into the Karachai AO and the Cherkess National *Okrug* (the latter became the Cherkess AO on 30 April 1928). In 1944, with the deportation of the Karachais, it was renamed the Cherkess AO; on 9 January 1957 it was reestablished as the Karachai-Cherkess AO. Its territory in 1977 was 14,100 square km. Its population in 1979 was 367,111, an increase of 7.1% on 1970. Its urban population in 1979 was 169,000 or 43% (32.6% in 1970). Its capital is Cherkessk.

The third national territory is the Karbardino-Balkar ASSR, founded on 1 September 1921 as the Kabard AO. On 16 January 1922 it was renamed Kabardino-Balkar AO and on 5 December 1936 this was changed to Kabardino-Balkar ASSR. In 1944, with the deportation of the Balkars, it was renamed the Kabard ASSR, and on 9 January 1957 it was reestablished as Kabardino-Balkar ASSR. Its population in 1979 was 666,546 (13.3% up on 1970). Urban dwellers in 1979 numbered 393,000 or 58% (47.6% in 1970). Its territory in 1977 was 12,500 square km. Its capital is Nal'chik (1979 population 207,000).

Demography. Between 1959 and 1970 and between 1970 and 1979, the increase of the Cherkess group was relatively modest compared to that of Central Asian and East Caucasian Muslims. In the Adyghe AO, the demographic progress of the natives is too slow to counterbalance the continuous and large immigration of Russians and other non-Muslims.

Table 8.v.1.   ADYGHE, CHERKESS & KABARDIAN POPULATIONS

	1926	1939	1959	1970	1970	% increase 1959–70	% increase 1970–9
Adyghes	79,000	88,000	79,631	99,855	108,711	25.4	9.2
Cherkess			30,785	39,785	46,470	30.6	15.6
Kabardians	140,000	164,100	203,620	279,928	321,719	37.5	15.0
Totals	219,000	252,100	313,704	419,568	476,900	33.7	13.7

In 1970, out of 99,855 Adyghes, 81,478 (81.6%) lived in the Adyghe AO and 18,377 outside of the republic. Of the latter, 13,693 were in neighbouring Russian areas of the Krasnodar *krai* (districts of Uspenskoe and Tuapse).

In 1970, out of 39,785 Cherkess, 31,190 (78.4%) lived in the Karachai-Cherkess AO and 8,595 (21.6%) outside their national territory. Of the latter 1,060 lived in Russian areas of the Stavropol' *krai* and 3,508 in the Krasnodar *krai* (including the Adyghe AO).

In 1970, of the 279,928 Kabardians, 264,675 (94.5%) lived in the

Kabardino-Balkar ASSR leaving only 15,253 outside their national territory. Of the latter 4,867 (1.7%) were in the Stavropol' *krai* (including
the Karachai-Cherkess AO); 2,168 (0.8%) in the North Ossetian ASSR
(Mozdok area); 5,725 (2.0%) in other areas of the RSFSR; and 2,493
(0.9%) in other Soviet republics.

Table 8.v.2.   LOCATION OF THE CHERKESS TRIBES, 1979

	Total (Soviet Union)	In their national national territory (and %)	Outside their national territory (and %)
Adyghes	108,711	86,388 (79.5)	22,323 (20.5)
Cherkess	46,470	34,430 (74.1)	12,040 (25.9)
Kabardians	321,719	303,604 (94.4)	18,115 (5.6)

The three Cherkess nationalities are non-migratory. They form
basically rural communities. The percentage of rural dwellers is even
higher among those established in their national territories: of the
Adyghes 87.3% are rural; of the Cherkess 88.3%; and of the Kabardians
78%. In 1970, of the 99,855 Adyghes, 21,603 (21.6%) were urban; of
the 89,785 Cherkess, 8,379 (10.7%); and of the 279,928 Kabardians,
66,820 (23.9%).

Unlike the eastern Caucasus, which remains a predominantly "native"
and Muslim area, the three Cherkess national territories of the western
and central Caucasus have a large non-Muslim population. Table 8.v.3
shows the composition of Muslim and non-Muslim populations.

The Adyghe AO is the *only* Muslim national territory in the Soviet
Union where the Muslim part of the total population is decreasing; it has
fallen from 23.8% in 1959 to 21.6% in 1970 and 21.4% in 1979, while
that of the Russians and other Europeans progressed from 76.2% to
78.4% in 1970 and 78.6% in 1979. The relatively modest natural
increase of the Adyghes in 1959–70 (23.6%), which fell to 6.0% between 1970 and 1979, is counterbalanced by the heavy immigration of
the Russians (an increase of 37.9% compared to the average 13% of
1959–70). It is probable that in the near future the Adyghe AO will be
completely swamped by Russian settlers.

An opposite example to the Adyghe AO is the Karachai-Cherkess
AO, which is steadily regaining a Muslim majority. The percentage of
Muslims went up from 43.1% in 1959 to 47.7% in 1970 and 49.2% in
1979. This is because of the return of the deported Karachais, the

Table 8.v.3. MUSLIMS AND NON-MUSLIMS IN THE KARACHAI-CHERKESS AO, 1959–79

	1959 population (and % of total)	1970 population (and % of total)	% increase 1959-70	1979 population (and % of total)	% increase 1970-9
Total	277,959	344,651	24.0	367,111	6.5
Muslims					
Karachais	67,839 (24.4)	97,104 (28.2)	43.1	109,196 (29.7)	12.4
Cherkess	24,145 (8.7)	31,190 (9.0)	29.2	34,130 (9.4)	10.4
Abazas	18,159 (6.5)	22,896 (6.6)	26.1	24,245 (6.6)	5.9
Daghestanis	9,331 (3.4)	11,760 (3.4)	23.4	12,381 (3.5)	9.5
Tatars		1,668 (0.5)			
Total Muslims	119,665 (43.1)	164,618 (47.7)	37.6	180,802 (49.2)	9.8
Non-Muslims					
Russians	141,843 (51.0)	162,442 (47.1)	14.5	165,451 (45.0)	1.8
Ukrainians	4,011 (1.4)	4,819 (1.4)	20.1		
Ossetians	3,644 (1.3)	3,724 (1.1)			
Greeks		1,744 (0.5)			
Belorussians		1,015 (0.3)			
Others	8,796 (3.2)	6,289 (1.9)			
Total non-Muslims	158,294 (56.9)	180,033 (52.3)	13.7		

Table 8.v.4.   MUSLIMS AND NON-MUSLIMS IN THE ADYGHE AO, 1959–79

	1959 population (and % of total)	*1970 population (and % of total)*	*% increase 1959–70*	*1979 population (and % of total)*	*% increase 1970–9*
Total	284,690	385,644	35.5	404,590	4.8
Muslims					
Adyghes	65,908 (23.1)	81,478 (21.0)	23.6	86,388 (21.4)	6.0
Tatars	1,886 (0.6)	2,154 (0.5)	14.2	?	?
Total Muslims	67,794 (23.8)	83,632 (21.6)	23.3	86,388 (21.4)	6.0
Non-Muslims					
Russians	200,492 (70.4)	276,537 (71.6)	37.9	285,626 (70.6)	3.3
Ukrainians	7,988 (2.8)	11,214 (3.6)	40.3	12,078 (3.0)	0.7
Armenians	3,013 (1.1)	5,217 (1.3)	73.1	6,359 (1.6)	21.0
Belorussians	?	2,088 (0.5)	?	13,939 (3.4)	—
Others	5,403 (1.9)	6,956 (1.6)	?		
Total non-Muslims	216,896 (76.2)	302,012 (78.4)	39.2	318,002(78.6)	6.3

weakness of Russian immigration, and the higher fertility rate of the native Muslims. In 1970 the Russian community increased by only 14.5% (only slightly above the average of 13%).

In the Kabardino-Balkar ASSR, between the three censuses (1959/70/79) Muslims have slightly improved their position, from 53.4% to 56.0%. This is due to the high fertility rate of all Muslim communities and the repatriation of the deported Balkars, which counterbalances the significant Russian immigration. Table 8.v.5 shows the Muslim and non-Muslim population distribution.

In the Karachai-Cherkess AO, Russians represent the urban element (77.0%, compared to 12.6% Karachais and 11.7% Cherkess in 1970). In the Kabardino-Balkar ASSR and the Adyghe AO the Russian community is almost equally divided between city and rural dwellers: 50.7% and 49.3%, respectively. The rural Russian communities are represented by the old Kuban Cossack settlers, established in the area since the late eighteenth century.

Ethnographic data. In the Kabardian community the tribal system disappeared long ago, and the largest unit of native society is the clan (*lepk*), which was disintegrating before 1917, but still retains certain traditions (such as exogamic taboos at the clan level and vendettas involving the whole clan). Before the Revolution, Kabardian society represented a curious and unique blend of patriarchal-clan elements on the one hand and an extremely complicated and sophisticated feudal structure on the other. This society was then divided into nine classes, from the princes at the top to the slaves at the bottom. The existence of a strong, wealthy and influential aristocracy allowed the Tsarist regime to coopt it into the Russian nobility during the conquest of the Caucasus and to obtain by this measure the obedience and loyalty of the Kabardian nation as a whole. The Kabardian nobility were not destroyed during the Revolution and the first years of the Soviet regime, and the pro-Russian tradition of the Kabardians survived the upheaval.

Before the Revolution the Kabardians were (as they still are) considered by all North Caucasian Muslims as models of gallantry and civility. The customs of *atalykat* (education of children by a related family) and *kunaklik* (hospitality) were strictly observed. The family structure remains today strictly traditional. The payment of *kalym* is still observed. Respect for elders, sobriety and, above all, an overwhelming sense of superiority are some of the factors that protect the Kabardians from any cultural or biological assimilation by the Russians.

Table 8.v.5.   MUSLIMS AND NON-MUSLIMS IN THE KABARDINO-BALKAR ASSR

	1959 population (& % of total)	1970 population (& % of total)	% increase 1959–70	1979 population (& % of total)	% increase 1970–9
Total	420,115	588,209		666,546	13.3
Muslims					
Kabardians	190,284 (45.3)	264,675 (45.0)	39.1	303,604 (45.5)	14.7
Balkars	34,018 (8.1)	51,356 (8.7)	50.6	59,710 (9.0)	16.2
Tatars		2,664 (0.4)		?	
Daghestanis		2,196 (0.4)		?	
Total Muslims	224,372 (53.4)	320,891 (54.5)	43.0	373,000 (54.5)	15.3
Non-Muslims					
Russians	162,586 (38.7)	218,595 (37.2)	34.4	234,137 (35.2)	7.1
Ukrainians	8,400 (2.0)	10,362 (1.7)	23.3	12,139 (1.8)	17.1
Ossetians	6,442 (1.5)	9,167 (1.5)	42.3	9,710 (1.4)	5.9
Jews	3,529 (0.8)	5,578 (0.9)	58.0	?	
Koreans	1,798 (0.4)	3,773 (0.6)	109.8	?	
Germans		5,262 (0.9)		9,905 (1.5)	88.2
Armenians		2,033 (0.4)		?	
Georgians		1,933 (0.3)		?	
Others	12,988 (3.1)	10,609 (1.8)		30,656 (4.6)	
Total non-Muslims	195,743 (46.6)	267,312 (45.5)	36.5	296,547 (44.5)	10.9

Unlike the Kabardians, the Adyghe and the Cherkess groups were traditionally divided into tribes, each one forming a political unit. Each of these units spoke its own dialect and possessed its own strictly delimited territory. This system was disrupted by the great exodus of the Cherkess after the Russian conquest in the 1860s. At present tribes constitute mainly "psychological" units, and tribal dialects, although they still survive, are disappearing.

Of the tribes still in existence, two make up most of the Adyghe population. The first is the Bzhedug, in the district of Teuchez, on the left bank of the lower Kuban, southeast of Krasnodar (Adyghe AO). They speak their own dialect. The second is the Temirgoy, along the upper Laba valley in the eastern part of the Adyghe AO, and in the districts of Shovgen, Krasnogvardeisk and Koshakhabl. They too speak their own dialect. A small tribe is the Shapsug, in five *auls* of the district of Oktiabrskii, along the lower Kuban valley, south of Krasnodar (Afipsin, Natukhay, Panakhes, Khastuk, Pseytuk: Adyghe AO) and in the Tuapse and Lazarevski districts of the Krasnodar *krai* (outside the Adyghe AO). They speak their own dialects. Another tribe is the Abadzekh, in onè *aul*, Shovgenovskiy, in the valley of the river Fars, south of the Kuban (Adyghe AO), which also speaks its own dialect. There is also the Besleney, the most important Cherkess tribe, in the Karachai-Cherkess AO and also in two *auls* of the Adyghe AO (Blechepsin and Uliap) and in two *auls* of the district of Uspenskoe of the Krasnodar *krai*. This tribe speaks a special dialect of Kabardian.

Language and assimilation. The Adyghes, Cherkess and Kabardians speak closely related dialects and use two literary languages. The Adyghe language is divided into four dialects: Shapsug, Bzhedug, Abadzekh and Temirgoy, the last of which serves as the basis of the Adyghe literary language. The Kabardian-Cherkess language is divided into three dialects: Baksan (basis of the literary Kabardian-Cherkess language), Besleney spoken by the Cherkess and in the Kuban, and three subdialects: Malka, Lesser Kabardian and Mozdok. Loyalty to the national spoken language in all three Cherkess territories is exceptionally high, despite intense Russian pressure.

Before the Revolution the three Cherkess groups had no national literary language and for this purpose used Ottoman Turkish and Arabic. There were some unsuccessful attempts to transcribe Adyghe and Kabardian into Arabic script in the 1800s and again in 1905. The Kabardo-Cherkess literary language was created only in 1924 and endowed immediately with Latin script, which was replaced in 1936 by Cyrillic. The Adyghe language was endowed with Arabic script in 1918, and the first Adyghe newspaper appeared in 1923. The Arabic script was replaced by the Latin in 1926 and Cyrillic in 1936.

However, the literary languages are little used. In the Kabardino-Balkar ASSR, out of 12 newspapers, only one (published in Nal'chik at the republican level) is in Kabardian. The local Kabardian newspapers, previously published in the districts of Baksan and Urban, disappeared in 1959. In the Karachai-Cherkess AO, out of 5 newspapers, only one is in Kabardian (with 3,900 copies in 1970); the other 4 are in Karachai-Balkar (10,000 copies), in Nogai (2,000 copies), in Abaza (2,800 copies), and in Russian (35,000 copies). In the Adyghe AO, out of the eight newspapers, only one — published in Maikop — is in Adyghe (4,000 copies).

Table 8.v.6.   KABARDIANS, ADYGHES AND CHERKESS DECLARING THEIR NATIONAL LANGUAGE AS NATIVE TONGUE

	% in Soviet Union, 1959	% in Soviet Union, 1970	% increase 1959–70	1970 % native language spoken in national territory
Kabardians	97.9	98.0	+ 0.1	99.1
Adyghes	96.8	96.5	− 0.3	99.1
Cherkess	92.0	89.7	− 2.3	98.8

		% in Soviet Union, 1979	% increase 1970–79	1979 % native language spoken in national territory
Kabardians		97.9	− 0.1	99.1
Adyghes		95.7	− 0.8	98.7
Cherkess		91.4	+ 1.7	98.6

The level of linguistic russification in urban and rural areas among the three Cherkess groups is unequal. The percentages of those russified in 1970 were as follows:

	In the Soviet Union as a whole		Within national territory	
	Urban	Rural	Urban	Rural
Kabardians	6.1%	0.5%	3.0%	0.2%
Cherkess	21.7	1.0	4.2	0.2
Adyghes	13.1	0.8	5.0	0.3

Religious data. All three Cherkess groups are Sunni Muslims of the Hanafi school. There is a small group of Christian Kabardians in the city of Mozdok and in neighbouring villages (North Ossetian ASSR). These are descendants of the serfs who escaped from Kabarda in the eighteenth and nineteenth centuries, took refuge behind the Terek Cossack line and were converted to Christianity.

Islam was brought to Kabarda in the fifteenth and sixteenth centuries by the Crimean Tatars and the Ottoman Turks, but Christianity and paganism survived until the seventeenth century. Before the Revolution, the Sufi brotherhoods never really took root in Kabarda (partly because of the successful opposition of the Kabardian nobility). The Kabardians did not join the Shamil holy war or the Chechen-Daghestani uprising of 1920–2. Islam remained more superficial in Kabarda than in nearby Chechnia. In 1926 there were only 200 adepts of the Sufi *tariqa* in the three Cherkess territories, compared to 60,000 among the Chechens and 10,000 among the Ingush.

Islam was brought to the Adyghe territory by the Ottoman Turks and by the Crimean Tatars even later in the sixteenth and seventeenth centuries, and all traces of Christianity and paganism disappeared only during the early 1800s. Contrary to what happened in Kabarda, Sufism in the form of the Naqshbandiya brotherhood was introduced — without much success — among the western Cherkess tribes in the early 1800s, and the Adyghes took an active part in the holy war against the Russians. Sufism disappeared, however, after the great exodus of the Adyghe tribes in 1865.

The number of working mosques in the three Cherkess territories is not known, but probably does not exceed ten. We located in 1980 the following working "cathedral" mosques: 2 in the Kabardino-Balkar ASSR, Nal'chik and Kyzburun, and 4 in the Karachai-Cherkess AO: Mirny, Uchekent, Khalsan and Kumysh. The number of registered clerics is certainly insignificant. There is little information concerning the religious life in these areas, but it would seem that there is a new slow expansion of the Sufi *tariqa* (especially of the Qadiriya in its Vis Haji form) from the Chechen-Ingush ASSR westward. Anti-religious propaganda is relatively strong. Between 1948 and 1975, 13 anti-Islamic works were published in Kabardian and 12 in Adyghe.

Nationalism and national awareness. The Kabardians, isolated throughout their history from other North Caucasian Muslims, did not participate in the wars of the eighteenth to the twentieth centuries against the

Russians (Imam Mansur, Shamil and the 1920–2 uprising). They were considered before 1917 the most pro-Russian of all North Caucasian Muslims; the Kabardian nobility was loyal as a rule to the Russian regime and less xenophobic than any other mountaineer nationality. The Kabardians did not participate in the 1943 revolt and were not deported (like the Chechens, Ingush, Karachais and Balkars).

The national awareness of the Kabardians corrresponds more or less to the definition of the modern Kabardian nation. Their religiosity is not strong enough to give them a supra-national pan-Islamic awareness, and their sub-national tribal loyalties have almost disappeared. On the other hand, because of their great sense of superiority, the Kabardians have always remained aloof from all other nationalities — including the Russians — and mixed marriages with Russians are rare.

Among the Adyghes and the Cherkess, tribal loyalties and the awareness of belonging to a tribe (Besleney or Temirgoy) are still stronger than the feeling of being part of an Adyghe or a Cherkess nation. As in Kabarda, pan-Islamic, supra-national awareness is weak. Anti-Russian feeling is stronger among the Cherkess and the Adyghes than among the Kabardians.

The same feeling exists within the numerous and influential Cherkess colonies abroad — in Turkey, Syria, Jordan, Israel and Lebanon (probably more than a million strong today). Contacts are maintained between the Cherkess of the Soviet Union and those colonies where the Adyghe language is still spoken and even written (in Arabic script). All three Cherkess groups have maintained a strong feeling of kinship between themselves and continue to call themselves "Adyghe".

(vi) THE ABAZAS

The Abazas (in Russian *Abaziny*) are Sunni Muslims of the Hanafi rite. There are no non-Muslims among them. This is a small national group speaking a language close to Abkhazian but living among the Cherkess tribes. In 1926 the Abazas numbered 13,825; in 1959, 19,591; in 1970, 25,448 (an increase of 29.9% since 1959) and in 1979, 29,000 (an increase of 14% since 1970).

In 1970, out of the 25,448 Abazas, 22,896 (or 90%) lived in the Karachai-Cherkess Autonomous *Oblast'*, where they formed 16 villages in the upper valleys of the rivers Kuban, Juma, and the Greater and Lesser Zelenchuk. The rest of the Abazas lived in 2 villages of the Stavropol' *krai*, near Kislovodsk. In 1979, out of the 29,497 Abazas, 24,245 (82.2%) lived in the Karachai-Cherkess Autonomous *Oblast'*. The Abazas are mainly a rural community; in 1959, 89.4% of them lived in the country and in 1970, 82.4%.

The Abazas are divided into two tribal federations: the southern or Shkarawa and the northern or Tapanta. During the century-long Caucasian wars, they were divided between the rival camps: the Tapanta sided with the Russians while the Shkarawa resisted the Russian invasion. After the final defeat of the mountaineers, the greater part of the Shkarawa tribes migrated to the Ottoman Empire. Today tribal awareness is disappearing, and the Abaza consider themselves part of the Adyghe-Cherkess-Kabardian nation.

The Abazas speak two different dialects: the southern (or Ashkara) and the northern (or Tapanta). The northern dialect is the basis of the literary Abaza language created in 1932 in Latin script, replaced in 1938 by Cyrillic. A newspaper in Abaza is published in Cherkessk (Karachai-Cherkess AO), with 2,800 copies in 1970. Loyalty to the native language is exceptionally high for a small group. In 1959, 94.8% of the Abazas claimed Abaza as their native language (only 86.2% among the town-dwellers). In 1970 the percentage of those claiming Abaza as their native language rose to 96.1% (86.3% among the town-dwellers). In 1979 it fell to 95.3% (97.7% in their national territory).

Islam was brought to the Abazas by the Nogais in the sixteenth century, but only in the eighteenth century did the Tapanta tribes become fully Islamised. The Shkarawa tribes adopted Islam only in the middle of the nineteenth century, a result of the missionary efforts of Shamil's *naib*, Mehmet Emin.

(vii) THE KARACHAI-BALKARS

The Karachais and the Balkars are split between two national territories: the Karachai-Cherkess Autonomous *Oblast'* and the Kabardino-Balkar ASSR, described previously in the section devoted to the Cherkess tribes. They are two Turkic groups belonging to the same nation; although living geographically isolated from each other in the high valleys of the central part of the Northern Caucasus, they speak the same Turkic language (of the Kypchak branch), divided into several dialects, and use the same literary language. They are descendants of the Kuban Bulgars and of the Kypchak (Polovtsy) tribes, pushed up the mountains by the Mongols in the thirteenth century, and vassals from the fifteenth century of the Kabardian and Adyghe nobility.

Demography. The Karachais occupy the upper and middle valleys of the Kuban and its tributaries Taberda, Zelenchuk and Aksut in the districts of Karachaevsk, Malo-Karachaevsk, Zelenchukskaya, Ust-Dzhegutinskaya, Elbruskaya and Predgradnenskaya of the Karachai-Cherkess AO. In 1959 they numbered 81,403; in 1970, 112,741 (38.5% up on 1959) and in 1979, 131,074 (15.9% up on 1970). The majority of the Karachais live in their national territory, the Karachai-Cherkess AO: 97,104 (83.5%) in 1970. In 1979, of the 131,074 Karachais of the Soviet Union, 109,196 (83.3%) lived in the Karachai-Cherkess AO. In the purely Russian areas of the Stavropol' *krai* in 1970, there were 6,125 Karachais (5.4%) while 3,602 others lived in various territories of the RSFSR (outside the Stavropol' *krai*) and 5,910 in other republics, mainly Kazakhstan and Kirghizia (these were former deportees who remained in Central Asia).

The Balkars inhabit the highest areas of the central Caucasus, the upper valleys of the rivers Baksan, Chegem and Cherek, corresponding to the districts of Elbrus, Chegem and Zol of the Kabardino-Balkar ASSR. In 1959 they numbered 42,408; in 1970, 59,501 (40.3% up on 1959); and in 1979, 66,000 (10% up on 1970). The majority of the Balkars live in their national territory, the Kabardino-Balkar ASSR. In 1979, out of the 66,334 Balkars of the Soviet Union, 59,710 (90.0%) lived in the Kabardino-Balkar ASSR. Table 8.vii.1 shows the population distribution of the Balkars in 1970. Both Karachais and Balkars are basically rural communities: of the Karachais 89.1% were rural dwellers in 1959 and 83.6% in 1970; of the Balkars 80.7% were rural dwellers in 1959 and 71.7% in 1970.

Table 8.vii.1.   BALKAR POPULATION DISTRIBUTION, 1970

Kabardino-Balkar ASSR	51,356 (86.3%)
Kazakhstan	2,714 (4.6)
Kirghizia	1,973 (3.3)
Armenia	983 (1.7)
Uzbekistan	254 (0.4)
Azerbaijan	184 (0.3)
Stavropol' *krai*	505 (0.8)
Other areas of the RSFSR	1,532

The Karachais and Balkars have the same social structure based on a strong clan system. The *tukhum* (clan) remains a psychological reality. It has its own cemetery (in the past it had its own mosque) and observes various traditional customs: the practice of vendettas involving the whole *tukhum*; exogamy within the *tukhum*; marriage by abduction, *atalykat* and levirate; extreme respect for the elders (*aksakalyk*) and sexual segregation. These customs protect the native society from any attempt at biological assimilation by the Russians.

Religious data. Islam was brought rather late to the Karachais and the Balkars by the Kabardians in the middle of the eighteenth century, but it put down deep roots. The Karachais and Balkars are considered more religious than the Cherkess tribes surrounding them, especially since their deportation. However, it seems that there are only a few working mosques left in their territories. It seems also that the relatively high level of religious practice among the Caucasian Turks has been maintained by the Qadiriya brotherhood originating from the Chechen area.

The Central Caucasian Turks did not take an active part in the Caucasian wars, nor in the 1920–2 Daghestani-Chechen uprising, and there is no indication of serious troubles in their area during the Second World War. Their deportation in 1943, together with the Chechens, the Ingush and some Muslim Ossetians, may be explained by the Russians' general anti-Muslim xenophobia rather than by any active resistance on their part.

Linguistic data. The Karachai-Balkar language is divided into several dialects, practically one dialect to each valley. The Baksan-Chegem dialect was taken as the basis of the literary language; it was endowed only in 1924 with a Latin alphabet, which was then replaced in 1939 by the Cyrillic. Despite 15 years spent in deportation, the North Caucasian Turks remain strongly attached to their own language. Between 1959 and 1970, the percentages of those claiming Karachai-Balkar as their native language were: (Karachais) 1959, 96.8%; 1970, 98.1%; 1979, 97.7%; (Balkars) 1959, 97.0%; 1970, 97.2%; 1979, 96.9% — a small rise and then a decline.

The Karachais are not being assimilated either by the Russians or by the Cherkess. The Balkars, on the contrary, seem to be undergoing assimilation by the Kabardians. This assimilation is the only factor that can explain their slow growth of only 10% between 1970 and 1979. In 1979 the proportion of linguistically "russified" Karachais and Balkars remained extremely small: 2,658 Karachais (2.0%) and 1,799 Balkars (2.7%). Loyalty to the native tongue was, of course, higher among the rural dwellers (Karachais 99.1%, Balkars 98.6%) than among the urban (Karachais 93.1%, Balkars 93.5%) — these are 1970 figures.

Two newspapers are published in Karachai-Balkar. In Cherkessk, Karachai-Cherkess AO, there is *Leninyn Bairaghy* (Lenin's Flag) (10,081 copies in 1970). In Nal'chik, Kabardino-Balkar ASSR, there is *Kommunizmge Zhol* (Road to Communism) (5,000 copies in 1970).

Nationalism and national awareness. The North Caucasian Turks have no awareness of belonging to a modern Soviet Karachai or Balkar nationality; both groups designate themselves by their clan or tribal origins. They define themselves as members of one of the four *tukhums*: Trama, Budian, Adurkhay or Nawruz. The identity of the Balkars is tribal or local: Baksanchy (from the valley of Baksan), Chegemli, Bezengili, Kholamlu (from the valley of Kholam), or Malkarly (or Balkarly — an expression which became the name of the entire group).

Supra-national awareness, that of being members of the community of mountaineers, is still very much alive. Both groups identify themselves as *Tawlu* — the Turkic equivalent of the Russian *gortsy*, or mountaineers. (In emigration, especially in the United States, the Karachai-Balkars mix with other Caucasian mountaineers rather than with their fellow Turks or Tatars.) Pan-Turkic awareness among them is non-existent. Pan-Islamic awareness, that of belonging to the *Umma* of the Believers, has been steadily growing since the Second World War.

(viii) THE MUSLIM OSSETIANS

Only a minority of the Ossetians are Muslims (Sunni of the Hanafi school) — probably less than 30%. Before the 1917 Revolution, the majority were Orthodox Christians.

Administrative data. The North Ossetian ASSR was formed on 7 July 1924, under the name of the North Ossetian Autonomous *Oblast'*; it became an Autonomous Republic in December 1936. Its territory covers 8,000 square km. Its population was 597,000 in 1979 (an increase of 7.9% on 1970). Its urban population was 68% in 1979 (64% in 1970). Its capital is Ordzhonikidze, which had a population in 1979 of 279,000.

The South Ossetian AO of the Georgian SSR was founded on 22 April 1922, and its territory is 3,959 square km. Its population was 98,000 in 1979, 1,421 less than in 1970. Its urban population was 42% in 1979 (36% in 1970). Its capital is Tskhinvali (formerly Staliniri).

Demography. The Ossetian population in the past sixty years has been: 1926, 272,000; 1939, 354,000; 1959, 413,000; 1970, 488,000 (18% up on 1959); 1979, 541,893 (11% up on 1970).

In 1979 67.2% of the Ossetians lived in their national territories: 55.2% (299,022) lived in the North Ossetian ASSR; and 12.0% (65,077) lived in the South Ossetian AO. The remaining 31.3% formed border or immigrant colonies in the following areas (1970 figures, 1979 figures not available except for Georgia (160,497) and the Kabardino-Balkar ASSR (9,710)).

Georgian SSR	84,112 (17.2%)
Kabardino-Balkar ASSR	9,167 (1.9)
Stavropol' *krai*	7,713 (1.6)
Moscow city	3,676 (0.8)
Chechen-Ingush ASSR	2,652 (0.5)
Rostov *oblast'*	1,666 (6.4)
Krasnodar *krai*	1,640 (0.3)
Daghestan ASSR	1,633 (0.3)
Tajik SSR	5,755 (0.2)
Ukrainian SSR	4,554 (0.9)
Uzbek SSR	4,003 (0.8)
Kazakh SSR	3,491 (0.7)
Azerbaijan SSR	2,315 (0.5)
Turkmen SSR	1,887 (0.4)

Religious data. The Ossetians of the South Ossetian AO are all Christians, as are the majority of Ossetian immigrants to non-Muslim territories. But it appears that the Ossetians living in the Chechen-Ingush and Daghestan ASSRs are mostly Muslims. The Ossetian colonies in Central Asia are probably mixed: at least part of the Central Asian Ossetians are former Muslim deportees (Digors) who remained in their place of exile.

The Ossetian community is divided into three major tribal formations, each speaking its own dialect. These dialects are very different from one another. The three formations are the Iron (eastern) in the North Ossetian ASSR; the Digor (western), whose self-denomination is *Digurata* (in Russian, *Digortsy*) in the North Ossetian ASSR; and the

Tual (southern) in the South Ossetian AO. The Digors are Muslim, while the Ironis and the Tuals are Christian.

Part of the Digor population was deported in 1943, together with the Chechens, Ingush, Karachais and Balkars, and it was only in the 1960s that they were allowed to return to their homeland.

Islam was brought to the Digors from Kabarda in the seventeenth and eighteenth centuries. Muslim Ossetians have always been lukewarm Muslims (just as the Christian Ossetians were but superficially Orthodox). It seems, however, that since the Second World War Sufism in its most radical form (the Vis Haji *tariqa*) is penetrating North Ossetia from the nearby Ingush area. As a possible consequence of this development, Islam in Ossetia might gain in ardour and aggressiveness. The total number of Muslim Ossetians may be roughly estimated at between 100,000 and, at most, 150,000. It would seem that their increase is more rapid than that of the Ossetian Christians.

The national awareness of the Ossetians is religious rather than ethnic. Muslim Ossetians (Digors) feel closer to the Muslim Kabardians than to their Christian kinsmen, the Iron or the Tual. Muslim Ossetians are traditionally anti-Russian, while the Christian Ossetians have generally been the most pro-Russian among the North Caucasian mountaineers.

Many attempts have been made to transcribe the Ossetian language: into the Church Slavonic alphabet in the late eighteenth century; into the Georgian alphabet in southern Ossetia in the early nineteenth century; into Arabic characters in 1923; and even into the Latin alphabet in 1924. Two Ossetian literary languages, Iron and Digor, co-existed for a short time from 1924 to 1938, Digor disappearing as a written language in 1938. Since then the Ossetian literary language, based on the Iron dialect, is transcribed in Cyrillic. The Ossetians (the Christians more than the Muslims) are subjected to the process of linguistic russification more than any other North Caucasian nationality. The percentage of Ossetians having declared Ossetian as their native language has been slowly decreasing: 1959, 89.1%; 1970, 88.6%; and 1979, 88.2%.

(ix) THE SHAH DAGH PEOPLES

The Shah Dagh peoples consist of three small ethnic groups living in three large villages: Budug, Kryz and Khinalug, in the area of Mount Shahdagh in the Konakhkent district of the Azerbaijan SSR. The groups are named after their villages and are Sunni Muslims of the Shafe'i school.

Besides these three *auls*, the Budugs are also found in those of Deli Gaya and Guney Budug, and the Kryz in the *auls* of Alik, Jek and Gapuk of the same Konakhkent district. Smaller *auls* of the Budugs and Kryz also exist in the districts of Khudat, Ismailly, Khachmass, Kuba, Kutkashen and Zardob of the Azerbaijan SSR.

Each group speaks a different language, belonging to the Samurian group of the Daghestani languages; Azeri is used as the literary language. Isolated from the outside world, the Shah Dagh peoples have preserved a patriarchal way of life, but endogamic taboos are disappearing.

The 1926 census listed 2,000 Budugs, 2,600 Kryz and 100 Khinalugs. The censuses of 1959, 1970 and 1979 did not list them. It is probable that the Shah Dagh peoples have been more or less assimilated by the Azeris.

(x) THE GEORGIAN MUSLIMS: ADJARS, INGILOIS, LAZ

ADJARS. The Adjars are Sunni Muslims of the Hanafi school. They are ethnically Georgians, and speak a Gurian dialect (with many Turkish words). Their literary language is Georgian. They were converted to Islam by the Ottoman Turks in the sixteenth and seventeenth centuries when the Turks occupied the western part of Transcaucasia.

The Adjars were listed in the 1926 census separately from the rest of the Georgians, as a distinct nationality; at that they numbered 71,498. In subsequent censuses (1939, 1959, 1970) they have been listed with other Georgians. Their number may be estimated at 130,000 (minimum) to 160,000.

The Adjars have their own national territorial unit — an Autonomous Soviet Socialist Republic, founded on 16 July 1921, and with a territory of 3,000 square km. Its population in 1979 was 355,000 of whom 45.3% were urban. In 1970 the population was 309,768 (33.1% urban). The capital is Batumi, with a population in 1979 of 124,000.

The foreign population (non-Muslims) of the Adjar ASSR comprises the groups (along with an unknown number of Christian Georgians) shown in the accompanying table. Batumi, the capital and a big industrial city, is a non-Muslim town, but the countryside remains Muslim. In 1979 the Georgians numbered 283,872, part of whom — mainly the city-dwellers — are Christian. The Abkhaz and the Azeris living in the Adjar ASSR are all Muslims as well.

Table 8.x.1.   FOREIGN POPULATION OF THE ADJAR ASSR, 1970–9

	1970	1979	Difference 1970/79 (%)
Russians	35,774 (31,638 urban)	34,544	– 3.6
Armenians	15,614 (14,859 urban)	16,101	+ 3.1
Ukrainians	7,181 (6,075 urban)	5,402	– 32.9
Greeks	6,867 (3,534 urban)	—	—
Jews	1,546 (1,511 urban)	—	—

Before the Second World War the Muslim population of the Adjar ASSR was larger. The 1926 census listed 3,295 Kurds and 629 Khemshins (Armenian Muslims) who were residents of Adjaristan, as well as a certain number of ''Turks''. All these Muslims were deported in November–December 1944 because of tension between the Soviet Union and Turkey and do not figure in the 1959 and 1970 censuses. It would appear that Adjars were not deported from their republic in 1944.

According to our limited information concerning the Adjars, it seems that they remain deeply attached to their faith (this is true at least of the masses). One working mosque operates in Batumi, and in 1979 the *imam* was an Adjar. It seems that there are few mixed marriages between Christians and Muslims.

The national awareness of the Adjars was in the past more religious than ethnic, and to a certain extent the position remains the same. The older generation of the Adjar intellectuals were oriented entirely towards Turkey, and before the Second World War most Adjars were bilingual in Georgian and Turkish, with Turkish being used as the language of culture.

INGILOIS. The Ingilois are Sunni Muslims of the Hanafi school. They are Georgians of eastern Kakhetia who were converted to Islam in the seventeenth century by the Ottoman Turks during their occupation of Transcaucasia, and who intermingled with the southern Daghestanis (Lezghins). However, the Ingilois are closer to the Azeris and the Daghestanis than to the Georgians, their ethnic brethren. The Ingilois (mainly a rural community) live in the northwestern districts of Azerbaijan (Kasum, Ismailly, Tauz, Shamkhor) and speak the Kakhetian dialect of Georgian with many loan-words from Azeri. Most Ingilois are bilingual in Georgian and Azeri, with Azeri being used as their literary language.

The number of the Ingilois is uncertain but may be estimated at 3,000 to 5,000 (maximum). We do not know whether they were listed in the 1970 census as Georgians living in Azerbaijan or as Azeris, but their assimilation by the Azeris is well advanced.

LAZ. The Laz are a small Ibero-Caucasian community of Sunni Muslims of the Hanafi school, who speak a language of the Mingrelian group. The majority of the Laz nation live in Turkey along the Black Sea coast between Trabzon and the Soviet border, where their number was estimated in the 1950s at 160,000.

In the Soviet Union, the 1926 census listed 645 Laz near Batumi in the Adjar ASSR. Despite their small number (and perhaps in order to use them as a show model for the Turkish Laz), they were at one time treated by the Soviet authorities as a distinct nationality. In 1927 the Laz language (which is not written in Turkey) was provided with a Latin alphabet, and some books in it were published in Batumi. This attempt was abandoned in 1938, and the Laz language lost its written form. In the 1939, 1959 and 1970 censuses, the Laz were considered merely as an ethnic group of the Georgian nation.

(xi) THE KURDS

The majority of the Kurds are Sunni Muslims of the Hanafi school. There is also a minority of Yezidis ("Devil Worshippers"), and there are Shi'a of the Ja'farite rite and a small group of Ali Illahis. The Soviet Kurds are descendants of immigrants from Turkey and Iran. The total Kurdish population — in Turkey, Iraq, Iran, Syria and Lebanon — is estimated at more than 10 million.

The Yezidis are ethnically Kurds speaking the Kurmanji dialect. Their secret religion is a modified Manichean dualism with a few elements borrowed from Islam. Muslims do not consider them to be co-religionists and call them "Devil Worshippers". The Yezidis have their own social and religious customs which differ considerably from those of their Muslim cousins. Muslim Kurdish intellectuals have recently adopted a more favourable attitude toward the Yezidis, and some even consider that in the Middle Ages (when almost all Kurdish tribes were Yezidis) Yezidism was the national religion of the Kurds. However, there are no contacts between Muslims and Yezidis at the mass level, the latter observing a strict endogamy within their community. In the 1926 census they were treated as a distinct nationality, and today they are supposed to form an ethnic group of the Kurdish nation.

In 1926 there were 69,000 Kurds in the Soviet Union, including some 15,000 Yezidis listed separately. In 1939 there were 45,900; in 1959, 52,949; in 1970, 88,930 (67.9% up on 1959); and in 1979, 115,858 (30.4% up on 1970).

The fluctuations between the 1926 and 1970 figures are due not to the assimilation of the Kurds by some other national group but to the imprecisions of the census operations. Thus it seems that in 1939 and 1959 many Kurds were listed as Azeris or even as Armenians. In 1970, because of the pro-Kurdish policy of the Soviets, many Kurds were once again, as in 1926, listed as such. Recently there has been no significant immigration of Kurds to the Soviet Union.

The first Kurds to settle in the Caucasus came from Iranian Kurdistan in the early nineteenth century and settled mainly in the districts of Lachin and Zangelan, in Azerbaijan. They were mostly Shi'a Muslims of the Ja'farite rite (with a Sunni minority). The second and most important migration from the Ottoman Empire took place in three waves during the Russian-Turkish wars of 1853–6, 1877–8 and 1914–18. These migrants were Sunni Muslims (from eastern Anatolia) and Yezidis from the Jebel Sinjar (in northern Iraq). The Yezidis were fleeing religious persecutions. They settled in Armenia, while a small minority moved straight to Georgia.

During the Soviet regime some changes occurred in the distribution of the Kurds in Transcaucasia. Some Azerbaijani Kurds (mainly the Sunni) moved to eastern Armenia in the 1920s, while others left Armenia for the Georgian cities. After the Second World War, Kurdish colonies (mainly rural) settled in Central Asia: Kazakhstan, Kirghizia, Turkmenistan. In 1970, of the total of 88,930 Soviet Kurds, 34,317 were town-dwellers — a rather high proportion (38.6%).

The majority of the Kurds lived in 1970 in the three Transcaucasian republics — 65,945 (74%). In the Armenian SSR, there were 50,822 Kurds in 1979 (25,627 in 1959 and 37,486 in 1970). They were established mostly in western Armenia — the districts of Apazan, Verin-Talin and Echmiadzin, with small groups in the districts of Ijevan, Sevan, Basargechar, Ashtarak, Oktemberian and Vedi. The Kurds of Armenia are largely Yezidis (15,000 in 1926 and probably some 25,000 today). The minority are Sunni.

In Azerbaijan there were 7,769 Kurds in 1970 (1,487 in 1959) of whom only 17% were town-dwellers. They live in the three western districts along the Armenian border — Lachin, Kubatli and Zangelan — and are mainly Shi'a. The 1979 figures are not available.

In Georgia there were 20,690 Kurds in 1970 (27.6% up on 1959), of whom 20,031 (97%) were town-dwellers (industrial workers). There were 26,688 Kurds in 1979 (an increase of 25.7%). In Tbilisi there were 18,409 Kurds (in 1970). The majority of Georgian Kurds are Sunni.

In 1970 some 20,000 Kurds (mainly Sunni) lived in Central Asia; these colonies consisted of immigrants or perhaps deportees, such as the Kurds from the area of Akhaltsikhe (Georgia) and from abroad (Iran). In Kazakhstan there were 12,313 Kurds of whom 1,448 (12%) were town-dwellers. The Kurds (the majority of whom were Muslims) were settled in the three southern regions of the republic: Alma-Ata 3,628, Dzhambul 4,657, and Chimkent 2,441. In Kirghizia there were 7,974 Kurds of whom 1,735 (22%) were town-dwellers; the majority (5,189) were living in the Osh region. A smaller group, mainly of industrial workers, settled after the Second World War in Turkmenistan: 2,263 in 1959, not mentioned in 1970. There are no Kurds in the RSFSR.

In 1970, of the 88,930 Kurds of the Soviet Union, 77,879 (or 87.6%) claimed Kurdish as their native language; in 1979 the proportion had decreased to 83.6%. The number of russified Kurds is comparatively high; these are essentially town-dwellers. In 1970, of the 3,399 Kurds who claimed Russian as their native language, 2,226 (65.5%) lived in Georgia. The linguistic assimilation of the Kurds is relatively rapid, but it varies greatly in different areas. The proportion of Kurds who claimed Kurdish as their native language was as follows in 1970 in these areas: Georgia 79% (75.2% in 1979), Azerbaijan 61%; Armenia 92% (84.6% in 1979); Kazakhstan 96.4%; and Kirghizia 98.4%. Assimilation is more advanced in Azerbaijan, where Kurds live among other Muslims (27% of rural Kurds claimed Azeri as their first language); it is also more advanced in Georgia, where almost all of the Kurds live in cities. In Armenia, we may assume that most of the 7,140 Kurds who claimed Armenian as their first language in 1979 were Yezidis.

Kurdish, divided among several dialects, has no real literary language. Some attempts have been made in Iran and Iraq to transliterate it in Arabic and, in Syria, in Latin script. In the Soviet Union a literary language based on the Kurmanji dialect spoken in eastern Anatolia, and different from the dialects spoken in Iraq and Iran, was created in 1922. It was endowed with a modified Armenian alphabet, replaced in 1929 by the Latin one and in 1944 by the Cyrillic.

Soviet Kurds enjoy in Armenia an authentic extraterritorial cultural autonomy. They have their own network of schools, an institute of Kurdish studies at the Academy of Sciences of Erevan, and a modest national press, which includes a bi-weekly Kurdish newspaper *Reiya Taze* (The New Way), published since March 1930 in Erevan with a circulation of 2,500–3,500 copies.

National awareness. Kurdish national awareness is difficult to analyse, although it is obviously very strong. All Kurds — intellectuals as well as the masses — have a strong sense of belonging to the Kurdish nation and of being bound together by a solid kinship. There are very few mixed marriages with other Muslims, and the endogamic taboos are still observed within the community. However, national awareness is hardly based on Islam. Muslim Kurds are, as a rule, tolerant toward their Yezidi brothers who have been persecuted for centuries by all other Muslims as well as by the Christians. Religion among the Kurds (Islam or Yezidism) remains a corpus of social traditions rather than a well-defined spiritual creed.

National awareness is also not based on loyalty to the Kurmanji language. The advanced linguistic assimilation of the Kurds to the use of various Christian languages (Russian, Georgian, Armenian) does not mean that they are losing their national identity and are being assimilated by their Christian neighbours. Similarly, there is no assimilation of the Kurds living in Azerbaijan by the Azeris.

We may say that Kurdish national identity is expressed in a specific way of life based on various social customs, clan solidarity, some specific purely Kurdish historical traditions, and a common oral literature. It is also based on their sense of superiority as a primitive warlike community, respected by other more peaceful (and more prosperous) nationalities surrounding them.

Kurdish nationlism should be taken seriously. All the Kurds in Turkey, Iraq and Iran feel that they form a numerically important, potentially wealthy nation, occupying a central and strategic position in the Middle East. The political cadres (young intellectuals) have not, as often happens in the Muslim world, cut their ties with the tribes. The long succession of bloody revolts in Iran and Iraq and political agitation in Turkey bolster the Kurds' belief that "their time will come", and that this is not a mere dream.

Soviet Kurds have a general notion of belonging to a Kurdish nation, but the vast majority of them are peasants or industrial workers whose political views do not go beyond purely local interests. However, there is a small but distinguished Kurdish élite consisting mainly of scholars working in various Armenian institutions and in Moscow who seem passionately interested in the Kurdish world abroad. Since the Second World War these Kurdish intellectuals have enjoyed favourable treatment by the Soviets, comparable with that given to the Uighurs and Dungans in Central Asia. They are in contact with the groups of Kurdish intellectuals abroad, in Damascus and Paris.

Soviet Armenia may thus appear as a kind of substitute national home, where Kurds enjoy cultural autonomy. But this national home is very small; the number of Kurdish intellectuals in the Soviet Union is negligible, and it is difficult to talk of the real use of the Soviet Kurds as agents or propagandists abroad, and even less of the Soviet government having a systematic Kurdish strategy. Such a strategy would be incompatible with a pro-Arab or pro-Iranian strategy and would permanently antagonise the Turks. It remains in reserve, as an eventual option. It seems, however, that the Soviet authorities do not trust their own Kurdish intellectuals, and that the Soviet Kurds may also be influenced by ideas from abroad, especially by the radical Kurdish revolutionaries in Iran and Iraq.

(xii) THE ABKHAZ

The Abkhaz are partly (50–70%) Orthodox Christians of the Gregorian Church and partly Sunni Muslims of the Hanafi rite. The Abkhaz ASSR was constituted on 4 March 1921 and its territory is 8,600 square km. Its population was 486,082 in 1979, compared with 486,959 in 1970. Town-dwellers numbered 238,000 (or 47% in 1979; 44.2% in 1970). Its capital is Sukhumi, which had a population in 1979 of 114,000.

The Abkhaz population in 1926 was 57,000. In 1939 it was 59,000 (an increase of 3.5%); in 1959, 65,430 (10.9% up on 1939); in 1970, 83,240 (27.2% up on 1959); and in 1979, 91,915 (9.6% up on 1970). The large fluctuations in the numerical increase of the Abkhaz may be explained by the more or less extensive degree of their "georgianisation".

In the middle of the nineteenth century the total number of Abkhaz was some 150,000. After the final conquest of the western Caucasus, almost half of them (all Muslims) left their homeland and emigrated to the Ottoman Empire, and their descendants still live in Turkey, Syria, Jordan, Iraq and Egypt, where they are known as "Cherkess".

The majority of the Abkhaz live in their own republic. In 1970, of the 83,240 persons of Abkhaz nationality, 77,276 (or 92.8%) lived in the Abkhaz ASSR. In 1979, of 90,915 Abkhaz in the Soviet Union, 83,097

(91.4%) lived in the Abkhaz ASSR and 2,188 in other areas of the Georgian SSR. The remainder were distributed between the city of Tbilisi, Georgia, and the Adjar Republic, where in 1970 there were 1,361 people in the villages of Bebokvati, Angisi and Gonia, all Muslims. In 1970 there were 2,427 in the RSFSR and 476 in the Ukraine. In their own republic, the Abkhaz represent only a minority. Table 8.xii.1 shows the population distribution of the republic.

In their own republic, the Abkhaz are grouped in the district of Ochamchiri (south of Sukhumi) and Gudauta (west of Sukhumi), and of the total 62.3% are rural dwellers. The town-dwellers live in Sukhumi, Gudauta, Ochamchiri, Tkvarcheli and Gagra, all of which have a large Georgian majority.

The Abkhazian language belongs to the Abasgo-Cherkess group of the Ibero-Caucasian languages, very different from Georgian. In 1970 the percentage of Abkhaz who claimed this language as their first was 97.2% in Georgia and 97.8% in Abkhazia. An attempt was made to create a Cyrillic alphabet for the Abkhaz in the nineteenth century, but this was only half-successful and up till 1928 Abkhazian remained a non-literary language. From 1918 to 1938 it was transliterated in the Latin script, but in 1938 the Latin alphabet was replaced by the Georgian instead of Cyrillic and, till 1954, there was a rapid process of "georgiani-sation". From 1945 to 1956, Georgian even replaced Abkhazian as the only language of the Abkhaz ASSR. In 1954 the Georgian alphabet was replaced by the Cyrillic, and in 1956 Abkhazian was, in theory at least, re-established as the language for schools. It remains at present a minor literary language, with Georgian and Russian being used as the languages of higher education.

In 1970, of the three republican-level newspapers published in Sukhumi (the capital of Abkhazia), the one in Abkhazian had the lowest circulation (14,000 copies, compared with 21,000 copies for the Georgian newspaper and 33,000 copies for the Russian one). Of the seven district newspapers, one was in Russian, one in Georgian, three in Russian and Georgian (mixed), one in Abkhazian and Russian (mixed), and one in Abkhazian and Georgian (mixed).

There are no quantitative data for the religions of the Abkhaz. We may surmise that approximately equal numbers of the Abkhaz are respec-tively Muslims and Christians, but both these religions form no more than a surface layer on the old paganism. The Abkhaz received Chris-tianity in its Greek form from Byzantium during the fourth to sixth centuries, but from the ninth to the fifteenth centuries Abkhazia was

Table 8.xii.1.   POPULATION OF THE ABKHAZ ASSR, 1959–79

	1959 population (and % of total)	*1970 population (and % of total)*	*increase (%) 1959–70*	*1979 (incomplete) and % of total)*	*increase (%) 1970–9*
Total	404,738	486,959	20.3	486,082	– 0.002
Abkhaz	61,193 (15.0)	77,276 (15.8)	26.3	83,097 (17.1)	7.5
Georgians	158,221 (39.1)	199,595 (41.0)	26.1	213,322 (43.9)	6.9
Russians	86,715 (21.4)	92,889 (19.1)	7.5	79,730 (16.4)	– 14.2
Armenians	64,425 (15.9)	74,850 (15.4)	16.2	73,350 (15.1)	– 0.007
Ukrainians	11,474 (2.8)	11,955 (2.5)	4.2	10,257 (2.1)	– 14.2
Greeks	9,101 (2.2)	—	—	13,642 (2.8)	?
Jews	3,332 (0.8)	4,372 (0.9)	31.2	?	?
Estonians	1,882 (0.5)	1,834 (0.4)	2.5	?	?
Belorussians	—	1,901 (0.4)	—	?	?
Tatars	—	1,738 (0.3)	—	?	?
Ossetians	—	1,212 (0.2)	—	?	?
Others	—	6,221	—	?	?

under the cultural and religious influence of Georgia. In the later fifteenth century, the Ottoman Turks occupied some fortresses on the coast (Sukhum Kale), and Islam began slowly to penetrate the hinterland, although it never rooted itself deeply. The ruling Abkhaz dynasty, the Sharvashidze, changed its religion in accordance with political necessities, and its subjects followed suit. However, by the middle of the nineteenth century, the majority of the Abkhaz seem to have professed Islam. After the massive exodus of the Muslim Abkhaz in the 1860s, a certain equilibrium was established between the two faiths. But unlike what we find elsewhere in similar cases of religiously split nationalities (e.g. the Ossetians), there is no opposition between the Christian and the Muslim Abkhaz, who are indifferent in matters of religion.

National awareness among the Abkhaz is limited to a small group of intellectuals. Two options have existed since the creation of the Abkhaz nation around 1924, and both these options still have champions among the Abkhaz leaders. The first is to become culturally "georgianised", with, as the final stage of the process, the total assimilation of the Abkhaz by the Georgians. The absence of a national Abkhaz culture, the closeness of the Abkhaz and the Georgian ways of life, a common historical tradition, a common church (in the case of Christians) — these are the arguments advanced by the supporters of georgianisation. The second option is to resist georgianisation with the help of the Russians in order to achieve a real Abkhaz identity. Abkhaz nationalism is thus used as a stake in the complicated game played since 1922 between Moscow and the Georgians.

However, the problem of Abkhaz national identity remains a minor and a theoretical one. The Abkhaz form but a small minority vis-à-vis a large and growing Georgian majority. Except for an improbable mass immigration by Russians into Abkhazia, it is difficult to imagine what could preserve the Abkhaz in the long run from total assimilation by the Georgians.

(xiii) THE MESKHETIANS

Of the Meskhetians the majority are Sunni Muslims of the Hanafi school; there are also small groups of Ali Illahis. "Meskhetian" is a collective self-denomination of several Muslim groups from southwestern Georgia and northern Armenia deported to Central Asia in November and December 1944, and since then forbidden to return to their original homeland.

Although our knowledge is incomplete in this field, it seems that the following more or less turkified groups today form the Meskhetian nationality. The Turks of Meskhetia are by far the most important group, with the addition of some smaller groups: the Karapapakhs of northern Armenia; the Khemshins of Adjaristan; some Kurds from Adjaristan; the Turkmen of Georgia; and possibly some turkified Adjars, Abkhaz and Laz from Adjaristan. The total number of Meskhetians has been estimated at 150,000 (S.E. Wimbush) and 200,000 (R. Conquest) and even 500,000 (*samizdat*).

THE TURKS OF MESKHETIA. In Soviet literature a distinction is made between *Turki* (the Turks of Turkey) and *Tiurki* (Turks), the latter being a general designation for all Turkic-speaking peoples. The denomination "*Tiurki*" was also applied before 1935 to the Azeris and in general to all Transcaucasian Turks.

The Turks, speaking Turkish, formerly lived along the Kura valley in the Akhaltsikhe, Adigeni, Aspindza, Akhalkalaki and Bogdanovka districts of the Georgian SSR, along the Turkish frontier. In 1926 the first Soviet census listed 137,921 Turks (*Tiurki*) in Georgia; this figure included the Azeris. In 1959 there were 153,600 Azeris in Georgia (excluding the Meskhi Turks); in 1970 they numbered 217,758. The Turks (*Turki*) listed in the 1959 census amounted to 35,000 but no indication was given of their place of establishment. The appellation "*Turki*" was probably limited to the Meskhi Turks already deported to Central Asia. In 1970 the preliminary data of the census (as published in the *Vestnik Statistiki*, 5, 1971) gave the figure of 79,000 Turks (with no locals). The Turks disappear completely from the final figures of the 1970 census as published in the fourth volume (Moscow 1973). The 1979 census lists 92,689 Turks (*Turki*); their location is not indicated. Out of this number, 78,513 (or 84.7%) spoke Turkish, 2,555 (2.7%) Russian, and 11,621 (or 12.6%) "other languages", probably Azeri and Uzbek.

It is probable that the 1970 figure of 79,000 Turks included almost the total of deported Meskhi Turks and also some members of other groups (Karapapakhs, Kurds, Khemshins) who were turkified in the deportation. Only this assimilation of smaller groups by the Meskhi Turks can explain the enormous increase (125.7%) in the number of Turks between 1959 and 1970.

In their original homeland, the Meskhi Turks were a rural, deeply religious community. As in the case of the deported North Caucasians, their religiousness became even more spectacular and aggressive during the deportation. According to reports received by Dr Rasma Karklins from Soviet German emigrants from Central Asia (see her *Ethnic Relations in the USSR*), the Turks of Central Asia, i.e. the deported Meskhi Turks, are the most religious of all Central Asian Muslims. Their national awareness is thus divided between Islam and their "Turkishness" — a strong sense of belonging to the *Turkish* (not Turkic) nation and culture.

THE KARAPAPAKHS OF NORTHERN ARMENIA. The 1926 census listed 6,316 Karapapakhs in northern Armenia near the Georgian border. The majority were Ali Illahis who had migrated to Turkey from Iran around 1820 and settled in Armenia at the end of the nineteenth century. The Karapapakhs are a Turkmen tribe speaking a dialect close to Azeri and using Turkish as their literary language. They disappear from later census registrations (1939, 1959, 1970), when they were listed either as Azeris or as Turks (*Turki*). Their knowledge of their secret religion and their religious awareness was weakened, and it is probable that they no longer perceive the differences which in the past had isolated them from other Muslims. Today they probably amount to a maximum of 10,000 individuals.

KHEMSHINS. Khemshins are Armenians converted to Sunni Islam, Hanafi school, by the Ottoman Turks in the eighteenth century. They are bilingual (Armenian and Turkish) and use Turkish as their literary language.

The 1926 census listed 629 Khemshins, almost all living in the Adjar ASSR. They disappeared from the following census. In fact, they were listed either as Armenians or as Azeris. Today their number is estimated at 1,000. The entire Khemshin community was deported in November 1944 to Central Asia, where they are called "Turks" by the local population, with whom they do not mix. The Khemshin identity is more religious than ethnic. At present they are being assimilated by the Turks.

KURDS. An old colony of Kurds (Sunni and Ali Illahi) was established in southern Georgia. In 1926 there were 4,024 Kurds living in the district of Akhaltsikhe and Akhalkalaki. Another group of some 2,000 lived in the Adjar ASSR. All were deported in November 1944. It is possible that these Kurds were subjected to a more intensive assimilation by the Turks than were those of Armenia.

OTHER GROUPS. The Turkmen of southern Georgia, a small tribe from eastern Anatolia speaking an Azeri dialect, were deported together with the Meskhi Turks in November 1944. It is possible that a certain number of turkified Adjars and Muslim Abkhaz living in the Adzhar ASSR were also deported.

The total number of Muslims from southwestern Georgia who were resettled in Central Asia (mainly in Uzbekistan, Tajikistan and Kirghizia) was estimated in 1970 to be between 100,000 and 150,000. In their exile all these disparate groups engaged in a curious process of nation-building. United by their faith, a deeply-rooted popular Islam (the Ali Illahis drawing nearer to the Sunnis), and by a common Turkish culture and language, they survived in an alien milieu by voluntarily relinquishing the particular characteristics that differentiated them. Thus they became one Meskhetian Turkish nationality. That this decision has been a conscious one is proved by several documents produced by the political leaders of the Meskhetian movement and published in *samizdat* since 1968. The Meskhetians have neither been rehabilitated in 1956 (as the other deported Caucasians were) nor permitted to migrate back to their homeland. On 30 May 1968, a decree of the Presidium of the Supreme Soviet of the Soviet Union declared that the Meskhetians have taken root in their place of exile. Since then the leaders of the Meskhetian movement have asked in vain either to be allowed to return to their homeland or to emigrate to Turkey. It seems, however, that some Meskhetian Turks have been permitted to settle in Azerbaijan. (In September 1985 a Georgian journal, *Komunisti* of Tbilisi, reported that some 14 Meskhetian families were allowed to return to Western Georgia. See Elisabeth Fuller, "Georgian Muslims deported by Stalin permitted to return", *Radio Liberty Research Bulletin*, RL 32/86, Jan. 14, 1986.)

(xiv) THE TALYSH

The Talysh are Shi'a Muslims of the Ja'farite rite ("Twelvers"). In the 1926 census their number was given as 77,323, and in 1931 it was estimated as 89,000. They were not listed in the 1939, 1959 and 1970 census registrations as a separate nationality but as Azeris.

In 1959, however, the census mentioned 10,616 individuals speaking Talyshi which they claimed to be their native language; 10,563 of them lived in Azerbaijan. Since all Talysh are bilingual (Talysh and Azeri), it is probable that the real number of people speaking Talyshi is much higher than the figures given in 1959. Some Soviet specialists give a minimum figure of 100,000.

The Talysh live in the extreme southern districts of Azerbaijan, bordering Iran: Astara and Lenkoran. They form the majority of the population there and in the districts of Lerik and Masally, where they are also mixed with the Azeris.

The Talysh language is a dialect of northern Iran. In 1930 it became a literary language endowed with the Latin alphabet. In 1931, a Talysh newspaper (*Kizil Talysh*) was published in Lenkoran and the first text-books in Talyshi were introduced in schools. In 1939, when Cyrillic replaced the Latin alphabet for the Caucasian languages, the Talysh were deprived of their literary tongue. Since then they have used Azeri for that purpose.

The Talysh constitute a purely rural community. In 1959, out of the 10,616 Talyshi-speaking individuals in the Soviet Union, only 152 were living in cities. Generally, they live in purely Talysh areas or in villages with a Talysh majority. Their assimilation by the Azeris is therefore very slow. The Talysh districts of Azerbaijan are reputed to be among the most religious of the republic. They are very conservative and still observe various traditional customs: *kalym*, levirate, sororate and polygamy.

(xv) THE MUSLIM TATS

The Muslim Tats are Shi'a Muslims of the Ja'farite rite ("Twelvers"). The term "Tats" was used before the Revolution by certain Turks to designate sedentaries of non-Turkic origin, but it is now applied to a small Caucasian national group speaking a southern dialect of the Iranian language. The group is divided into three separate religious communities. First are the Jewish Tats or "mountain Jews" (*Dagh Chufut*), established mainly in southern Daghestan and in the villages of Krasnaya Sloboda (Kuba district) and Vartashen, and in the city of Baku. Second are the Christian Tats of the Armeno-Gregorian faith, established in the villages of Matrosa (Shemakha district) and Kilvan (Divichi district). And third are the Muslim Tats (Shi'a), living mainly in Baku, in the Apsheron peninsula, and in the districts of Siazan, Divichi, Kuba, Konakhkent, Shemakha and Ismailly (i.e. mainly in northern and northeastern Azerbaijan).

It is not easy to secure data determining the numerical importance of the three Tati communities. In fact, the Armenian Tats have been listed in the last census registrations (1959 and 1970) as Armenians. The mountain Jews have been, theoretically, listed as Jews, but we know that a certain number of Tati-speaking Jews preferred in 1970 to be listed as Tats.

In 1926 the number of Tats was 28,443 and in 1959 11,463. Soviet demographers explain this decrease by the assimilation of the Muslim Tats by the Azeris. In the 1959 census the total number of individuals speaking Tati was 46,316, of whom 25,225 were Jewish Tats. The remaining 21,091 speaking Tati were probably for the most part Muslim Tats, with a minority of Armenian Tats.

The 1970 census does not give the total number of people speaking Tati. Those who were listed as Tats by nationality numbered 17,109, which indicates a large increase of 49.2% since 1959. Since there is no reason to believe that the assimilation of the Muslim Tats by the Azeris has been halted, there are only two possible explanations of the sharp increase of the Tats: first, that a certain number of mountain Jews have declared themselves as Tats to escape anti-Semitic discrimination (we know that this explanation is at least partly true); and secondly, that the 1959 census concerning the Tats grossly exaggerated the importance of their assimilation by the Azeris, and that in 1970 a certain number of those who declared themselves to be Azeris in 1959 were once again listed as Tats.

In 1970, out of 17,109 Tats, 7,769 lived in Azerbaijan and 6,440 in southern Daghestan. The remaining 2,990 lived in the neighbouring Caucasian republics (Georgia, Armenia and Checheno-Ingushetia). The Tats are essentially an urban community. In 1970, there were 16,604 (out of a total of 17,109, i.e. 97%) living in the cities. In Daghestan, the percentage of city-dwellers is only slightly lower, at 96.3%; but in Azerbaijan, out of 7,769 Tats, 7,524 (96.8%) live in the city of Baku. In 1979 the number of Tats in the Soviet Union was 22,441, of whom 7,437 (33.1%) lived in southern Daghestan and 8,848 (39.4%) in Azerbaijan.

There is no alphabet proper for the tongue of the Muslim Tats, and they use Azeri as their literary language. The special dialect of the Tati-speaking Jews, strongly flavoured by Hebrew, possesses (in theory) a written language in the Cyrillic alphabet. Before the Revolution, the Hebrew alphabet was used; this was changed to the Latin alphabet in 1929 and the Cyrillic in 1939.

In 1959, 70.9% of the Tats claimed Tati as their native language while 24.6% claimed Russian. In 1970 the percentage of those speaking Tati increased to 72.6%.

The Tats represent a fairly developed urban community, mainly of oil-workers, who practise inter-ethnic endogamy and live in a closed society. Their national identity is based on their Iranian language. To our knowledge, there are no indications of any Tat nationalism, nor is there any attempt by the Soviet authorities to sponsor the emergence of some national Tat opposition to the Azeris. The Muslim Tat community seems to be condemned in the long run to assimilation by the Azeris.

In 1979 the proportion of Tati-speakers fell to 67.4% and that of Russian speakers rose to 29.4%. In Azerbaijan, out of 8,848 Tats, 44.8% claimed Tati only as their first mother-tongue and 49.2% claimed Russian. In the Daghestan ASSR, out of 7,437 Tats, 91.5% were Tati-speakers and only 8.0% Russian-speakers.

9

MUSLIMS OF EUROPEAN RUSSIA AND SIBERIA

(i) THE TATARS

The Tatars are Sunni Muslims of the Hanafi school, although it should be noted that since the sixteenth century there has been an important Tatar Christian community — the Kryashens — consisting of between 200,000 and 250,000 individuals. Several ethnic groups which differ according to historical background, locale and language have been listed in the last three Soviet censuses under the general name of Tatars. Those groups are the Volga (or Kazan) Tatars, the Crimean Tatars (deported in 1943 and rehabilitated though not allowed to return to their Crimean homeland), the Siberian Tatars, the Astrakhan Tatars and the Lithuanian Tatars.

The Tatar ASSR was founded on 27 May 1920, and in 1979 its territory covered 68,000 square km. Its population in 1979 was 3,436,000, compared to 3,131,238 in 1970. Its urban population in 1979 was 2,172,000 (1,613,555 in 1970 — an increase of 34.6%); its rural population in 1979 was 1,264,000 (1,517,283 in 1970, a decrease of 250,000). The capital of the Tatar ASSR is Kazan, with a population in 1979 of 993,000 (869,000 in 1970 and 667,000 in 1959).

Demography

Table 9.i.1.   THE TATAR POPULATION

	Population	*Increase %*
1939	4,300,000	
1959	4,967,701	
1970	5,930,670	19.4
1979	6,317,468	6.5

The exceptionally low population growth of the Tatars between 1970 and 1979 may be explained by two factors: first, the low natural increase of the *urban* Tatar colonies (55% of the community) and, secondly, the assimilation of the Tatars by the host-nationalities of the numerous diaspora colonies. The Volga Tatars are the only migratory Muslim nation in

223

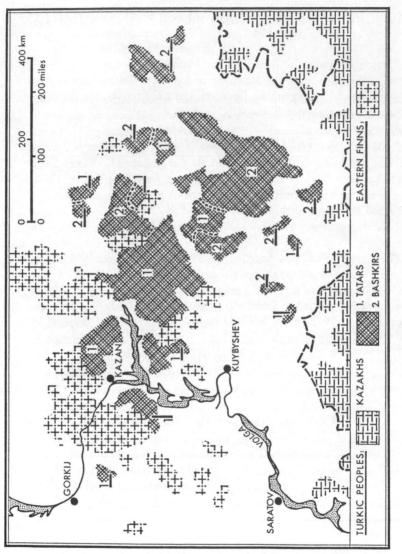

THE MUSLIM PEOPLES OF THE MIDDLE VOLGA

TURKIC PEOPLES: KAZAKHS   1. TATARS   2. BASHKIRS

EASTERN FINNS:

224

the Soviet Union. Only 25.5% of the Tatars lived in their national territory in 1970 and 25.9% in 1979. Since the fall of the Khanate of Kazan in 1552, the Tatars are the only Muslim Turkic nationality of the Russian empire or the Soviet Union to have formed important diaspora colonies. Since the Second World War these colonies have been deprived of national schools and their own press and are therefore susceptible to assimilation either by the Russians or by other Turkic nationalities. According to the incomplete figures of the 1979 census, the Tatars are distributed as shown in Table 9.i.2.

Table 9.i.2.   TATAR POPULATION DISTRIBUTION, 1970–9

	1970 *(and % of total)*		1979 *(and % of total)*		*Increase* %
Total Tatars	5,930,000		6,317,468		6.5
RSFSR	4,757,913	(80.2)	5,010,922	(79.3)	– 5.3
Uzbekistan	573,733	(9.7)	649,764	(10.3)	– 13.1
Kazakhstan	287,712	(4.9)	313,460	(4.9)	– 8.8
Azerbaijan	31,787	(0.5)	31,350	(0.5)	– 0.14
Kirghizia	69,373	(1.2)	72,018	(1.1)	– 3.8
Turkmenistan	36,457	(0.6)	40,432	(0.6)	– 9.7
Tajikistan	70,803	(1.2)	79,529	(1.3)	– 13.0
Ukraine	76,212	(1.3)	90,542	(1.4)	
Belorussia, Moldavia	36,680	(0.4)	30,451	(0.6)	

It would seem that between 1970 and 1979 there was a continuous immigration of Tatars from the Middle Volga to Uzbekistan (+ 13.1%), to Tajikistan (+ 13.0%) and, to a less degree, to Turkmenistan (+ 9.7%) and to Kazakhstan (+ 8.8%). The immigrants were mainly technical and professional urban cadres. It is likely that between 1970 and 1979 only a few of the Tatars living in Central Asia have been assimilated either by the local nationalities or by the Russians. On the other hand, there has been a steady assimilation of the Tatar urban colonies outside their national territories. In Azerbaijan the decrease in the number of Tatars may be explained both by out-migration and by the assimilation of the Tatars by the Azeris.

The 1970 census provides complete figures concerning the distribution of the Tatars. They form four main categories of colonies.

1. *The Middle Volga and Urals.* This is the original territory of the Volga Tatars, in which they generally constitute rural communities.

Table 9.i.3.   TATARS IN THE MIDDLE VOLGA AND URALS, 1970–9

Administrative territory	Tatar population 1970	Tatars in the urban community (and %)	Tatar population 1979
Tatar ASSR	1,536,431	593,665 (38.5)	1,641,60
Bashkir ASSR	944,507	408,769 (43.3)	940,46
Perm' *oblast'*	169,372	111,054 (65.6)	157,72
Orenburg *oblast'*	145,376	54,156 (37.2)	151,38
Ul'ianovsk *oblast'*	122,409	45,054 (36.8)	134,76
Kuibyshev *oblast'*	93,687	48,246 (51.5)	103,60
Gorki *oblast'*	71,798	28,320 (39.4)	68,63
Kirov *oblast'*	45,309	23,037 (50.8)	44,90
Mordovian ASSR	44,955	11,075 (24.6)	45,76
Saratov *oblast'*	43,238	23,841 (55.0)	47,94
Mari ASSR	40,280	18,440 (45.8)	40,91
Penza *oblast'*	74,838	11,659 (15.6)	78,23
Chuvash ASSR	36,217	9,697 (26.3)	37,57
Volgograd *oblast'*	23,518	14,378 (61.6)	25,53

2. *The original homelands of other historical Tatar groups.* In these areas the Tatars represent small minorities with a high proportion of country-dwellers (see Table 9.i.4).

3. *The urban Tatar diaspora.* Tatar colonies exist everywhere in the Soviet Union from the western borderlands to the Pacific Ocean. Some are old colonies dating from the sixteenth to eighteenth centuries; this is especially true of those established in Siberia between Kazan and China. The Central Asian diaspora is mainly a nineteenth-century phenomenon, and the out-migration of the Tatars was still in progress between 1959 and 1970.

The detailed 1979 census figures have not yet been published, and in order to study the migratory trends among the Volga Tatars we are compelled to compare the 1959 and 1970 census numerical data. During this period there was a steady movement of the Tatars from their Middle Volga homeland in the following directions:

— Towards all five Central Asian republics (this movement continued between 1970 and 1979);

— Towards the large cities (Leningrad, Moscow — in Moscow the increase in the Tatar community was 36%);

Table 9.i.4.   TATARS IN THE NATIVE HOMELAND, 1970

Administrative territory	Tatar group	Population	Tatars in the urban community (and %)	1979 (incomplete) figures
Astrakhan *oblast'*	Astrakhan Tatars	67,062	37,064 (55.3)	70,781
Kalmyk ASSR	Astrakhan Tatars	1,230	564 (45.8)	
Omsk *oblast'*	Siberian Tatars	44,330	18,860 (42.5)	46,714
Novosibirsk *oblast'*	Siberian Tatars	28,825	5,088 (21.3)	28,549
Kurgan *oblast'*	Siberian and Volga Tatars	23,932	5,088 (21.3)	23,507
Tiumen' *oblast'*	Siberian and Volga Tatars	102,861	35,674 (34.7)	136,757
Tomsk *oblast'*	Siberian Tatars	15,226	9,303 (61.1)	17,630
Riazan *oblast'*	Kasymov Tatars	4,057	1,659 (40.9)	
Belorussian SSR	Lithuanian Tatars	10,031	5,346 (53.3)	
Latvian SSR	Lithuanian Tatars	2,688	1,472 (54.7)	
Lithuanian SSR	Lithuanian Tatars	3,460	2,323 (67.1)	
Krasnodar *krai*	"Tatarised" Nogais	17,709	10,135 (57.2)	26,072
Stavropol' *krai*	"Tatarised" Nogais	9,405	4,229 (44.9)	
Moldavian SSR	"Tatarised" Nogais	1,859	1,029 (55.4)	

— Towards some areas in western Siberia (in the Tiumen' and Omsk *oblasts* the increase of the Tatars between 1959 and 1970 was 42% and 22% respectively);
— Towards the Lower Volga territory: Kuibyshev (+ 26%), Saratov (+ 27%), and Volgograd (+ 32%).

Table 9.i.5.   TATAR COLONIES

Administrative territory	1970		1979 (incomplete)	
	Tatar population	Tatars in urban communities (and %)	Tatar population	Increase %
Chelyabinsk oblast'	216,809	151,527 (69.9)	219,744	+ 1.3
Sverdlovsk oblast'	176,029	134,288 (76.3)	179,347	+ 1.9
Moscow city	109,293	109,293(100.0)	—	—
Moscow oblast'	49,193	39,650 (80.5)	52,141	+ 6.0
Udmurt ASSR	87,193	69,171 (79.4)	99,141	+13.8
Kemerovo oblast'	69,313	59,450 (85.8)	64,821	– 6.5
Krasoyarsk krai	46,623	28,416 (60.9)	49,894	+ 7.0
Irkutsk oblast'	41,500	28,333 (68.7)	41,474	– 0.1
Leningrad	32,861	32,861(100.0)	—	—
Primorskiy krai	18,256	15,289 (86.3)	19,464	+ 6.6
Rostov oblast'	16,106	12,543 (77.9)	?	—
Altai krai	8,052	5,519 (86.5)	?	—
Khabarovsk krai	14,571	11,657 (80.0)	16,591	+13.9*
Amur oblast'	5,369	3,501 (65.2)	?	—
Arkhangel'sk oblast'	4,613	3,739 (81.0)	4,906	+ 6.4
Vladimir oblast'	8,747	7,873 (90.0)	9,202	+ 5.2
Ivanov oblast'	10,511	9,967 (94.8)	11,061	+ 5.2
Kaliningrad oblast'	2,752	2,288 (83.1)	?	—
Kalinin oblast'	4,712	3,877 (82.3)	?	—
Kamchatka oblast'	3,728	2,922 (78.4)	?	—
Kostroma oblast'	3,355	2,851 (85.0)	?	—

Magadan *oblsat'*	5,295	3,872 (73.1)	6,793	+ 28.3*
Murmansk *oblast'*	7,521	6,654 (88.5)	?	—
Sakhalin *oblast'*	11,153	8,691 (77.9)	?	—
Chita *oblast*	14,283	8,313 (52.2)	13,372	– 6.4
Tula *oblast'*	11,500	10,521 (91.5)	?	—
Yaroslav *oblast'*	7,211	6,792 (94.2)	?	—
Daghestan ASSR	5,770	4,832 (83.7)	?	—
Kabardino-Balkar ASSR	2,664	1,853 (69.5)	?	—
Karelian ASSR	2,603	1,707 (65.6)	?	—
Komi ASSR	11,908	9,307 (78.1)	17,837	+ 49.8*
North Ossetian ASSR	1,658	1,405 (34.7)	?	—
Tuva ASSR	822	670 (81.5)	?	—
Chechen-Ingush ASSR	5,571	4,335 (77.8)	?	—
Buryat ASSR	9,991	4,010 (40.1)	10,291	+ 3.0
Yakut ASSR	7,679	6,515 (84.8)	10,980	+ 43.0
Georgian SSR	3,102	2,320 (74.8)	?	—
Estonian SSR	2,205	1,168 (53.0)	?	—
Khanty-Mansii National *Okrug*			36,899	
Chukot National *Okrug*			1,995	
Yamalo-Nenets National *Okrug*			8,556	
Ust'-Orda Buryat National *Okrug*)			4,782	

*Eastern Siberia

There were other less important movements: in the direction of eastern Siberia (the Yakut ASSR, increase of 49%; Kamchatka, increase of 28%; and even Magadan, increase of 76%), and towards northern Russia (Murmansk, increase of 35%; the Komi ASSR, increase of 41%). The newly immigrated Tatars settled in cities as technicians and workers. These immigrants came principally from the original Tatar homeland — Perm' *oblast'*, Gor'kiy, the Mari ASSR, Kirov, the Tatar ASSR — and also from the central area of northern Russia: Vladimir and Ivanovo *oblasts*, Yaroslavl', Tula.

In their national territory, the Autonomous Tatar Republic, the Tatars are in a minority: 47.6% in 1979 compared to 49.1% in 1970 and 47.2% in 1959.

4. *Central Asia, Azerbaijan, and the Ukraine*, as illustrated in Table 9.i.6. In the Ukraine the most important Tatar colony is in the Donets region, and consists mainly of industrial workers who are being subjected to a process of russification which is already well advanced. In 1979, out of the 26,027 Tatars living in the Donets region, only 52.3% claimed Tatar as their first mother tongue.

Table 9.i.6.   TATAR COLONIES IN
CENTRAL ASIA, AZERBAIJAN AND THE UKRAINE

	1970 population		% of urban communities	1979 population	% increase 1970–9
	Total	Urban			
Uzbekistan	573,733	421,022	73.4	648,764	13.1
Kazakhstan	287,712	203,110	70.6	313,764	8.8
Tajikistan	70,803	63,536	89.7	79,529	13.0
Kirghizia	69,373	55,719	80.3	72,018	3.8
Turkmenistan	36,457	33,464	91.8	40,432	9.7
Azerbaijan	31,787	31,043	97.6	31,350	stable
Ukraine	76,212	67,368	88.4	90,542	18.8

15,078 Tatars (mainly Crimean) were listed in the Crimean region in 1979. They represent only 0.7% of the total population of the Crimea.

Ethnographic data. As described earlier, several historical, ethnic or geographical groups have been listed in the last three censuses under the denomination of Tatar. Some have been more or less completely assimilated by the Volga Tatars; others maintain a certain specific identity. The Crimean Tatars are dealt with separately.

The Siberian Tatars call themselves the *Top Ierli Khalk* (Older Inhabitants) to distinguish themselves from the new Volga Tatar immigrants. In pre-revolutionary Russian sources they were often called *Yasachnye Tatary* (Tatars paying the *yasak* or tribute). This denomination covers half a dozen autochthonous Turkic groups, all Sunni Muslims of the Hanafi school, who form scattered rural settlements in the vast territory of western Siberia, delimitated by the Ural mountains in the west, the Tavda river in the north, the Ishim steppe in the south, and the Baraba steppe in the east.

Siberian Tatars belonged in the past to the eastern part of the Ulus of Sibir, which in 1582 had been destroyed and annexed to the empire of Ivan the Terrible. They were converted to Islam in the fourteenth and fifteenth centuries. Geographically, the Siberian Tatars are divided into five main groups, each speaking its own dialect.

— *The Tiumen' and the Tobol Tatars*, self-denomination "Tiumenli" and "Tobolik". In 1926, there were 22,636 Tiumen' Tatars and 32,102 Tobol Tatars established in the districts of Baikalovsk, Volzhansk, Vagaisk, Dubrovinsk, Tobol'sk, Tiumen', Yalutorov and Yarkov of the Tiumen' and Kurgan *oblasts* (along the valleys of the rivers Tobol, Tura, Tavda, Iset, Pyshma, Achiry, Noska and Laima).

— *The Tara Tatars*, self-denomination Tarlyk, a smaller group in the valleys of the Irtysh and Tara, in the district of Tara of the Omsk *oblast'*. In 1926 there were 11,517 Tara Tatars.

— *Baraba Tatars*, self-denomination Baraba, located farther to the southeast, along the valley of the river Om' and its tributaries and in the steppe of Baraba, in the districts of Barabinsk, Kuibyshev, Chanov, Kargatsk, Khyshtov and Severnyi *oblast'* of Novosibirsk. In 1926, the census listed 7,528 Baraba Tatars.

— *Tomsk Tatars*, around the city of Tomsk. In 1926, they were not listed separately. They numbered probably 2,000–3,000.

— *Bukharlyks*, originally fifteenth- and sixteenth-century fur merchant colonies from Central Asia in western Siberia. With time, they blended with the autochthonous Siberian Tatars and adopted their spoken dialects. In the 1926 census, they were listed as an ethnic group composed of 11,659 individuals.

The Volga Tatars began to settle on the territory populated by the Siberian Tatars in the eighteenth century, but in spite of the similarity of their spoken dialects, the two groups did not mix until the Revolution and were treated differently by the Russian administration. The *Inorodtsy* or "foreign" nationalities assimilated the Siberian Tatars, and the Russian peasants assimilated the Volga Tatars. Until the Revolution, the Siberian Tatars maintained their tribal and clan structure that the Volga Tatars had lost centuries earlier.

Nowadays, the Siberian Tatars number about 150,000. They represent rural communities, and they still do not mix much with the Volga Tatars (basically city-dwellers in western Siberia) or with the Russians.

The second ethnic group is that of the *Astrakhan Tatars*, whose self-denomination is *Karagashly*. Other denominations include "Tatars of Yurt" and "Tatars of Kundorov". The fifteenth- and sixteenth-century forefathers of the Astrakhan Tatars founded the Khanate of Astrakhan and mixed with the Nogais, whom they assimilated. They speak and write the same language as the Kazan Tatars but have different historical and cultural traditions. The 1926 census listed them as a separate ethnic group formed of 43,000 individuals. Today there is nothing to distinguish them from the Volga Tatars.

The *Kasymov Tatars* comprise the third group. They are an historical group constituted in the fifteenth century by refugees from the Kazan Khanate who settled in the region of Riazan' under the command of a junior Chingissid, Khan Kasym. The Khans of Kasymov became vassals of the Moscow grand prince. The capital of this small Khanate was called Kasymov. Isolated among non-Muslims, Kasymov Tatars preserve their identity thanks to their firm attachment to their religion. The Russian census of 1897 listed them separately; at the time there were 7,399 of them. Neither the 1926 census nor the later ones maintained their separate listing. In 1970, the total number of the Tatars in the Riazan' *oblast'* was 4,000.

The fourth group is composed of Lithuanian Tatars, called also Polish and Belorussian Tatars. They are descendants of a small Nogai Horde to whom the Grand Duke Vitautas applied for assistance in his struggle against the Teutonic Order. After they had won a victory in the battle of Grünwald (1410) the Lithuanian ruler invited the Horde to settle in Lithuania and endowed its members with the status of nobility. The new immigrants married local women (Lithuanian, Polish or Belorussian), and the use of their Turkic language was rapidly abandoned and replaced by local languages. Nevertheless, they remained faithful to Islam. Before the Revolution, the Lithuanian Muslims were considered by other Muslims of Russia as models of good education and religiousness.

The majority of Lithuanian Tatars lived in Poland and spoke Polish. Some of them migrated to the United States, and they constitute today the most important Tatar community of America (around 2,000 families). The Polish Tatar mosque in Brooklyn is used by other Muslims from the Soviet Union. The Lithuanian Tatars living in the Soviet Union represent a small community speaking Belorussian and Lithuanian. Their total number in the Soviet Union probably does not exceed 5,000.

The *Volga Tatars* are the fifth ethnic group. The Volga Tatar nation is not yet completely consolidated: it is divided into several of its own ethnic groups, differing from each other by their historical, ethnic and even religious background:

1. *The Volga Tatars* proper, also called the Kazan Tatars. Before the Revolution they called themselves "Turks" and in some cases even Bulgars. They are descendants of the Volga Bulgars, of turkicised Eastern Finns and of the Golden Horde Turkic tribes. The ethnic type of the Volga Tatar varies from the purely Finnic (blond with blue eyes) to the mongoloid type close to the Kazakh. They speak a unique language with no secondary dialects. The Volga Tatars are an old sedentary nation of peasants and merchants and have completely lost their tribal and clanic structure.

2. *The Mishars*, who are turkicised Eastern Finns (Meshchera and Mordvinians). They were converted to Islam at the time of the Bulgar kingdom and of the Golden Horde but have nevertheless preserved their Finnic ethnic type and speak a special (western) dialect of the Kazan Tatars. The Mishars differ from the Volga Tatars (proper) by the fact that they are essentially a peasant community. Their home territory is between the Oka and the Volga, where they form purely Mishar villages or groups of villages (Gor'kiy, Ul'ianovsk, Penza, Saratov, Tambov *oblast'*, southern region of the Tatar ASSR, the Chuvash ASSR and the Mordvinian ASSR). Isolated Mishar villages are also found in the Kuibyshev and Sverdlovsk *oblasts* and in the Bashkir ASSR, the inhabitants of which are called Meshcheriaks. In 1912 the Mishars numbered some 200,000. They are distinctly aware of forming a separate ethnic group. They have been listed as Tatars in the 1926, 1959, 1970 and 1979 censuses.

3. *The Teptiars*, Volga Tatars who after the Russian conquest of Kazan in 1552 migrated eastward and settled as peasants among the Bashkirs to whom they paid a tribute inscribed in a special register (in Tatar *tepter*,

from the Persian *defter*), hence their name. Despite many centuries of association with the Bashkirs, the Teptiars have preserved their Tatar identity. They speak a special dialect, half-way between Kazan Tatar and Bashkir. Because of their peculiar historical tradition and because they are basically a peasant community, they have not been completely assimilated either by the Bashkirs or by the Tatars living in Bashkiria. In 1912, the Teptiars numbered some 300,000 individuals. In the 1926, 1959, 1970 and 1979 censuses, they have been listed as Tatars.

4. *The Kryashens*, Volga Tatars, who converted to Orthodox Christianity, mainly during two campaigns. In the second half of the sixteenth century, following the conquest of the Kazan Khanate, a relatively large number of Muslim Tatars and animist Turks or Finns were converted. Those early converts were called "old converts" (in Russian *Starokryasheny*; in Tatar *Taze Kryash* or Pure Kryashens). For their benefit the Gospels, the Orthodox religious books and the liturgy were translated into Tatar (in Cyrillic script). They became authentic Christians but were not russified, and their community survived until the Revolution. The *Starokryashens* speak a special dialect, different from Tatar, with very few Arabic and Persian words.

In the first half of the eighteenth century, during the reign of the Tsarina Anna, a large number of Muslim Tatars were forced to convert. These so-called "new converts" (in Russian *Novo-kryasheny*; in Tatar *Yangi Kryash*) remained crypto-Muslims in the majority and after 1905 reverted to Islam.

Both Kryashen communities were considered till 1928 as a separate nationality. In the 1926 census they were listed as such, and numbered 101,477. They had their own written language in Cyrillic while the Tatars used Arabic script. A newspaper in Kryashen appeared in Kazan in 1927–8, but their press disappeared after 1929.

Kryashens are basically a peasant community, living in their own Christian villages. Since 1928 they have been subjected to a steady process of assimilation by both Tatars and Russians. They are closer to the Russians than to the Tatars, and mixed marriages with Russians are frequent. At most, the present population amounts to 250,000.

Language and the problem of assimilation. The territory of the Middle Volga has been an Islamic bastion since the ninth century. The ancestors of the Volga Tatars attained a high level of urban civilisation in the tenth, eleventh and twelfth centuries, and their culture was not destroyed either by the Mongol invasion of the thirteenth century or by the Russian conquest of the sixteenth. In the nineteenth century the Tatar cities of Kazan, Orenburg, Troitsk, and Astrakhan ranked among the greatest cultural centres of the Islamic world.

This background explains the Tatar community's exceptional capacity for survival. Not only has it resisted pressure over four centuries aimed at their assimilation by the Russians, but they even succeeded in converting to Islam and Tatarising some Eastern Finns (Udmurts, Maris, Mordvinians) and Christian Turks (Chuvash). The exact number of these conversions is not known but it is certainly considerable. This process was especially strong between 1905 and 1928 (it is impossible to evaluate it statistically because conversion to Islam was followed by immediate Tatarisation). At the same time, the Tatars are the only Muslim Turkic nationality which, because of its diaspora, is being linguistically assimilated by the Russians. The process started after 1929 and is still going on.

In 1935 the Tatar press was still the most important Muslim press in the Soviet Union. Altogether 208 Tatar newspapers were published: 129 in the Tatar Republic and 79 in the diaspora (37 in Bashkiria, 10 in other territories of the Middle and Lower Volga, 22 in the Urals, 5 in Siberia, 2 in Ukraine, 1 in Leningrad, 1 in Moscow, and 1 in Baku). Kazan Tatar was at the time an authentic *lingua franca* of Soviet Islam. After 1935 the Tatar language rapidly lost its position; the number of Tatar newspapers published outside the Tatar Republic dropped to 44 in 1936, to 41 in 1938, and to 38 in 1956. In 1970 there remained only three Tatar newspapers outside the Tatar and the Bashkir Republics (in the Kirov, Kuibyshev and Cheliabinsk *oblasts*). In the Tatar ASSR in 1970, there were 38 newspapers in Tatar, compared to 35 in Russian, 4 in Chuvash, and 1 in Udmurt. There are no Tatar schools outside the Tatar and Bashkir Republics.

In the middle-lower Volga and Ural homeland, the Tatars are maintaining the use of their language. In this area, the proportion of those who claim Tatar as their native language remains exceptionally high (above 90%).

In some areas, where the Tatars constitute only small scattered urban colonies, their linguistic assimilation is well advanced. With more than 30% of the Tatars claiming Russian as their true mother tongue, their disappearance in a not too distant future may be predicted, as shown in Table 9.i.8.

Table 9.i.7.   TATARS IN MIDDLE VOLGA AND URAL AREAS
CLAIMING TATAR AS THEIR NATIVE LANGUAGE 1959–70 (%)

	1959	1970	Difference 1959–70	1979	Difference 1970–9
Gorkiy *oblast'*	93.7	90.5	– 3.2	88.8	– 1.7
Kirov *oblast'*	93.7	91.7	– 2.0	88.7	– 3.0
Mari ASSR	96.4	93.6	– 2.8	93.0	– 0.6
Mordvinian ASSR	99.2	97.1	– 2.1	96.5	– 0.6
Chuvash ASSR	97.5	95.9	– 1.6	93.5	– 2.4
Astrakhan *oblast'*	96.3	94.6	– 1.7	93.8	– 0.8
Penza *oblast'*	98.0	97.3	– 0.7	96.8	– 0.5
Ul'ianovsk *oblast'*	98.0	96.9	– 1.1	94.9	– 2.0
Tatar ASSR	98.9	98.5	– 0.4	99.9	+ 1.4
Kurgan *oblast'*	94.2	91.8	– 2.4	89.1	– 2.7
Orenburg *oblast'*	95.2	92.2	– 3.0	89.4	– 3.0
Tiumen' *oblast'*	96.2	92.0	– 4.2	88.2	– 3.8
Bashkir ASSR	97.6	96.3	– 1.3	94.2	– 2.1
Udmurt ASSR	94.7	90.4	– 4.3	86.9	– 3.5

Table 9.i.8.   TATARS IN SCATTERED URBAN COLONIES
CLAIMING TATAR AS THEIR NATIVE LANGUAGE (%)
(1979 figures incomplete)

	1959	1970	1979	Difference 1959–70	Difference 1970–9
Komi ASSR	82.7	69.8	69.1	– 12.9	– 0.7
Yaroslav *oblast'*	77.2	66.4	43.9	– 10.8	– 22.5
Rostov *oblast'*	74.3	67.2		– 7.1	
Chita *oblast'*	65.1	61.4	54.9	– 3.7	– 6.5
Primor'e *krai*	63.8	44.9	45.0	– 18.9	+ 0.1
Khabarovsk *krai*	59.1	46.7	44.0	– 12.4	– 2.7
Kamchatka *oblast'*	59.9	55.0		– 4.9	
Magadan *oblast'*	66.2	58.6	52.1	– 7.6	– 6.5
Sakhalin *oblast'*	60.1	53.3		– 6.8	

The process of assimilation is especially rapid in the industrial areas, as
shown in Table 9.i.9.

It is noteworthy that only in two areas was there a percentage increase
between 1959 and 1970 of Tatars claiming the Tatar language as their
native tongue; these areas are the Daghestan and the Chechen-Ingush
ASSRs, in both of which anti-Russian xenophobia is exceptionally strong.

Table 9.i.9.   TATARS IN INDUSTRIAL AREAS CLAIMING TATAR
AS THEIR NATIVE LANGUAGE
(*1979 figures incomplete*)

	1959	1970	1979	Difference 1959–70	Difference 1970–9
Moscow city	77.7	67.2		– 12.5	
Sverdlovsk *oblast'*	87.2	76.6	73.1	– 10.6	– 3.5
Tula *oblast'*	83.1	70.6		– 12.5	
Cheliabinsk *oblast'*	90.5	82.2	77.7	– 8.3	– 4.5
Kemerovo *oblast'*	85.8	73.3	70.2	– 12.5	– 3.1
Irkutsk *krai*	81.3	70.6	62.8	– 10.7	– 7.8

In Daghestan the percentage grew from 85.7% in 1959 to 87.6% in 1970 (+ 1.9%) and in the Chechen-Ingush Republic from 77.2% to 78.0% (+ 0.8%).

The Tatars who lose the use of their native tongue are russified (and not assimilated through the use of some other Turkic language). This is true of Central Asia as well as of all other Turkic areas of the Soviet Union. Table 9.i.10 lists percentages of Tatars claiming other languages than Tatar as their native language.

Table 9.i.10.   LINGUISTICALLY ASSIMILATED TATARS, 1970–9

	Russian		Other languages (mainly Turkic)	
	1970	1979	1970	1979
Uzbekistan	8.4	12.4	1.7	4.7
Kazakhstan	15.8	21.9	2.5	2.8
Azerbaijan	23.8	32.4	1.9	1.7
Kirghizia	11.8	17.6	1.4	1.5
Tajikistan	11.2	16.9	2.3	1.2
Turkmenistan	15.8	19.6	1.6	0.4
Baskhir ASSR	3.3	5.4	0.4	0.4
Chuvash ASSR	4.0	6.3	0.2	0.2

Religious data. After four centuries of pressure aimed at eradicating Islam, which constitutes the very basis of their society, the Volga Tatars have developed an extraordinary capacity for surviving as Muslims. The response of the Tatar intellectual élite to the final effort of Tsarist Russia (during the reign of Alexander III) to convert them to Christianity was the modernist *Jadid* movement. This was a most interesting attempt made by the Muslim religious leaders to sponsor both religion and technical progress and to secure for Islam a place in the modern world. Before the 1917 Revolution, the Volga Tatars were among the most advanced members of the *Dar ul-Islam* in the field of education and Islamic theology. This exceptionally brilliant liberal Islam survived the first years of the Soviet regime and, although sorely tried by the purges of the 1930s, it left an enduring heritage.

Today the Tatars remain — at least in their original homeland of the middle Volga and Urals — deeply attached to Islam. In the 1970s, according to various surveys, 50% of them practised their religion in one way or another, in spite of the proportion of firm believers being only 20%. Islam among the Tatars remains more liberal and more intellectual than in Central Asia or the Caucasus. However, religion is fast disappearing among the Tatar urban diaspora in its purely Slavic environment.

Tatar official Islam is controlled by the Muslim Spiritual Board of Ufa, dominated by Volga Tatars: Chairman, the Mufti Tolgat Taziev (nominated in 1980); Vice-Chairman, Faiz ur-Rahman Sattar(ov). The language is Kazan Tatar. The board has a modest publishing activity (one edition of the Quran has been published since the Second World War) but has no *medressehs* under its jurisdiction. The number of working mosques seems considerable; there are probably several hundred, but these are mainly small village mosques. More important "cathedral" mosques exist (in 1980) in Moscow, Leningrad, Rostov, Kazan (one), Ufa (one), Gor'kiy, Orenburg, Cheliabinsk, Astrakhan, Saratov, Omsk, Chistopol', Izhevsk, Ishimbai, Novosibirsk, Bugul'ma, Irkutsk, Magnitogorsk, Kuibyshev, Tatarsk (Novosibirsk *oblast'*), Kargala (Orenburg *oblast'*), Zelenodol'sk (Tatar ASSR), Starye Urgary (Tatar ASSR), Sterlitamak (Bashkir ASSR), Zagitiak (Bashkir ASSR) and the village of Oktiabr'skii (Bashkir ASSR). Volga Tatars still provide a relatively high percentage of registered clerics and of students attending the two Central Asian *medressehs*.

Parallel Islam exercises no deep influence among the Tatars, at least in our times. The Naqshbandi order, which played an important part among them before the Revolution, seems to have disappeared after 1924.

Anti-religious literature is not greatly developed. Between 1948 and 1970, 65 anti-religious books and pamphlets were published in the Tatar language, which places the Tatars in seventh place, after the Uzbeks (177 books), the Daghestanis (140), the Kazakhs (126), the Azeris (96), the Tajiks (70), and the Kirghiz (69).

Nationalism and national awareness. A distinction must be made between the Tatar masses, both urban and rural, and the numerous Tatar intelligentsia. The Tatar workers, especially in the small colonies of the diaspora, are isolated in a purely Russian milieu where they are steadily losing their identity, their russification already well advanced. Among the rural masses living in their original Middle Volga homeland, the religious awareness ("we are Muslims") still seems stronger than the awareness of belonging to a modern Tatar nation.

The situation of the Tatar intelligentsia is more complicated. Before the Revolution they had several possible identities: purely religious or pan-Islamic; pan-Turkic ("we are Turks"); or limited, purely Tatar. Between 1900 and 1917, Tatar political life was dominated by the conflict between the upholders of Turkism (the *Türkchüler*) and those of Tatarism (the *Tatarchylar*), also called the localists (*Toprakchylar*).

During the first ten years of the Soviet regime, pan-Turkic or pan-Islamic identity gained the upper hand and was accepted as the basis of Tatar nationalism by the Tatar National Communists (Sultan Galiev and his comrades). During this period, Tatars appeared as the leaders of Soviet Islam, and the Volga Tatar language was its *lingua franca*. Up till 1930 newspapers in Tatar appeared all over the Soviet Union. However, Tatar National Communism was physically liquidated during the bloody purges of the 1930s, and supra-national pan-Turkic or pan-Islamic identity was banned as the worst kind of "bourgeois nationalism".

The situation today may be summarised as follows:

1. There is no sub-national, tribal or clan awareness among the Tatars.

2. The various small surviving ethnic groups, such as the Mishars and Siberian Tatars, are rapidly losing their sense of specificity.

3. The limited, purely Tatar identity is the only officially recognised one.

4. The supra-national pan-Turkic or pan-Islamic identity is officially condemned as a dangerous deviation. However, Tatar intellectuals seem to understand that their nation, isolated among Russians, can survive only by identifying itself with other Muslim Turks of the Soviet Union.

5. During a few centuries, the Tatars had full access to Russian culture. Nowadays they are the most westernised and russified of all Soviet Muslims. In 1979 the percentage of Tatars fluent in Russian as their second language was 69%, which places them ahead not only of all other Muslims but also of the Ukrainians (49.8%), Belorussians (49.0%), Armenians (38.6%) and Georgians (26.7%). Nevertheless, the Tatar

intelligentsia is the most attached to its traditional past. Since 1964, the Tatars are ahead of all other Soviet Muslims in the rehabilitation of their literature and political history.

6. Islam, even reduced to a minimal practice, remains the basis of the Tatar identity. Muslim Tatars feel themselves closer to a Central Asian Muslim than to a Kryashen (a Tatar convert to Orthodoxy).

7. Besides the Crimean Tatars and the Meskhetian Turks, only the Volga Tatars of all the Muslim nationalities have produced a *samizdat* (published underground) literature.

8. Tatar nationalism is the most difficult one to detect and analyse. It is less outspoken, more sophisticated, and centred for the time being around the problem of rehabilitating the *Jadid* movement of the late nineteenth century.

(ii) THE CRIMEAN TATARS

From its beginning the Crimean ASSR, founded in October 1921, had a mixed population. In 1923, out of a total of 623,000 inhabitants, there were 306,000 Russians and Ukrainians, 150,000 Tatars (25% of the total population), 50,000 Jews, 40,000 Germans, 12,000 Armenians and 12,000 Bulgarians. According to *samizdat*, the deportation of the Tatar population to Central Asia in 1944 involved some 238,000 individuals. On 30 November 1945, a year after the deportation, the Crimean ASSR was officially abolished and the territory renamed the Crimean region (*oblast'*) of the RSFSR. On 19 February 1954 it was removed from the RSFSR and became part of the Ukrainian SSR.

The present legal status of the Crimean Tatars is difficult to analyse. Officially, they have been cleared of the accusation of treason (decree of the Presidium of the Supreme Soviet of 9 September 1967) and have a kind of semi-legal existence. A newspaper in Crimean Tatar, *Lenin Bayraghy* ('Lenin's Flag', formerly *Stalin Bayraghy:*), is published in Tashkent; in the region of Dzhizak (Uzbek SSR) the Tatars enjoy a very modest cultural autonomy (Tatar language schools and a Tatar theatre). But although partly rehabilitated, the Crimean Tatars were listed in the 1970 and 1979 censuses together with the Volga Tatars, and despite their efforts are not permitted to resettle in the Crimea, which is now densely occupied by Russians and Ukrainians.

The present location of the Crimean Tatars are difficult to establish with precision. Only an insignificant number of Tatars have been allowed to return to the Crimea, 15,087 according to the 1979 census, but this figure could include a certain number of Volga Tatars. An unknown number live in Moscow, but the bulk of the population are in Uzbekistan and Kirghizia. According to Abdulhamidoglu, there were 406,000 Crimean Tatars in these two republics in the 1970s, distributed as follows:

Uzbekistan	
Tashkent city	64,000
Tashkent *oblast'*	139,000
Samarkand *oblast'*	70,000
Andizhan *oblast'*	54,000
Ferghana *oblast'*	51,000
Kirghizia	
Osh *oblast'*	38,000

In view of the terrible conditions of the deportation and the first years that the Crimean Tatars spent in Central Asia, a large number of them died, so that the figures above seem exaggerated.

Unlike the Volga Tatars, the Crimean Tatars are not assimilated by the Russians or by the native Muslims. They prefer marriage within their own community. Their struggle for rehabilitation and the right to return to the Crimea is a solitary one. It does not seem that they have received, or will receive, any serious backing from the Uzbeks among whom they live.

(iii) THE BASHKIRS

The Bashkirs are Sunni Muslims of the Hanafi school. There is a small Bashkir group, the Nagaibaks (*ca.* 12,000 in 1926) living in the district of Verkhneural'sk, who are Orthodox Christians, converted in the eighteenth century. Today they have been almost entirely assimilated by the Muslim Bashkirs. The Bashkir ASSR was founded on 23 March 1919; in 1979 it had a territory of 143,600 square km. Its population in 1979 was 3,848,000 (0.8% more than in 1970). Its urban population was 57% (48.2% in 1970). The capital is Ufa, which had a population in 1979 of 969,000 (771,000 in 1970 and 547,000 in 1959).

Demography. The total number of Bashkirs has been as follows at different times during the twentieth century:

1926   983,000
1939   842,000
1959   989,000
1970   1,239,681 (25% up from 1959)
1979   1,371,452 (19.6% up from 1970)

Between 1926 and 1970, the Bashkirs were subjected to a steady process of linguistic assimilation by the Volga Tatars, whose language they used as a literary and even as a spoken language. Between 1970 and 1979, the relatively slow increase of the Bashkirs (one of the slowest growths of all Muslim peoples except the Volga Tatars) may be explained not by any dramatic decrease of their natural fertility rate but by the assimilation of the Bashkir diaspora colonies either by other Muslim Turks or by the Russians (especially in the case of city-dwellers).

According to the incomplete 1979 census figures, 1,290,994 (or 94.2%) Bashkirs lived in the RSFSR, and some 80,000 lived in Central

Table 9.iii.1.   BASKHIR TERRITORIAL DISTRIBUTION IN
THE SOVIET UNION, 1970–9
(1979 incomplete)

	Population (and %)		Population and %	
Bashkir ASSR	892,248	(72.0)	935,880	(68.2)
Cheliabinsk *oblast'*	117,537	(9.5)	133,682	(9.7)
Perm' *oblast'*	47,812	(3.9)	48,752	(3.5)
Orenburg *oblast'*	37,501	(3.0)	43,269	(3.1)
Sverdlovsk *oblast'*	21,428	(1.7)	30,051	(2.2)
Kurgan *oblast'*	17,525	(1.4)	17,664	(1.3)
Kuibyshev *oblast'*	5,800	(0.5)		
Kemerovo *oblast'*	3,979	(0.3)		
Kazakhstan SSR	21,442	(1.7)		
Uzbekistan SSR	20,761	(1.7)		
Tajikistan SSR	4,842	(0.4)		
Kirghizia SSR	3,250	(0.3)		
Ukraine SSR	3,672	(0.3)		
Tatar ASSR	2,888	(0.3)		
Udmurt ASSR	2,005	(0.2)		

Asia and the Ukraine. It seems that between 1970 and 1979 there was, and maybe there still is, a significant out-migration of Bashkirs to Central Asia. Of the total Bashkir population in 1970 of 1,239,681, those in the RSFSR numbered 1,180,913 (95.3%).

The greater part of the Bashkir people live in their original homeland in the southern Urals, but only 68% live in their national territory (the Bashkir ASSR). Those Bashkirs who live in Cheliabinsk, Perm', Orenburg, Sverdlovsk, Kurgan and Kemerovo represent minorities in a territory heavily dominated by the Russians.

The Bashkirs as a whole are a peasant community; in 1970, 73.4% were rural-dwellers. In Bashkiria and neighbouring regions the percentage of rural-dwellers is as great or even greater. In the Bashkir ASSR, 80.3% are rural-dwellers; in Cheliabinsk *oblast'*, 66.3%; in Perm', 77%; in Orenburg, 76.7%; in Kurgan, 95%; and in Kuibyshev, 63%. As a rule, the peasant colonies are better able to preserve their national identity and resist assimilation by the Russians.

In the Sverdlovsk *oblast'* and in Central Asia, the Bashkirs essentially constitute urban colonies of industrial workers, who are *per se* more vulnerable to assimilation by the Russians. In these areas the number of rural-dwellers is considerably less. According to 1970 figures, in the Sverdlovsk *oblast'* 15.5% are rural-dwellers; in Kazakhstan, 38.8%; in Uzbekistan, 30.5%; and in Kirghizia, 28.8%.

In 1970, in the Bashkir ASSR, the Bashkirs represented only 23.4% of the total population (24.3% in 1979). Together with the Volga Tatars, they represented 48.1% of the total population in 1970, and 48.9% in 1979. Together, the three Turkic nationalities (Bashkirs, Tatars and the non-Muslim Chuvash) numbered 1,963,393 in 1970, or 51.4% of the population of the republic, and 1,998,670, or 52%, in 1979.

The Russians (71.1%), the Jews (98.6%), the Germans (69.9%), the Ukrainians (65.4%), the Belorussians (62.9%), and to a lesser degree the Tatars (56.7%) are mainly city-dwellers. The Bashkirs (19.7%), the Udmurts (10.5%), the Maris (14.4%), the Chuvash (22.5%) and to a less degree the Mordvinians (42.9%) are basically rural communities (1970 figures). In 1970 the various non-Muslim communities represented 67.6% of the urban population of the Bashkir Republic. The capital, Ufa, in particular remains a purely Russian town.

Ethnographic data. The Bashkirs were regarded before the Russian Revolution as a simple ethnic group of Tatars speaking several dialects, all of them slightly different from the Volga Tatars. The Bashkir nation was created in 1923 (when Bashkir became a literary language), and the nation is still not entirely consolidated.

The ancestors of the northern and western Bashkirs were Ugrian or Finnic tribes, turkified and Islamised during the period of the Golden

Table 9.iii.2.   ETHNIC COMPOSITION OF POPULATION,
BASHKIR ASSR, 1959–70

	1959 population (and % of total)		1970 population (and % of total)		increase (%) 1959–70
Total population	3,340,267		3,818,075		14.3
Bashkirs	737,711	(22.1)	892,258	(23.4)	20.9
Tatars	768,566	(23.0)	944,507	(24.7)	22.9
Total Muslims	1,506,277	(45.1)	1,836,755	(48.1)	21.9
Russians	1,416,805	(42.4)	1,546,304	(40.5)	9.1
Chuvash	109,970	(3.3)	126,638	(3.3)	15.1
Maris	93,902	(2.8)	109,638	(2.9)	16.7
Ukrainians	83,594	(2.5)	76,005	(2.0)	− 9.1
Mordvinians	43,582	(1.3)	40,745	(1.1)	− 6.5
Udmurts	25,388	(0.8)	27,918	(0.7)	9.9
Others (Belorussians, Jews, Germans)	60,749	(1.8)	54,072	(1.4)	− 11.0

*The population decrease of the Ukrainians and the Mordvinians, as well as the slow increase of the Udmurts, may be explained by the assimilation of these communities by the Russians and not by any migration out of the Bashkir ASSR.

Horde and the Khanate of Kazan. They are old sedentaries who have lost all memory of their clan-tribal origin. The southern and eastern Bashkirs are descendants of Turkic nomadic tribes closely related to the Kazakhs and the Nogais. They have preserved the memory of their tribal structure. The major southern Bashkir tribes are the same as are found among the Nogais, the Kazakhs and the Karakalpaks: Nayman, Ktay, Mangyt, Zilair (Jalair), Kypchak, and Tabyn. The sense of kinship and loyalty to kinsmen is still felt — especially among the Bashkir intelligentsia.

Language and assimilation. As already mentioned, there are only slight phonetic differences between the Bashkir dialects and those of the Volga Tatars. The Bashkir literary language was created in 1923, based on a southeastern (Kuvakan) dialect which is the most different from the Volga Tatar and most similar to Kazakh. However, the literary language remains semi-literary; many Bashkirs still use Volga Tatar as their written language.

Of all the Turkic Muslim peoples in the Soviet Union, the Bashkirs are also the least attached to their spoken national language, probably because it is still thought of as a simple Tatar dialect. Because of its greater sophistication and its similarity to Bashkir, Volga Tatar is still the native language of almost 30% of the Bashkirs, as shown in Table 9.iii.3.

Table 9.iii.3.   NATIVE LANGUAGES OF BASHKIRS, 1959–79

	1959	1970	1979 (incomplete)
Total Bashkirs	989,040	1,239,681	1,371,452
Language			
Bashkir	612,169 (61.9%)	820,390 (66.2%)	918,570 (67.0%)
Tatar	350,713 (35.4)	362,974 (29.3)	452,430 (33.0)
Russian	26,158 (2.6)	56,317 (4.5)	

Since the 1960s, the proportion of Bashkirs who declared Tatar to be their native language has decreased very slowly, while the proportionate increase of russified Bashkirs remained insignificant.

The detailed figures of the 1979 census show a rather paradoxical situation: there are more "tatarised" Bashkirs in their national republic than abroad, which demonstrates the artificial character of the Bashkir nation: 32.9% Tatar-speaking Bashkirs in the Bashkir ASSR, compared to 27% in the RSFSR, and 26% in the Soviet Union as a whole. Another apparently paradoxical picture is that the proportion of Bashkirs who declared Tatar as their native language is higher among peasants than among city-dwellers.

Outside the Bashkir ASSR, the Bashkir colonies are deprived of national schools and of a press in their own language and are therefore subjected to a steady assimilation process by the Russians, by the Tatars and to a less degree, in Central Asia, by the locally dominant Turkic nationalities. As a rule, the urban elements (especially the industrial workers) are being steadily russified. The Tatar influence on the country dwellers is stronger in the area west of the Urals (Perm') and weaker in the area south and east of the Urals (Orenburg, Kurgan, Cheliabinsk).

The relative indifference of the Bashkirs towards their own official language is illustrated by the situation of the periodical press in the Bashkir ASSR. Of the three newspapers published in Ufa in 1970, the Bashkir newspaper distributed 68,000 copies, the Tatar 108,000 copies, and the Russian 192,000 copies. Out of the 112 district newspapers published in the republic, only 21 were in Bashkir, while 30 were in Tatar, 55 in Russian, 2 in Chuvash, 2 in Mari and 2 in Udmurt.

Religious data. The Bashkirs were not subjected to the same missionary Christian pressure as the Volga Tatars. Only a relatively short and unsuccessful attempt was made by the Orthodox Church in the early eighteenth century to convert the Bashkirs to Christianity; this produced the small group of Nagaibaks. As a consequence, Bashkir Islam is less defensive and less militant than Tatar Islam. It is also less deeply rooted, especially among the formerly nomadic southeastern Bashkirs.

Table 9.iii.4.   ASSIMILATION OF BASHKIR COLONIES ABROAD, 1970–9 (%)

	Speaking Bashkir		Speaking Russian		Speaking Tatar		Speaking another Turkic language
	1970	1979	1970	1979	1970	1979	
Cheliabinsk *oblast'*	91.1	88.2	8.0	10.9	0.9	0.9	—
Sverdlovsk *oblast'*	63.3	63.5	26.6	28.0	10.1	8.5	—
Perm' *oblast'*	22.1	29.2	4.4	7.9	73.5	62.9	—
Orenburg *oblast'*	93.1	90.3	5.7	8.6	1.2	1.2	—
Kurgan *oblat'*	96.6	96.1	3.0	3.5	0.4	0.4	—
Kuibyshev *oblast'*	88.4		9.0		2.6		—
Kazakhstan SSR	74.5		17.7		6.2		—
Uzbekistan SSR	75.3		13.9		8.6		—
Kirghizia SSR	69.1		17.3		12.5		—

Ufa, the capital of Bashkiria, has been the centre of religious life for European Russian Muslims since the eighteenth century. Several *medressehs*, some of them famous throughout the entire Muslim world, as well as several Muslim periodicals are located there. Compared to the more advanced modernist Tatar centres such as Kazan, Orenburg and Troitsk, Ufa was a bastion of moderate conservatism.

The Ufa *muftiat*, created by Catherine II, was reestablished in 1943. Today Ufa is the seat of the Muslim Spiritual Board for European Russia and Siberia. Official Islam seems to be well represented by a relatively important number of working mosques: possibly more than 100 in the territory of the Bashkir ASSR. However, it is impossible to ascertain the nationality of the official clerics (including that of Mufti Abdul Bari Isaev, replaced in 1980 by T.S. Taziev); they may be Tatars as well as Bashkirs.

Sufi Islam was only weakly represented before the Russian Revolution by the Tatar Naqshbandis. We do not know if the new wave of

Sufism which originated in Kazakhstan reached Bashkiria after World War II.

The level of religiousness of the Bashkirs remains relatively low when compared to the Tatars. Anti-religious propaganda in Bashkiria is not very active. Between 1948 and 1975, 24 anti-Islamic books and pamphlets were published in Bashkir in Ufa (compared to 65 in Tatar and 177 in Uzbek).

Nationalism and national awareness. Bashkir national identity is difficult to describe, but it is obvious that even today, more than half a century after the official creation of a socialist Bashkir nation, the Bashkirs have not acquired a modern Soviet awareness of being a specific Bashkir nation. In the past they never organized themselves in a political formation higher than a tribe; the sub-national, religious (Islamic) or ethnic (pan-Turkic) awareness was never developed among the Bashkirs and today may have disappeared completely.

There is no historical Bashkir identity. Before the Russian conquest, the Bashkirs were divided between three main Muslim poles of attraction. The western Bashkirs belonged to the Khanate of Kazan and were subjected to a strong Tatar influence. The eastern Bashkirs belonged to the Khanate of Sibir and later (in the seventeenth century) depended on the Kazakh hordes; they feel closer to the Central Asian nomads. The southern Bashkir tribes were part of the Great Nogai Horde and have also maintained a sense of kinship with Central Asian nomads.

Before the Russian Revolution, a specific Bashkir culture simply did not exist. Their oral literature (epic songs such as *Idiku*) is the same as that of the Tatars, and Bashkir writers used literary Tatar (e.g. Majid Gafuri, who is regarded as the "founder of Bashkir literature"). Also, before the Revolution, most Bashkir intellectuals defined themselves simply as Tatars.

The main difference between the Bashkirs and the Tatars is social and economic rather than political: the Bashkir peasantry was liberated from serfdom in the eighteenth century. The Bashkirs never developed a merchant bourgeoisie comparable to that of the Tatars. The former tribal nobility preserved a certain influence until the Revolution, especially in southeastern Bashkiria.

In the seventeenth and eighteenth centuries the Bashkirs, because they had preserved their tribal structure, opposed Russian occupation with a fierce resistance that was almost uninterrupted from 1662 to 1774. The Bashkirs took an active part in all peasant revolts of eastern Russia: such as those of Stefan Razin and Pugachev (whose best lieutenant, Salavat Yulaev, was a Bashkir). No other Turkic Muslim nationality can boast of a comparable resistance to the Russians. This heroic resistance is part of the national pride of the Bashkirs and probably the best bond of Bashkir national awareness (at least among the intellectuals). The anti-Russian fighting tradition of the Bashkirs has a different profile from the more subtle resistance of the Tatars.

Since the foundation of the Bashkir ASSR, the Soviet authorities have tried to foster the Bashkirs' national identity and divide them from the Tatars in order to weaken any potential Tatar national movement. How successful has this policy been? It is doubtful whether the Soviets have succeeded in providing the Bashkirs with a specific national culture and a Bashkir historical tradition. On the contrary, the development of education in Bashkiria and in Tataristan tends to bring the two separated nations closer together.

GLOSSARY

adat — traditional or customary law thought to be of religious origin.

akhund — religious authority in the Shi'a areas, equivalent of *mullah*.

AO — *Avtonomnaia Oblast'* (Autonomous Region), an administrative region within a Soviet republic.

amengerstvo — levirate and sororate (see separate entries).

atalykat — education of children by a related family.

aksakal — (white beards) elders; "aksakalism" is used to denote the practice of investing the local *aksakal* with special decision-making powers; his decisions have both social and quasi-legal status within his own group.

ASSR — *Avtonomnaia Sovetskaia Sotsialisticheskaia Respublika* (Soviet Socialist Autonomous Republic), an administrative unit within a Soviet republic.

awlad — holy tribes of the Turkmen, supposed to descend from the Prophet.

Dar-ul-Islam — Literally the house of Islam, that is, all Muslim lands, as opposed to the *Dar ul-Harb*, the House of War, which includes all non- Islamic lands.

dinsiz — (lit., in Turkish, "without religion") atheist.

fetwa — legal opinion given by a *mufti*.

hadith — tradition concerning the life and the sayings of the Prophet.

hadj — pilgrimage to Mecca.

Hijra — the year of the arrival of the Prophet Mohammed in Medina.

ijtihad — the doctrine condoning individual interpretation of the sacred law, the *shari'at*, by qualified doctors of law.

imam — leader of a congregational prayer; or among the Shi'a, the term used for the leader of the World of Islam.

imam-khatib — head of a mosque.

ishan — head of a Sufi *tariqa*.

jema'at — assembly.

kadi — judge of the *shari'at* law.

kafir — infidel.

kalym — bride purchase price.

karshylyk — a sister and a brother married to a brother and a sister.

kawm — clan.

kolkhoz — collective farm.

krai — (territory) an administrative unit within the RSFSR.

kunaklik — hospitality.

Kurban Bairam — the feast of sacrifice celebrated on the 10th day of the month of the *hadj* when the pilgrims make sacrifices in Mina near Mecca.

levirate — the custom of a widow marrying the brother of her deceased husband.

mahalle — a native quarter in a city.

masjid — small mosque.

masjid-e juma — cathedral mosque in which Friday prayers can be performed.

mazar — shrine; tomb of a saint.

mazhab — a school of law within Sunni Islam. There are four of these schools: Hanafi, Shafe'i, Maleki and Hanbali.

249

medresseh — Muslim high school.
mekteb — Muslim elementary school.
millet — nation.
mirasizm — rediscovery of national past.
mudarris — professor in a *medresseh*.
muezzin — a minor cleric in a mosque who calls the faithful to prayers.
mufti — canon lawyer.
mullah — general term used to designate Muslim clerics.
murid — adept of a Sufi brotherhood.
murshid — leader of a Sufi *tariqa*.
mutevvali — caretaker of a mosque.
naib — representative of the *imam*, or of a ruler.
oblast' — region, an administrative unit within a Soviet republic.
paranja — veil worn by Muslim women.
pir — shrine, holy place of pilgrimage. Also sheikh, synonymous with *murshid*.
raion — district, an adminstrative unit within an *oblast'*.
RSFSR — *Rossiiskaia Sovetskaia Federativnaia Sotsialisticheskaia Respublika* (Russian Soviet Federated Socialist Republic).
ru — clan.
sadaka — voluntary contributions of believers to aid mosques.
salat — private prayer said five times a day by Muslims.
sawm — fasting during the month of Ramadan.
shafe'i — one of the four schools (*mazhab*) of legal interpretation of Muslim law. In the Soviet Union this school is found only in Daghestan. It is distinguished by its conservatism.
shahada — a private profession of belief in one God and the recognition that Mohammed is His prophet.
shaman — priest or priest-doctor among northern tribes of Asia.
shari'at — Quranic law.
sheikh — leader of Sufi order.
sororate — custom of a widower marrying the sister of his deceased wife.
sovkhoz — state farm.
SSR — *Sovetskaia Sotsialisticheskaia Respublika* (Soviet Socialist Republic), one of the Soviet socialist (federal) republics forming the Soviet Union.
Sufism — from the Arabic *al-Suf* (wool); a mystical doctrine of Islam based on initiation and leading to personal union with God.
taip — clan or division of a clan.
taqlid — literally, "imitation", implying an uncritical acceptance of traditional interpretations of the *shari'at*.
tariqa — "Path" (leading to god); Sufi brotherhood.
tukhum — large extended family; in some areas, a tribe.
ulema — scholar in theology. (plural of *alim*).
waqfs — an endowment used to support a pious foundation, such as a *medresseh, mekteb* or mosque.
zakat — obligatory alms destined to assist the poor.
zhuz — horde.
ziarat — shrine, holy place of pilgrimage.
zikr — individual or collective prayers (silent or aloud) of a Sufi brotherhood.

BIBLIOGRAPHY

GENERAL

Akiner, S. *The Islamic Peoples of the Soviet Union.* London, 1984.

Aristov, N.A. "Zametki ob etnicheskom sostave tiurkskikh plemen i narodnostei i svedeniia ob ikh chislennosti", *Zhivaia Starina*, vols III–IV, St Petersburg, 1896.

Arsharuni, A., and Gabidullin, Kh. *Ocherki panislamizma i pantiurkizma v Rossii.* Moscow, 1931.

Baskakov, N.A. *Tiurkskie iazyki.* Moscow, 1960.

Bennigsen, A. "La famille musulmane en Union Soviétique", *Cahiers du Monde Russe et Soviétique*, vol. 1, no. 1, 1960, pp.83–108.

——. "Panturkism and Panislamism in History and Today". *Central Asian Survey*, vo. 3, no. 3, July 1984, pp.39–51.

Bennigsen, A., and Broxup, M. *The Islamic Threat to the Soviet State.* London, 1983.

Bennigsen, A., and Lemercier-Quelquejay, C. *Islam in the Soviet Union.* London, 1967.

——. *Les Musulmans oubliés.* Paris, 1981.

——. *La presse et le mouvement national chez les Musulmans de Russie avant 1920.* Paris, 1964.

Bennigsen, A., and Wimbush, S.E. *Muslim National Communism in the Soviet Union: A Revolutionary Strategy for the Colonial World.* Chicago, 1979.

Benzing, J. *Einführung in der Studium der altaischen Philologie und der Turkologie.* Wiesbaden, 1952.

Bigi, M.J. *Eslahat Esaslary.* Petrograd, 1915–17.

Bräker, H. *Kommunismus und Weltreligionen Asiens: Kommunismus und Islam.* 2 vols, Tübingen, 1969–71.

Bütün Rusiya Müsülmanlarinin 1917 nci yilda, 1–11 Mayda Meskvede bulgan umumi Isiyezdinin Protokollari. Petrograd, 1917.

Carrère d'Encausse, H. *L'Empire éclaté.* Paris, 1978.

Castagné, J. *Le Bolchévisme et l'Islam: Revue du monde musulman.* Paris, 1922.

Dimanshtein, S. (ed.) *Revoliutsiia i natsional'nyi vopros.* Moscow, 1930.

Feshbach, M. "The Soviet Union: Population Trends and Dilemmas", *Population Bulletin*, vol. 37, no. 3, Aug. 1982.

Grousset, R. *L'Empire des Steppes.* 4th edn. Paris, 1980.

Hostler, C.W. *Turkism and the Soviets: The Turks of the world and their potential objectives.* London-New York, 1957.

Johelson, W. *Peoples of Asiatic Russia.* New York, 1928.

Karklins, Rasma. *Ethnic Relations in the USSR: The view from below.* London, 1985.

Katanov, N. *Etnograficheskii obzor turetsko-tatarskikh plemen.* Kazan, 1894.

Kolarz, W. *Russia and her Colonies.* New York, 1952.

Lemercier-Quelquejay, C. "From Tribe to Umma", *Central Asian Survey*, vol. 3, No. 3, July 1984, pp.15–27.

——. "Les Missions Orthodoxes en pays musulmans de Moyenne et Basse-Volga, 1552–1865", *Cahiers du Monde Russe et Soviétique*, vol. 8, no. 3, pp 369–403.

——. "Les sources de documentation sur la religion musulmane en Union Soviétique", *Cahiers du Monde Russe et Soviétique*, vol. 1, no. 1, pp.184–98, and vol. 1, no. 2, pp.373–81.

Mende, G. von. *Der Nationale Kampf der Russlands Turken*. Berlin, 1936.

Markov, G.E. *Kochevniki Azii: struktura khoziaistva i obshchestvennoi organisatsii*. Moscow, 1976.

Monteil, V. *Les Musulmans soviétiques*. Paris, 1957.

Mühlen, Patrik von. *Zwischen Hakenkreuz und Sowjetstern — Der Nationalismus der sowjetische Orientvölker im Zweiten Weltkrieg*. Düsseldorf, 1971.

Narody Srednei Azii. "Narody Mira" series. Moscow, 1957.

Ocherki obshchei etnografii: Aziatskaia chast' SSSR. Moscow, 1960.

Pipes, R. *The Formation of the Soviet Union*. Cambridge, Mass., 1957.

Razvitie narodov SSSR za 60 let. Moscow, 1983.

Ro'i, Y. (ed.) *The USSR and the Muslim World*. London, 1984.

Ryskulov, T. *Izbrannye trudy*. Alma-Ata, 1984.

Rywkin, M. "First Muslim or First Soviet", *Journal of Muslim Minority Affairs*, vol. 3, no. 2, Winter 1981, pp.277–9.

——. *Moscow's Muslim Challenge: Soviet Central Asia*. Armonk, NY, and London, 1982.

——. "The Soviet Nationalities Policy and the Communist Party Structure in Uzbekistan: A Study in the Methods of Soviet Russian Control." Unpubl. Ph. D. thesis, New York University, 1960.

Sultan-Galiev, M.S. "Sotsial'naia revoliutsiia i Vostok", in *Zhizn' natsional'nostei*, nos 38(46), 39(47), 42(50), 1919.

Tokarev, C.A. *Narody Srednei Azii*, vol. V of series *Etnografiia narodov SSSR: Istoricheskie osnovy byta i kul'tury*. Moscow, 1958.

Veinstein, G., Lemercier-Quelquejay, C. and Wimbush, S.E. (eds) *Passé turko-tatar — Présent soviétique*. Brussels, 1986.

"Vsesoiuznaia perepis naseleniia: sostav sem'i", *Vestnik Statistiki*, no. 8, 1983, pp.60–80.

Wimbush, S.E. (ed.) *Soviet Nationalities in Strategic Perspective*. London, 1985.

Wixman, R. *The Peoples of the USSR: An ethnographic handbook*. New York, 1984.

Wurm, S. *Turkic Peoples of the USSR: Their historical background, their languages and the development of Soviet linguistic policy*. London, 1954.

ISLAM IN THE SOVIET UNION

Abdulaev, M.A., Vagabov, M.V. *Aktual'nye problemy kritiki i preodoleniia islama*. Makhach-Qala, 1975.

Ashirov, Nugman. *Evoliutsiia islama v SSSR*. Moscow, 1973.

——. *Islam i natsii*. Moscow 1975.

——. "Islam i natsional'nye otnosheniia", *Nauka i religiia*, no. 10, 1973, pp. 54–9; no. 12, 1973, pp.41–6; no. 2, 1974, pp.34–8.

——. *Musul'manskaiia propoved'*. Moscow, 1978.

——. *Nravstvennye poucheniia sovremennogo islama*. Moscow, 1977.

Basilov, V.N. *Kul't sviatykh v islame*. Moscow, 1970.

Duisenbin, Z.H. *K voprosu o sovremennom islame*. Alma-Ata, 1961.

Izimbetov, G. *Islam i sovremennost'*. Nukhus, 1963.

Klimovich, L. *Islam*. 2nd edn, Moscow, 1965.

——. *Islam v Tsarskoi Rossii*. Moscow, 1936.

Makatov, I.A. *Islam, veruiushchii, sovremennost'*. Makhach-Qala, 1974.

——. *Sovetskoe obshchestvo i religiia*. Makhach-Qala, 1962.

Materialy nauchnoi konferentsii modernizatsiia islama i aktual'nye voprosy teorii nauchnogo ateizma. Moscow, 1968.

Mavliutov, R.R. *Islam*. 1st edn, Moscow, 1969, 2nd edn, Moscow, 1974.

Pivovarov, V.G. *Na etapakh sotsialisticheskogo issledovaniia*. Groznyi, 1974.

——. *Struktura religioznoi obshchiny*. Groznyi, 1970.

Rodinson, M. *Marxisme et le monde musulman*. Paris, 1972.

Saidbaev, T.S. *Islam i obshchestvo — opyt istoriko-sotsiologicheskogo issledovaniia*. Moscow, 1978.

Snesarev, G., and Basilov, V. *Domusul 'manskie verovaniia i obriady Srednei Azii*. Moscow, 1975.

Sukhareva, O.A. *K voprosu o kul'te musul'manskikh sviatykh v Srednei Azii*. Works of the Institute of History and Archaeology, Academy of Science of the Uzbek SSR, vol. II. Tashkent, 1950.

Sultan-Galiev, M.S. "Metody antireligioznoi propagandy sredi musul'man", *Zhizn' natsional'nostei*, 29 (127), 14 Dec. 1920; 30(128), 23 Dec. 1920.

Tolstov, S.P. "Religiia narodov Srednei Azii", *Religioznye verovaniia narodov SSSR — Sbornik etnograficheskikh materialov*, vol. 1. Moscow–Leningrad, 1931.

Vagabov, M.A. *Islam i sem'ia*. Makhach-Qala, 1973.

——. *Islam i sem'ia*. Moscow, 1980.

Vakhabov, A. *Islam v SSSR*. Moscow, 1972.

——. *Musul'mane v SSSR*. Moscow, 1980.

CENTRAL ASIA: GENERAL

Abramzon, S.M. *K voprosu o patriarkhal'noi sem'e u kochevnikov Srednei Azii*. Short Reports of the Institute of Ethnography. Academy of Sciences of the

USSR (hereafter ANSSSR), no. XXVIII. Moscow, 1958.

Allworth, E. *Central Asia: A Century of Russian Rule.* New York and London, 1967.

—— (ed.). *The Nationality Question in Central Asia.* New York, 1973.

Aminov, A.M. *Ekonomicheskoe razvitie Srednei Azii (kolonial'nyi period) — Ot vtoroi poloviny XIX stoletiia do pervoi mirovoi voiny.* Tashkent, 1959.

Andrianov, B.V. *Karta narodov Srednei Azii i Kazakhstana (po dannym perepisi 1926 g.). Materialy k istoriko-etnograficheskomu atlasu Srednei Azii i Kazakhstana.* Works of the Institute of Ethnography, ANSSSR, vol. XLVIII. Moscow and Leningrad, 1961.

Bacon, E. *Central Asia under Russian Rule.* Ithaca, NY, 1966.

Bartol'd, V.V. *Istoriia kul'turnoi zhizni Turkestana.* Leningrad, 1927.

——. *Istoriia turetsko-mongol'skikh narodov. Konspekt lektsii chitannykh studentam Kazakhskogo Vysshego Pedagogicheskogo Instituta v 1926-1927.* Tashkent, 1928.

——. *Turkestan v epokhu mongol'skogo nashestviia.* St Petersburg, 1898-1900.

Bendrikov, K.E. *Ocherki po istorii narodnogo obrazovaniia v Turkestane (1865-1924).* Moscow, 1960.

Becker, S. *Russia's Protectorates in Central Asia: Bukhara and Khiva, 1965-1924.* Cambridge, Mass., 1968.

Broxup, M. "The Basmachi", *Central Asian Survey*, vol. 2, no. 1 (July 1983), pp. 57-83.

Caroe, Sir Olaf. *The Soviet Empire: The Turks of Central Asia and Stalinism.* London, 1953.

Carrère d'Encausse, H. *Réforme et révolution chez les Musulmans de l'empire russe: Bukhara 1867-1927.* Paris, 1966.

Castagné, J. *Les Basmatchis.* Paris, 1925.

——. *Le Turkestan depuis la Révolution russe (1917-1921).* Paris, 1922.

Chokaev, M. *Turkestan pod vlast'iu Sovetov.* Paris, 1925.

Etnicheskie protsessy u natsional'nykh grupp Srednei Azii i Kazakhstana. Moscow, 1980.

Galutso, P.G. *Turkestan-Koloniia..* Tashkent, 1935.

Ginzburg, V.V. *Drevnie i sovremennye antropologicheskie tipy Srednei Azii. Proiskhozhdenie cheloveka i drevnee rasselenie chelovechestva.* Works of the Institute of Ethnography, ANSSSR, vol. XVI. Moscow, 1951.

Hambly, G. (ed.) *Central Asia.* London, 1969.

Hayit, B. "Bugünkü Türkistan", *Egitim Kültür*, no. 14 (March 1982).

——. "Demographic and Economic Situation of the Muslims of Turkestan", *ABN Correspondence*, vol. 23, nos. 1-2 (Jan.–Apr. 1982).

——. "Die Nationalen Regierungen von Kokand und der Alash Orda." Unpubl. Ph. D. thesis, University of Münster, 1950.

——. "Some Reflections on the Subject of the Annexation of Turkestan and Kazakhstan by Russia," *Central Asian Survey*, vol. 3, no. 4 (Nov. 1984), pp. 61-77.

——. *Soviet Russian Colonialism and Imperialism in Turkestan as an Example of the Soviet Type of Colonialism of an Islamic People in Asia*. 1965 (place of publication not stated).

——. *Turkestan im Herzen Eurasiens*. Cologne, 1980.

——. *Turkestan im XX Jahrhundert*. Darmstadt, 1956.

Henze, P.B. "The Central Asian Muslims and their Brethren Abroad: Marxist Solidarity or Muslim Brotherhood", *Central Asian Survey*, vol. 3, no. 3 (July 1984), pp. 51–69.

Holdworth, M. *Turkestan in the Nineteenth Century*. London, 1959.

Inoiatov, Kh. Sh. *Pobeda sovetskoi vlasti v Turkestane*. Moscow, 1978.

Istoriia i etnografiia narodov Srednei Azii — Sbornik statei. Dushanbe, 1981.

Istoriia kommunisticheskikh organizatsii Srednei Azii. Tashkent, 1967.

Kommunisticheskaia partiia Turkestana i Uzbekistana v tsifrakh – Sbornik statisticheskikh materialov, 1918–1967. Tashkent, 1968.

Kononov, A.N. *Rodoslovnaia Turkmen — Sochinenie Abul Gazi khana khivinskogo*. Moscow-Leningrad, 1958.

Krader, L. *The Peoples of Central Asia*. Bloomington, Ind., 1962.

Logofet, D.N. *Bukharskoe khanstvo pod russkim protektoratom*. Petrograd, 1922. 2 vols.

Maliavkin, A.G. *Istoricheskaia geografiia Tsentral'noi Azii*. Novosibirsk, 1981.

Materialy po istorii prisoedineniia Srednei Azii k Rossii. Tashkent, 1969.

McCagg, W.O., and Silver, Brian S. (ed). *Soviet-Asian Ethnic Frontiers*. New York, 1979.

Micklin, P.P. "Soviet Water Diversion Plans: Implications for Kazakhstan and Central Asia", *Central Asian Survey*, vol. 1, no. 4 (April 1983), pp. 9–45.

Nemchenko, M. *Natsional'noe razmezhevanie v Srednei Azii*. Moscow, 1925.

Nove, A., and Newth, G.A. *The Soviet Middle East: A model for development*. New York, 1963.

Olzscha, R. *Turkestan. Die politisch-historischen und wirtschaftlichen Probleme Zentralasiens*. Leipzig, 1942.

Pahlen, K.V. *Mission to Turkestan*. London, 1964.

Park, A.G. *Bolshevism in Turkestan, 1917–1927*. New York, 1957.

Pierce, R. *Russian Central Asia, 1867–1917: A study in colonial rule*. Berkeley, Calif., 1960.

Poliakov, Iu. A., and Chugunov, A.I. *Bor'ba s Basmachestvom v Sredneaziatskikh respublikakh SSSR*. Moscow, 1983.

Rakowska-Harmstone, T. "Islam and Nationalism: Central Asia and Kazakhstan under Soviet Rule", *Central Asian Survey*, vol. 2, no. 2 (Sept. 1983), pp. 7–89.

Ryskulov, T.R. *Revoliutsiia i korennoe naselenie Turkestana*. Tashkent, 1925.

Rywkin, M. *Russia in Central Asia*. New York, 1963.

Safarov, G. *Kolonial'naia revoliutsiia — opyt Turkestana*. Moscow, 1921.

Saray, M. "The Russian Conquest of Central Asia", *Central Asian Survey*, vol. l, nos. 2/3 (Nov. 1982), pp. 1–31.

Schuyler, E. *Turkistan: Notes of a Journey in Russian Turkistan, Khokhand, Bukhara and Kuldja*. London-New York, 1877. 2 vols.

Sem'ia i semeinye obrazy u narodov Srednei Azii i Kazakhstana. Sbornik statei. Moscow, 1978.

Togan, A.Z.V. *Bugünkü Türkili (Türkistan) ve Yakin Tarihi*. Istanbul, 1947.

——. *Hatiralar*. Istanbul, 1969.

Tursunov, Kh. T. *O natsional'no-gosudarstvennom razmezhevanii Srednei Azii*. Tashkent, 1957.

Vambéry, A. *Travels in Central Asia*. London, 1864.

Vinnikov, Ia. R. *Sovremennoe rasselenie narodov i etnograficheskikh grupp v Ferganskoi doline — Sredneaziatskii etnograficheskii sbornik*. Works of the Institute of Ethnography, ANSSSR. Moscow, 1959.

Wheeler, G. *The Modern History of Central Asia*. London-New York, 1964.

——. *The Peoples of Soviet Central Asia*. London, 1966.

——. *Racial Problems in Soviet Muslim Asia*. London, 1960.

Wimbush, S.E. "The Politics of Identity Change in Soviet Central Asia", *Central Asian Survey*, vol. 3, no. 3 (July 1984), pp. 69–79.

Zarudin, I.I. *Spisok narodnostei Turkestanskogo kraia*. Leningrad, 1925.

Uzbeks

Abdusamedov, A.I. *Osnovnye etapy razvitiia ateizma v Uzbekistane*. Tashkent, 1979.

Agzamkhodzhaev, A. *Obrazovanie i razvitie Uzbekskoi SSR*. Tashkent, 1971.

Aiupov, M.T. *Nekotorye voprosy istorii profsoiuznogo dvizheniia v Uzbekistane*. Tashkent, 1969.

Allworth, Edward. *Uzbek Literary Politics*. London, 1964.

Aminova, R.H., Akhbunova, M.A., and Inoiatov, Kh.Sh. *Pobeda velikoi oktiabr'skoi sotsialisticheskoi revoliutsii i postroenie sotsializma v Uzbekistane (1917–1937 gg)*. Tashkent, 1967.

Bakhanov, M.G. *Formirovanie Uzbekskoi sotsialisticheskoi natsii*. Tashkent, 1961.

Bezrukova, N.T. *Kommunisticheskaia partiia Uzbekistana v tsifrakh. (Sbornik statisticheskikh materialov). 1924–1964 godu*. Tashkent, 1964.

Dzhabbarov, I. *Obshchestvennyi progress, byt i religiia. (Sotsial'no filosofskoe issledovanie na materialakh Uzbekskoi SSR)*. Tashkent, 1973.

Fierman, William. "Two Young Uzbek Writers' Perspectives on Assimilation", *Central Asian Survey*, vol. 2, no. 3 (Nov. 1983), pp. 63–79.

Iakubovskii, A. Iu. *K voprosu ob etnogeneze Uzbekskogo naroda*. Tashkent, 1941.

Inoiatov, Kh.Sh. *Oktiabr'skaia revoliutsiia v Uzbekistane*. Moscow, 1958.

Istoriia Bukharskoi i Khorezmskoi narodnykh sovetskikh respublik. Moscow, 1971.

Istoriia narodov Uzbekistana. 2 vol. Tashkent, 1960–7.

Istoriia rabochego klassa Uzbekistana. 3 vol. Tashkent, 1964–6.

Istoriia Samarkanda v dvukh tomakh. Tashkent, 1969–70.

Istoriia sovetskogo gosudarstva i prava Uzbekistana. Vol. 1. Tashkent, 1960.

Istoriia Uzbekskoi SSR. 4 vols. Tashkent 1967–8.

Karmysheva, B.Kh. *Uzbeki-Lokaitsy iuzhnogo Tadzhikistana, vyp. 1: istoriko-etnograficheskii ocherk zhivotnovodstva v dorevoliutsionnyi period*. Dushanbe, 1954.

Kary-Niiazov, T.N. *Ocherki istorii kul'tury sovetskogo Uzbekistana*. Moscow, 1955.

——. *O kul'turnom nasledii Uzbekskogo naroda*. Tashkent, 1960.

KPSS i sovetskoe pravitel'stvo v Uzbekistane. Sbornik dokumentov, 1925–1970 gg. Tashkent 1972.

Logofet, D.N. *Bukharskoe khanstvo pod russkim protektoratom*. 2 vols. St Petersburg, 1911.

Materialy po istorii Uzbekistana. Tashkent 1963.

Medlin, W.K., Cave, W.M., and Carpenter, F. *Education and Development in Central Asia: A Case Study of Social Change in Uzbekistan*. Leiden, 1971.

Ostroumov, N.P. *Sarty — Etnograficheskie materialy*, vol. I. Tashkent, 1890.

——. *Sarty — Etnograficheskie materialy*, vol. II. Tashkent, 1908.

Rywkin, M. *Soviet Nationalities Policy and the Communist Party Structure in Uzbekistan*. New York, 1960.

Sazonova, M.V. *K etnografii Uzbekov iuzhnogo Khorezma — Trudy Khorezmskoi arkheologo-etnograficheskoi ekspeditsii*, vol. I. Moscow, 1952.

Shaniiazov, K. Sh. *Istoriko-etnograficheskii ocherk Karlukov iuzhnykh i zapadnykh raionov Uzbekistana*. Leningrad, 1960.

——. *K etnicheskoi istorii Uzbekskogo naroda*. Tashkent, 1974.

Snesarev, G.P. *Relikty domusul'manskikh verovanii i obriadov u Uzbekov Khorezma*. Moscow, 1969.

Soper, J. "Shakeup in the Uzbek Literary Elite", *Central Asian Survey*, vol. 1, no. 4 (April 1983), pp. 59–83.

Sovremennyi aul Srednei Azii (Sotsial'no-ekonomicheskii ocherk). Tashkent, 1927.

Sukhareva, O.A. *Islam v Uzbekistane*. Tashkent, 1960.

Uzbekistan za 60 let sovetskoi vlasti — statisticheskii sbornik. Tashkent, 1958.

Zadykhina, K.L. *Uzbeki del'ty Amu-Dar'i — Trudy Khorezmskoi arkheologo-etnograficheskoi ekspeditsii*, vol. I. Moscow, 1952.

Kazakhs

Abramzon, S.M. "Preobrazovaniia v khoziaistve i kul'ture Kazakhov za gody sotialisticheskogo stroitel'stva", *Sovetskaia etnografiia*, no. 1, 1961.

Amanturlin, Sh. B. *Predrassudki i sueveriia i ikh preodolenie*. Alma-Ata, 1984.

Argynbaev, Kh. *Istoriko-kul'turnye sviazi russkogo i kazakhskogo narodov i ikh vliianie na material'nuiu kul'turu Kazakhov v seredine XIX i nachale XX vv. (Po materialam vostochnogo Kazakhstana)*. Alma-Ata, 1959.

Asfendiiarov, S.D., and Kunte, P.A. *Istoriia Kazakhstana s drevneiskikh vremen*. Alma-Ata, 1971.

Baishev, S. *Pobeda sotializma v Kazakhstane.* Alma-Ata, 1961.

Bekmakhanov, E.B. *Prisoedinenie Kazakhstana k Rossii.* Moscow, 1957.

Bukeikhanov, A. "Kirgizy", in A.I. Kostelianskii, *Formy natsional'nogo dvizheniia v sovremmenykh gosudarstvakh.* St Petersburg, 1910, pp. 577–600.

Demko, G.J. *The Russian Colonization of Kazakhstan, 1896–1916.* Bloomington, Ind., 1969.

Dimanstein, S. "K 15 letiiu Kazakhstana", *Revoliutsiia i natsional'nosti,* no. 10 (68), Oct. 1935.

Goloshchekin, F. *Partiinoe stroitel'stvo v Kazakhstane — sbornik statei.* Moscow, 1930.

Grodekov, N.I. *Kirgizy i Kara-Kirgizy Syr-Dar'inskoi oblasti.* Tashkent, 1889.

Istoriia Kazakhskoi SSR. 2 vols, Alma-Ata, 1957 and 1959.

Istoriia Kazakhskoi SSR — epokha sotsializma. Alma-Ata, 1967.

Iusupov, Sh. "Iz istorii perekhoda kochevogo kazakhskogo naseleniia k osedlosti", *Voprosy istorii,* no. 3, 1960.

Iz istorii partiinogo stoitel'stva v Kazakhstane — sbornik statei i materialov. Alma-Ata, 1936.

Kazakhstan za 40 let — statisticheskii sbornik. Alma-Ata, 1960.

Kharuzin, A.N. *Kirgizy bukeevskoi ordy — antropologo-etnologicheskii ocherk.* News of the Society for Lovers of Nature, Anthropology and Ethnography of Moscow University, vol. LXIII, Moscow, 1889, and vol. LXXII, Moscow, 1891.

Korbe, O.A. "Kul'tura i byt kazakhskogo kolkhoznogo aula", *Sovetskaia etnografiia,* no. 4, 1950.

Kreindler, I. "Ibrahim Altynsarin, Nicolas Il'minskii and the Kazakh National Awakening", *Central Asian Survey,* vol. 2, no. 3. (Nov. 1983), pp. 99–117.

Kul'turnoe stroitelstvo Kazakhstana — statisticheskii sbornik. Alma-Ata, 1960.

Kuzembaev, N. *O kul'ture i byte naseleniia aula i sela.* Alma-Ata, 1948.

Levshin, A.I. *Opisanie kirgiz-kazakhskikh ili kirgiz-kaisatskikh ord i stepei.* St Petersburg, 1832.

Materialy i issledovaniia po etnografii kazakhskogo naroda. Alma-Ata, 1963.

Nurmukhamedov, S.B., Savos'ko, V.K., and Suleimenov, R.B. *Ocherki istorii sotsialisticheskogo stroitel'stva v Kazakhstane 1933–1940.* Alma-Ata, 1966.

Obrazovanie Kazakhskoi SSR. Alma-Ata, 1957.

Rudenko, S.I. "Ocherk byta severo-vostochnykh kazakhov", "Sbornik statei antropologicheskogo otriada kazakhstanskoi ekspeditsii-issledovanie 1927", *Materialy Komissii ekspeditsionykh issledovanii,* no. 15. Leningrad, 1930.

Ryskulov, T.R. *Kazakhstan.* Moscow, 1927.

Shakhmatov, B.F. *Kazakhskaia past'bishchno-kochevaia obshchina — Voprosy obrazovanie, evoliutsii i razlozheniia.* Alma-Ata, 1964.

Shulembaev, K.Sh. *Obraz zhizni, religiia, ateizm: obshchee i osobennoe v obraze zhizni i religioznykh verovanniiakh kazakhov i voprosy ateisticheskogo vospitaniia.* Alma-Ata, 1983.

Vostrov, V.V. *Rodoplemennyi sostav i rasselenie kazakhov na territorii Semirechenskoi oblasti. Novye materialy po arkheologii i etnografii Kazakhstana.*

Works of the Institute of History, Archaeology and Ethnography, Academy of Sciences of the Kazakh SSR, vol. 12. Alma-Ata, 1961.

Vostrov, V.V., and Mukanov, M.S. *Rodoplemennyi sostav i rasselenie kazakhov — konets XIX, nachalo XX v.* Alma-Ata, 1968.

Tajiks

Andreev, M.S. *Tadzhiki doliny Khuf (verkhov'ia Amu-Dar'i),* vols. 1–2. Moscow, 1953–8.

Bartol'd, V.V. *Tadzhiki. Istoricheskii ocherk.* Tashkent, 1925.

Bobrinskii, A.A. "Sekta ismail'ia v russkikh i bukharskikh predelakh Srednei Azii", *Etnograficheskoe obozrenie,* no. 2, 1902.

Braginskii, I.S. *Ocherki po istorii tadzhikskoi literatury.* Dushanbe, 1956.

Gadzhiev, A.Kh. *Reaktsionnaia sushchnost' ideologii sektanstva v Islame.* Dushanbe, 1963.

Gafurov, B.G. *Istoriia tadzhikskogo naroda,* 2nd edn, vol. I. Moscow, 1952.

Irkaev, M.I. *Ocherk po istorii sovetskogo Tadzhikistana (1917–1957).* Dushanbe, 1957.

Iz istorii kul'turnogo stroitel'stva v Tadzhikistane. Sbornik statei, vol. 1. Dushanbe, 1973.

Kadyrov, A. *Prichiny sushchestvovaniia i puti preodolenia perezhitkov islama.* Leninabad, 1966.

Kisliakov, N.A. *Ocherk po istorii karategina — K istorii Tadzhikistana,* 2nd edn. Dushanbe, 1954.

——. *Sem'ia i brak u tadzhikov.* Works of the Institute of Ethnography, ANSSSR, vol. XLIII, Moscow-Leningrad, 1953.

Materialy po istorii kompartii Tadzhikistana, vol. 1. Dushanbe, 1963.

Monogarova, L.F. *Preobrazovanie v bytu i kul'ture pripamirskikh narodnostei.* Moscow, 1972.

Naselenie Tadzhikskoi SSR. Po dannym vsesoiuznoi perepisi naseleniia 1979 goda. Dushanbe, 1980.

Radzhabov, Z.Sh. *Iz istorii obshchestvenno-politicheskoi mysli tadzhikskogo naroda vo vtoroi polovine XIX i v nachale XX v.* Dushanbe, 1957.

Rakowska-Harmstone, T. *Russia and Nationalism in Central Asia: The Case of Tadzhikistan.* Baltimore, Md., 1966.

Kirghiz

Abramzon, S.M. *Etnicheskii sostav kirgizskogo naseleniia severnoi Kirgizii. Trudy kirgizskoi arkheologo-etnograficheskoi ekspeditsii,* vol. IV. Moscow, 1960.

——. *Kirgizy i ikh etnogeneticheskie i istoriko-kul'turnye sviazi.* Leningrad, 1971.

——. "Kirgizskaia sem'ia v epokhu sotsializma", *Sovetskaia etnografiia,* no. 5, 1957.

——. *Ocherk kul'tury kirgizskogo naroda.* Frunze, 1946.

——. *Voprosy etnogeneza kirgizov po dannym etnografii. Trudy kirgizskoi arkheologo-etnograficheskoi ekspeditsii*, vol. III. Frunze, 1959.

Altmyshbaev, A.A. *Obshchestvennaia mysl' kirgizov domarksova perioda.* Frunze, 1984.

Amanaliev, B. *Kyrgyzstan dinii zhana erkin oiloonun tarykhynan.* Frunze, 1967.

——. *Religiia i religioznye perezhitki. Sbornik statei.* Frunze, 1969.

Arystanbekov, S. *Nekotorye kharakternye osobennosti religioznykh perezhitkov.* Frunze, 1965.

Baktygulov, Dzh. S. *Sotsialisticheskoe preobrazovanie kirgizskogo aula (1928–1940).* Frunze, 1978.

Balaieva, T.D. *Do islamskie verovaniia i ikh perezhitki u kirgizov.* Frunze, 1972.

——. *Religioznye perezhitki u kirgizov i ikh preodolenie.* Frunze, 1981.

Bartol'd, V.V. *Kirgizy (Istoricheskii ocherk).* Frunze, 1943.

Dorzhenov, S.B. *Islam bugünkü kündö.* Frunze, 1980.

——. *Kyrgyzstandagy islamdyn tarykhynan.* Frunze, 1968.

——. *Perezhitki islama v Kirgizii i prichiny ikh suschestvovaniia.* Scholarly Notes of the Kirghiz Medical Institute, vol. 62. Frunze, 1969.

Dor, R. *Contribution à l'étude des Kirghizes du Pamir afghan.* Paris, 1975.

Formirovanie i razvitie kirgizskoi sotsialisticheskoi natsii. Frunze, 1957.

Istoriia Kirgizii vols I–II. Frunze, 1956.

Karakaeva, I.G. *Sovremennaia kirgizskaia gorodskaia sem'ia.* Frunze, 1981.

Mambetaliev, S. *Kyrguzstandagy müsülman sektalary.* Frunze, 1966.

——. *Perezhitki nekotorykh musul'manskikh techenii v Kirgizii i ikh istoriia.* Frunze, 1969.

——. *Sufizm zhana anyn Kyrgyzstanodagy agymdary.* Frunze, 1972.

Protiv religioznogo obmana i mrakobesiia. (Sbornik materialov o reaktsionnoi roli religii i antiobshchestvennoi deiatel'nosti sluzhitelei kul'ta v Kirgizii.) Frunze, 1970.

Ryskulov, T.R. *Kirgizstan.* Moscow, 1935.

Vinnikov, Ia. R. *Rodoplemennoi sostav i rasselenie kirgizov na territorii iuzhnoi Kirgizii. Trudy kirgizskoi arkheologo-etnograficheskoi ekspeditsii*, vol. I. Moscow, 1956.

Turkmen

Agaev, Kh. *Vzaimootnosheniia prikaspiiskikh turkmen s Rossiei v XIX v. do prisoedineniia k Rossii.* Ashkhabad, 1965.

Ataev, K. *Nekotorye dannye po etnografii turkmen-shikhov.* Works of the Institute of History, Archaeology and Ethnography ANTSSR, vol. VII. Ashkhabad, 1963.

Bartol'd, V.V. *Ocherki istorii turkmenskogo naroda.* Sbornik "Turkmeniia", vol. 1. Leningrad, 1929.

Basilov, V.N. *K voprosu o proiskhozhdenii turkmenskikh ovliadov*. Theses of reports of the conference of young scientific workers and candidates, Institute of Ethnography, ANSSSR, Moscow, 1967.

Bayramsakhatov, N., ed. *Religioznye perezhitki i put' ikh preodoleniia v Turkmenistane*. Ashkhabad, 1977.

Bregel', Iu. E. *Khorezmskie turkmeny v XIX veke*. Moscow, 1961.

Demidov, S.M. *Sufizm v Turkmenii (evoliutsiia i perezhitki)*. Ashkhabad, 1978.

——. *Turkmenski ovliady*. Ashkhabad, 1976.

Dzhikiev, A. *Turkmeny iugo-vostochnogo poberezh'ia Kaspiiskogo moria (Istoriko-etnograficheskii ocherk)*. Ashkhabad, 1961.

Istoriia Turkmenskoi SSR, vol. I (Books 1–2) and vol. II. Ashkhabad, 1957.

Karpov, G.I. *Plemenoi i rodovoi sostav turkmen*. Poltoratsk, 1925.

——. "Turkmeniia i turkmeny (Istoriko-etnograficheskii ocherk)", *Turkmenovedeniie*, nos 10–11, 1929.

Markov, G.E. *Iz etnicheskoi istorii turkmenskogo naroda*. Short reports of the Institute of Ethnography, vol. XXIX, Moscow, 1958.

Materialy po istorii turkmen i Turkmenii, vols 1–2. Moscow-Leningrad, 1938–9.

Mikhailov, F.I. *Tuzemtsy Zakaspiiskoi oblasti i ikh zhizni'*. Ashkhabad, 1900.

Oshanin, L.V. *Antropologicheskii sostav turkmenskikh plemen i etnogenez turkmenskogo naroda*. Works of the Southern Turkmenistan archaeological expedition, vol. IX. Ashkhabad, 1959.

Rosliakov, A.A. "K voprosu ob etnogeneze turkmen (o vremeni i usloviiakh obrazovaniia turkmenskoi narodnosti)", News of the Turkmen Branch of the ANSSSR, no. 5, 1950.

Saray, M. "Russo-Turkmen Relations up to 1874", *Central Asian Survey*, vol. 3, no.4 (Nov. 1984), pp. 15–49.

Tumanovich, O. *Turkmenistan i turkmeny*. Ashkhabad, 1926.

Vasil'eva, G.P. *Turkmeny-Nokhurli (Istoriko-etnograficheskii ocherk)*. Central Asian Ethnographic Collection, I. Works of the Institute of Ethnography, vol. XX. Moscow, 1954.

Karakalpaks

Andrianov, B.V. *Etnicheskaia territoriia karakalpakov v severnom Khorezme (XVIII–XIX v)*. *Materialy i issledovaniia po etnografii karakalpakov*. Works of the Khorezm Archaeological-Ethnographic Expedition, vol. III. Moscow, 1958.

Bazarbaev, Zh. *Opyt sotsiologicheskogo izucheniia ateizma i religii*. Nukus, 1979.

——. *Sekuliarizatsiia naseleniia sotsialisticheskoi Karakalpakii*. Nukus, 1973.

Dosymov, Ia.M. *Ocherki po istorii karakalpaksoi literatury*. Tashkent, 1960.

Esbergenov, Kh.B. "Ob izuchenii religioznykh verovanii karakalpakov", *Konkretnye issledovaniia sovremennykh religioznykh verovanii*. Moscow, 1967.

Izimbetov, T. *Islam i sovremennost'*. Nukus, 1963.

Materialy po istorii karakalpakov. Leningrad-Moscow, 1935.

Nurmukhamedov, M.K., Zhdanko, T., and Kamalov, S.K. *Karakalpaki (Kratkii ocherk istorii s drevneishikh vremen do nashikh dnei).* Tashkent, 1971.
Ocherki istorii Karakalpakskoi ASSR, 2 vols. Tashkent, 1964.
Tatybaev, S.U. *Obrazovanie i razvitie Kara-Kalpakskoi Avtonomnoi Sovetskoi Sotsialisticheskoi Respubliki (1932–1937).* Tashkent 1959.
Tsapenko, N., and Tadzhimov, T. *Kara-Kalpakskaia ASSR (Kratkii spravochnik).* Tashkent, 1960.
Zhdanov, T.A. "Etnogenez karakalpakov", *Vestnik Karakalpakskogo Filiala ANUzSSR*, no. 1, 1961.
——. *Karakalpaki khorezmskogo oazisa — arkheologicheskie i etnograficheskie raboty khorezmskoi ekspeditsii (1945–1948).* Works of the Khorezm Archaeological-Ethnographic Expedition, vol. III. Moscow, 1958.
——. *Ocherki istoricheskoi etnografii karakalpakov. Rodoplemennaia struktura i rasselenie v XIX–nachale XX v.* Works of the Institute of Ethnography ANSSSR, vol. IX. Moscow-Leningrad, 1950.

Uighurs

Galuzo, P.G. "Uigurskoe i dunganskoe krest'ianstvo v dorevoliutsionnom Semirech'e", *Voprosy istorii Kazakhstana XIX–nachala XX v.* Works of the Institute of History, Archaeology and Ethnography, Academy of Sciences of the Kazakh SSR, vol. 11. Alma-Ata, 1961.
Kabirov, M.N. *Pereselenie Iliiskikh uigur v Semirech'e.* Alma-Ata. 1951.
Materialy po istorii i kul'tury uigurskogo naroda. Alma-Ata, 1978.
Materialy po obsledovaniiu tuzemnogo i russkogo staro-zhil'cheskogo khoziaistva i zemlepol'zovaniia v Semirechenskoi oblasti, vol. V. St Petersburg, 1914.
Vinogradski, A.V. "Taranchi (ocherk)", *Estestvoznanie i geografiia*, no.7, 1907.
Zakharova, I.V. *Material'naia kul'tura uigurov Sovetskogo Soiuza.* Central Asian Ethnographic Collection, II. Works of the Institute of Ethnography, vol. XLVII. Moscow, 1959.

Dungans

Iusupov, Kh. *Pereselenie Dungan na territoriie Kirgizii i Kazakhstana.* Frunze, 1961.
Stratanovich, G.G. *Otchet ob ekspeditsii k dunganam Kirgizii (1945).* Short reports of the Institute of Ethnography, no. III. Moscow, 1947.
——. *U dungan Oshskoi gruppy.* Short reports of the Institute of Ethnography, no. IV. Moscow, 1948.
Sushanlo, M. *Dungane Semirech'ia.* Frunze, 1959.
Vasil'ev, V.A. *Dungane. Kultura i Pis'mennost' Vostoka*, books VII–VIII. Moscow, 1931.

Small Minorities: Arabs, Baluchis, Turks, Tsiganes

Gaffenberg, E.G. "Poezdka k beludzham Turkmenii v 1958", *Sovetskaia etnografiia*, no.6, 1958.

Karmysheva, B.Kh. "Etnograficheskaia gruppa 'Tiurk' v sostave uzbekov", *Sovietskaia etnografiia*, no.1, 1960.

Snesarev, G.P. *Sredneaziatskie tsygane*. Short reports of the Institute of Ethnography, no. XXXIV. Moscow, 1960.

Tsereteli, G.V. *Arabskie dialekty v Srednee Azii. Doklady sovetskoi delegatsii na XXIII mezhdunarodnom kongresse vostokovedov. Sektsii semitologii*. Moscow, 1954.

Vinnikov, I.N. "Araby v SSSR", *Sovetskaia etnografiia*, no.4, 1940.

Vinnikov, Ia.R "Beludzhi Turkmenskoi SSR", *Sovetskaia etnografiia*, no.1, 1952.

THE CAUCASUS: GENERAL

Allen, W.E.D., and Muratoff, P. *Caucasian Battlefields: A history of the wars on the Turco-Caucasian border, 1828–1921*. Cambridge, 1953.

Avksent'ev, A.V. *Islam na Severnom Kavkaze*, 1st edn. Stavropol, 1973.

——. *Islam na severnom kavkaze*. 2nd edn. Stavropol, 1984.

Belokurov, S.A. *Snosheniia Rossii s Kavkazom. Materialy izvlechennye iz Moskovskogo glavnogo arkhiva*. Ministry of Foreign Affairs, vol. 1, 1578–1613. Moscow, 1889.

Baddeley, John F. *The Rugged Flanks of the Caucasus*, 2 vols. Oxford, 1940.

——. *The Russian Conquest of the Caucasus*. London, 1908.

Bagirov, M.D. *K voprosu o kharaktere dvizheniia miuridizma i Shamilia*. Moscow, 1950.

Bammate, H. *The Caucasus Problem*. Bern, 1919.

——. *Le Caucase et la révolution russe*. Paris, 1929.

Benckendorff, C. de. *Souvenir intime d'une campagne au Caucase pendant l'été de l'année 1845*. Paris, 1858.

Bennigsen, A. "Muslim Guerilla Warfare in the Caucasus (1918–1928)", *Central Asian Survey*, vol.2, no.1 (July 1983), pp.45–57.

Berkok, I. *Tarihte Kavkasya*. Istanbul, 1958.

Bodenstedt, F. *Les peuples des Caucases et leur guerre d'indépendance contre la Russie*. Paris, 1859.

Borisenko, I. *Sovetskie respubliki na Severnom Kavkaze v 1918 godu*. 2 vols. Rostov-on-Don, 1930.

Bushuev, S.K. *Bor'ba gortsev za nezavisimost' pod rukovodstvom Shamilia*. Moscow, 1939.

Chursin, G.F. *Ocherki po etnologii Kavkaza*. Tiflis, 1913.

Daniialov, A.A. *O dvizhenii gortsev Dagestana i Chechni pod rukovodstvom Shamilia*. Makhach-Qala, 1966.

Djabagui, V.G. "Soviet Nationality Policy and Genocide", *Caucasian Review*, Munich, 1955, pp. 71–80.

Dokumenty po russkoi politike v Zakavkaz'i, vol. I. Baku, 1920.

Dubrovin, N.F. *Istoriia voiny i vladychestva russkikh na Kavkaze.* 6 vols. St Petersburg, 1871.

Dvizhenie gortsev severo-vostochnogo Kavkaza v 20–50 g. XIX veka. Makhach-Qala, 1959.

Fadeev, A.V. *Rossiia i Kavkaz v pervoi treti XIX v.* Moscow, 1960.

Fadeev, R.A. *Shest'desiat let kavkazskoi voiny.* St Petersburg, 1880.

——. *Sobranie sochinenii.* vol. I. St Petersburg, 1889.

Fuller, E. "The Azeris in Georgia and the Ingilois: Ethnic minorities in the limelight", *Central Asian Survey*, vol. 3, no.2 (April 1984), pp. 75–87.

Gadzhiev, I.B. *Sovmestnaia bor'ba bakinskogo proletariata i trudiashchikhsia Dagestana protiv angliiskikh interventov i denikinskoi kontrerevoliutsii v 1919–1920 g.* Makhach-Qala, 1960.

——. *Sovmestnaia bor'ba trudiashchikhsia Azerbaidzhana i Dagestana za vlast' sovetov (1919–1920).* Makhach-Qala, 1968.

Gadzhiev, S.M. *Puti preodoleniia ideologii islama. (Po materialam severnogo Kavkaza i Dagestana).* Makhach-Qala, 1963.

Gadzhiev, V.G. Ramazanov, Kh. Kh., and Danialov, G.A. *Dvizhenie gortsev severo-vostochnogo Kavkaza v 20–50 gg XIX v. Sbornik dokumentov.* Makhach-Qala, 1959.

Henze, M.L. "The Religion of the Central Caucasus: An analysis from 19th-century travellers' accounts", *Central Asian Survey*, vol.1, no.4 (April 1983), pp. 45–58.

——. "Thirty Cows for an Eye: The traditional economy of the Central Caucasus. Analysis from 19th-century travellers' accounts", *Central Asian Survey*, vol.4, no.3 (1985).

Henze, P.B. "Fire and Sword in the Caucasus: The 19th-century resistance of the North Caucasian mountaineers", *Central Asian Survey*, vol.2, no.1 (July 1983), pp. 5–44.

Iandarov, A.D. *Sufizm i ideologiia natsional'no-osvoboditel'nogo dvizheniia. (Iz istorii razvitiia obshchestvennykh idei v Checheno-Ingushetii v 20–70 g. XIX v.)* Alma-Ata, 1975.

Karamulov, N.A. *Svedeniia arabskikh pisatelei o Kavkaze, Armenii i Azerbaidzhane. Sbornik materialov dlia opisaniia mestnostei i plemen Kavkaza.* Vol. XXIX, Tiflis, 1901; vol. XXXI, Tiflis, 1902; vol. XXXII, Tiflis, 1903; vol. XXXVIII, Tiflis, 1908.

Kavkazskii etnograficheskii sbornik. Vol. I, Moscow-Leningrad, 1957; vol. II, Moscow, 1958.

Kosok, P. *Kuzey Kafkasya, Hürriyet ve istiklal Savasi Tarihinden Yapraklar.* Istanbul, 1962.

——. "Revolution and Sovietization in the North Caucasus", *Caucasian Review*, no. 1, 1956, pp. 47–54; and no. 3, 1956, pp. 45–53.

Kosven, M.O. *Etnografiia i istoriia Kavkaza. Issledovaniia i materialy.* Moscow, 1961.
——. *Materialy po istorii etnograficheskogo izucheniia Kavkaza v russkoi nauke. Kavkazskii etnograficheskii sbornik,* 2 vols. Moscow, 1955 and 1959.
——. "Ocherki po etnografii Kavkaza", *Sovetskaia etnografiia,* no.2, 1946.
Kul'tura i byt narodov severnogo Kavkaza (1917–1967). Moscow, 1968.
Lavrov, L.I. *Etnografiia Kavkaza. Po polevym materialm 1924–1978 gg.* Leningrad, 1982.
——. *Istoriko-etnograficheskie ocherki Kavkaza.* Leningrad, 1978.
Leontovich, F.I. *Adaty kavkazskikh gortsev. Materialy po obychnomu pravu severnogo i vostochnogo Kavkaza,* vols. 1–2. Odessa, 1882.
Magomaev, R.M. *O dvizhenii Shamilia.* Makhach-Qala, 1949.
Magomedov, R.M. *Bor'ba gortsev za nezavisimost' pod rukovodstvom Shamilia.* Makhach-Qala, 1939.
Mahommed, T.K. *Tri imama. Memuary murida Shamilia.* Makhach-Qala, 1926.
Marr, N. Ia. *Plemennoi sostav naseleniia Kavkaza.* Petrograd, 1920.
Marx, K. *The Eastern Question: Letters written 1853–1856 dealing with the events of the Crimean War.* London, 1897.
Mokhir, M.V. *Aksai (ili tashkichu). Sbornik materialov dlia opisaniia mestnostei i plemen Kavkaza,* vol. XVI. Tiflis, 1893.
Narody Kavkaza, vols 1–2. Moscow, 1960–2.
Pikman, A.M. "O bor'be kavkazskikh gortsev s tsarskimi kolonizatorami", *Voprosy istorii,* March 1956.
Pokrovskii, M.V. "O kharaktere dvizheniia gortsev zapadnogo Kavkaza v 40–60 godakh XIX v.", *Voprosy istorii,* no.2, 1957.
Popov, M.Ia. "Narody severnogo Kavkaza v epokhe feodalizma", *Voprosy istorii,* no.7, 1966.
Pozhidaev, V.P. *Gortsy severnogo Kavkaza. Ingushi, Chechentsy, Khevsury, Osetiny i Kabardintsy. Kratkii istoriko-etnograficheskii ocherk.* Moscow-Leningrad, 1926.
Semenov, N. *Tuzemtsy severo-vostochnogo Kavkaza.* St Petersburg, 1895.
Smirnov, N.Ia. *Miuridizm na Kavkaze.* Moscow, 1963.
Uslar, P.K. *Etnografiia Kavkaza,* vols. 1–6. Tiflis, 1887–96.
Volkova, N.G. *Etnicheskii sostav naseleniia severnogo Kavkaza v XVIII–nachale XX veka.* Moscow, 1974.
Wixman, R. *Language Aspects and Ethnic Patterns and Processes in the North Caucasus.* Department of Geography Research Paper no. 191, University of Chicago, 1980.

Daghestan

Akhmedov, D.N., Vagabov, M.V., and Magometov, M.S. *Dagestan.* 2nd edn, Makhach-Qala, 1971.
Akhmetov, SH.B. "K voprosu o rasprostranenii islama v Dagestane", *Voprosy istorii Dagestana,* no.2, 1975.

Aliev, A.I. *Istoricheskii opyt stroitel'stva sotsializma v Dagestane.* Makhach-Qala, 1969.

Alikberov, G.A. *Pobeda sotsialisticheskoi revoliutsii v Dagestane.* Makhach-Qala, 1968.

Allen, W.E.D. "Military Operations in Daghestan, 1917–1921", *Army Quarterly*, vol.XXIX, 1934–5.

Astemirov. "Itogi kul'tstroitel'stva Dagestana k 15 letiiu Oktiabria", *Revoliutsiia i natsional'nosti*, nos 10–11, 1932.

Autlev, M.G., and Etenko, L.A. "Istoriia Dagestana", *Istoriia SSSR*, no.6, 1970.

Bor'ba za ustanovlenie i uprochnenie sovetskoi vlasti v Dagestane, 1917–1920. Sbornik dokumentov i materialov. Moscow, 1958.

Bulatova, A. *Svad'ba laktsev v XIX–XX v.* Makhach-Qala, 1968.

Chursin, G.F. "Etnograficheskii ocherk avarov", *Biulleten' Kavkazskogo Istoriko-arkheologicheskogo Instituta v Tiflise*, no. 4, 1928.

Daniialov, A.D. *Sovetskiy Dagestan.* Moscow, 1960.

——. *Stroitel'stvo sotsializma v Dagestane, 1921–1940. Uglovye problemy.* Moscow, 1975.

Daniialov, G.D. *Klassovaia bor'ba v Dagestane vo vtoroi polovine XIX–nachale XX v.* Makhach-Qala, 1970.

——. *Sotsialisticheskoe preobrazovanie v Dagestane (1920–1941 gg).* Makhach-Qala, 1960.

Desiat' let avtonomii Dagestana. Makhach-Qala, 1931.

Emirov, N.P. *Iz istorii voennoi interventsii i grazhdanskoi voiny v Dagestane.* Makhach-Qala, 1972.

Erel, S. *Dagistan ve Dağistanlilar.* Istanbul, 1961.

Evstigneev, Iu. A. "Natsional'no-smeshannye braki v Makhachkale", *Sovetskaia etnografiia*, no.4, 1971.

Feodal'nye otnosheniia v Dagestane, XIX–nachalo XX v. Arkhivnye materialy, sostavlenie, predislovie i primechaniia Kh. M. Khashaeva. Moscow, 1969.

Gabiev, S. *Laki, ikh proshloe i byt. Sbornik materialov dlia opisaniia mestnostei i plemen Kavkaza*, vol. XXXVI. Tiflis, 1906.

Gadzhiev, V.G. *Rol' Rossii v istorii Dagestana.* Moscow, 1965.

Gadzhieva, S. Sh. *Kaiakentskie kumyki.* Works of the Institute of Ethnography, ANSSSR (new series), vol. XLVI. Moscow, 1958.

——. *Kumyki-istoriko-etnograficheskoe issledovanie.* Moscow, 1961.

——. *Material'naia kul'tura kumykov, XIX v. — nachalo XX v.* Makhach-Qala, 1960.

——. *Sem'ia i semeinyi byt' narodov Dagestana.* Makhach-Qala, 1967.

Isaev, A.A. *O formirovanii i razvitii pis'mennosti narodov Dagestana.* Sociological collection, vol. 1. Makhach-Qala, 1970.

Kaloev, B.A. *Aguly.* Makhach-Qala, 1954.

Kazanbiev, M.A. *Sozdanie i ukreplenie natsional'noi gosudarstvennosti narodov Dagestana.* Makhach-Qala, 1970.

Khashaev, Kh.M. (ed). *Feoldal'nye otnosheniia v Dagestane XIX–nachalo XX v. Arkhivnye materialy.* Moscow, 1969.

——. *Obshchestvennyi stroi Dagestana v XIX veke.* Moscow, 1961.

Lavrov, L.I. 'Rutul'tsy,' *Sovetskaia etnografiia*, no.4, 1953.

Leshifov, A.L. *Vozniknovenie i razvitie sovetskoi natsional'noi gosudarstvennosti narodov Dagestana.* Makhach-Qala, 1968.

Magomedov, R.M. *Dagestan. Istoricheskie etiudy.* Makhach-Kala, 1971.

——. *Istoriia Dagestana s drevneishikh vremen do kontsa XIX veka.* Makhach-Qala, 1968.

——. *Khronologiia istorii Dagestana.* Makhach-Qala, 1959.

——. *Obshchestvenno-ekonomicheskii i politicheskii stroi Dagestana v XVIII–nachale XIX vekov.* Makhach-Qala, 1957.

Magomedov, R., and Nazarevich, A. *Dagestanskaia ASSR. 25 let bor'by i truda v sostave Rossiiskoi federatsii.* Makhach-Qala, 1945.

Narody Dagestana. Moscow, 1935.

Narody Dagestana. Sbornik statei. Moscow, 1955.

Navruzov, M. "Dagestanskaia ASSR", *Vestnik statistiki*, no.2, 1973.

Pantiukhov, I.I. *Sovremennye Lezginy.* Tiflis, 1901.

50 let Dagestanskoi ASSR. Materialy torzhestvennogo zasedaniia Dagestanskogo obkoma KPSS i verkhovnogo soveta DASSR, posviashchennogo 50-letiiu obrazovaniia Dagestanskoi ASSR. Makhach-Qala, 1971.

Ocherki istorii Dagestana, vols 1–2. Makhach-Qala, 1957.

Oktiabr'skaia revoliutsiia i reshenie natsional'nogo voprosa v Dagestane. Makhach-Qala, 1967.

Samurski (Efendiev), N. *Dagestan.* Moscow-Leningrad, 1925.

——. "Desiatiletie sovetskoi vlasti v Dagestane", *Sovetskoe stroitel'stvo*, no.2, 1931.

——. *Grazhdanskaia voina v Dagestane.* Makhach-Qala, 1925.

Shiksaidov, A. *Kogda i kak nasazhdalsia v Dagestane islam. Iz istorii musul'manskoi religii v Daghestane (VII–XV vv).* Makhach-Qala, 1962.

Shilling, E.M. *Kubachintsy i ikh kul'tura. Istoriko-etnograficheskie etiudy.* Works of the Institute of Ethnography, ANSSSR (new series), vol. VIII, 1949.

Sotsiologicheskii sbornik. Daghestan branch of the ANSSSR. Makhach-Qala, 1970.

Takho-Godi, A.A. *Revoliutsiia i kontrrevoliutsiia v Dagestane.* Moscow, 1927.

Vagabov, M.V. *Bor'ba partiinoi organizatsii Dagestana za internatsional'noe edinstvo trudiashchikhsia v gody grazhdanskoi voiny (1918–1921).* Makhach-Qala, 1967.

Vasil'ev, A.T. "Kazi-Kumuktsy (etnograficheskie ocherki)", *Etnograficheskoe obozrenie*, XLII, nos. 3–4, 1899.

Chechens — Ingush

Avtorkhanov, A.K. *Osnovnym voprosam istorii Chechni.* Groznyi, 1930.
——. *Kratkii istoriko-kul'turno ekonomicheskii ocherk o Chechne.* Rostov, 1931.
——. (A. Uralov). *Narodo-ubiistvo v SSSR. Ubiistvo chechenskogo naroda.* Munich, 1952.
——. *Revoliutsiia i konttrevoliutsiia v Chechne.* Groznyi, 1933.
Berzhe, A.P. *Chechnia i chechentsy. Kavkazskii kalendar' na 1860 g.* Tiflis, 1859.
Bryan, F.E. "Anti-religious Activities in the Chechen-Ingush Republic of the USSR and the Survival of Islam", *Central Asian Survey*, vol.3, no.2, 1984, pp. 99–116.
Desiat' let Chechni. Rostov, 1928.
Ippolitov, A.P. *Etnograficheskie ocherki argunskogo okruga. Sbornik svedenii o kavkazskikh gortsakh*, vol. I. Tiflis, 1868.
——. *Uchenie 'zikr' i ego posledovateli v Chechne i Argunskom okruge. Sbornik svedenii o kavkazskikh gortsakh*, vol. II. Tiflis, 1869.
Kashbulatov, A. *Checheno-Ingushetiia nakanune pervoi russkoi burzhuaznoi demokraticheskoi revoliutsii.* Groznyi, 1963.
Laudaev, U. *Chechenskoe plemia. Sbornik svedenii o kavkazskikh gortsakh*, vol. VI. Tiflis, 1872.
Maksimov, E. *Chechentsy. Istoriko-geograficheskii i statistiko-ekonomicheskii ocherk*, vol. III, book 2. Vladikavkaz, 1893.
Mamleev, Kh.B. *Nekotorye osobennosti islama v Checheno-Ingushetii.* Groznyi, 1970.
Mankiev, A.A. *Iz istorii klerikal'no-musul'manskoi mysli v Checheno-Ingushetii. Sotsiologiia, ateizm, religiia.* Groznyi, 1972.
Mustafinov, M.M. *Zikrizm i ego sotsial'naia sushchnost'.* Groznyi, 1971.
Oshaev, Kh. *Ocherk nachala revoliutsionnogo dvizheniia v Chechne.* Groznii, 1927.
Pantiukhov, I.I. *Ingushi*, News of the Caucasian Department of the Russian Geographical Society, vol. XIII, no. 6. Tiflis, 1900.
Pivovarov, V.G. *Byt, kul'tura, natsional'nye traditsii i verovaniia naseleniia Checheno-Ingushskoi ASSR.* Groznyi, 1971.
——. "Sotsiologicheskoe issledovanie problem byta, kul'tury natsional'nykh traditsii i verovanii v Checheno-Ingushskoi ASSR", *Voprosy nauchnogo ateizma*, XVII, 1975.
Sheripov, Z. *Ocherk o Chechne.* Groznyi, 1929.
Sotsiologiia, ateizm, religiia. News of the Chechen-Ingush Scientific Research Institute of History, Language and Literature of the Soviet Ministry of the Chechen-Ingush ASSR, vol. I. no. I. Groznyi, 1972.

Kabardians and the Kabardino-Balkar ASSR

Anisimov, S.S. *Kabardino-Balkariia*. Moscow, 1937.

Bushuev, S.K. *Iz istorii russko-kabardinskikh otnoshenii*. Nal'chik, 1956.

Dokumenty po istorii Balkarii, 40–90 g. XIX v. Nal'chik, 1959.

Dokumenty po istorii bor'by za sovetskuiu vlast' i obrazovaniia avtonomii Kabardino-Balkarii 1917–1922. Nal'chik, 1983.

Gardanov, B.A. *Opisanie kabardinskogo naroda, sostavlennoe v 1784 g. P.S. Potemkinym. Sbornik statei po istorii Kabardy*, vol. 5. Nal'chik, 1956.

Gugov, R.Kh., and Uligov, U.A. *Ocherki revoliutsionnogo dvizheniia v Kabardino-Balkarii*. Nal'chik, 1967.

——. *Bor'ba trudiashchikhsia za vlast' Sovetov v Kabarde i Balkarii*. Nal'chik, 1957.

Istoriia Kabardino-Balkarskoi ASSR c drevneishikh vremen do velikoi okt. sots. revoliutsiia. Moscow, 1967.

Istoriia Kabardy s drevneishikh vremen do nashikh dnei. Moscow, 1957.

Karaulov, N.A. *Balkary na Kavkaze. Sbornik materialov dlia opisaniia mestnostei i plemen Kavkaza*, vol. XXXVIII. Tiflis, 1908.

Lavrov, L.I. *O proiskhozhdenii narodov severo-zapadnogo Kavkaza. Sbornik statei po istorii Kabardy*, vol. 3. Nal'chik, 1954.

——. *Proiskhozdenie balkartsev i karachaevtsev*. Short reports of the Institute of Ethnography, ANSSSR, no. XXXII. Moscow, 1959.

——. "Proiskhozhdenie Kabardintsev i zaselenie imi nyneshnei territorii", *Sovetskaia etnografiia*, no.1, 1956.

Maksimov, E. *Kabardintsy. Statistiko-ekonomicheskii ocherk. Terskii sbornik*, vol. 2, book 2. Vladikavkaz, 1892.

Tsavkilov, B.K. *Prichiny zhivuchesti religioznykh perezhitkov i puti ikh preodoleniia*. Nal'chik, 1959.

Vorob'ev, S. "Kabarda i Balkariia za 10 let svoei avtonomii (1921–1931)", *Revoliutsiia i natsional'nosti*, no.1(22), 1932.

Karachais and the Karachai-Cherkess Autonomous Oblast'

Alekseeva, E.P. *Drevniaia i srednevekovaia istoriia Karachaevo-Cherkesii. Voprosy etnicheskogo i sotsial'no-ekonomicheskogo razvitiia*. Moscow, 1971.

Ivanenkov, N.S. *Karachaevtsy*. News of the Society of Lovers of Learning of the Kuban *oblast'*, vol. V. Ekaterinodar, 1912.

Kataev, A. *Perezhitki islama i puti ikh preodoleniia (Na materialakh Karachaevo-Cherkesskoi avtonomnoi oblasti)*. Cherkessk, 1968.

Nevskaia, V.P. *Karachaevtsy. Sbornik narody Karachaevo-Cherkessii (Istoriko-etnograficheskie ocherki)*. Stavropol', 1957.

Problemy ateisticheskogo vospitaniia v usloviiakh Karachaevo-Cherkessii. Cherkessk, 1979.

Adyghes and Cherkess

Antlev, M.G., Zevakin, E.S., and Khoretlev, A.O. *Adygi-istoriko-etnograficheskii ocherk. K 400–letiiu dobrovol'nogo prisoedineniia k Rossii.* Maikop, 1957.

Kalmykov, I.Kh. *Cherkesy. Sbornik narody Karachaevo-Cherkessi.* Stavropol', 1957.

Khashkhozheva, Kh.R. *Adygeiskie prosvetiteli vtoroi poloviny XIX–nachala XX veka.* Nal'chik, 1983.

Lavrov, L.I. *Doislamskie verovaniia adygeitsev i kabardintsev. Issledovaniia i materialy po voprosam pervobytnykh religioznykh verovanii.* Works of the Institute of Ethnography, ANSSSR (new series), vol. LI. Moscow, 1959.

Liul'e, L. Ia. *Cherkesiia. Istoriko-etnograficheskie stat'i.* Krasnodar, 1927.

Nogmov, Sh.B. *Istoriia adygeiskogo naroda. Sostavlennaia po predaniiam kabardintsev.* Nal'chik, 1958.

Ocherk istorii Adygei, vol. I. Maikop, 1957.

Pokrovskii, M.V. *Adygeiskie plemena v kontse XVIII–pervoi polovine XIX v. Kavkazskaia etnografia,* coll. 2. Works of the Institute of Ethnography, ANSSSR (new series), vol. XLVI. Moscow, 1958.

Traho, R. "Literature on Circassia and the Circassians", *Caucasian Review,* no.1, 1956, pp. 145–62.

Nogais

Alekseeva, E.P. *Nogaitsy. Sbornik narody Karachaevo-Cherkessii.* Stavropol', 1957.

Alieva, U. *Kara-Khalk (Karakhalk — chernyi narod).* Rostov-on-Don, 1927.

Farforovskii, S.V. *Nogaitsy Stavropol'skoi gubernii. Istoriko-etnograficheskii ocherk.* Notes of the Caucasian Department of the Russian Geographical Society, vol. XXVI, book 7. Tiflis, 1909.

Gadzhieva, S.Sh. *Ocherki istorii sem'i i braka u nogaitsev, XIX–nachalo XX v.* Moscow, 1979.

Kochekaev, B. *Sotsial'no-ekonomicheskoe i politicheskoe razvitie nogaiskogo obshchestva v XIX–nachale XX.* Alma-Ata, 1973.

Abkhaz

Adzhindzhal. I.A. *Iz etnografii Abkhazii. Materialy i issledovaniia.* Sukhumi, 1969.

Antelava, I.G. *Ocherk po istorii Abkhazii XVII–XVIII v.* Sukhumi, 1951.

Dzhanashvili, M. *Abkhaziia i abkhaztsy.* Notes of the Caucasian Department of the Russian Geographical Society, vol. 16. Tiflis, 1894.

Dzidzariia, G.A. "Iz istorii ustanovleniia sovetskoi vlasti v Abkhazii", *Istoricheskie Zapiski',* no. 44, Moscow, 1959.

Inal-Ipa, Sh.D. *Abkhazy.* Sukhumi, 1960.

Kobakhia, V.O. "V bratskoi sem'e narodov", *Ekonomicheskaia gazeta*, no. 10, March 1971.

Marr, N. Ia. *Abkhazovedenie i abkhazy. Izbrannye raboty*, vol. V. Moscow-Leningrad, 1935.

Ocherki istorii Abkhazskoi ASSR. Sukhumi, 1960.

50 let sovetskoi Abkhazii. Sukhumi, 1971.

Smyr, G.V. *Islam v Abkhazii i puti preodoleniia ego perezhitkov v sovremennykh usloviiakh.* Tbilisi, 1972.

———. *Perezhitki islama i puti ikh preodolenii v sovremennykh usloviiakh Abkhazii.* Sukhumi, 1967.

Ossetians

Chursin, G.F. *Osetiny.* Tiflis (Tbilisi), 1925.

Dzoblaev, Sh.D. "Peredovaia politicheskaia mysl' Osetii kontsa XIX–nachala XX v", *Vestnik Moskovskogo universiteta* (Pravo), no.3, 1971.

Gil'chenko, N.V. *Materialy dlia antropologii Kavkaza. Osetiny.* St Petersburg, 1890.

Istoriia Severo Osetinskoi ASSR. 2 vols, Ordzhonikidze, 1966.

Lavrov, D. *Zametki ob Osetii i osetinakh. Sbornik materialov dlia opisaniia mestnostei i plemen Kavkaza* vol. III. Tiflis, 1883.

Ocherki istorii Severo-Osetinskoi partiinoi organizatsii. Ordzhonikidze, 1969.

Pfaf, V.B. *Etnologicheskie issledovaniia ob osetinakh. Sbornik sved. o Severnom Kavkaze*, vol. II. Moscow, 1872.

Abazas

Genko, A.N. *Abazinskii iazyk.* Moscow, 1955.

Lavrov, L.I. *Abaziny. Istoriko-etnograficheskii ocherk. Kavkazskaia etnografiia, sbornik I.* Works of the Institute of Ethnography, ANSSSR (new series): vol. XXVI. Moscow, 1955.

Small Minorities: Yezidis, Tats, Kurds

Anisimov, I.Sh. *Kavkazskie Evrei-gortsy.* Moscow, 1888.

Aristova, T.F. *Kurdy Zakavkaz'ia. Istoriko-etnograficheskii ocherk.* Moscow, 1966.

———. "Poezdka k kurdam Zakavkaz'ia", *Sovetskaia etnografiia*, no.6, 1958.

Bennigsen, A. "Les Kurdes et la Kurdologie en Union Soviétique", *Cahiers du Monde Russe et Soviétique*, XIII(1), pp. 57–113.

Chursin, R.F. *Talyshi.* Tiflis, 1926.

Egiazarov, S.A. *Kratkii etnograficheskii ocherk kurdov Erivanskoi gubernii.* Notes of the Caucasian Dept. of the Russian Geographical Society, vol. II, book XIII. Tiflis, 1891.

Komarov. *Taty.* Notes of the Caucasian Dept. of the Russian Geographical Society, vo. 8. Tiflis, 1879.

Kurdov, K.M. "Taty Dagestana", *Russkii antropologicheskii zhurnal*, nos 3–4, 1907.

Miller, B.V. *Taty, ikh rasselenie i govory.* Baku, 1929.

Mokri, M. *Kurdologie et enseignement de la langue kurde en URSS.* Paris, 1963.

Vip'chevskii, O.L. "Ocherki po istorii ezidstva", *Ateist*, no.51, Moscow, 1930.

Wimbush, S.E., and Wixman, R. "The Meskhetian Turks: A new voice in Soviet Central Asia", *Canadian Slavonic Papers*, Summer-Fall 1974.

Azeris

Alekperov, A.K. *Issledovaniia po arkheologii i etnografii Azerbaidzhana.* Baku, 1960.

Alieva, L.M. *Rabochie-tekstil'shchiki Baku v nachale XX v.* Baku, 1969.

Anserov, N.I. *Tiurki sovetskogo Azerbaidzhana. K kharakeristike ikh fizicheskogo tipa.* Baku, 1930.

Azerbaidzhan. Istoricheskie i dostoprimechatel'nye mesta. Baku. 1960.

Azerbaidzhan v gody pervoi russkoi revoliutsii. Sbornik statei. Baku, 1965.

Azerbaidzhanskii etnograficheskii sbornik. Issledovaniia i materialy, vol. 1. Baku, 1964.

Azizbekova, P., Mnachakanian, A., and Traskunov, M. *Sovetskaia Rossia i bor'ba za ustanovlenie i uprochenie vlasti sovetov v Zakavkaz'e.* Baku, 1969.

Baykara, H. *Azerbaycan Istiklal Mucadelesi Tarihi.* Istanbul, 1975.

Guliev, Dzh.B. *Bor'ba kommunisticheskoi partii za osushchestvlenie leninskoi natsional'noi politiki v Azerbaidzhane.* Baku, 1970.

Guliev, G.A. "Etnografiia Azerbaidzhana za 40 let", *Sovetskaia etnografiia*, no.4, 1961.

Guseinov, G. *Iz istorii obshchestvennoi i filosofskoi mysli v Azerbaidzhane, XIX veka.* 2nd edn. Baku, 1958.

Guseinov, M.D. *Tiurkskaia demokraticheskaia partiia Musavat v proshlom i nastoiashchem: programma i taktika.* Tiflis, 1927.

Ibragimbeili, Kh.M. *Rossiia i Azerbaidzhan v pervoi treti XIX veka. Iz voenno-politicheskoi istorii.* Moscow, 1969.

Imart, G. "Un intellectuel azerbaidjanais face à la Révolution de 1917: Samad-Aga Agamaly-oglu", *Cahiers du Monde Russe et Soviétique*, VIII(4), 1967, pp. 528–59.

Islam i ego nekotorye perezhitki. Batumi, 1959.

Ismailov, M. *Sotsial'no-ekonomicheskaia struktura Azerbaidzhana v epokhu imperializma.* Baku, 1982.

Istoriia Azerbaidzhana v 3 tomakh. Baku, 1958–63.

Iz istorii sovetskogo rabochego klassa Azerbaidzhana. Baku, 1964.

Karakashly, K. *Ob airumakh.* Izvestia obshchestva obsledovaniia i izucheniia Azerbaidzhana, vol.1, no. 8. Baku, 1929.

Kazemzadeh. F. *The Struggle for Transcaucasia (1917–1921).* New York, 1951.

Kaziev, M.A. *Iz istorii revoliutsionnoi bor'by bakinskogo proletariata.* Baku, 1956.

Khadzhibeyli, Dzh. *Antiislamistskaia propaganda i ee metody v Azerbaidzhane.* Munich, 1959.

Kolonial'naia politika rossiiskogo tsarizma v Azerbaidzhane v 20–60 g. XX v. Moscow-Leningrad, 1936.

Kommunisticheskaia partiia Azerbaidzhana v tsifrakh-statisticheskii sbornik. Baku, 1970.

Kurbanov, M.K. *Kul'tura sovetskogo Azerbaidzhana.* Baku, 1959.

Lemercier-Quelquejay, C. "Islam and Identity in Azerbaijan", *Central Asian Survey,* vol.3, no.2, April 1984, pp. 29–57.

Nadzhafov, A.I. *Formirovanie i razvitie Azerbaidzhanskoi sotsialisticheskoi natsii.* Baku, 1955.

Pobeda sovetskoi vlasti v Zakavkaz'e. Tbilisi, 1971.

Prisoedinenie Azerbaidzhana k Rossii i ego progessivnye posledstviia v oblasti ekonomiki i kul'tury. Baku, 1955.

Rasul Zade, M.E. *L'Azerbaidjan en lutte pour l'indépendance.* Paris, 1930.

Sattarov, M.M. *Islam dini galyglary.* Baku, 1967.

Sovetskii Azerbaidzhan. Baku, 1958.

Trofimova, A.G. *K voprosu ob etnograficheskikh zonakh Azerbaidzhanskoi SSR.* Short reports of the Institute of Ethnography, ANSSSR, no. XXXII. Moscow, 1959.

THE MIDDLE VOLGA

Tatars

Abdullin, Ia. G. *Tatarskaia prosvetitel'naia mysl'.* Kazan, 1976.

Abdullin, M. and Batyev, S. "Tatarskaia ASSR. Real'nost' i burzhuaznye mify", in *Sultangalievshchina i ee burzhuaznye zashchitniki.* Kazan, 1977.

Arutiunian, Iu.V. "Opyt sotsial'no-etnicheskogo issledovaniia po materialam Tatarskoi ASSR", *Sovetskaia etnografiia,* no.4, 1968.

Battal-Taymas, A. *Kazan Türkleri: Tarihi ve Siyasi Görüsler.* Istanbul, 1925.

Bennigsen, A., and Lemercier-Quelquejay, C. *Les mouvements nationaux chez les musulmans de Russie: Le Sultangalievisme au Tatarstan.* Paris, 1960.

Devletshin, T. *Cultural Life in the Tatar Autonomous Republic.* New York, 1953.

Desiat' let sotsialisticheskogo stroitel'stva v Tatarstane (1920–1930). Sbornik. Kazan, 1930.

Desiatiletie sovetskogo Tatarstana, 1920–1930. Kazan, 1930.

Devlet, N. "A Specimen of Russification: The Turks of Kazan", *Central Asian Survey*, vol.2, no.3 (Nov. 1983), pp. 79–89.

Dvadtsat' let Tatarskoi ASSR. Kazan, 1940.

Faseev, K.F. *Iz istorii tatarskoi peredovoi obshchestvennoi mysli — Vtoraiia polovina XIX–nachalo XX veka.* Kazan, 1955.

Gabidullin, Kh. *Tatarstan za sem' let (1920–1927).* Kazan, 1927.

Gorokhov, V.M. *Reaktsionnaia shkol'naia politika tsarizma v otnoshenii tatar Povolzh'ia.* Kazan, 1941.

Grigor'ev, A.N. *Khristianizatsia nerusskikh narodnostei kak odin iz metodov natsional'no-kolonial'noi politiki tsarizma v Tatarii. S poloviny XVI v. do fevralia 1917 g.* Kazan, 1948.

Gyil'fanov, I. *Islam dine turynde.* Kazan, 1965.

Ibragimov, G. *Kak vesti antireligioznuiu propagandu sredi tatarok i bashkirok.* Moscow, 1928.

——. *Tatary v revoliutsii 1905 goda.* Kazan, 1926.

Ishaky, A. *Idel-Oural.* Paris, 1933.

Ishmukhamedov, Z.A. *Islam i ego ideologiia.* Kazan, 1983.

——. *Sotsial'naia rol' i evoliutsiia islama v Tatarii (Istoricheskie ocherki).* Kazan, 1979.

Istoriia Tatarii v materialakh i dokumentakh. Moscow, 1937.

Kasymov, G. *Ocherki po religioznomu i antireligioznomu dvizheniiu sredi tatar do i posle revoliutsii.* Kazan, 1932.

——. *Pantiurkistskaia kontrrevoliutsiia i ee agentura sultangalievshchina.* Kazan, 1931.

Khasanov, M.A. "Kul'turnoe stroitel'stvo Tatarii za 15 let", *Revoliutsiia i natsional'nosti*, no.11, 1933.

Klimov, I.M.*Obrazovanie i razvitie Tatarskoi ASSR, 1920–1926.* Kazan, 1960.

Klimovich', L.I. "Religioznoe dvizhenie v Tatarskoi respublike", *Antireligioznik* (Moscow), no.4, 1927.

Lemercier-Quelquejay, C. "Abdul Kayum al-Nasyri: A Tatar Reformer of the 19th Century", *Central Asian Survey*, vol.1, no.4 (April 1983), pp. 109–33.

Malov, E. *Ocherk religioznogo sostoianiia kreshchenykh tatar, podvergshikhsia vliianiiu magometanstva. Missionerskii dnevnik.* Kazan, 1872.

——. *O novokreshchenskoi kontore.* Kazan, 1878.

Materialy po izucheniiu Tatarstana. Sbornik statei, vol. 2. Kazan, 1925.

Mozharovskii, A.T. *Izlozhenie khoda missionerskogo dela po prosveshcheniiu kazanskikh inorodtsev s 1552 po 1867 godu.* Moscow, 1880.

Mukhametshin, Iu.G. *Tatary kriasheny.* Moscow, 1977.

Obrazovanie Tatarskoi ASSR. Sbornik dokumentov i materialov. Kazan, 1963.

Protiv sultangalievshchiny i velikoderzhavnosti. Sbornik. Kazan, 1929.

Radlov, V.V. *Etnograficheskii obzor turetskikh plemen Sibiri i Mongolii.* Irkutsk, 1929.

Rorlich, A.A. "Which Way will Tatar Culture Go? A controversial essay by

Galimdzhan Ibragimov", *Cahiers du Monde Russe et Soviétique*, XV(3–4), pp. 363–71.

Rubinshtein, L. *V bor'be za leninskuiu natsional'nuiu politiku*. Kazan, 1930.

Saadi, A. *Tatar edebiyaty tarihi*. Kazan, 1926.

Spuler, B. "Die Wolga Tataren und Bashkiren unter russischen Herrschaft", *Der Islam*, XXIX–2, 1949, pp. 142–216.

Struktura naseleniia i gorodov Tatarii. Kazan, 1971.

Sultan Galiev, M.S. "Tatarskaia avtonomnaia respublika", *Zhizn' natsional'nostei*, no.1, 1923, pp. 25–39.

——. "Tatary i okt'iabrskaia revoliutsiia", *Zhizn' natsional'nostei*, 21(122), 1921.

Tatariia v proshlom i nastoiashchem. Kazan, 1975.

Tatary Srednego Povolzh'ia i Priural'ia. Moscow, 1967.

Tomilov, N.A. *Sovremennye etnicheskie protsessy sredi Sibirskikh Tatar*. Tomsk, 1978.

Torzhestvo leninskoi natsional'noi politiki v Tatarii. Kazan, 1968.

Validov, Dzh. *Ocherki istorii obrazovannosti i literatury Tatar do revoliutsii 1917 goda*. Moscow, 1923.

Ziiasev, Kh.K. *K istorii bukhartsev i tashkentsev v Sibirii (XVII-pervaia polovina XIX v.)*, News of the Academy of Sciences of the Uzbek SSR, Sociological series, No. 10, 1956.

Bashkirs

Abdullin, M.I. "Istoriia obrazovaniia Bashkirskoi ASSR v sovremennoi burzhuaznoi istoriografii", *Istoriia SSSR*, no.6, 1972, pp. 194–205.

Bashkiriia za 50 let. Statisticheskii sbornik. Ufa, 1969.

Bikbulatov, N.V., and Ilimbetov, F.F. "Nauchnaia sessiia po etnogenezu bashkir", *Sovetskaia etnografiia*, no.3, 1970, pp.162–7.

Formirovanie i razvitie sovetskogo rabochego klassa Baskhirskoi ASSR. Chast' I. Ufa, 1971.

Ishkulov, F.A. *O nekotorykh momentakh i osobennostiakh provedeniia leninskoi natsional'noi politiki v Bashkirii v pervye gody sovetskoi vlasti*. Ufa, 1970.

Iz istorii feodalizma i kapitalizma v Bashkirii. Ufa, 1971.

Iz istorii rabochego klassa Bashkirskoi ASSR. Ufa, 1967.

Iz istorii sotsialisticheskogo stroitel'stva v avtonomnykh respublikakh. Ufa, 1970.

Iz istorii sovetskoi Bashkirii. Ufa, 1969.

Materialy po istorii Bashkirskoi ASSR, vol. I. Moscow, 1936.

Novye vremena — novye obriady. Ufa, 1979.

Obrazovanie bashkirskoi avtonomnoi sovetskoi sotsialisticheskoi respubliski. Sbornik dokumentov i materialov. Ufa, 1959.

Patrushev, D. *Islam i ego reaktsionnaia sushchnost'*. Ufa, 1962.

Tipeev, Sh. *K istorii natsional'nogo dvizheniia v sovetskoi Bashkirii*. Ufa, 1929.

Voprosy istorii Bashkirii, vol. 1. Ufa, 1972.

CRIMEAN TATARS

Abdulhamitoglu, N. *Türksüz Kırım — Yüzbinlerin Surgünü.* Istanbul, 1974.

Bochagov, A.K. *Milli Firka. Natsional'naia kontrrevoliutsiia v Krymu. Ocherk.* Simferopol', 1930.

Dubrovin, N. *Prisoedinenie Kryma k Rossii — Reskripty, pis'ma, reliatsii i doneseniia,* vol. 1. St Petersburg, 1885.

Elagin, V. "Natsionalisticheskie illiuzii Krymskikh tatar v revoliutsionnye gody", *Novyi vostok,* no.5 (1924), pp. 190–216; and no.6 (1924), pp. 205–25.

Fisher, A. *The Crimean Tatars.* Stanford, Calif., 1978.

Grigorenko, A. *A kogda my vernemsia.* New York, 1977.

Kirimal, E. *Der nationale kampf der Krimturken.* Emsdetten, 1952.

Krichinskii, A. *Ocherki russkoi politiki na okrainakh. Iz istorii religioznykh pritesnenii Krymskikh tatar.* Baku, 1919.

Özenbashly, A. *Çarlik hakimietinde Krim faciasï yahut Tatar Hicretleri.* Simferopol', 1925.

Sheehy, A. *The Crimean Tatars and the Volga Germans: Soviet Treatment of Two National Minorities.* London, 1971.

Ülküsal, M. *Kırım Türk — Tatarlari (Dünü-Bugünü-Yarini).* Istanbul, 1980.

Usov, S.A. *Istoriko-ekonomicheskie ocherki Kryma. Proshloe i nastoiashchee Krymskogo sel'skogo khoziaistva.* Simferopol', 1925.

INDEX

279